FELIDS AND HYENAS OF THE WORLD

Wildcats, Panthers, Lynx, Pumas,
Ocelots, Caracals, and Relatives

José R. Castelló

Foreword by
Alexander Sliwa and Andrew Kitchener

PRINCETON UNIVERSITY PRESS
PRINCETON AND OXFORD

Copyright © 2020 by José R. Castelló

Copyright of the photographs remains with the individual photographers

Requests for permission to reproduce material from this work should be sent to Permissions, Princeton University Press

Published by Princeton University Press
41 William Street, Princeton, New Jersey 08540
6 Oxford Street, Woodstock, Oxfordshire OX20 1TR
press.princeton.edu

ISBN 978-0-691-20845-9
ISBN (pbk.) 978-0-691-20597-7
ISBN (e-book) 978-0-691-21186-2

British Library Cataloging-in-Publication Data is available

Production and design by José R. Castelló, Madrid, Spain
This book has been composed in Helvetica Neue
Printed on acid-free paper ∞
Printed in Italy

10 9 8 7 6 5 4 3 2 1

CONTENTS

FOREWORD 5

ACKNOWLEDGMENTS 7

INTRODUCTION 8

PANTHERA LINEAGE
Tigers, Lions, Jaguars, and Leopards 30

PUMA LINEAGE
Puma, Jaguarundi, and Cheetah 80

OCELOT LINEAGE
Ocelot, Margay, Guiña, Colocolo, and Related Species 96

LEOPARD CAT LINEAGE
Leopard Cat, Pallas's Cat, and Related Species 134

CARACAL LINEAGE
Caracal, Serval, and African Golden Cat 156

WILDCAT LINEAGE
Domestic Cat, Wildcats, and Related Species 174

LYNX LINEAGE
Lynx and Bobcat 202

BAY CAT LINEAGE
Asiatic Golden Cat, Marbled Cat, and Borneo Bay Cat 226

HYENAS
Hyenas and Aardwolf 238

SKULLS 258

GLOSSARY 263

REFERENCES 267

INDEX 277

FOREWORD

It is with great pleasure and admiration that I write the foreword to *Felids and Hyenas of the World*. José Castelló has set the gold standard with his two major preceding books *Bovids of the World* (2016, Princeton University Press) and *Canids of the World* (2018, Princeton University Press) for practical, affordable, and visually stunning reference guide books on these mammalian families. Not only is he a gifted photographer himself, he is unrelenting in searching for the best available images on the World Wide Web to show the characteristics of the depicted species and subspecies. There are billions of images of one of man's favorite companions and majestic sources of fear and admiration, the small and large cats in their diverse family that roam all continents, apart from Antarctica, and that prowl through all terrestrial habitats. What book can satisfy our urge to revel in the beauty, elegance, and diversity better than this current one, which systematically strives to depict the full glory of the Felidae? This tome reflects painstaking dedication to deliver a reference without comparison.

All wild living cat species and the domestic cat are depicted with a full page, most often showing currently recognized subspecies on their own spread with several pictures of adults and kittens. For each species information about its morphology, distribution, habitat, ecology, biology, and diet, as well as its main threats and current conservation efforts is provided, taken from the most current literature available, and here again José Castelló has delved deeply into both reasonably available and cryptic (gray) literature. This is no small feat as there is substantial references on some members of the cat family, particularly the European and North American species and the classic *Panthera* cats, while information on particularly the smaller species is comparatively scarce and hard to obtain. Synthesizing all of this into digestible form requires great stamina and systematic rigor, which is presented here.

I am certain that this book will find high acclaim and wide readership and will foster even more admiration and a drive toward deeper research into the lesser known felid species, leading to concerted efforts to protect individuals, populations, and species by providing an affordable and portable current reference.

Alexander Sliwa
PhD, Curator, Cologne Zoo, Germany
Felid Taxon Advisory Group (TAG) Chair of the European Association of Zoos and Aquaria (EAZA)
Invited Member of IUCN SSC Cat Specialist Group
Black-Footed Cat Working Group Project Leader; Sand Cat Sahara Team Co-Leader

I have been waiting a very long time for a book like this one. My interest in wild cats dates back to when I was in my mid-teens when a new charity, the Cat Survival Trust, was established locally where I lived. Fascinated by opportunities to get close to many of the world's smaller cat species, I became ever eager to find out more, but good books about cats were lacking. However, my first significant encounter with a wild cat was when I was seven years old, with a young female Puma on Sandown Beach in the Isle of Wight, where the famous lion tamer Nyoka was taking it for a walk on a lead. When it chased after me, dragging Nyoka with it, I quickly became terrified and was too upset to meet it once it was under its owner's control. When I started work at National Museums Scotland, I met Dr. Nigel Easterbee, who was carrying out a status survey on European Wildcats in Scotland and research on how to distinguish wildcats from domestic cats and their hybrids. When Nigel died tragically in a car accident, I took up this important area of research and added hundreds of specimens of road-killed wild-living cats to the museum's collection, which recently helped to show the imminent extinction of the European Wildcat in Scotland today through hybridization. At the same time that I met Nigel, I was finishing off my first book, *Wild Cats of the World* (1991, Cristopher Helm), which was a synthesis of what was known of the behavior and ecology of the world's cats, but it wasn't an identification guide to all taxa, which seemed an ever-distant dream. Soon after, I was invited to join the IUCN Cat Specialist Group by the late Peter Jackson. My feline career continued with research on geographical variation in Tigers in the 1990s and Clouded Leopards in the 2000s, resulting in the recognition of the first new big cat species, the Sunda Clouded Leopard, in 180 years. In 2010 I was asked by Urs and Christine Breitenmoser to lead the IUCN Cat Specialist Group's Cat Classification Task Force, which published its final report in 2017. This report reduced the number of cat subspecies dramatically, with only a modest increase in the number of species. But it was beyond the scope of this report to show what they looked like. So, I am delighted that the first comprehensive book that illustrates all the world's species and subspecies of cat has at last been published. José Castelló's *Felids and Hyenas of the World* is a magnificent guide to these two important families of carnivorous mammals.

Having been very impressed by José's two earlier books, *Bovids of the World*, published in 2016, and *Canids of the World*, published in 2018, I wondered whether he had turned his attention to the felids. So, I contacted him out of the blue, offering him any assistance that I could. By return email José confirmed that he was indeed working on the felids, and possibly the hyaenids, for his next volume. José's books follow a well-established pattern with an introductory chapter that provides a brief but interesting, summary of different aspects of our knowledge of felid and hyaenid morphology, both inside and out, classification and taxonomy, behavior, including social organization, feeding and diet, reproduction and communication, with subsequent sections looking at distribution and habitat, evolution and the fossil record, domestication and conservation status, and ending with a guide on how to use the book. What enriches this book and brings it to life is the stunning photographs of a wide variety of cats and hyenas showing different aspects of their appearance, anatomy, and behaviors.

The meat of this book is the series of chapters that correspond to the main felid phylogenetic lineages identified by molecular studies led by Steve O'Brien and his many colleagues over the last few decades, with the lesser known hyenas and aardwolves in the final chapter. After an introductory section to each chapter, each species and subspecies gets a two-page spread with a description, other names in multiple languages, taxonomy, similar species, reproduction, behavior, distribution, habitat, and conservation status. What makes this book remarkable and very useful to a cat specialist like myself is the array of photographs showing lateral, frontal, posterior, and other views of each taxon, including differences between the sexes and also juveniles and younger animals where their appearance differs significantly. José has established an incredible network of people around the world who have sent him photos of all species and subspecies from these two mammalian families. Having worked for seven years in revising their taxonomy, I find it fascinating to be able to look at the differences between all the subspecies that are recognized in the IUCN's *A revised taxonomy of the Felidae*.

Cats, of course, have been animals of endless fascination for people over many millennia. Recorded in cave paintings dating to tens of thousands of years ago, to images on pottery, standing stones, mosaics, and sculptures from across a wide array of ancient civilizations from the Incas to the Ancient Egyptians, cats have continually captured our imaginations with their grace and beauty as well as their power and strength. Sadly, our fascination with cats has not prevented us from killing them as troublesome consumers of livestock and people, or exploiting them for their fur or bones for our vanity or medicine. Hyenas, in contrast, have been much neglected and vilified as mere scavengers or cruel killers that are much persecuted wherever they live. Only the small and dainty Aardwolf, which feeds almost exclusively on termites, is excluded from these stereotypes, but as a consequence we know little about it. However, it is important that we are aware that the few hyaenid species that survive today are a vestige of a much more widespread and diverse family that populated the Old World, and that despite their canid-like appearance, they are closely related to the felids and are equally fascinating. *Felids and Hyenas of the World* offers a new opportunity to get to know the world's hyaenids better. I hope you will take the opportunity to use this stunning guide, whether in the wild or in captivity, to brush up your knowledge of and ability to identify the diverse, beautiful, and captivating felids and hyaenids of the world. I certainly will!

Andrew Kitchener
PhD, Principal Curator of Vertebrates, National Museums Scotland, UK
Member of the IUCN Cat Specialist Group
Chair of the IUCN Cat Specialist Group's Cat Classification Task Force
Honorary Fellow of the Royal Zoological Society of Scotland

ACKNOWLEDGMENTS

This book is dedicated to my wife, Beatriz, and my children, Alejandro and Beatriz, for their love and support during the long hours that I spent working on this book. Also, I need to thank my parents, who taught me the value of hard work and education. Compiling a book like this one would be impossible without the help of dozens of experts and wildlife photographers. I am deeply grateful to all the colleagues and friends who have been part of this long endeavor.

A special thanks to Alexander Sliwa for his expert and gracious assistance in preparing this book, for sharing his collection of photographs, and his vast knowledge of felids and hyenas. Alexander is a conservation biologist, Curator at the Cologne Zoo, Felid Taxon Advisory Group Chair of the European Association of Zoos and Aquaria, member of the IUCN SSC Cat Specialist Group, and a major expert in the behavioral ecology of many species of wild cats.

I am also particularly grateful to Andrew Kitchener, Principal Curator of Vertebrates in the Department of Natural Sciences at the National Museums Scotland, Chair of the Cat Classification Task Force, member of the IUCN SSC Cat Specialist Group, and the author of *The Natural History of the Wild Cats* (1991, Cornell University Press).

A very special thanks goes also to my friend Sergey Chichagov, a Latvian biologist and passionate photographer, who has shared his profound knowledge of wild cats and hyenas and hundreds of photographs with me. I wish also to acknowledge the help provided by Roland Wirth, founder of the Zoological Society for the Conservation of Species and Populations; Klaus Rudloff, Curator Emeritus at Tierpark Berlin; and Pierre de Chabannes, a photographer specializing in animal conservation. My grateful thanks are also extended to Alex Kantorovich, curator of Hai Park Kiryat Motzkin; Jonas Livet, a French biologist and consultant in zoology; Juan S. Villalba-Macías, an Uruguayan conservationist and Curator at Bioparque M'Bopicuá; Balázs Buzás, a Hungarian conservationist and wildlife photographer; and Phil Myers, Professor Emeritus and Curator Emeritus at the Museum of Zoology, University of Michigan-Ann Arbor.

Finally, many thanks also to Jim Sanderson, Sebastian Kennerknecht, Laila Bahaa-el-din, Gregory Breton, Guillaume Dupuy, Francisco Javier Erize, Mike Gordon, Eyal Bartov, Jaime San Román, Daniel López Velasco, Jesús Rodriguez-Osorio Martín, Igor Antuna, Javier Amores, Francisco Erize, Valeriy Maleev, Vladimír Cech, Rodrigo Villalobos, Nayer Youakim, Ricky Reino, Tomasz Doron, Johannes Pfleiderer, Paulo Barreiros, Michal Sloviak, Alexander Meyer, Alexander Coke Smith, Otgonbayar Baatargal, Arno Meintjes, Ulrike Joerres, Johan Bordonné, Milan Korínek, Antonio Núñez Lemos, Kevin Schafer, Santiago M. Carrillo, Ricardo Fernández Chaves, Arjan Haverkamp, Minor Torres Salazar, Agustín Emoris, Bruna Zafalon da Silva, Puch Corinne, Cochahuasi Animal Sanctuary, Mendis Wickramasinghe, Michael Lorentz, Jonas Van de Voorde, Jean-Francois Potier, Florent Doko, Joachim S. Müller, Peggy and Marc Faucher, Verónica Araya García, Nikhil B. Vatsal, Christopher Momberg, Nate Hart, Bharath-Shreyas Photography, Jorge Serpa, Anda Ciurezu, David Howlett, Javier Gómez Aoiz, Elena Mashkova, Andrea Riveros Díaz, La Senda Verde Wildlife Sanctuary, Bruna Zafalon da Silva, Demis Bucci, Tim Sagorski, Gustavo Muniz, Avijit Sarkhel, Angela Meyers, Huilo Huilo Biological Reserve, Reserva Nacional Mocho Choshuenco, Parque Nacional Laguna San Rafael, Eduardo Minte Hess, Enrique Couve, Alfredo Boettiger, Luiz Mosca, Carmelo Pamies Boluda, David Piaggio De Casanova, SERFOR, Markus Lilje, Lukas Blazek, McKenzie Greenly, Murthy Kantimahanti, Vishwanath M. K. Mysore, Vickey Chauhan, Yoann Lombard, Ezra Hadad, Eric François, Erwin & Annemieke, Greg Pierson, Esteban Argerich, Juan Reppucci, Eliraz Dvir, Yossi Eshbol, Javier Muñoz Gutiérrez, Parinya Padungtin, Vivek Sharma, Raymond De Smet, Willie van Schalkwyk, Juan José Part Oliver, Vijaybabu Kaliappan, Shahab Mirzaean, Narong Suwannarong, Tambako the Jaguar, Jeremy Holden, Kedar Nath Timsina, Mike & Glen Heramb Wildlife Photography, Radhakrishnan Rajagopalan, Tin Man Lee, Ron Gallagher, Zoo Praha, Iman Memarian, Debankur Biswas, Bjorn Olesen Wildlife Photography, Young Photography, Sid Bramhankar, Stephen Young, Kevin Hatfield, Cede Prudente, Santiago F. Burneo, Thomas Retterath, Jasmine Curtis, Ronny Graf, Josh More, Jaime E. Jiménez, Aditya Singh, Dominique Salé, Armand Meding, Bram Demeulemeester, Jaime López, Marie Reed, Anuroop Krishnan, Warren Metcalf, Alcey Kangit, Steven Metildi, Paul Sebastian Ellis, Emmanuel Keller, Ron Tzur, Peter Dunn, Alex Martín Ros, Antonio Rivas, Sam Carrera, Robert Kok, Iding A. Haidir, Lennart Verheuvel, Ken Kawata, Kimio Honda, and to all the great photographers for their enormous generosity in sharing their photographs; without them, this work would be impossible. I also want to acknowledge and thank Flickr and ZooChat, and their community of wildlife photographers.

RECOGNITION

The family Felidae is a lineage of highly specialized mammalian carnivores adapted for a predatory lifestyle; it includes Wildcats, Lions, Leopards, Tigers, Ocelots, Pumas, Lynx, Caracals, and other cats, with a total of 14 genera and at least 42 extant species. Felids are often considered to be the most typical carnivores: they are strictly carnivorous and their morphology is the most highly specialized of all carnivorans for catching, killing, and devouring prey. All felids bear a strong resemblance to one another, but exhibit the most diverse fur pattern of all terrestrial carnivores. Most species are solitary, territorial, and largely nocturnal or crepuscular. They occupy diverse habitats and are distributed naturally on all continents except Australia, where they have been introduced by humans, and Antarctica. The karyotype of all cats is 2n=38, except in the Ocelot lineage where it is 2n=36.

The family Hyaenidae contains only four species of non-arboreal, cursorial hunters, each in its own genus. Three species hunt and scavenge large vertebrate prey, while the Aardwolf (*Proteles cristatus*) subsists almost exclusively on termites. Although phylogenetically closer to felids, hyenas are behaviorally and morphologically similar to canids, with complex social lives. Hyenas are restricted to Africa and Asia. The karyotype of all hyenas is 2n=40.

Size and body shape (figs. 1 and 2): Felids vary widely in size, from the male Amur Tiger (*Panthera tigris altaica*), which may be up to 300 cm long and can weigh up to 300 kg, to the tiny Rusty-Spotted Cat (*Prionailurus rubiginosus*) and Black-Footed Cat (*Felis nigripes*), which weigh less than 2 kg. Felids are remarkably uniform in body shape and proportions, with rounded heads, short muzzles, long vibrissae, highly sectorial carnassials, sharp retractile claws, and compact, muscular bodies, with distinctive coat markings. The recent radiation of the cat family as we know it today, coupled with the constraints of prey capture and the processing of a highly carnivorous diet, has resulted in a limited range of variation within the Felidae. Males are generally larger and more muscular than females, have relatively larger, broader heads, thicker necks, larger teeth, and greater biting force than females, but otherwise there is minimal sexual dimorphism, with the notable exception of Lions.

Figure 1. Variety of size and body shape in felids: (1) Amur Tiger (*Panthera tigris*); (2) Cheetah (*Acinonyx jubatus*); (3) Canada Lynx (*Lynx canadensis*); (4) Caracal (*Caracal caracal*); (5) Sunda Leopard Cat (*Prionailurus javanensis*); (6) Black-Footed Cat (*Felis nigripes*). Sizes compared to an adult human.

The three large species of hyenas are dog-like, with large necks and massive heads, strongly developed masticatory musculature, blunt muzzles, large eyes and ears, powerful forequarters, less well-developed hindquarters, and medium-length tails. The Aardwolf (*Proteles cristatus*), in contrast, is diminutive, weighing about 10 kg. All species have well-developed anal pouches.

Coat (fig. 3): The cat family exhibits a wide diversity of coat colors and patterns, from pale gray to reddish and yellowish-brown, and there are often stripes, spots, or rosettes. In many species, even plain ones, distinctive facial markings are apparent, and in about half of all cat species, most of them forest-dwellers, prominent white spots adorn the backs of their ears. Melanistic (black) forms have

Figure 2. Variety of size and body shape in hyaenids: (1) Spotted Hyena (*Crocuta crocuta*); (2) Brown Hyena (*Parahyaena brunnea*); (3) Striped Hyena (*Hyaena hyaena*); (4) Aardwolf (*Proteles cristatus*). Sizes compared to an adult human.

been described in at least 13 wild species, but leucistic (white) forms occur rarely. Some species display different color phases; for example, in the Jaguarundi (*Herpailurus yagouaroundi*), coloration varies from dark brown or gray to light reddish. Young often have different markings from the adult coloration; for example, newborn Cheetah (*Acinonyx jubatus*) cubs have a long, white-gray mane, absent in the adult, while Puma (*Puma concolor*) or Lion (*Panthera leo*) cubs are spotted; these spots gradually disappear as they mature. Pelage coloration and markings are important in preventing a hunting cat from being seen while waiting in ambush. Many smaller cats are also likely to be camouflaged for protection from predation. Melanism can provide an adaptive advantage in wetter areas with dense vegetation, and it has been postulated that it may be associated with mutations that provide resistance to viral infections. Pelage is usually soft and woolly, with a glossy appearance maintained by frequent cleaning with the tongue and paws. Pelage also insulates cats from their ambient climate, and some species with a wide geographical distribution (e.g., Tiger, Leopard) have variable fur length depending on their geographical origin. Fur length may also vary seasonally through the annual temperature cycle. Male Lions develop a minimal to abundant mane of very long hairs on the neck and chest; Cheetahs have a dense but relatively short nuchal crest. The tail is well haired, but not bushy, and the facial whiskers are well developed and often thought to be an adaptation to nocturnal movement in dense cover.

Figure 3. Variations in pelage length and color in Leopards (*Panthera pardus*): There is a high degree of variation in coloring of Leopards across their broad geographical range: (1) Melanistic Indochinese Leopard (*P. pardus delacouri*), also know as Black Panther, which is most populous in humid forests; (2) Persian Leopard (*P. pardus tulliana*), a pale subspecies lacking the rich reddish-tawny hue characteristic of other subspecies; (3) African Leopard (*P. pardus pardus*), with the typical yellowish fur covered with black rosettes; (4) North Chinese Leopard (*P. pardus orientalis*), with long, dense hair, bright and lustrous in color, and large black rosettes.

The pelage of hyenas is a mix of spots, stripes, and muted shades of brown and black. The coat of the Spotted Hyena (*Crocuta crocuta*) is short and sparse, but in the other species it is long and shaggy with an erectile mane. The tail is bushy.

Skeleton (figs. 4 and 5): The skeleton of most felids is designed for speed and power, for flexible bodies with muscular limbs, and a number of morphological adaptations that have allowed them to become the most adept hunters in the order Carnivora. Its anatomy is conservative, with only the size and relative proportions of the various bones varying much from species to species. All cats have a very flexible vertebral column, allowing rotation along the length of the spine. As a result, cats can twist and turn easily, and flex and arch the back to increase stride length and speed. The number of vertebrae in the spinal column is remarkably consistent in all felids: 7 cervical, 13 thoracic, 7 lumbar, and 3 sacral vertebrae. Caudal vertebrae, which make up the tail, vary from 14 to 28. Some species, such as the Cheetah (*Acinonyx jubatus*) and Marbled Cat (*Pardofelis marmorata*), have very long tails that serve an important function in counterbalancing the weight of the body when running or climbing. Other cats, such as the Lynx (*Lynx* spp.) and the Caracal (*Caracal caracal*), have short tails. Felids have a vestigial baculum (os penis).

Hyenas have relatively short torsos and are fairly massive, with a short, thick neck, low hindquarters, high withers, giving a sloping-back posture. Their skeletons are adapted to long-distance, energy-efficient foraging in open environments. The axial skeleton of hyenas has a total of 47-58 vertebrae: 7 cervical, 15-16 thoracic, 4-5 lumbar, 2-4 sacral, and 19-26 caudal vertebrae. They show limited mobility, even in the cervical area, which is enlarged and robust to maintain the powerful muscles involved in the bone-crushing system. Hyenas lack a baculum (os penis).

Limbs (fig. 6): All cats are digitigrade and have five toes on the forefoot and four on the hind foot. The first digit on the front foot, the dewclaw, is mostly small and does not touch the ground (in Cheetahs the dewclaw is long and is used to snag and drag down prey). All cats have protractile claws, being retracted in the resting position in a fleshy sheath. Cats use their claws to help grab prey, to climb

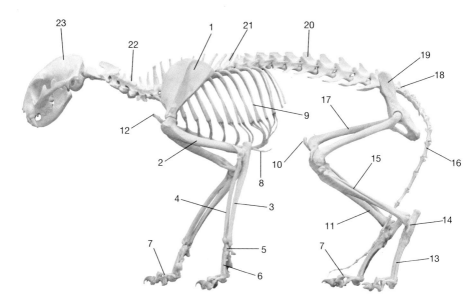

Figure 4. The skeleton of the Domestic Cat (*Felis catus*): (1) scapula; (2) humerus; (3) ulna; (4) radius; (5) carpals; (6) metacarpals; (7) phalanges; (8) sternum; (9) ribs; (10) patella; (11) tibia; (12) clavicle; (13) metatarsals; (14) tarsus; (15) fibula; (16) caudal vertebrae; (17) femur; (18) sacral vertebrae; (19) pelvis; (20) lumbar vertebrae; (21) thoracic vertebrae; (22) cervical vertebrae; (23) skull. Photo credit: *Sascha Uncia*.

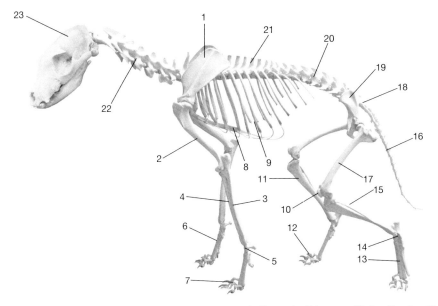

Figure 5. The skeleton of the Aardwolf (*Proteles cristatus*): (1) scapula; (2) humerus; (3) ulna; (4) radius; (5) carpals; (6) metacarpals; (7) phalanges; (8) sternum; (9) ribs; (10) patella; (11) tibia; (12) phalanges; (13) metatarsals; (14) tarsus; (15) fibula; (16) caudal vertebrae; (17) femur; (18) sacral vertebrae; (19) pelvis; (20) lumbar vertebrae; (21) thoracic vertebrae; (22) cervical vertebrae; (23) skull. Photo credit: *Polyoutis*, Museum of Osteology, OK (USA).

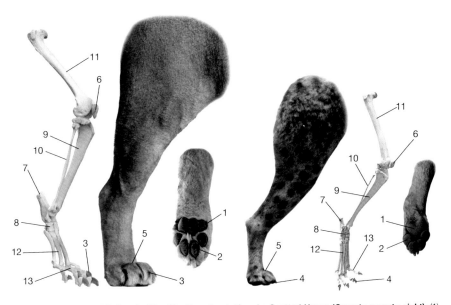

Figure 6. Right hind limbs of a Lion (*Panthera leo*, left) and a Spotted Hyena (*Crocuta crocuta*, right): (1) metatarsal pad; (2) digital pads; (3) protactile claw; (4) non-retractable claw; (5) paw; (6) patella; (7) tuber calcanei; (8) tarsal bones; (9) tibia; (10) fibula; (11) femur; (12) metatarsal bones; (13) phalanges. Photo credit: *Suphakit73*, Eric Isselée.

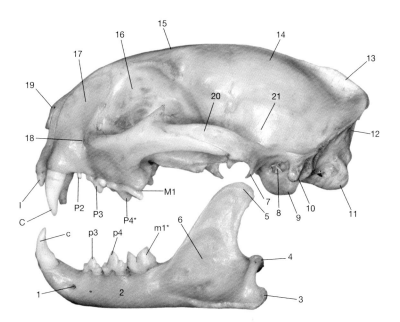

Figure 7. The skull of the Serval (*Leptailurus serval*), side view: (I) incisors; (C) canines; (P) premolars; (M) molars; (*) carnassials; (1) mental foramen; (2) mandible; (3) angular process; (4) condyloid process; (5) coronoid process; (6) masseteric fossa; (7) retroauricular process; (8) external acoustic meatus; (9) auditory bulla; (10) paraoccipital process; (11) occipital condyle; (12) occipital; (13) sagittal crest; (14) parietal; (15) frontal; (16) orbit; (17) maxilla; (18) infraorbital foramen; (19) nasal; (20) zygomatic arch; (21) temporal. Photo credit: *Phil Myers, Museum of Zoology, University of Michigan-Ann Arbor (USA)*.

trees, and as weapons in fights. The purpose of this skin sheath is to protect the claws from excessive wear. When needed, the claws are actively extended, or protracted. The sheaths are vestigial in the Cheetah (*Acinonyx jubatus*), as well as in the Fishing Cat (*Prionailurus viverrinus*) and Flat-Headed Cat (*Prionailurus planiceps*), such that the claws protrude visibly. The bottoms of the paws have soft pads, in the center and one at the tip of each toe, which help cats to move silently when stalking game. Species living in extreme climates, such as Sand Cats (*Felis margarita*) living in deserts and Canada Lynx (*Lynx canadensis*) living in boreal forests, have fur-covered foot pads to insulate the feet from extreme surface temperatures and to facilitate traveling on both sand and snow. Arboreal cats, such as Margays (*Leopardus wiedii*) and Marbled Cats (*Pardofelis marmorata*), have very wide paws, to grip large branches, and a flexible ankle joint allows them to climb down trees head first. The legs in felids may be very long or relatively short. Forelimbs are used for locomotion and prey-killing. Hind limbs are generally longer, an important feature for acceleration and jumping, and provide more force than forelimbs. The tibia and fibula bones in the hind limbs are joined by fibrous tissue in most species (with the exception of some arboreal cats, such as the Margay), with the tarsal bones below them also being fused, giving increased stability when running. The reduction or the clavicle (collar bone) in felids increases stride length and absorbs shocks after a jump.

Hyenas are also digitigrade and highly cursorially adapted. They have four toes on each foot, except in the forefeet of the Aardwolf (*Proteles cristatus*), which has five. Front feet are far larger than hind feet, giving a distinctive track. Paws have supporting bulging pads and short, blunt claws, not protractile, unlike those of felids. Forelimbs are longer than hind limbs, with a sloping-back posture and somewhat rocking-horse running gait. The well-developed forelimbs provide ample power to prey on animals much larger in size than themselves, and take the weight of prey parts that hyenas often carry away, while the relatively weak hind limbs sustain long-distance loping, which is advantageous when hunting faster. Bones are generally more curved than in felids, more closely resembling those of canids, although more robust. The Spotted Hyena (*Crocuta crocuta*) displays more robust limbs than the remaining genera. The curved and stocky girdles further resemble more closely those of canids, rather than the more slender, straight, and elongated girdles of felids.

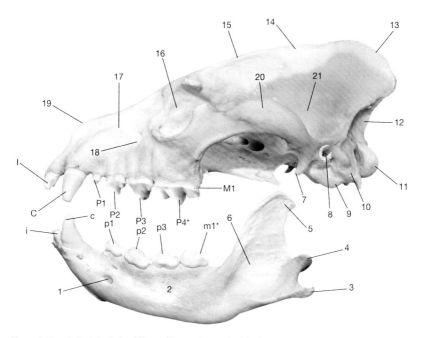

Figure 8. The skull of the Striped Hyena (Hyaena hyaena), side view: (I) Incisors; (C) canines; (P) premolars; (M) molars; (*) carnassials; (1) mental foramen; (2) mandible; (3) angular process; (4) condyloid process; (5) coronoid process; (6) masseteric fossa; (7) retroauricular process; (8) external acoustic meatus; (9) auditory bulla; (10) paraoccipital process; (11) occipital condyle; (12) occipital; (13) sagittal crest; (14) parietal; (15) frontal; (16) orbit; (17) maxilla; (18) infraorbital foramen; (19) nasal; (20) zygomatic arch; (21) temporal. Photo credit: *Phil Myers*, Museum of Zoology, University of Michigan-Ann Arbor (USA).

Skull (figs. 7 and 8): Felids have a short and rounded rostrum with large eyes, powerful jaws, and specialized sharp-edged carnassials. The skull in most small cats is rounded, with a domed braincase, and a very short, broad rostrum. Large cats have a more elongated skull, with a more extended muzzle. The masticatory apparatus and dentition are highly specialized for vertebrate prey-killing and meat-shearing functions. Large cat species and males in medium-sized species have sagittal and nuchal crests along the top of the skull, providing the necessary surface area for strong jaw-closing muscles (temporal muscles) to attach and creating even greater jaw strength. The zygomatic arches are strongly built and widely bowed, leaving room for these large temporal muscles. Small cats show only limited sagittal crests, although the Flat-Headed Cat (*Prionailurus planiceps*), one of the smaller cats, also has a well-developed crest, suggesting that this fish-eater has great biting power. The orbital space in the skull is large and faces more or less forward providing space for relatively large eyes with binocular vision, as many species rely on their eyesight to detect potential prey. The orbit is normally open to the side, though in many cases, especially in small cats, it can be closed by cartilage.

The skull of the three large hyenas is long and robust, characterized by a series of features that provide an enhanced ability to break bones: massive jaws with strong teeth, a high sagittal crest, and broad zygomatic arches that swing out at the back, enabling the presence of large masticatory muscles. The muzzle is generally shorter, but wider than in canids. The distal elongation of the frontal sinuses, which completely overlap the brain, is also characteristic and unique among the Carnivora. The skull of the Aardwolf (*Proteles cristatus*) is highly adapted to an insect diet. It displays a dog-like morphology, with a long muzzle, and the skull lacks a sagittal crest, the elongated frontal sinuses, and the wide and opened zygomatic arches that are characteristic of other hyenas. The mandible is shallow and thin.

Dentition (figs. 7, 8, and 9): The basic dental formula of felids is: incisors (I) 3/3, canines (C) 1/1, premolars (P) 3/2, molars (M) 1/1 = 30, but some species (the four species of Lynx, the Pallas's Cat, Asian Golden Cat, Jungle Cat, Ocelot, Andean Mountain Cat, and Clouded Leopard) may have 28. The reduced dentition allows for a reduced length of the skull and mandibles, which improves efficiency of the muscles that close the jaw. Cats can move their jaws slightly laterally so that they can engage their carnassials, which normally do not shear past each other when using a killing bite; the mandibular condyle is tubular. They cut and tear their food into chunks they can swallow. Cats have a more powerful bite relative to muscle mass than any other carnivore except mustelids. The tongue is also covered with sharp papillae capable of cutting or ripping flesh and useful for grooming the fur. All felid premolars and molars show carnassial modifications and the third premolar has an extra feature: an anterior cusp for crushing bones. The incisors are small and arranged in a straight line, and are used to maintain a grip on prey and for nipping flesh from carcasses. Canines are exceptionally long, strong, slightly curved, and sharply pointed, often with a lengthwise groove in the enamel, and are used to kill prey.

The dental formula in hyenas is: incisors (I) 3/3, canines (C) 1/1, premolars (P) 4/3, molars (M) 1/1 = 34, except for the Aardwolf (*Proteles cristatus*), which often has a reduced number of premolars and molars. The dentition is similar to that of felids, although the teeth are overall wider and stouter. The carnassials are very powerful and shifted far back to allow for a very powerful bite to crush bone. The remaining premolars are robust, with broad bases and cutting edges. Bone-cracking hyenas rely on the premolars for breaking bones instead of the molars, like canids. The canines are short, thick, and robust, and the incisors are unspecialized. Dentition in the termite-eating Aardwolf is more distinctive, being characterized by reduced and widely spaced peg-like cheek teeth that contrast with the still large canines.

CLASSIFICATION

The family Felidae belongs to the order Carnivora, a monophyletic group comprising 16 extant families. Carnivorans have teeth and claws adapted for catching and eating prey. The order Carnivora is characterized by functional specializations for shearing in the fourth upper premolar and the first lower molar. These teeth, called carnassials, have a blade-like morphology, and remain as the central character complex that unites members of the order Carnivora. Other features shared by all carnivores include the fusion of certain bones in the foot (scaphoid, lunar, and central bones) to form the scapholunar, an ossified auditory bulla, a relatively undeveloped clavicle, and a penis containing an elongated bony structure known as the baculum (lost in hyenas).

Carnivora are grouped into two suborders (fig. 10): Feliformia (cat-like carnivorans) and Caniformia (dog-like carnivorans). Feliformia includes seven families: Nandiniidae (African Palm Civet), Felidae (cats), Prionodontidae (linsangs), Viverridae (civets and genets), Hyaenidae (hyenas), Eupleridae (Malagasy

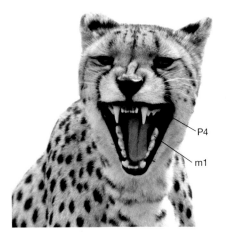

Figure 9. Dentition in the Cheetah (*Acinonyx jubatus*) and Spotted Hyena (*Crocuta crocuta*): The generalized felid dental formula is I 3/3, C 1/1, P 3/2, M 1/1 = 30. The upper third premolar and lower molar are adapted as carnassial teeth and the third premolar has an extra feature: an anterior cusp for crushing bones. The dental formula of the large hyenas is I 3/3, C 1/1, P 4/3, M 1/1 = 34. The dentition is similar to that of felids, although the teeth are overall wider and stouter. The carnassials are very powerful and shifted far back to the point of exertion of peak pressure on the jaws. Carnassial teeth are the last upper premolar, P4, and the first lower molar, m1. Photo credits: *Lucasdm, Tambako*.

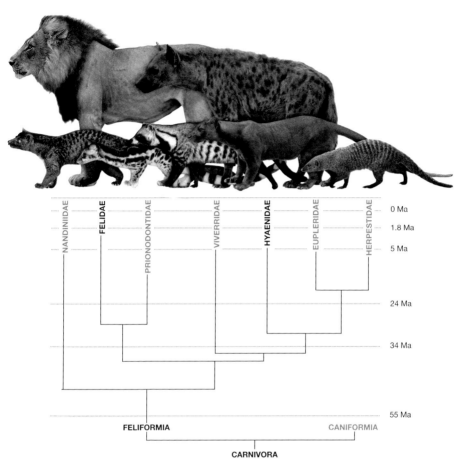

Figure 10. Schematic phylogenetic tree of the Carnivora, based on molecular data, with estimated divergence times, and illustrations of representative taxa (from left): Nandiniidae: African Palm Civet (*Nandinia binotata*); Felidae: Lion (*Panthera leo*); Prionodontidae: Banded Linsang (*Prionodon linsang*); Viverridae: African Civet (*Civettictis civetta*); Hyaenidae: Spotted Hyena (*Crocuta crocuta*); Eupleridae: Fossa (*Cryptoprocta ferox*); Herpestidae: Banded Mongoose (*Mungos mungo*) (Modified from Zhou et al. 2017). Photo credits: *Klaus Rudloff, Thomas Retterath, Ondrej Prosický, Dominique Salé, José R. Castelló, Iakov Filimonov.*

carnivorans), and Herpestidae (mongooses). Caniformia includes Canidae (dogs, wolves, coyotes, jackals, and foxes), Ursidae (bears), Ailuridae (Red Panda), Mephitidae (skunks and stink badgers), Procyonidae (raccoons and relatives), Mustelidae (weasels, badgers, and otters), and three marine mammal families: Phocidae (true seals), Otariidae (seals and sea-lions), and Odobenidae (walruses).

Feliforms share a common attribute: the auditory bullae are double-chambered, composed of two bones joined by a septum, while caniforms have single-chambered or partially divided auditory bullae, composed of a single bone. Feliforms tend to have shorter rostra than caniforms, fewer teeth, and more specialized carnassials. They tend to be more carnivorous and are generally ambush hunters.

The family Felidae comprises two subfamilies: the Pantherinae, which includes the larger-bodied cats of the genera *Panthera* and *Neofelis*, with 7 species, and the Felinae, comprising 12 genera and 34 species. The key characteristic to separate the big cats from the smaller cats is the presence of a partially ossified hyoid bone (which allows big cats to roar, but not purr), while the hyoid of smaller cats is completely ossified and rigid (allowing them to purr but not roar). However, it has been found that

15

the fundamental difference between the mostly roaring non-purring cats and the rest is the structure of the larynx: long, fleshy, elasticat vocal folds within the larynx of big cats resonate to produce a roar, whereas the smaller cats, including the Cheetah, have simpler vocal folds that only allow purring. Molecular studies support the existence of eight major phylogenetic groups or lineages of extant felids (fig. 11): the Panthera lineage consists of the five big, roaring cats belonging to the genus *Panthera*, as well as the two closely related species of Clouded Leopards; the Puma lineage is composed of three species in three genera: Puma, Jaguarundi, and Cheetah; the Ocelot lineage, essentially a Neotropical group, comprises nine species belonging to the genus *Leopardus*; the Leopard Cat lineage consists of six Asian wild cats, five in the genus *Prionailurus* and one in the genus *Otocolobus*; the Caracal lineage comprises three medium-sized cats, two species in the genus *Caracal* and one in *Leptailurus*; the Wildcat lineage consists of six small wild cats in the genus *Felis* as well as the Domestic Cat: European and African Wildcats, Chinese Mountain Cat, Jungle Cat, Sand Cat, and Black-Footed Cat; the Lynx lineage comprises four cats in the genus *Lynx*: the Canadian, Iberian, and Eurasian Lynx, and the Bobcat; and the Bay Cat Lineage has three species in the genera *Pardofelis* and *Catopuma*: Marbled Cat, Asiatic Golden Cat, and Bay Cat.

The family Hyaenidae also forms part of the suborder Feliformia. The four extant species of the Hyaenidae are divided into two subfamilies. The subfamily Hyaeninae contains the Spotted Hyena, the Brown Hyena, and the Striped Hyena. The Aardwolf is the only member of the subfamily Protelinae (fig. 12).

TAXONOMY

The taxonomy of felids has undergone considerable changes in the past, not only at the level of species and subspecies, but even at the level of genus. Based on new molecular, morphological, and biogeographical studies, the Cat Classification Task Force (CCTF) of the IUCN Cat Specialist Group recently reviewed the current taxonomy of the Felidae (Kitchener et al., 2017). A total of 14 genera, 42 species, and 77 subspecies are currently recognized by the CCTF, which is a considerable change from the classification proposed by Wozencraft in 2005, the last major revision of the Felidae. The Clouded Leopard (*Neofelis nebulosa*) has now been separated into two species: Sunda Clouded Leopard (*Neofelis diardi*) and Indochinese Clouded Leopard (*Neofelis nebulosa*). The Sunda Leopard Cat (*Prionailurus javanensis*) was determined to be its own species separate from the Leopard Cat, now called the Mainland Leopard Cat (*Prionailurus bengalensis*). The Iriomote Cat is no longer recognized as a subspecies, being now included with the Amur Leopard Cat (*Prionailurus bengalensis euptilurus*). The Wildcat is now categorized into two separate species: the European Wildcat (*Felis silvestris*), and the African and Asian Wildcat (*Felis lybica*), which includes the steppe and bush cats of Africa and Asia. The Chinese Mountain Cat (*Felis bieti*), formerly classified as a Wildcat subspecies, is now recognized as a valid species. All the small cats of South and Central America are now brought together in the genus *Leopardus,* and the Tigrina is now categorized in three different species. The Snow Leopard, formerly placed in the genus *Uncia*, is now assigned to the genus *Panthera* (*P. uncia*). The Lion (*Panthera leo*) consists now of only two subspecies, and the Asian Lion is no longer considered a valid subspecies, being subsumed within the subspecies *P. leo leo*. Only two Tiger subspecies have been proposed: the nominal *P. t. tigris* of mainland Asia, and *P. t. sondaica* of Sumatra, Java, and Bali, although new genome-wide studies suggest that there may be six Tiger subspecies. Only further research will be able to resolve the potential conflicts in existing data. We will follow this new taxonomic proposal for the description of most species and subspecies in this book.

Hyenas have been the subject of a number of systematic studies during the last two centuries, due in large part to the extensive fossil record of the group, with nearly 70 described fossil species. The Aardwolf was formerly placed in its own family, Protelidae, but is now included as a subfamily in the Hyaenidae. The Brown Hyena was previously classified in the genus *Hyaena*, but later placed in its own genus, *Parahyaena*. The subspecific status of Striped Hyenas and Aardwolves is unclear. Because of its disjunct distribution in Africa, occurring in two discrete areas 1,500 kilometers apart from one another, the Aardwolf is provisionally categorized into two separate subspecies, but their validity requires confirmation. Five subspecies of Striped Hyena have been described on the basis of pelage characters, but they are inadequately characterized, and probably form only two larger groups, a northeast African-Arabian group, and a northwest African-Asian group. Neither the Spotted Hyena nor the Brown Hyena is currently recognized to have subspecies.

BEHAVIOR

Social Organization: With the exception of Lions, Cheetahs, and feral cats, felids do not live in social groups, but only come together to mate, probably because most hunt more efficiently as individuals. Even where large prey is abundant, they do not form groups to take advantage

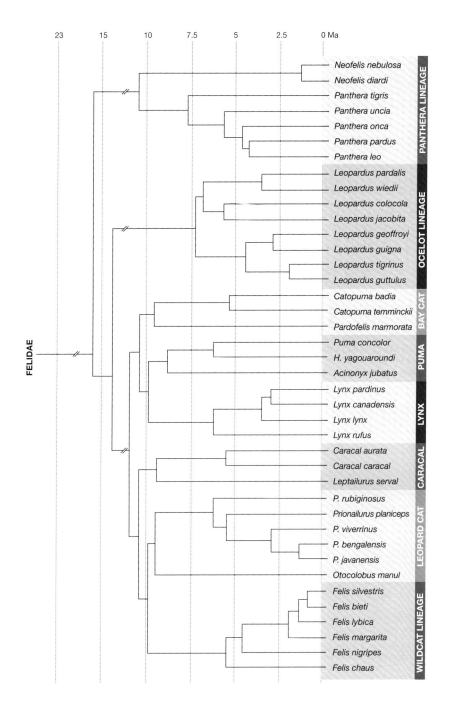

Figure 11. Phylogenetic tree of the Felidae, based on molecular data, with estimated divergence times. Modified from *Zhou et al., 2017*.

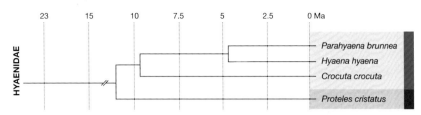

Figure 12. Phylogenetic tree of the Hyaenidae, based on molecular data, with estimated divergence times. Modified from *Westbury et al., 2019.*

of some of the potential benefits of sociality. Unlike cats, canids cannot bring down large prey animals alone, and their chasing style of hunting lends itself to cooperation. With the exception of Lions and Cheetah males, felids are generally intolerant of conspecifics. Females live spaced apart in home ranges, which are usually mutually exclusive or overlap to some degree. Young leave their mother's home range upon reaching adult size, although in some species, female offspring may take over part of their mother's home range. However, female cats and their female young do not stick together, except in Lions. Most felids are primarily nocturnal, with activity peaks during dusk and dawn, with the exception of Cheetahs and Jaguarundis. This nocturnal pattern of activity, the use of densely vegetated habitat, wide-ranging movements, and often wariness preclude obtaining information *in situ* for most species, especially the small cats. Most cats are exceptional climbers and some species are skilled swimmers. Scent-marking is used to mark home-range boundaries and communicate dominance and fertility. Cats, unlike canids, make little use of shelters either for their daily rest or for breeding.

Hyenas differ greatly in behavior and social organization depending on the species, ranging from weakly to highly social, with complex behaviors in large societies. Spotted Hyenas are gregarious and live in large matrilineal social groups known as clans whose members play different roles and hunt cooperatively. The remaining two species of larger hyenas only form small groups, although the interaction between individuals and their social behaviors is complex. Brown Hyenas have intricate relationships between individuals, with carcasses as important socializing focal points. Aardwolves, in turn, are socially monogamous, but primarily solitary foragers except when accompanied by cubs.

Figure 13. Mating in Lions (*Panthera leo*): A female presents her ano-genital region to the male by backing toward him with her tail deflected to one side and assumes a crouching posture (lordosis) resting on her extended forelimbs. The male mounts by stepping over and behind the female with forelegs straddling her on either side. During intromission, the male makes quick bites at the nape of the female's neck. The female usually turns toward the male and may swing a paw at him immediately after copulation. The female may show an after-reaction, consisting of vigorous rolling on the ground. Copulation in other felids is similiar but less frequent. Photo credit: *Alexandra Giese.*

Figure 14. Spotted Hyena (*Crocuta crocuta*) mating: Owing to its pseudopenis, a female maintains complete control over the mating process. Males are forced to mate in a very unstable position. They depend on the full cooperation of the female. The glans of the male's penis swells slightly in the female's reproductive tract, so that the sex partners remain in a brief "copulatory lock" for some minutes. Photo credit: *Mike Dexter.*

Feeding behavior and diet: Members of the Felidae differ little in their diets. They are all hypercarnivores that specialize on vertebrates, but may differ in their choice of prey and prey-size preferences. Unlike most canids, which frequently eat fruits and vegetation, cats are almost entirely carnivorous. Large cats prey on very large mammals (mostly ungulates), with only a few species making up the bulk of their diet. Medium-sized felids eat smaller prey but a larger number of different species. Small felids prey on mammals, birds, reptiles, amphibians, and insects. Fishing Cats and Flat-Headed Cats are unique among felids, as they are especially adapted for preying upon fish and frogs. All wild cats hunt and kill their own prey, but some will scavenge opportunistically. Felids most often hunt alone. Typically, they come across or flush prey when patrolling their home ranges or they lie in ambush by trails or burrow entrances waiting for prey to appear. Once the prey has been detected, most cats stalk by crouching low to the ground and approaching slowly, making use of any intervening cover. When within striking distance, the cat rushes forward or pounces on the prey. Some cats may also hunt arboreally, or hunt out of trees for terrestrial prey, or may hunt in water. Cooperative hunting is observed in a few species, but Lions display this behavior more often, and in a more organized way, than other species. However, cooperative hunting comparable to that found in canids is not seen in felids. Food caching is not common, although large kills may be cached by covering with leaves, grass, or dirt, or carried into trees. Large cats usually remain near a kill for several days and consume it at their leisure. Among the smaller cats, the prey is mostly consumed at one meal. Cats are stimulated to stalk and catch prey even when satiated, which explains why most felids may kill many more animals than they can eat. Cats mainly hunt at night, though the Cheetah is diurnal. Cats rarely chase their prey over any great distance (except for the Cheetah), although they may make a short rush before striking. Felids usually kill their prey with a single strangulating bite to the throat for large prey or a bite to the nape of the neck to sever the spinal cord of small prey. Their truncated jaws, long canines, and powerful forelimbs with protractile claws enable them to kill swiftly once they have made contact with the prey. Hunting strategies used by small cats for birds, reptiles, and fishes are also very consistent among species, usually involving stalking and sit-and-wait ambushes. Most small cats feed by crouching over their prey without using their paws, whereas large cats (excepting the Snow Leopard) eat while lying down. Like most carnivores, felids are independent of free water, but will utilize water when available.

The dentition of the three larger hyenas is adapted to meat-eating and bone-crushing, while the Aardwolf displays a reduced dentition because its diet is based almost solely on termites. Hyenas' ability to break open bones and extract marrow, and also to digest bone, gives them access to a food source unavailable to other carnivores. Spotted Hyenas eat almost everything they can, and scavenge to a large extent, although they also actively hunt. Striped Hyenas are not efficient hunters and rely

Figure 15. Different facial expressions in the Tiger: (1, 2) flehmen (open mouth, wrinkled nose, raised chin and gaping tongue), facilitating the transfer of scents into the vomeronasal organ located in the roof of the mouth; (3) yawning face, usually signaling a tired animal; (4) threat, defensive face, with upper lips curled, mouth open to show the canines, and ears lowered and turned backward; (5) aggressive, stalking; (6) neutral face. Photo credits: *Georg Sander, Marie Reed, Eric Gevaert, Alexander Sliwa.*

on foraging, feeding mainly on carrion, especially the bony remains of carcasses. Brown Hyenas are also generalist, opportunistic, and scavenging carnivores that eat almost everything they can. Hyenas may cache food and accumulate bones in waterholes, under bushes, or in tall grass. The presence of water is essential to Spotted Hyenas and Striped Hyenas, and they cannot inhabit arid regions without it. The Brown Hyena drinks water when it is available, but is independent of it. Aardwolves are also independent of water as they get all their moisture from the termites eaten.

Reproduction: Felids are annually polyestrous or seasonal breeders. Both male and female cats spend much time in exploring the urine and skin gland secretions of strange cats who may come into their range. The urine and cheek gland secretions of females generally contain pheromones and males commonly show flehmen in response to these messages. Receptive females exhibit a characteristic lordosis essential for a successful mating. They lie on the ground with the rump raised and make alternate treading movements with the hind legs. During copulation, the male grips the neck of the female, especially at ejaculation (fig. 13). There may be repeated copulations over a short period of time. Gestation period varies greatly depending upon body size, with larger species having longer gestation periods, ranging from 2 to 3.5 months, and litter sizes from 1 to 5. Larger cat species produce litters every two to five years, while smaller cats do so annually or, rarely, twice a year. If the first litter is lost, females will mate soon and may rear a second litter. Females have no aid from males in provisioning the young and must cope with rearing offspring and teaching them to hunt without assistance of other adults. Felids are not burrowers and they generally do not excavate dens, but young are typically born at secluded sites (crevices, hollow logs, caves, tree dens). Young cats are born in a slightly more precocial state than is the case with canids. Except for Lions, male and female cats seldom meet face to face, and they do not maintain permanent pair bonds. Male home ranges overlap those of more than one female.

The three larger species of hyenas are polyestrous and non-seasonal breeders, with reproductive periods occurring throughout the year and depending on resource availability. Aardwolves, in contrast, have a single estrus per year, commonly during the winter. Mating systems are diverse. Spotted Hyena males and females possess similar external genitalia. Female Spotted Hyenas have a peniform and erectile clitoris, as well as a false scrotum. Male Spotted Hyenas can only mate when they are dominant in their clan, although all the males can court females, making their mating highly polygynous (fig. 14). Mating in the smaller Brown Hyena clans takes place between resident clan females and nomadic males, and generally only a single female per clan gives birth to cubs each year. Male Striped Hyenas mate by following an estrous female for days. The monogamous Aardwolf displays cuckoldry as a common trait: neighboring males paste and visit the female while the resident male is away foraging, so that when the time comes the resident male is not the only one that has copulated with the female. Gestation time is variable between hyaenid species, around 90 days, and litter size is from one to four. They keep their young in breeding dens, which are usually holes in the ground or sometimes caves. The cubs leave the communal den when they are older.

Visual communication (fig. 15): Visual signals do not differ greatly among Felidae. Complex expressive movements are highly developed, despite most species being solitary. When conspecifics meet, their tail posture, position of the ears, and exposure of teeth reveal their level of tolerance. The long ear tufts of some species accentuate the movements of ears when signaling visually. Long ringed tails with prominent black tips may also be important as visual signals. Often visual communication is associated with vocalizations to accentuate the desired effect. Cats have acute, binocular, dichromatic vision, with very good night vision, helped by a layer inside the eye, the tapetum lucidum, which reflects back light, and accounts for the eye shine we see in cats' eyes at night. Whiskers are sensitive to touch, which also helps the animals move around at night and direct the killing bite.

Hyenas use a variety of tactile, visual, vocal, and olfactory systems of communication. Spotted Hyenas have the most developed visual patterns in the family, using a greater variety of head and tail movements, with an elaborate meeting ceremony. The most striking visual display of hyenas is pilo-erection of the long hair over the back and neck, which occurs in any situation where there is a tendency to either attack or flee. Spotted Hyenas can erect the hairs on their necks during aggressive encounters, but the display is less prominent as they have much shorter hair.

Olfactory communication (fig. 16): The sense of smell is less important in cats than vision and hearing, with a major role in communication and social interaction, maintaining home ranges, and advertising that females are ready to mate. Felids produce and deposit odors from their anal glands, as well as from the cheek and submandibular glands, and the glands between the foot pads. Urine is undoubtedly an important information carrier, but feces may also serve a demarcation purpose in big cats (but not in Lions), often combined with anal gland secretions. Males mark with urine by raising the tail and marking to the rear on vertical objects, such as bushes and tree trunks. Females generally leave urine marks by squatting, but at a lower frequency than males, but they will spray too. One

Figure 16. Tigers mark their home ranges with scent and visual cues: (1) sniffing a tree; (2) spraying urine on a tree trunk to signal the boundaries of and trails within its territory; (3) scratching its claws and marking a tree with secretions from the perioral, submandibular, and interdigital glands. Photo credits: *Ndp, Andy Rouse, Francois Savigny*.

combined olfactory and visual signal involves scratching on tree branches. Both large and small cats tend to rub their cheeks on those scratched areas, and urination may occur in the immediate vicinity of a scratching tree.

Hyenas scent-mark in several ways, such as pasting, scratching, and using latrines, but unlike other carnivorans do not use urine for scent-marking. Pasting is a scent-marking method exclusive to hyenas, consisting of smearing strong-smelling anal gland secretions, produced in the anal pouch, onto objects in their range. The anal pouch, located above the anus, is anatomically and histologically very similar in the four species. The pouch itself is formed by large numbers of sebaceous glands, with their internal secretory area being eversible and retractable. Scratching involves scent-marking objects with secretions from the interdigital glands and is complementary to pasting.

Vocal Communication: Felids have numerous vocalizations for communicating with conspecifics. Close contact calls are employed in encounters, while long-distance vocalizations not only bring sexes together for breeding but allow for the maintenance of spacing among adult individuals of the same sex. Meow-type calls are common to all species: low-intensity meows usually occur between mothers and kittens at close range; high-intensity meows are used by adults for home-range advertisement and mate attraction. Most species spit, hiss, and growl in agonistic situations. In close-contact situations, cats frequently purr. Most big cats, however, seem incapable of purring (or they purr only while exhaling). Whereas purring cats tend to have a rigid hyoid bone connected to the skull by a series of other small bones, the large, non-purring, roaring cats (Lions, Tigers, Leopards, and Jaguars) have large pads of fibro-elastic tissue near the forward portion of their vocal folds, and a more flexible, incompletely ossified hyoid bone. Roaring is utilized in long-range communication, during mating, and sometimes after a successful kill, but never during the attack, which is carried out in silence. Felids have acute hearing, well beyond the human ear. The ability to hear very high frequency sounds is especially useful to small cats, as it allows them to detect the ultrasonic communication of small rodents. The large ears of some species allow them also to detect small rodents running through the undergrowth. These large ears can be moved together or independently to listen to these sounds.

Spotted Hyenas have a wide range of different vocalizations, which they use for individual recognition, to defend their territory, and to communicate between individuals, but also to maintain the complex social organization of clans. The vocalizations in the remaining three species of hyenas, which lack the developed social skills of Spotted Hyenas, are less complex. Striped Hyenas have a wide range of vocalizations, which have not been studied in depth but apparently resemble those of Spotted Hyenas, although they are less varied. Striped Hyenas vocalize much less in Africa than in Asia, being almost silent in East Africa, in order to avoid the dominant carnivores of the area. Brown Hyenas have eight types of vocalizations, which they mainly use for short-range communications between individuals when foraging. Aardwolves use diverse acoustic signals when interacting with conspecifics at close and medium range but seem to lack a true long-range vocalization.

DISTRIBUTION AND HABITAT

Felids are found the world over, with the exception of Australia, the polar regions, and some oceanic islands. Domestic Cats have been introduced to almost all places settled by humans, including Australia and other islands, where they are usually considered a serious pest, causing extinctions of many endemic species. Some species have extremely wide geographical distributions: Leopards inhabit most of Asia and Africa, the Eurasian Lynx lives across northern Europe and Asia, Wildcats live in Europe, Africa, and Asia, Pumas live in much of North, Central, and South America, and the Leopard Cat's range stretches from Southeast Asia into parts of India in the south, extending to the Russian Far East in the north. Other species have very restricted ranges: the Iberian Lynx lives only on the Iberian Peninsula, the Andean Mountain Cat lives in the central Andes, the Chinese Mountain Cat lives only in central China, the Bay Cat is restricted to the island of Borneo, the Sunda Clouded Leopard lives on the islands of Borneo and Sumatra, the Black-Footed Cats lives only in southern Africa and has the most restricted distribution of any African cat species, while the distribution of the Guiña is limited to the Chilean and Argentinian temperate forests, having the smallest geographical range of the New World felids. Cats have colonized almost all major habitat types from desert to equatorial rainforest, swamps, and high mountains, and most species are not habitat specialists and can be found in a range of environments.

The diversity and geographic distribution of the family Hyaenidae was much greater in the past, with more than 60 species known from the fossil record, distributed throughout Africa, Eurasia, and, intermittently, even North America. Hyenas now occur mainly in sub-Saharan Africa, with no species being found in the rainforests of the Congo and only the Striped Hyena occurring in North Africa, continuing through into southern Asia as far as India. Hyenas have a wide habitat tolerance from semi-desert, savanna, and open woodland to dense dry woodland. The Spotted Hyena also occupies montane habitats.

EVOLUTION AND FOSSIL RECORD

The order Carnivora first appeared about 60 Ma, in the middle Paleocene, and throughout the Eocene was represented by a single family, the Miacidae, composed of small species that did not diversify very much. Toward the end of the Eocene and early Oligocene, about 35-40 Ma, miacids underwent a rapid evolutionary radiation that produced several of the modern carnivoran families. The Felidae diverged from a common ancestor with the Viverridae, Hyaenidae, Herpestidae, and Eupleridae. The family Felidae later diverged into two major lineages, Pantherinae and Felinae, about 15 Ma. The Pantherinae diverged in Asia from a common felid ancestor during the late Miocene (11 Ma), and Clouded Leopards (*Neofelis*) split very early (6.5 Ma) from *Panthera* species. The Bay Cat lineage is the second oldest Felidae lineage to diverge from the ancestral cat species in Asia at 9.4 Ma, and three species evolved in Southeast Asia. The Caracal lineage is the third oldest lineage of the family and diverged at 8.5 Ma; the precursor of this lineage spread trans-continentally from Asia into Africa, when the sea level lowered, creating a land bridge between Africa and the Arabian Peninsula. The ancestors of the Ocelot lineage probably diverged in North America 8 Ma, and later migrated over the Panama land bridge to South America and evolved recently and rapidly. The Lynx lineage descends from a common ancestor that diverged from other cat species 7.2 Ma and dispersed to the Americas via the reopening of the Bering land bridge. The Puma lineage diverged from other felids approximately 6.7 Ma in Eurasia. The Leopard Cat lineage probably diverged from Eurasian forebears that either remained in Asia or derived from American migrants that crossed the Bering Strait between 6.7 and 6.2 Ma. The Wildcat lineage is the most recent to diverge at 3.4 Ma around the Mediterranean basin and western Asia.

Hyenas diverged from their sister feliform group around 29 Ma, in the middle Oligocene period. The family Hyaenidae consisted of at least 24 species at the peak of hyaenid diversity, in the late Miocene some 12-6 Ma. Fossil remains of hyaenids have been found in Africa, Europe, Asia, and North America. The smallest and oldest member of the Hyaenidae family, the Aardwolf, diverged ca. 10.6 Ma from its bone-cracking living relatives, while the divergence between *Crocuta* and *Hyaena* plus *Parahyaena* occurred ca. 8.6 Ma.

DOMESTICATION

Humans seem to be fascinated with felid species, and Domestic Cats rank among the most venerated companion animals. Wild felids have been tamed for use in hunting, as pets or companions, and as status symbols. However, only one species, the Afro-Asian Wildcat, was ever domesticated. The Cheetah has been kept in captivity since 5,000 years ago, when the Sumerians tamed them as pets and for hunting. Other ancient civilizations tamed Cheetahs for hunting, including those in Egypt, Assyria, India, and China. However, Cheetahs failed to breed in captivity until the 1950s, and thus domestication was impossible. At the beginning of Egyptian history, and much later in the Middle East, larger species such as Lions and Leopards were also tamed and kept in royal palaces for companionship, protection, and prestige. Tigers were popular in aristocratic collections in Asia for centuries, and were also trained to hunt by early Chinese emperors. Ancient Egyptians appear to have trained Jungle Cats to hunt without domesticating them. Servals and Caracals were also tamed in ancient Egypt; several centuries later, Caracals were trained for hunting birds and gazelles in Iran and India. In pre-Columbian times, the Jaguarundi is thought to have been tamed as a rodent-catcher in South and Central America. Similarly, other South American felids (e.g., Geoffroy's Cat, Ocelot, Margay, and Puma) are easily trapped and tamed, and many local people have kept and continue to keep them as pets and for rodent control. Probably most were tamed after capture as kittens as a by-product of hunting for food or pelts.

The modern cat is not fully domesticated in the classic sense. The most widely accepted account of cat domestication posits that cats essentially domesticated themselves. Most cats do not live in social

Figure 17. Phenotypic heterogeneity in Domestic Cat (*Felis catus*): The basic size and shape of Domestic Cats has remained more or less the same, certainly more so than in dogs. Most breeds of cats have been developed over the last 200 years through selective breeding, mostly in Europe and the USA. Examples of breeds include: (1) Siamese; (2) Sphynx, a hairless cat breed; (3) Abyssinian; (4) Kurilian Bobtail; (5) Bengal, created from hybrids with Asian Leopard Cats; (6) Mekong Bobtail; (7) Norwegian Forest, adapted to a very cold climate; (8) Colorpoint Persian, characterized by its round face and short muzzle. Photo credits: *Iakov Filimonov, Eric Isselée, Nelikz, Cynoclub, Leigh Warner, Sergey Taran.*

groups, they lack a hierarchical social structure, and they are solitary hunters, features that make them poor candidates for domestication. Evidence points to a commensal relationship between cats and humans lasting thousands of years before humans exerted substantial influence on their breeding. Wildcats likely colonized Neolithic villages drawn by the local abundance of food and were simply tolerated by humans, who saw the benefits of allowing these animals to live around their rodent-infested homes and granaries. Wildcats may have also been an integral feature of village life as a result of people actively adopting, hand-rearing, and socializing young Wildcats to keep as pets. This domestication process has not profoundly altered the morphological, physiological, behavioral, and ecological features of cats. Unlike many other domesticated mammals bred for food, herding, hunting, or security, most of the cat breeds (fig. 17) originated recently, within the past 200 years, largely due to selection for aesthetic rather than functional traits. This domestication of cats resulted in widespread adoption of cats as pets, and expansion of the range and populations of cats to virtually every corner of the inhabited world. Today there are nearly 1 billion domestic cats worldwide.

Studies of mitochondrial DNA from modern Wildcats and Domestic Cats demonstrate that ancient populations of Near Eastern/North African Wildcats (*Felis lybica*) were the maternal ancestors of Domestic Cats, and that domestication probably occurred somewhere in the Fertile Crescent (the Levant, southern Turkey, and Iraq) of western Asia, when humans ceased following wild herds of animals and adopted more agricultural lifestyles. Despite the long history of cats with humans, there is little archaeological evidence for their domestication. A Wildcat phalanx from the site of Klimonas shows that they were introduced to Cyprus 11,000 years ago, providing the earliest connection between humans and cats. The earliest cat to demonstrate a close association with humans is also from Cyprus, where a young Wildcat was interred next to a human ca. 9,500 years ago. However, little is known about the crucial period for cat domestication between 9,000 and 4,000 years ago. The first evidence for Domestic Cats is based on Egyptian paintings dated to 4,000 years ago, and by about 1,600 years ago, Domestic Cats clearly and frequently appear in art, shown sitting under chairs, eating fish, playing, and helping people hunt birds in the Nile Delta's papyrus swamps. From Egypt, cats were probably exported to Greece around 3,000 years ago and from there to Europe. Cats were thought to have first appeared in China around 2,000 years ago.

CONSERVATION STATUS

Wild cats are among the most threatened groups of mammals. At least 50% of felid species are threatened and in need of urgent protection according to the International Union for Conservation of Nature (IUCN). Wild cats are predators requiring large areas of habitat with suitable prey density. Human population growth and deforestation, especially in tropical Asia, have negatively impacted both these requirements, resulting in a decline in all cat species in range and number. Larger species are heavily persecuted because of the danger they pose to livestock and humans, while small cats are also persecuted for the fur trade. Illegal poaching driven by a demand for cat body parts for use in traditional Asian medicine is still a major problem. Despite the immense attention paid to charismatic big cats, many of the highly threatened smaller species are elusive and poorly studied, and they may appear as low priorities on the conservation agenda.

Hyenas are often misunderstood and persecuted, and they are often regarded as vermin and a liability to local communities. Their body parts are also used for traditional medicines and rituals. The Spotted Hyena is considered to be safe, although there is a continuing decline in populations outside protected areas. The Striped Hyena is listed as Near Threatened, being endangered in many parts of its range, with only six countries having populations estimated above 100 individuals, and, of those, only Egypt and Kenya have estimated populations over 1,000. However, no conservation efforts have targeted this species and the lack of information about its behavior makes effective management difficult. It is often hunted or poisoned throughout its range. The Brown Hyena is also listed as Near Threatened, with a population size estimated at between 5,000 and 8,000 animals, which makes it one of the rarest large African carnivores. They are often persecuted based on the mistaken belief that they are harmful to livestock. Aardwolves are not considered endangered, and they are widespread, although they are not common throughout their range.

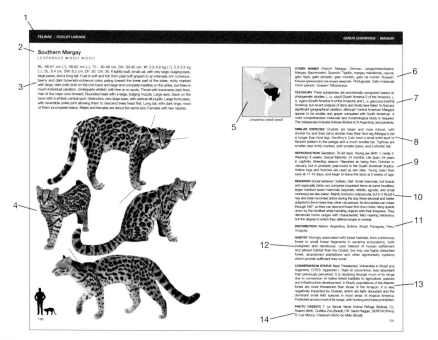

Figure 18. Understanding a page layout: (1) Phylogenetic group; (2) scientific and common name; (3) measurements and description; (4) color plates and silhouette comparing size with a human figure; (5) distribution maps; (6) other names, including foreign and local names; (7) subspecies and taxonomy; (8) similar species or subspecies; (9) reproductive biology; (10) behavior; (11) distribution; (12) habitat; (13) conservation status and estimated population; (14) photo credits.

HOW TO USE THIS BOOK

The main purpose of this guide is to enable the observer to identify all known species of wild felids and hyenas from all over the world. Information is presented in the same format throughout, with maps showing geographic ranges, and photographs highlighting the specific identification criteria in each case. We have packed as much detail into this volume as possible, but also worked hard to keep it concise and efficient, so that it is not unwieldy in the field. All the information for a given taxon is displayed on two facing pages.

Most felids and hyenas can be identified from field sightings by using the photographs and descriptions in this guide. Look through the color plates and determine what type of animal you saw. Turn to the text page for the species that most resembles your sighting and look at the distribution map. If the map is not shaded for your area, then return to the color plates and try another similar species or subspecies. Keep in mind that many species may vary in color from one region to another and that not all color morphs can be illustrated in a guide. When you find a species that resembles your sighting and occurs in the correct geographic area, read the text to see if the description fits the habitat that you are in and any behavior you may have observed. Also check the Similar Species section for other possibilities.

The overall structure of this guide is based on the taxonomic classification of the family Felidae into eight recognized groups, and is organized to provide the maximum ease of use for its readers. Each account in this book is organized as follows (fig. 18):

(1) **Classification**: To help the reader grasp the scientific arrangement, the pages for each group have a distinctive color on their top margin. This organization also helps to clarify a species' relationship to other species in the same group. When trying to identify an unfamiliar wild cat or hyena, it can often be helpful to first place it into a group, which will reduce your search.

(2) **Name**: The most common name as well as the scientific name is included for each entry. There is no official list of vernacular names for felids and hyenas, and common names have developed through long usage. They are convenient labels but they carry no deeper meaning, and some are actually inappropriate. Some species are named for people (Geoffroy's Cat), for geographic locations (Andean Cat), for habitats (Chinese Mountain Cat), or for their behavior (Fishing Cat). Furthermore, common names differ widely around the world. The scientific names, although less accessible, are much more valuable, since they impart real information about relationships among species. The scientific names are governed by rules of nomenclature and are standardized worldwide so that they transcend language barriers. The first word of the scientific name (always capitalized) is the genus. The second word, in lowercase, is the species name. For polytypic species (species with two or more subspecies), the third word, also in lowercase, is the subspecies name.

(3) **Description**: The identification section begins with a list of external measurements and weights, recorded in centimeters and kilograms, respectively. Measurements and weights are given as averages or ranges. They are intended as aids to identification and to give a clearer impression of the animal. Keep in mind that many felids may exhibit tremendous variability in size and weight, and that males and females may differ in size. Where applicable, differences between the sexes are outlined. Explanations of the most common standard measurements for felids and hyenas are as follows: Body length (BL) is measured from the tip of the muzzle to the base of the tail. Tail length (TL) is measured from its junction with the body to the end of the vertebrae. Shoulder height (SH) is measured from the base of the foot pad to the top of the shoulder. Weight (W) is expressed in kilograms (weight is influenced by seasonal changes and body condition). Skull length (SL) is the condylobasal length of the skull, measured from the anterior points of the premaxilla to the posterior surfaces of the occipital condyles. Skull width (SW) is the zygomatic width of the skull, the maximum width across the zygomatic arches. Dental formula (DF) is the number of each type of tooth in each half of the upper and lower jaw. Chromosome number (CN) is the diploid number of chromosomes. Descriptions in this guide concentrate on external features that can be observed in a live animal, and will assist the reader in species or subspecies identification, including pelage characteristics and coloration, and notable morphological traits.

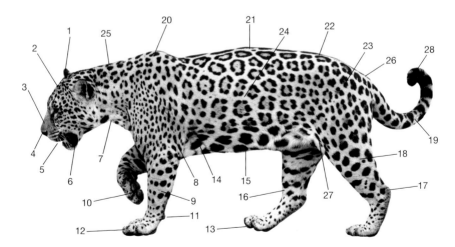

Figure 19. Topography of a typical felid: Jaguar (*Panthera onca*): All felids have a similar basic form, although the relative length of limbs, ears, and tail varies considerably between species. (1) Ear (pinna); (2) forehead; (3) muzzle; (4) rhinarium; (5) whiskers (vibrissae); (6) lip; (7) throat; (8) elbow; (9) foreleg; (10) forefoot (paw); (11) dewclaw; (12) toes and claws; (13) pads; (14) chest; (15) belly (abdomen); (16) hind leg; (17) hock (ankle); (18) thigh; (19) tail; (20) shoulder; (21) back; (22) loin; (23) hip; (24) flank; (25) neck; (26) rump; (27) stifle (knee); (28) tip of tail. Photo credit: *Javier Amores*, Pantanal (Brazil).

(4) **Color plates**: The color plates, which are based on real photographs, are the core of this guide and will be the most useful component for identification. The illustrations show each species described. Occasionally, coat variations and young forms are also illustrated. Features that are most important for identification are indicated by bars. Silhouette drawings illustrate the species on each page to a common scale in order to relate its size to a human figure 180 cm tall.

(5) **Distribution maps**: The black parts of the maps represent the approximate area within which a species or subspecies occurs at present, although within this area it would not be found in unsuitable habitat. The gray parts of the maps represent the species' distribution when a subspecies is depicted. Areas of hybridization between subspecies may occur. Former distribution has not been taken into account. A glance at the range map will give a quick indication of a species' or subspecies' distribution. It should be remembered that the scale of the maps is such that only general distribution patterns can be given. Always consult the Distribution section to obtain a more detailed indication of range.

(6) **Other names**: Following the English and scientific names in each species account, this section lists alternative and colloquial English names, and French, German, Spanish, Russian, and local names where appropriate.

(7) **Taxonomy**: This section lists the subspecies for a polytypic species. The identification of subspecies can be a rewarding and exciting challenge. However, the differences between subspecies are usually less distinct than the differences between species. When a subspecies may be identified based on external features that can be observed in a live animal, a short description with their distinguishing features is included. Sometimes subspecies may only be identified based on their geographic range, which is also described in this section and illustrated in the distribution map. Keep in mind that some authors may disagree over the validity of certain subspecies, or whether a certain population is a subspecies or a full species. Additionally, animals that belong to different subspecies of the same species are capable of interbreeding and producing fertile offspring.

(8) **Similar species**: This section lists those species or subspecies that are similar to or could be confused with another species, or that have a similar range, and their distinguishing features are mentioned. Before you finalize your decision on the species identity, check this section.

(9) **Reproduction**: A brief description of breeding biology is given, including gestation length, litter size, weaning time, sexual maturity, and maximum life span (generally in captivity).

(10) **Behavior**: This section includes information on group composition and structure, range size, diet, predators, daily and seasonal activity patterns, and social interactions. Behavioral characteristics that may aid in identification are given preference, but other aspects of interest are also mentioned.

(11) **Distribution**: This section describes the actual countries in which a species is native and the general geographic space that it occupies. Distribution and habitat must be considered together to determine if a given animal is likely to be found in a given area.

(12) **Habitat**: Includes the local conditions of climate, vegetation, soil types, water availability, elevation, and terrain. Some animals have very specific habitat requirements, while others may occupy just about any habitat within their range.

(13) **Status**: This section indicates the species' relative abundance and lists its conservation status in cases where the species is threatened or endangered. When available, estimated population of a species is also given. The conservation status is based on up-to-date information published in the IUCN Red List of Threatened Species. The IUCN (International Union for Conservation of Nature) is a global conservation group that researches threatened species and coordinates practical conservation plans. Listed statuses in this guide are adapted from the IUCN Red List of Threatened Species (version 14, August 2019). The IUCN Red List of Threatened Species places species into one of the following categories: Extinct: There is no reasonable doubt that there are no remaining individuals alive. Extinct in the Wild: A species is known to survive only in captivity or as a naturalized population well outside the former range. Critically Endangered: A species has an extremely high risk of extinction in the wild or is already likely to be extinct, but for which confirmation is required. Within this category, it is often difficult to be certain that a species is extinct, as the last few individuals may still be holding on and in need of conservation attention. Endangered: A species has a very high risk of extinction in the wild. Vulnerable: A species is likely to become Endangered unless the circumstances that are threatening its

survival and reproduction improve, and it is therefore considered to be facing a high risk of extinction in the wild. Near Threatened: A species is likely to become Vulnerable in the near future and has been evaluated against the criteria but does not qualify for Critically Endangered, Endangered, or Vulnerable for now, but is close to qualifying for or is likely to qualify for a threatened category in the near future. Least Concern: A species is widespread and abundant. Data Deficient: There is not enough information to assess the risk of extinction. Not Evaluated: A species has not yet been evaluated. Domesticated: This is not an official category of the IUCN Red List; this category overlaps Least Concern but has been applied to domesticated animals, for which the IUCN criteria are not valid. CITES listings are also included. CITES (the Convention on International Trade in Endangered Species of Wild Fauna and Flora) is an international agreement between governments, aimed to ensure that international trade in specimens of wild animals and plants does not threaten their survival. CITES Appendix I lists species that are the most endangered and for which international trade is prohibited, except when the purpose is not commercial. Appendix II lists species that are not necessarily threatened with extinction but that may become so unless trade is closely controlled; international trade may be authorized by the granting of an export permit or re-export certificate. Appendix III is a list of species included at the request of a particular country/state that already regulates trade in the species and that needs the cooperation of other countries to prevent unsustainable or illegal exploitation.

(14) **Photo credits**: The contribution of every photographer is gratefully acknowledged and their names and the place where the photograph was taken appear in each entry. Copyright rests with the individual photographers. Some photos have been enhanced through the use of graphics editing programs to highlight identification marks and remove distracting background features.

ABBREVIATIONS

The following abbreviations, contractions, and symbols have been used in the book to make it simpler for the reader to access the information.

ca.: circa (approximate date)

cm: centimeters

g: grams

kg: kilograms

m: meters

km: kilometers

km^2: square kilometers

ha: hectares

kmph: kilometers per hour

BL: body length (without tail)

TL: tail length

SH: shoulder height

W: weight, west, western

SL: skull length (condylobasal length)

SW: skull width (zygomatic width)

CN: chromosome number

DF: dental formula

Ma: million years ago

N: north, northern

NE: northeast, northeastern

NW: northwest, northwestern

S: south, southern

SE: southeast, southeastern

SW: southwest, southwestern

E: east, eastern

♂: male, males

♀: female, females

†: extinct

T, TR, TL: Top, top-right, top-left

C, CR, CL: Center, center-right, center-left

B, BR, BL: Bottom, bottom-right, botton-left

NP: National Park

Panthera lineage
TIGERS, LIONS, JAGUARS, AND LEOPARDS

RECOGNITION The Panthera lineage, placed taxonomically in the Pantherinae subfamily, consists of the five big cats of the genus *Panthera*, *P. tigris* (Tiger), *P. leo* (Lion), *P. pardus* (Leopard), *P. onca* (Jaguar), and *P. uncia* (Snow Leopard), as well as the two closely related *Neofelis* species (Mainland and Sunda Clouded Leopards). The Snow Leopard was considered the only member of the genus *Uncia*, but genetic analysis has confirmed its inclusion within *Panthera,* as a sister species to the Tiger. *Panthera* species are large-sized cats, with a thickset body, muscular forequarters, large and broad feet, a long tail, and a heavily built head. All *Panthera* species have long vocal folds with an incompletely ossified hyoid bone, allowing them, except for the Snow Leopard, to roar (the reason behind their vernacular name, roaring cats, as opposed to the small cats, often referred to as purring cats). *Neofelis* species are medium-sized cats, with a long body, relatively short, robust legs with large feet, a very long tail, elongated canine teeth, and a completely ossified hyoid bone. Melanism has been reported for Leopards, Jaguars, and Clouded Leopards. This group is sexually dimorphic, with males being larger and heavier than females. All species have the typical felid dental formula (I 3/3, C 1/1, P 3/2, M 1/1 = 30). Chromosome number is 2n=38.

PHYLOGENY The Pantherinae diverged in Asia from a common felid ancestor during the late Miocene (11 Ma). Clouded Leopards (*Neofelis*) diverged first, approximately 6.5 Ma, as would be expected from their distinctive morphology implying a long separate evolutionary lineage. Today's *Panthera* species diverged from a common ancestor 2-4 Ma. The oldest known species in *Panthera* are those referable to *P. blytheae*, from the late Miocene-early Pliocene of the Himalayan region, and *P. palaeosinensis* and *P. zdanskyi*, from the Plio-Pleistocene of China. The oldest modern Tiger fossils date from 2 Ma, from northern China and Java. By the late Pliocene and early Pleistocene, Tigers were widely distributed in eastern Asia. Fossil Tigers have not been recorded outside Asia. The oldest modern Lion fossils are from Tanzania, at about 2-3 Ma. During the middle Pleistocene Lions extended their range outside Africa, and by about 500,000 years ago they were found throughout Europe and Asia. By 300,000 years ago Lions probably crossed the Bering Strait into North America, and during the last interglacial period they spread farther into North America. Lions became extinct in the Americas and large parts of Asia at the end of the latest glaciation. The oldest Leopard fossils are also from Tanzania, at about 2-3 Ma. During the earlier middle Pleistocene, the first Leopards appear in Eurasia. The earliest Jaguars dispersed across Europe at least 1.5-1.9 Ma, and entered the American continent through Beringia in the early Pleistocene. In North America the oldest definitive Jaguar fossils date from approximately 850,000 years ago.

BEHAVIOR The lion is the most social of all cat species, living in complex social systems called prides, while the rest of the species follow the fundamental felid pattern of being largely solitary hunters. This group is primarily nocturnal and crepuscular, but can also be active during the day. They mark and defend their home ranges and have a marked preference for medium-sized to large ungulates.

DISTRIBUTION Tigers are currently restricted to Southeast Asia, India, the Russian Far East, and northeastern and extreme southwestern China. Lions have a patchy distribution in Africa, south of the Sahara, and in the Gir Forest of India. The Leopard has the largest distribution of all wild cats, and occurs in many parts of Africa and Asia. Jaguars are found in tropical or subtropical forest, from northern Mexico to northern Argentina. The Snow Leopard inhabits the mountains of Central Asia and northwestern India, at elevations between 3,000 and 5,000 m. Clouded Leopards are closely associated with dense habitat and are considered forest dependent. Mainland Clouded Leopards range from the southeastern Himalayas across southeastern Asia, extending through southern China and into peninsular Malaysia, while the Sunda Clouded Leopard is endemic to Borneo and Sumatra.

CONSERVATION All these species have suffered a marked reduction of range and population sizes, due to loss of habitat, widespread hunting of their prey, intense persecution, and illegal hunting for the Asian medicinal trade. The Tiger, classified as Endangered, occurs in only 5% of its historical range, with an estimated population of fewer than 4,000. Lions have disappeared over the last century from 85% of their former range, with a total population of 25,000, in populations with a high risk of local extinction. Leopards have been extirpated from at least 40% of their African range and more than 50% of their Asian range, while Jaguars have been extirpated from 50% of their range. The Snow Leopard has an estimated population of 6,000 individuals, but its status is poorly known. Clouded Leopards are listed as Vulnerable, being naturally rare; very little is known about its population trends, since they inhabit very dense vegetation and are very elusive. All these species are fully protected.

white form   pseudomelanistic form

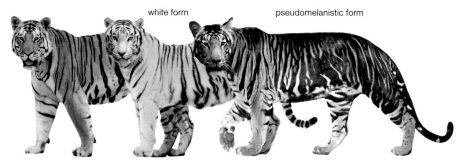

Bengal Tiger
Panthera tigris tigris, 34

Amur Tiger
Panthera tigris tigris, 36

Indochinese Tiger
Panthera tigris tigris, 40

Malayan Tiger
Panthera tigris tigris, 42

South China Tiger
Panthera tigris tigris, 38

Sunda Tiger
Panthera tigris sondaica, 44

African Leopard
Panthera pardus pardus, 52

Arabian Leopard
Panthera pardus nimr, 54

Persian Leopard
Panthera pardus tulliana, 56

Indian Leopard
Panthera pardus fusca, 58

Sri Lankan Leopard
Panthera pardus kotiya, 60

Indochinese Leopard
Panthera pardus delacouri, 62

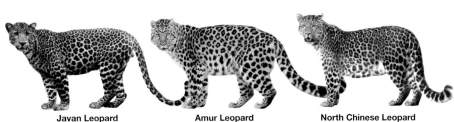

Javan Leopard
Panthera pardus melas, 64

Amur Leopard
Panthera pardus orientalis, 66

North Chinese Leopard
Panthera pardus orientalis, 68

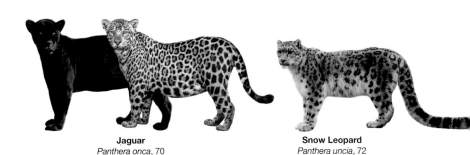

Jaguar
Panthera onca, 70

Snow Leopard
Panthera uncia, 72

West and Central African Lion
Panthera leo leo, 46

Asian Lion
Panthera leo leo, 48

Southern African Lion
Panthera leo melanochaita, 50

Indochinese Clouded Leopard
Neofelis nebulosa, 74

Sumatran Clouded Leopard
Neofelis diardi diardi, 76

Bornean Clouded Leopard
Neofelis diardi borneensis, 78

Bengal Tiger
PANTHERA TIGRIS TIGRIS

BL: 173-221 cm (♂), 157-175 cm (♀). TL: 85-110 cm. SH: 90-110 cm. W: 175-260 kg (♂), 100-160 kg (♀). SL: 31.1 cm (♂), 26.8 cm (♀). SW: 25.1 cm (♂), 19.6 cm (♀). DF: 30. CN: 38. The largest cat, with a deep chest, muscular forequarters, and heavily built limbs. A large subspecies. Coat is short and glossy, rich orange to rufous-fawn in color, patterned with black stripes, often doubled, from shoulder to root of tail. White underparts. Pseudomelanism (very wide and merged stripes, giving an almost entirely black appearance) and erythrism (strawberry tigers) may occur; complete melanism is unknown. White forms with blue eyes and chocolate-colored stripes on a white background are very rare. Males with a cheek ruff. White patches around eyes and on cheeks. Ears small and rounded, black on the back, with a large, conspicuous white spot. Nose pad flesh colored. Long whiskers. Powerful forelimbs with large paws, shorter than hind limbs. Tail is long, slim, and banded with black rings almost to the tip. Females are smaller and lighter than males.

white form

Young

34

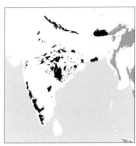

Panthera tigris tigris
(Bengal population)

OTHER NAMES *French*: Tigre du Bengale. *German*: Königstiger, Indischer Tiger, Bengaltiger. *Spanish*: Tigre de Bengala, tigre indio. *Russian*: Бенгальский тигр. *Hindi*: Bagh, sher. *Kannada*: Hoole. *Malayalam*: Kaduwa, naree. *Marathi*: Patery, dhanya wagh.

TAXONOMY The IUCN Cat Specialist Group recognizes only two subspecies: *P. t. tigris* (comprising Bengal, Malayan, Indochinese, South Chinese, Siberian, and extinct Caspian Tiger populations), and *P. t. sondaica* (Sumatran and extinct Javan and Balinese populations). A recent genetic study supports six monophyletic tiger clades: *tigris* (Bengal), *altaica* (Amur), *amoyensis* (South China), *corbetti* (Indochinese), *jacksoni* (Malayan), and *sumatrae* (Sumatran), with *virgata* (Caspian), *sondaica* (Javan), and *balica* (Balinese) having become extinct within the 20th century.

REPRODUCTION *Gestation*: 93-106 days. *Young per Birth*: 1-4. *Weaning*: 6 months. *Sexual Maturity*: 3-4 years (♀), 4-5 years (♂). *Life Span*: 15 years, over 20 years in captivity. *Breeding Season*: Throughout the year, with most births occurring in December and April. Cubs are born in a shelter situated in tall grass, thick bush, or in caves, with eyes and ears closed. At 5-6 months of age they begin to take part in hunting, and at 2-3 years, they slowly start to separate from the family group and become transient.

BEHAVIOR *Social Behavior*: Solitary. *Diet*: Mainly sambar, but also wild pig, spotted deer, or even fish from mangroves; large animals such as rhinos, elephant calves, and gaur are taken opportunistically; they may attack humans if prey is unavailable, or if the tiger is old or injured. They hunt nocturnally, but in certain protected areas are diurnal due to tourist presence. They stalk their prey through high grass cover or undergrowth and, with one sudden onrush, take it down with a bite to the throat, and hold on until prey is lifeless; suffocation is also practiced. Tigers tend to eat the prey from the rump forward as opposed to Leopards, which eat from the belly up.

DISTRIBUTION *Native*: Bangladesh, Bhutan, India, Nepal. *Regionally Extinct*: China, Pakistan. In India, it is distributed along the Terai foothills of the Himalayas, in NE India, in central India, the Eastern Ghats and the Western Ghats including the Nilgiri plateau. The states of Madhya Pradesh, Maharashtra, Odisha, Bihar, West Bengal, Arunachal Pradesh, and Andhra Pradesh have large Tiger habitats left while those in Assam, Karnataka, Uttarakhand and Rajasthan support large numbers in protected areas.

HABITAT Tropical moist evergreen forests, tropical dry forests, tropical and subtropical moist deciduous forests, mangroves, subtropical and temperate upland forests, and alluvial grasslands. In the Sundarbans, it is adapted to a mangrove habitat, in the Terai it frequents a moist deciduous-grassland-riverine habitat complex, and in higher altitudes such as Sikkim and Arunachal Pradesh, it inhabits coniferous, oak, and rhododendron forests.

CONSERVATION STATUS Endangered. CITES: Appendix I. Estimated population of this subspecies was 2,400 animals in 2010 (1,700 in India, 440 in Bangladesh, 200 in Nepal, 75 in Bhutan), with no subpopulation larger than 250. India is home to the largest number of Bengal Tigers and the largest number of Tigers among all Tiger range states.

PHOTO CREDITS TL: *Oakdalecat*, Kanha (India); TR: *Kirill Kurashov*; CL: *Amit Rane*, Tadoba Andhari (India); CR, Young: *Vladimir Cech*, Ranthambhore NP (India) B: *EPhotocorp*, Ranthambhore NP (India).

Amur Tiger

PANTHERA TIGRIS TIGRIS

BL: 190-280 cm (♂), 140-200 cm (♀). TL: 86-115 cm. SH: 105-124 cm. W: 180-306 kg (♂), 160 kg (♀). SL: 31.6 cm (♂), 26.2 cm (♀). SW: 24.4 cm (♂), 19.9 cm (♀). DF: 30. CN: 38. The largest subspecies, thicker coated and much paler colored, particularly the winter coat, with larger white parts around the eyes, cheeks, lower part of the body, and bottom half of the tail. Stripes not so strongly colored, often brownish in older animals, relatively narrow, long, often bifurcated at the ends, or occur in pairs throughout. Number of stripes relatively small. Winter coat long and dense, with a washed-out appearance compared to summer pelage, ocherous-yellow in color, with a fairly intense admixture of reddish-rust. Color and pattern very variable. Underside of body and inner surface of legs white. White color on flanks usually extends quite far up. Summer coat brighter and more reddish. Males with a long facial ruff on the cheeks. Tail is long, banded with 7-8 black rings. Females smaller than males.

Young

Panthera tigris tigris
(Amur population)

OTHER NAMES Siberian Tiger, Manchurian Tiger, Korean Tiger. *French*: Tigre de Sibérie, tigre de l'Amour. *German*: Sibirischer Tiger, Amurtiger. *Spanish*: Tigre de Amur, tigre siberiano. *Russian*: Амурский тигр.

TAXONOMY Recognized as a *P. t. tigris* population since the revision of felid taxonomy in 2017. Formerly considered as a distinct subspecies (*P. t. altaica*). Includes *amurensis*, *coreensis*, *mikadoi*, *mandshurica*, and *longipilis*. The Caspian Tiger (*virgata*), extinct since the 1970s, is sometimes considered as an E population of Siberian Tiger, though slightly smaller in size and less massive in appearance.

REPRODUCTION *Gestation*: 93-106 days. *Young per Birth*: 1-4. *Weaning*: 6 months. *Sexual Maturity*: 3-4 years (♀), 4-5 years (♂). *Life Span*: 15 years, over 20 years in captivity. *Breeding Season*: Throughout the year, with most births occurring in July and August. Cubs disperse from their natal home ranges on average at 2 years.

BEHAVIOR *Social Behavior*: Solitary. *Diet*: Large ungulates (wild pig, elk, musk deer, roe deer, brown bear), but also small animals (rodents, fishes, turtles, crayfish, insects). This is the northernmost population, faced with harsh environmental conditions including severe winters and low prey population densities. They are very reclusive compared to their tropical counterparts and avoid contact with humans. ♂ territories are 20 times larger than those of Tigers in Nepal and India, averaging 1,380 km² (large area requirements are not an intrinsic characteristic of this subspecies, but a consequence of their need for adequate prey, which occur at low population densities in the N temperate forests). The home ranges of ♂ overlap one or more of the smaller ♀ home ranges. ♂ compete for access to breeding ♀ and home range sizes expand and contract depending on the number of resident ♀ a ♂ can successfully defend. Intraspecific fighting and infanticide, especially in high-population-density Tiger populations, often accompany changes in home-range holders. They commonly travel 15-20 km per day. They avoid hunting in areas with deep snow cover, partly because few prey frequent these areas, but also because the unstable snow crust makes walking difficult and noisy. When moving through areas with deep snow, they often take advantage of frozen riverbeds, paths made by ungulates, valley bottoms, or anywhere the snow depth is less and travel is easier. They usually spend 2-3 days with a large kill before abandoning the carcass, but small prey is consumed quickly.

DISTRIBUTION *Native*: China, Russia. It is virtually confined to the Russian Far East (Primorye territory with a smaller population in Khabarovsk), although a few survive along China's NE border area and possibly also in North Korea.

HABITAT Temperate deciduous forest (Korean pine and Mongolian oak forests), but also riverine forests. They avoid high-elevation and more N forest types (spruce-fir, larch), where deep snows limit movement of ungulates and Tigers, and where forage is limited.

CONSERVATION STATUS Endangered. CITES: Appendix I. The Russian Tiger population fell as low as 20-30 animals in the 1930s. In 2010 the population was estimated to number between 430 and 500 individuals, but the population is again declining. Main threats include poaching, hunting of wild prey species, and diseases (canine distemper from domestic dogs); it is particularly susceptible to habitat destruction and fragmentation as it requires large areas. Its genetic diversity seems to be markedly low.

PHOTO CREDITS T: *Alexey Golovanov* (Russia); C, Young: *Sergey Chichagov*, Riga Zoo (Latvia); B: *Lerka555*.

South China Tiger

PANTHERA TIGRIS TIGRIS

BL: 162 cm (♂), 154 cm (♀). TL: 76 cm. SH: 90 cm. W: 127-177 kg (♂), 100-118 kg (♀). SL: 25.9 cm (♂), 22.5 cm (♀). SW: 21 cm (♂), 19 cm (♀). DF: 30. CN: 38. A small Tiger, darker, more fully striped, with a somewhat longer and softer, though variable, coat than that of the Bengal subspecies. Coat is ochraceous-tawny, usually clear on the feet and the nose, patterned with black stripes. Underparts are white. White patches around eyes and on cheeks. Ears are small and rounded, placed apart on the top of the head, black on the back, with a large, conspicuous white spot. Nose pad flesh colored. Long whiskers. Forelimbs are thick and powerful with large paws. Tail is long, slim, and banded with black rings almost to the tip. Females considerably smaller and lighter than males.

Young

Panthera tigris tigris
(South China population)

OTHER NAMES Amoy Tiger. *French*: Tigre de Chine méridionale. *German*: Südchinesischer Tiger. *Spanish*: Tigre de Amoy, tigre del sur de China, tigre de Xiamen. *Russian*: Южнокитайский тигр. *Chinese*: Hu.

TAXONOMY Recognized as a *P. t. tigris* population since the revision of felid taxonomy in 2017. Formerly considered as a distinct subspecies (*P. t. amoyensis*). It was recognized as a subspecies only on the basis of a limited sample of 5 captive animals. Includes *styani*.

REPRODUCTION *Gestation*: 93-106 days. *Young per Birth*: 1-4. *Weaning*: 6 months. *Sexual Maturity*: 3-4 years (♀), 4-5 years (♂). *Life Span*: 15 years, over 20 years in captivity. *Breeding Season*: Throughout the year.

BEHAVIOR *Social Behavior*: Solitary, but there are reports of ♂ associating with ♀ and cubs. *Diet*: In the former range of this subspecies, prey species include mainly large mammals, especially ungulates (sambar, wild pig, roe deer, red deer) that weigh between 10 and 100 kg. There is no information about this population living in the wild and very little information on its natural behaviors. In captivity, they are solitary and they can be aggressive toward each other. They may hunt at any time of the day or night, but in areas disturbed by human activities they are principally nocturnal. They are ambush predators, springing onto their prey and taking it down with their muscular front limbs. They kill small prey by a bite to the back of the head and neck, and large prey by a throat bite, causing suffocation. They may spend several days feeding on a large prey item, covering it up with leaves and grass each time they depart. They may range over 15–30 km in a single night of hunting. Unlike most other cats, Tigers will enter water without hesitation and are excellent swimmers.

DISTRIBUTION *Native*: China. The historical range of this subspecies stretched over a vast landscape of 2,000 km from E to W and 1,500 km from N to S in China; from the E it ranged from Jiangxi and Zhejiang Provinces westward through Guizhou and Sichuan Provinces. The most northerly extension was in the Qinling Mountain and Yellow River area. This population is now functionally extinct in the wild and survives as a captive population derived from six wild-caught founders.

HABITAT In China they have been found in tropical evergreen, deciduous, coniferous, scrub-oak, and birch forests, mangrove swamps, and dry thorn forests. They range as high as 3,900 m.

CONSERVATION STATUS Critically Endangered, probably Extinct in the Wild. CITES: Appendix I. Field surveys in 2001 revealed no signs of South China Tigers and strongly indicated that there is no remaining viable Tiger population. As of 2011, 108 South China Tigers were in managed captive breeding programs in China and in a private facility in Africa. The population shows a low level of juvenile survivorship, and reproductive difficulties, due to inbreeding depression and genetic diversity decline, facing a huge conservation challenge. The total population of all Chinese Tigers is estimated at fewer than 200. This dramatic drop in numbers is principally due to habitat destruction and hunting. Tiger bone has been an important ingredient in traditional Chinese medicine.

PHOTO CREDITS CL: *SUN Ge*, Chongqing Zoo (China); Young: *Harvey Barrison*, Chongqing Zoo (China); T, B, CR: Chengdu Zoo (China).

Indochinese Tiger
PANTHERA TIGRIS TIGRIS

BL: 170-259 cm (♂), 140-239 cm (♀). TL: 60-110 cm. SH: 58-114 cm. W: 150-195 kg (♂), 100-130 kg (♀). SL: 28.9 cm (♂), 25.9 cm (♀). SW: 22.3 cm (♂), 19.5 cm (♀). DF: 30. CN: 38. A medium-sized Tiger, darker in color, and more richly striped than the Bengal and Amur populations. Indistinguishable in appearance from the Malayan Tiger. Coat is short and glossy, dark orange, almost golden in color, patterned with rather short and narrow dark single stripes. Underparts are white. Males have a cheek ruff. White patches around eyes and on cheeks. Ears are small and rounded, placed apart on the top of the head, black on the back, with a large, conspicuous white spot. Nose pad flesh colored. Long whiskers. Forelimbs are thick and powerful with large paws. Tail is long, slim, and banded with black rings almost to the tip. Females are smaller and lighter than males.

Young

Panthera tigris tigris
(Indochinese population)

OTHER NAMES Northern Indochinese Tiger, Corbett's Tiger. *French*: Tigre de l'Indochine. *German*: Hinterindischer Tiger. *Spanish*: Tigre de Indochina. *Russian*: Индокитайский тигр.

TAXONOMY Recognized as a *P. t. tigris* population since the revision of felid taxonomy in 2017. Formerly considered as a distinct subspecies (*P. t. corbetti*).

REPRODUCTION *Gestation*: 93-106 days. *Young per Birth*: 1-4. *Weaning*: 6 months. *Sexual Maturity*: 3-4 years (♀), 4-5 years (♂). *Life Span*: 15 years, over 20 years in captivity. *Breeding Season*: Throughout the year, but most frequently during November through early April. Cubs are born with their eyes and ears closed.

BEHAVIOR *Social Behavior*: Solitary. *Diet*: Medium-sized to large mammals such as gaur, sambar, and Eurasian wild pig. Tigers also prey on smaller prey, such as muntjac, porcupines, macaques, and hog badgers in areas where the large ungulate numbers have been seriously depressed by human activity. However, Tigers living on a diet of muntjac would be unable to rear young. There is little specific information about the behavior of this population in the wild. It tends to hunt more at night. A strong swimmer, it likes to spend the hotter parts of the day half-submerged in cool water in streams and lakes. Predominantly terrestrial but a strong tree climber. Territorial, maintaining a large territory whose size is dictated by the availability of prey. The ♂ has a larger home range that usually overlaps those of a number of ♀. They rarely begin feeding at the kill site, but commonly drag the kill into dense cover before commencing to feed.

DISTRIBUTION *Native*: India, Laos, Myanmar, Thailand. *Possibly Extinct*: Cambodia, China, Vietnam. In Cambodia and Vietnam there is no evidence of breeding and only a few confirmed records, in Myanmar only one potential viable population remains and in Laos only one Tiger population with fewer than 20 mature individuals remains. In China (Yunnan Province along the boundary with Laos) its status is unclear and there are few recent confirmed records.

HABITAT Found in a variety of habitats, but requires intact forest, favoring dense vegetation with secluded locations suitable for dens, with abundant prey and access to water. Tigers reach highest population densities in fertile mosaics of grass, shrubs, and woodland; closed forest is a relatively poor habitat.

CONSERVATION STATUS Endangered. CITES: Appendix I. Its status is poorly known. Indochinese Tigers generally occur at very low population densities compared with those Tigers recorded in optimal habitats in parts of India, and have been poached severely in many parts of their range. In the 1980s it was still considered widespread but is now absent from many areas. Its population is estimated to be no more than 342 individuals with 200 in Thailand, 85 in Myanmar, 20 in Vietnam, 20 in Cambodia, and 17 in Laos. Owing to its need for large areas of intact habitat that support its prey, the range of the Tiger has become seriously fragmented; hunting and poaching have also led to a rapid decline in populations, and it is now extinct from many parts of Southeast Asia. It is the least represented population in captivity.

PHOTO CREDITS T: *Kantapat*, Khao Kheow Open Zoo (Thailand); CR: *LightSecond* (Thailand); Young: *Dssimages* and *Josh More*, Henry Doorly Zoo, NE (USA); B: *Alexander Sliwa*, Khao Kheow Open Zoo (Thailand).

Malayan Tiger
PANTHERA TIGRIS TIGRIS

BL: 259 cm (♂), 239 cm (♀). TL: 65-110 cm. SH: 58-114 cm. W: 47-129 kg (♂), 24-88 kg (♀). DF: 30. CN: 38. A medium-sized Tiger, darker in color and more richly striped than the Bengal and Amur populations. Indistinguishable in appearance from the Indochinese population. Coat is short and glossy, dark orange, almost golden in color, patterned with rather short and narrow dark single stripes. Underparts are white. Males have a cheek ruff. White patches around eyes and on cheeks. Ears are small and rounded, placed apart on the top of the head, black on the back, with a large, conspicuous white spot. Nose pad flesh colored. Long whiskers. Forelimbs are thick and powerful with large paws. Tail is long, slim, and banded with black rings almost to the tip. Females are smaller and lighter than males.

Young

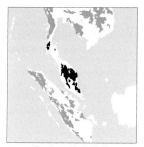

Panthera tigris tigris
(Malayan population)

OTHER NAMES Southern Indochinese Tiger. *French*: Tigre de Malaisie. *German*: Malaysischer Tiger. *Spanish*: Tigre de Malasia. *Russian*: Малайский тигр. *Malay*: Harimau.

TAXONOMY Recognized as a *P. t. tigris* population since the revision of felid taxonomy in 2017. Formerly included in *P. t. corbetti*, and later recognized as a distinct subspecies. There are however no clear differences when specimens from the two regions are compared cranially or in pelage.

REPRODUCTION *Gestation*: 93-106 days. *Young per Birth*: 1-4. *Weaning*: 6 months. *Sexual Maturity*: 3-4 years (♀), 4-5 years (♂). *Life Span*: 15 years, over 20 years in captivity. *Breeding Season*: Probably throughout the year. Cubs are born with their eyes and ears closed.

BEHAVIOR *Social Behavior*: Solitary. *Diet*: Wild pigs, muntjac, sambar, bearded pigs, and serows; they may also prey on sun bears, young elephants, rhino calves, and occasionally on livestock. They occur at very low population densities of 1.1-1.98 tigers per 100 km^2 in the rainforest as a result of low prey population densities; thus to maintain viable Tiger populations of a minimum of 6 breeding females, reserves need to be larger than 1,000 km^2.

DISTRIBUTION *Native*: Malaysia. The geographical division between Malayan and Indochinese Tigers is unclear as populations in N Malaysia are contiguous with those in S Thailand. They have been reported from early-succession vegetation fields, agricultural areas outside forests in Kelantan, Terengganu, Pahang, and Johor, and many riparian habitats outside forests in Pahang, Perak, Kelantan, Terengganu, and Johor. Most of the major rivers that drain into the South China Sea had some evidence of tigers, whereas those draining into the Straits of Malacca in the west did not.

HABITAT Evergreen dipterocarp rainforest, but also occur in non-forested lands, such as riverine woodlands, belukar (early-succession scrub), agricultural lands, and abandoned fields.

CONSERVATION STATUS Critically Endangered. CITES: Appendix I. The population was estimated at 250-340 adult individuals in 2014; it likely comprises fewer than 200 mature breeding individuals and has a declining trend. Habitat fragmentation due to development projects and agriculture is a serious threat. In Malaysia there is a substantial domestic market in recent years for Tiger meat and manufactured Tiger bone medicines. Tiger predation reduces the numbers of wild pigs, which can become a serious pest in plantations and other croplands.

PHOTO CREDITS T: *Sharon Morris*; Young: *Petr Mašek*, Zoo Prag (Czech Republic); CR: *Alexander Sliwa*, Zoo Melaka (Malaysia); CL: *Alexander Sliwa*, Zoo Negara (Malaysia); B: *Alexander Sliwa,* Berlin Tierpark (Germany).

Sunda Tiger
PANTHERA TIGRIS SONDAICA

BL: 170-195 cm (♂), 150-165 cm (♀). TL: 50-75 cm. SH: 75 cm. W: 100-140 kg (♂), 75-110 kg (♀). SL: 28.1 cm (♂), 24.7 cm (♀). SW: 21.6 cm (♂), 18.3 cm (♀). DF: 30. CN: 38. The smallest and darkest subspecies, with numerous, relatively narrow black stripes, much closer together, sometimes degenerating into rows of small spots. Lines of small dark spots between regular stripes on the back, flanks, and hind legs. White of the belly is limited to a narrow striped area, and the light color encircling the eyes is smaller than in mainland subspecies. Males have a prominent facial ruff on the cheeks, more marked than in other subspecies. Ears are small and rounded, black on the back, with a large, conspicuous white spot. Nose pad flesh colored. Long whiskers. Hind limbs are much longer than the forelimbs. Forelegs with striking black markings on their inner and hind parts. Tail is long, slim, and banded with 12 or more black rings almost to the tip. Sexual dimorphism is well marked.

Young

44

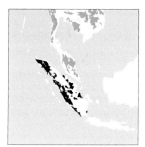

Panthera tigris sondaica

OTHER NAMES Sumatran Tiger. *French*: Tigre du Sumatra. *German*: Sumatra Tiger. *Spanish*: Tigre de Sumatra. *Russian*: Суматранский тигр.

TAXONOMY Considered as a subspecies of Tiger (*P. tigris*). The island populations of the Sunda region have been revised and merged into a single subspecies, the Sunda Tiger. It is distinguishable by both genetic and morphological analysis, and some authors consider it to be a separate species. It includes *balica* (Bali Tiger), extinct since the 1940s; *sondaica* (Javan Tiger), extinct since the early 1980s; and *sumatrae* (Sumatran Tiger), the only extant population. Includes *bintana*.

REPRODUCTION *Gestation*: 93-106 days. *Young per Birth*: 1-4. *Weaning*: 6 months. *Sexual Maturity*: 3-4 years (♀), 4-5 years (♂). *Life Span*: 15 years, over 20 years in captivity. *Breeding Season*: Throughout the year, but usually from November to April. The pair remain together for 5-6 days after which the ♂ moves off and the ♀ is left to raise the young by herself. Cubs open their eyes at 2 weeks and leave the den for the first time at 2 months. Both ♂ and ♀ disperse at 19 months, but ♀ usually exhibit natal philopatry and occupy part of mother's home range. ♂ disperse over much longer distances to find vacant home ranges. Cubs are fully independent at 2 years of age. Tigers communicate by marking with urine and feces, and by rubbing heads, roaring, purring, and grunting.

BEHAVIOR *Social Behavior*: Solitary. *Diet*: Sambar, red muntjac, wild pig, pig-tailed macaque, and Malayan tapir. Mostly nocturnal, resting during the day in the shade, but at dusk they begin to roam through their range and may travel more than 32 km in a night. This subspecies has extremely long whiskers, which form effective sensors when moving through the particularly dense undergrowth. They stalk prey through often dense cover until close enough to pounce. The carcass is dragged to a secluded area where it is consumed. They are efficient and fast swimmers; if given the chance, they will run ungulates into the water where the animals are at a much greater disadvantage. Home ranges are established and secured by marking the boundaries with urine and feces. In Sumatra, ♂ home range sizes averaged 110 to 400 km²; ♀ sizes were significantly smaller. There was extensive overlap of both ♂ and ♀ home ranges. ♂ tended to show greater site persistence than ♀.

DISTRIBUTION *Native*: Indonesia (Sumatra). Tigers were once widely distributed on the islands of Sumatra, Java, and Bali. Today, both the Bali and Java populations are extinct. The only remaining population, the Sumatran Tiger, persists dispersed between the NP of Berbak, Bukit Barisan Selatan, Gunung Leuser, Way Kambas, and Kerinci Seblat.

HABITAT Lowland forest with dense understory cover and steep slopes, farther from forest edge, and closer to forest centers. They strongly avoid forest areas with high human influence and make little use of plantations of acacia and oil palm.

CONSERVATION STATUS Critically Endangered. CITES: Appendix I. The current wild population has declined from an estimated 1,000 individuals in the 1970s to approximately fewer than 400. Main threats include poaching for domestic and international markets, prey depletion from human hunting, as well as loss of habitat to human settlement, which also occurs partly inside protected areas. Illegal trade of Tiger parts and human-Tiger conflict remain a threat.

PHOTO CREDITS T: *James Taylor*, Thrigby Hall Wildlife Gardens (UK); Young: *Eric Isselée* and *Arjan Haverkamp*, Burgers Zoo (Netherlands); CR: *Andrey Kotkin*, Berlin Tierpark (Germany); B: *Philip Bird*, Fuengirola Zoo (Spain).

West and Central African Lion

PANTHERA LEO LEO

BL: 247-284 cm (♂). W: 148-190 kg (♂), 110-120 kg (♀). SL: 33 cm (♂), 26.5 cm (♀). SW: 24.8 cm (♂), 20.1 cm (♀). DF: 30. CN: 38. A large, muscular, and deep-chested cat, with an unpatterned body, and a long naked tail with a tuft at the tip. Smaller than *melanochaita*, with smaller manes. Pelage is short and harsh, from dull yellowish to medium reddish-brown in color, sometimes darkened by an abundance of black tipping to the hairs. Males with a moderate mane growth or maneless, shorter and sparser than in East and South African Lions. Relatively short muzzle, with prominent whiskers. White chin. Ears small and round, backs of the ears black. Eyes from pale yellow to dark brown. Limbs heavy and muscular. Lionesses are slightly smaller and colored similar to males, and do not have a mane. Cubs have a faint spotted pattern that fades as they mature.

♂

Young

♀

Panthera leo leo
(African population)

OTHER NAMES *French*: Lion d'Afrique occidentale et centrale. *German*: Westafrikanischer Löwe, Senegallöwe. *Spanish*: León de África occidental y central. *Russian*: Лев (западноафриканский и центральноафриканский).

TAXONOMY Two subspecies are recognized: *P. leo leo* (Asia and W, Central and N Africa); and *P. leo melanochaita* (S and E Africa). The old classification was *P. leo leo* for Lions in Africa and *P. leo persica* for Lions in India. The subspecies are separated from each other by the African Rift Valley and the Central African rainforest. Results of genetic analyses indicate that Lions in W Africa and N parts of Central Africa form different Lion clades, which are more closely related to N African and Asian Lions than to Lions in S Africa and S parts of E Africa. Includes *azandica, senegalensis, gambianus, kamptzi*, and *nobilis*.

REPRODUCTION *Gestation*: 100-119 days. *Young per Birth*: 1-4, up to 7. *Weaning*: 6 months. *Sexual Maturity*: 3-4 years (♀), 5-8 years (♂); in captivity they can breed within 2.5 to 3 years. *Life Span*: 16 years, over 25 years in captivity. *Breeding Season*: Throughout the year.

BEHAVIOR *Social Behavior*: Small prides (2-4 animals), but may form larger groups. *Diet*: Medium-sized to large ungulates (buffalo, kob, roan antelope, hartebeest, waterbuck), but will take almost any animal, from warthogs to hippopotamus; smaller prey such as oribi and duiker are usually not favored; they also scavenge, displacing other predators (such as the Spotted Hyena) from their kills; they drink regularly when water is available, but are capable of obtaining their moisture requirements from prey and even plants. In W and Central Africa the knowledge of the species is very limited. They hunt mostly at night and in groups but have a relatively low hunting success rate. Population densities in this region are 0.7-3 Lions/100 km². Lions in this region thus tend to form small groups, probably due to dependence on domestic livestock, low mean prey body size, and low prey population density. Home range sizes in Pendjari (Benin) are 115-400 km², similar to those across Africa.

DISTRIBUTION *Native*: Benin, Burkina Faso, Cameroon, Central African Republic, Chad, Ethiopia, Niger, Nigeria, Senegal, Sudan. *Possibly Extinct*: Ghana, Guinea. *Regionally Extinct*: Côte d'Ivoire, Gambia, Guinea-Bissau, Mali, Mauritania, Sierra Leone, Togo.

HABITAT During the dry season, they show a preference for riparian forests and habitats around water, dry forests, and woodlands. In the wet period, vegetation on rocks and hills, woodlands, and dry forests are favored.

CONSERVATION STATUS Critically Endangered. CITES: Appendix II. In W Africa the population is currently estimated at just above 400 animals, being isolated from the populations in Central Africa, with 2,400 individuals; they are declining in some protected areas and have virtually disappeared from non-protected areas, except S Chad and N Central African Republic. Main threats include habitat conversion, prey base depletion, retaliatory or indiscriminate killing due to human-Lion conflict, bushmeat poaching, and excessive or poorly monitored trophy hunting.

PHOTO CREDITS TR: *Michael Lorentz*, Zakouma NP (Chad); TL, B: *Jorge Serpa*, Pendjari NP (Benin); Young: *Jean-Francois Potier* and *Florent Doko*, Pendjari NP (Chad); CL: *Jonas Van de Voorde*, Pendjari NP (Benin); CR: *Yoann Lombard*, Pendjari NP (Benin).

Asian Lion

PANTHERA LEO LEO

BL: 160-250 cm (♂), 110-180 cm (♀). TL: 71-105 cm. SH: 80-120 cm. W: 160-190 kg (♂), 110-120 kg (♀). SL: 30.6 cm (♂), 27.1 cm (♀). SW: 22.6 cm (♂), 20.2 cm (♀). DF: 30. CN: 38. A large cat, with an unpatterned body, and a long naked tail with a tuft at the tip. Slightly smaller than African Lions. Pelage ranges from ruddy-tawny, heavily speckled with black, to sandy or buff-gray, sometimes with a silvery sheen. Prominent fold of skin that spans the length of the abdomen (the abdominal fold is seldom observed in African Lions). Males have a moderate mane growth, shorter and sparser than their African counterparts. Manes can vary in color from pale blond to jet black. Ears are always visible. Lionesses are slightly smaller and colored similar to males, and do not have a mane. Cubs have a faint spotted pattern that fades as they mature.

♂

Young

♀

Panthera leo leo
(Asian population)

OTHER NAMES *French*: Lion d'Asie. *German*: Asiatischer Löwe. *Spanish*: León asiático. *Russian*: Азиатский лев. *Kathiawari*: Sawach. *Hindi*: Sher babbar. *Gujarati*: Sinh, sinhan, untia bagh.

TAXONOMY Frequently recognized as a distinct subspecies (*P. leo persica*), they are now subsumed under *P. l. leo* due to the close morphological and genetic similarities with N African Lions. Asian Lions have only colonized SW Asia within the last 20,000 years. Recent studies indicate that Lions from Asia and W and Central Africa are more closely related to each other than to Lions from E and S Africa.

SIMILAR SPECIES Asian Lions often have a bifurcation of the infraorbital foramen of the skull, and a longitudinal fold of skin running along their belly, which is rarely seen in African Lions. On the average, Asian Lions are smaller in size, have a scantier mane than the African Lion, with a fuller coat, a longer tassel of hair at the end of the tail, and a more pronounced tuft of hair on the elbows.

REPRODUCTION *Gestation*: 100-119 days. *Young per Birth*: 1-4, up to 7. *Weaning*: 6 months. *Sexual Maturity*: 3-4 years (♀), 5-8 years (♂); in captivity they can breed within 2.5 to 3 years. *Life Span*: 20 years in captivity. *Breeding Season*: Year-round (with a peak between October and November); most births occur between January and February. Birth interval is 18-26 months. Cubs are born blind and open their eyes after 11 days. They start walking when they are 15 days old. They are taken care of by all the ♀ of a pride. Infanticide can be quite high, causing up to 60% of cub mortality, and seems to occur especially in the first year after birth. ♀ tend to stay in natal pride while young ♂ disperse and adult ♂ may shift between prides under competition after 2-4 years.

BEHAVIOR *Social Behavior*: Less social than African Lions; prides of 2 ♀ and their young; ♂ joins only to mate. *Diet*: Wild ungulates (chital, sambar deer, wild pig, nilgai); livestock now makes up less than 25% of its diet. Mainly nocturnal and crepuscular. They spend major part of the day resting. During the day, they seem to prefer densely vegetated areas but at night their movement is more widespread and they may even move through agricultural fields and human habitations. ♂ defend home ranges that vary between 11 and 174 km^2 and the home ranges of ♀ are between 26 and 43 km^2. They mark their home range by roaring, urine spraying, and scuff-marking. They are very vocal and their roaring is audible over several km to advertise home-range occupancy.

DISTRIBUTION *Native*: India. It had a wide historic distribution across SW Asia but is now restricted to a single population in and around Gir Forest in the SW part of the Saurashtra region in the state of Gujarat (India).

HABITAT Dry deciduous teak, scrub jungle, dry savanna forests.

CONSERVATION STATUS Endangered. CITES: Appendix I. Fully protected in India. It exists as a single isolated population in Gujurat State (India), numbering approximately 500 animals, all occurring within one population, but in four separate areas, three of which are outside of the Gir Forest protected area. Major threats include poaching, habitat fragmentation, and inbreeding arising from a single population in one place.

PHOTO CREDITS TL: *Sanjay Shrishrimal*; TR: *Santanu Nandy*; CL: *Vladimír Cech*; Young: *Anuroop Krishnan*; C, B: *Kshitij30*. All photos taken at Gir NP (India).

Southern African Lion

PANTHERA LEO MELANOCHAITA

BL: 170-208 cm (♂), 158-184 cm (♀). TL: 61-100 cm. SH: 107-125 cm. W: 160-272 kg (♂), 90-152 kg (♀). SL: 32 cm (♂), 30 cm (♀). SW: 23.4 cm (♂), 19.5 cm (♀). DF: 30. CN: 38. A large, muscular, and deep-chested cat, with an unpatterned body, and a long naked tail. On average, the largest member of the family Felidae. Pelage is short and dense, from pale gold to amber in color, with pale or white inner limbs and ventral surface. Melanistic forms are extremely rare. Very pale forms (leucistic) are known. Adult males have a mane of longer hair covering the head, neck, chest, elbows, and occasionally belly, from platinum to black in color, with lighter hair surrounding the face. Sometimes maneless on the equator. Relatively short muzzle, with prominent whiskers. White chin. Ears small and round, backs of the ears black. Eyes from pale yellow to dark brown. Limbs heavy and muscular. Tail thick, muscular, and tapered, tip with a tuft of long, dark or black hairs. Lionesses are slightly smaller and colored similar to males, and do not have a mane. Cubs are spotted with rosettes that fade at maturity.

♂

Young

♀

Panthera leo melanochaita

OTHER NAMES *French*: Lion d'Afrique. *German*: Afrikanischer Löwe. *Spanish*: León africano. *Russian*: Лев (южноафриканский и восточноафриканский). *Afrikaans*: Leeu. *Ndebele*: Isilwane. *Sepedi, Sesotho, Setswana*: Tau. *Tshivenda*: Ndau. *Xhosa*: IsiGidi, iNgwenyama. *Xitsonga*: Nghala. *Zulu*: IBhubesi, iNgonyama.

TAXONOMY Considered as a subspecies of *P. leo* (Lion). Includes *massaica, sabakiensis, roosevelti, nyanzae, hollisteri, webbiensis, nubica, bleyenberghi, krugeri,* and *vernayi*.

REPRODUCTION *Gestation*: 100-119 days. *Young per Birth*: 1-4, up to 7. *Weaning*: 6 months. *Sexual Maturity*: 3-4 years (♀), 5-8 years (♂); 2.5-3 years in captivity. *Life Span*: 16 years. *Breeding Season*: Throughout the year. When cubs survive, the interbirth interval is typically about 2-3 years, with longer interbirth intervals in ecosystems with relatively high resident prey biomass and thus high Lion population densities. ♂ leave their natal pride at 3-4 years. Most ♀ stay in their natal prides, but about 30% disperse at approximately 2.5 years.

BEHAVIOR *Social Behavior*: Prides of 12-16 individuals: 4-6 adult ♀ (from 1 to 21), typically defended by coalitions of 2 ♂ (from 1 to 9), with a number of cubs or subadults. In areas with high human hunting pressure and reduced prey base, pride sizes tend to be smaller. *Diet*: Medium-sized to large ungulates, but will take almost any animal; they also scavenge. They drink regularly when water is available, but are capable of obtaining their moisture requirements from prey and even plants. Mainly nocturnal and crepuscular, spending large parts of the day and night resting. It is the most social felid species, living in complex social systems (prides) and exhibiting group territorial behavior. ♀ engage in several cooperative behaviors and often give birth in synchrony; the young are reared communally. There seems to be a complex division of labor among hunting lionesses. ♂ form coalitions to compete for tenure of a pride. Only very large coalitions, typically 3-5 individuals, tend to regularly have tenure over multiple prides. When a pride is taken over by new ♂, infanticide is common if there are young cubs, and ♀ come into estrus quite soon after the takeover. Both sexes defend the group home range against same-sex intruders. ♂ pride holders scent-mark and roar very frequently to demarcate and announce their presence. The Lion's roar can be heard for about 5-10 km and serves to warn other ♂ not to enter their home range.

DISTRIBUTION *Native*: Botswana, Ethiopia, Kenya, Malawi, Mozambique, Namibia, Somalia, South Africa, Swaziland, Tanzania, Uganda, Zambia, Zimbabwe.

HABITAT High habitat tolerance, inhabiting forested areas, dry forests, bushlands, and deserts, but is largely a species of the savannas. Recorded at elevations of up to 4,240 m. It prefers open areas such as scrub and grass complexes, and open to closed woodland, and requires areas with sufficient shelter and cover for hunting and denning, sufficient suitable prey, and minimal disturbance from humans.

CONSERVATION STATUS Vulnerable. CITES: Appendix II. In E and S Africa many large Lion populations have been stable over the last decades. Estimated population in S and E Africa is 25,000 Lions.

PHOTO CREDITS TR: *Peter Betts,* Kruger NP (South Africa); TL: *Thomas Retterath*, Okavango Delta (Botswana); CL: *Dennis Donohue* (Kenya); Young: *Altaoosthuizen*, Kalahari (South Africa); CR: *Riaan Albrecht*, Pilanesberg NP and *Arno Meintjes*, Kruger NP (South Africa); B: *Mogens Trolle*, Etosha NP (Namibia).

African Leopard
PANTHERA PARDUS PARDUS

BL: 92-183 cm (♂), 95-127 cm (♀). TL: 51-93 cm. SH: 57-70 cm. W: 28-72 kg (♂), 18-43 kg (♀). SL: 17.5 cm. SW: 12.9 cm. DF: 30. CN: 38. A large spotted cat, with robust forequarters, slender hindquarters, and relatively short legs. Pelage highly variable, short, close-lying and rather coarse, from a pale yellow to rich ocher. Underparts white to off-white. Melanism uncommon. Body with rosettes, each a cluster of small, black spots surrounding a normally unspotted center darker than the ground color. Solid black spots on the limbs, belly, throat, face, neck, and tail. Long thin tail, black tip with a white underside. Round ears, back with a prominent pale patch, bounded by black. Mature males may develop a distinctive throat dewlap and a belly fold. Females lighter than males, with 2 pairs of abdominal nipples. Cubs with blue eyes that mature to yellow-green. Leopards inhabiting the mountains of the Cape Provinces are much smaller.

Young

Panthera pardus pardus

OTHER NAMES *French*: Léopard d'Afrique. *German*: Afrikanischer Leopard. *Spanish*: Leopardo africano. *Russian*: Африканский леопард. *Afrikaans*: Luiperd. *Swati, Zulu*: Ingwe. *Sesotho*: Nkwe. *Shona*: Isngwe, mdaba. *Swahili*: Chui.

TAXONOMY Eight subspecies are recognized: *P. p. pardus* (African Leopard); *P. p. nimr* (Arabian Leopard); *P. p. tulliana* (Persian Leopard); *P. p. fusca* (Indian Leopard); *P. p. kotiya* (Sri Lankan Leopard), *P. p. melas* (Javan Leopard); *P. p. delacouri* (Indochinese Leopard); and *P. p. orientalis* (Amur and North Chinese Leopard). There are two main clades in Africa, but both occur in S Africa and appear to be partly sympatric. No subspecies can be distinguished within Africa.

SIMILAR SPECIES Cheetah is more slender, has longer legs and facial tearmarks, and is uniformly marked with circular, solid spots. Servals are much smaller and slender, with long legs, a shorter tail, and overly large ears. African Golden Cat is smaller, dark golden to smoky gray in color with less distinct spotting, and small, black-backed ears; melanistic African Golden Cat might be confused for a young black Leopard.

REPRODUCTION *Gestation*: 90-106 days. *Young per Birth*: 1-3. *Weaning*: 100 days. *Sexual Maturity*: 22-28 months. *Life Span*: 12 years, 23 years in captivity. *Breeding Season*: Throughout the year. Copulation lasts for 30 seconds to 1 minute at 6-minute intervals. They tend to copulate over a few days. Cubs are denned in thick vegetation, among rocks, tree roots, or in caves or aardvark burrows and open their eyes at 1 week. Cubs reach independence at 11-18 months.

BEHAVIOR *Social Behavior*: Solitary; adults socialize when mating; familiar non-mating pairs regularly meet without aggression, and ♂ are tolerant of cubs and interact with mothers and cubs, but may commit infanticide. *Diet*: Broad diet, ranging from arthropods to large antelope; they rarely feed from rotten carcasses. *Main Predators*: Lion, Spotted Hyena, African wild dog. Nocturnal, hunts at dusk and dawn. Solitary hunter. The home range of a ♂ often overlaps those of several ♀. Home ranges are marked with urine, scats, and scratches on trees. Ambush predator, creeping up to about a few meters from its potential prey before making a final pounce and delivering a fatal bite to the neck; they rarely chase after prey. They drag the carcass into a tree or under dense brush away from the reach of other predators. Good climber. It rarely swims.

DISTRIBUTION *Native*: Angola, Benin, Botswana, Burkina Faso, Burundi, Cameroon, Central African Republic, Chad, Congo, Côte d'Ivoire, Djibouti, DR Congo, Egypt, Equatorial Guinea, Eritrea, Ethiopia, Gabon, Ghana, Guinea, Guinea-Bissau, Kenya, Liberia, Malawi, Mali, Mozambique, Namibia, Niger, Nigeria, Rwanda, Senegal, Sierra Leone, Somalia, South Africa, South Sudan, Sudan, Swaziland, Tanzania, Uganda, Zambia, Zimbabwe. *Possibly Extinct*: Algeria, Gambia, Lesotho. *Regionally Extinct*: Mauritania, Morocco, Syria, Togo, Tunisia.

HABITAT Wide habitat tolerance. Woodland, grassland savanna and mountain habitats but also occur in coastal scrub, shrubland and semi-desert. Densely wooded and rocky areas are preferred.

CONSERVATION STATUS Vulnerable, N African population is Critically Endangered. CITES: Appendix I. Declining within large portions of their range, particularly outside of protected areas.

PHOTO CREDITS T: *Chris Fourie* (South Africa); CL, C: *Simon Eeman*, Kruger (South Africa); Young: *Chris Eason*, Mpumalanga (South Africa); CR: *Villiers Steyn* (South Africa); B: *Lauren Pretorius*, Kruger (South Africa).

Arabian Leopard
PANTHERA PARDUS NIMR

BL: 114-122 cm (♂), 93-113 cm (♀). TL: 66-81 cm. SH: 50-75 cm. W: 26-34 kg (♂), 18-23.5 kg (♀). SL: 17.7 cm. SW: 12.1 cm. DF: 30. CN: 38. A large, robust spotted cat with robust forequarters, slender hindquarters, relatively short legs, and a long tail. The smallest and palest subspecies of Leopard, and the largest Arabian cat. Pelage is very light in color; the deep golden-yellow between the black rosettes is only present on the back, while the rest of the body is beige to grayish-white, almost white. Underparts white. Less densely spotted below and inside the legs. Head large and powerful, spotted more finely than the rest of the body. Chin white. Ears rather small, marked black and white behind. Tail long, spotted as body. Females are smaller and lighter than males. Cubs are paler and grayer with longer fur.

Panthera pardus nimr

OTHER NAMES Sinai Leopard, South Arabian Leopard. *French*: Léopard d'Arabie. *German*: Arabischer Leopard. *Spanish*: Leopardo de Arabia. *Russian*: Южноаравийский леопард. *Arabic*: Nimr.

TAXONOMY Considered as a subspecies of *P. pardus* (Leopard). May prove to be consubspecific with subspecies *pardus*, although should be retained as a separate management unit. Includes *jarvisi* (Sinai).

REPRODUCTION *Gestation*: 90-106 days. *Young per Birth*: 1-3. *Weaning*: 100 days. *Sexual Maturity*: 22-28 months. *Life Span*: 22 years in captivity. *Breeding Season*: Throughout the year. Mating lasts an average of 6 days with frequent copulation occurring throughout that period. ♂ are vocal during copulation with most noise occurring just prior to dismounting. Cubs are born in a sheltered area, such as a small cave or under a rock overhang. During the first few weeks the ♀ frequently moves her cubs to different hiding places. Cubs open their eyes after about 1 week, and remain with their mother for up to 16 months. Although Leopards do occasionally bring food to their young, they usually prefer to take the young to the kill.

BEHAVIOR *Social Behavior*: Solitary. *Diet*: Arabian gazelle, Nubian ibex, Cape hare, rock hyrax, birds, Indian crested porcupine, Ethiopian hedgehog, small rodents, and insects; may also take goats, young camels, young donkeys, and cattle; they usually store carcasses of large prey in caves or lairs but not in trees. Adapted to live in arid and semi-arid regions, so it has small body size and a pale coat. Mostly nocturnal but may be diurnal in areas without human activity. Two daily peaks in activity, avoiding the midday heat; high temperatures are considered to inhibit their movements. Extremely wary and elusive. Home ranges marked by scent-marks, including scrapes, scats, urine spraying, and cheek rubbing. ♂ and ♀ avoid each other, presumably by staggering activities in different parts of shared ranges. The extensive scent-marking is presumably the key activity that allows overlap with minimal direct encounters while also enabling animals to come together for breeding.

DISTRIBUTION *Native*: Israel, Oman, Saudi Arabia, Yemen. *Regionally Extinct*: Kuwait, Lebanon, United Arab Emirates. Formerly widespread in the mountain periphery of the Arabian Peninsula, Sinai Peninsula, and in arid areas of Jordan and Israel. Known extant populations are confined to the mountains of Dhofar in southern Oman, parts of northern Yemen, the Hijaz and Sarawat Mountains in Saudi Arabia, and the Judean Desert and Negev Highlands in Israel.

HABITAT Remote and rugged mountain areas, semi-desert areas, and scrub, close to permanent waterholes and high in the mountains (> 1,000 m above sea level). Unlike some large mammalian carnivore species it seems to have a high tolerance of people.

CONSERVATION STATUS Critically Endangered. CITES: Appendix I. The estimated total number of individuals is 80–290 but distribution is patchy and many populations are at risk of extirpation. Leopards in Sinai are near extinction and the Jordanian population has been reduced to a few individuals. Leopards of the Al Wada'a area in Yemen are under great pressure from killing and from capture for trade. In Oman the Leopards of the Dhofar Mountains have benefited from comprehensive conservation measures. Leopards are often blamed for kills by wolves and for livestock losses.

PHOTO CREDITS TR: *Johannes Pfleiderer*, Sharjah (UAE); T, CL: *Jonas Livet*, Sharjah (UAE); CR: *Alexander Sliwa*, Al Hefaya (UAE); B: *Arun Somanathan* (UAE).

Persian Leopard
PANTHERA PARDUS TULLIANA

BL: 126-171 cm. TL: 94-106 cm. SH: 50-80 cm. W: 40-91 kg (♂), 26-60 kg (♀). SL: 20.6 cm (♂), 18.7 cm (♀). SW: 15.6 cm (♂), 12.8 cm (♀). DF: 30. CN: 38. A large, robust spotted cat with robust forequarters, slender hindquarters, relatively short legs, and a long tail. A large and pale subspecies of Leopard. Pelage highly variable, from a light grayish-yellow to a pale fulvous-buff, lacking the rich yellowish or reddish-tawny hue characteristic of other subspecies. Color more vivid on back. Underparts white. Hair cover varies significantly from dense and long in high mountains to short at lower elevations. Spots relatively few, usually not pure black, with a brownish tinge; light-colored centers of rosettes usually not darker than main background of coat. Long and thick tail. Round ears, back with a prominent pale patch, bounded by black. Females smaller than males. Cubs are light brown, uniformly speckled with tiny dark brown and black spots.

Young

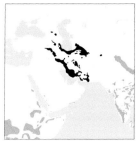

Panthera pardus tulliana

OTHER NAMES Anatolian Leopard, North Persian Leopard, Central Asian Leopard, Caucasian Leopard, West Asian Leopard, Baluchistan Leopard, Armenian Leopard. *French*: Panthère de Perse. *German*: Nordpersischer Leopard, Kleinasiatischer Leopard. *Spanish*: Leopardo de Persia. *Russian*: Переднеазиатский (персидский) леопард. *Farsi*: Palang-Kuh.

TAXONOMY Considered as a subspecies of *P. pardus* (Leopard). Includes *dathei*, *saxicolor*, *sindica*, *transcaucasica*, and *ciscaucasica*.

REPRODUCTION *Gestation*: 90-106 days. *Young per Birth*: 1-3. *Weaning*: 100 days. *Sexual Maturity*: 22-28 months. *Life Span*: 12 years, 21 years in captivity. *Breeding Season*: From mid-January to a peak in mid-February (mid-winter).

BEHAVIOR *Social Behavior*: Solitary; ♂ and ♀ associate briefly during mating periods, which may last for 2-7 days, and just after the short mating period, they separate. *Diet*: Ungulates including wild sheep, wild goat, wild pig, and roe deer are the most important prey species; they may also feed on small prey, including birds, rodents, and pikas; livestock predation has also been reported. One of the least-studied subspecies of Leopard. More active during the night. Territorial. Both sexes patrol their ranges and scent-mark trees, bushes, and rocks with urine mixed with anal gland secretions, scraping, and tree-clawing. ♂ scent-mark significantly more frequently than ♀ with and without cubs, especially on days preceding mating and when mating occurs. Leopard encounters with sympatric carnivores such as red fox, Caracal, Cheetah, and jackal are usually lethal. Consequently, smaller carnivores avoid such encounters by temporal and spatial niche segregation.

DISTRIBUTION *Native*: Armenia, Azerbaijan, Georgia, Iraq, Iran, Kazakhstan, Russia, Turkey, Turkmenistan. *Possibly Extinct*: Tajikistan, Uzbekistan. *Regionally Extinct*: Dagestan. They have a wide distribution in Iran, mostly in the region of the Alborz and Zagros mountain chains, and in Golestan NP in NE Iran. They are scarce in Iraq and Turkey, with a few records from the mountainous areas of Kurdistan. There is a small population on the Zangezur Ridge in Armenia and Azerbaijan. In Azerbaijan, there are records in the Talysh Mountains and in the Nakhchivan Autonomous Republic. Recently, a Leopard was video-trapped in North Ossetia, Georgia. There is some indication of its presence in the Babatag and Kugitang Mountains of Uzbekistan, Kazakhstan, and Afghanistan in Bamyan Province. In Pakistan, they are found in Waziristan, Baluchistan, Sindh Kohistan, and in Ayubia NP.

HABITAT Broken hilly or mountainous country, in association with acacia scrub forest, sparse juniper forest with precipitous and often inaccessible massifs, and broadleaf temperate forest in the Caucasus. Leopards occupy habitats where their major prey is abundant. They avoid areas with long-duration snow cover, deserts, and areas that are easily accessed from urban development.

CONSERVATION STATUS Endangered. CITES: Appendix I. Estimated population of 800-1,290 animals; Iran hosts the largest population of this subspecies. Persecuted primarily as a result of conflict with people over livestock predation. Other threats include habitat disturbances, poaching, depletion of their prey base due to poaching, and excess livestock in Leopard habitats.

PHOTO CREDITS TL, TR: *Ulli Joerres,* Beauval Zoo (France), Mulhouse Zoo (France); Young: *Eric Isselée*; CR, CL: *Sergey Chichagov*; B: *Alexander Sliwa*, Cologne Zoo (Germany).

Indian Leopard

PANTHERA PARDUS FUSCA

BL: 128-137 cm (♂), 104-102 cm (♀). TL: 76-106 cm. SH: 50-75 cm. W: 45-77 kg (♂), 30-45 kg (♀). SL: 21.4 cm (♂), 17.2 cm (♀). DF: 30. CN: 38. A large subspecies of Leopard, with larger rosettes. Pelage varies considerably from pale yellow to yellowish-brown or golden, paler in desert habitats, grayer in colder climes, more ocher in rainforest habitats. Spots fade toward the white underbelly and insides and lower parts of the legs. Large rosettes, with a darker tawny center as compared to the background, most prominent on the back, flanks, and hindquarters. Melanistic forms have dark rosettes against a dark brown or black background. Short ears, with a black back with a white spot in the center. Small, yellowish-gray eyes. Long tail, white underneath, with rosettes except toward the end, where the spots form incomplete bands. Females smaller than males. Juveniles have woolly fur, and appear dark due to the densely arranged spots.

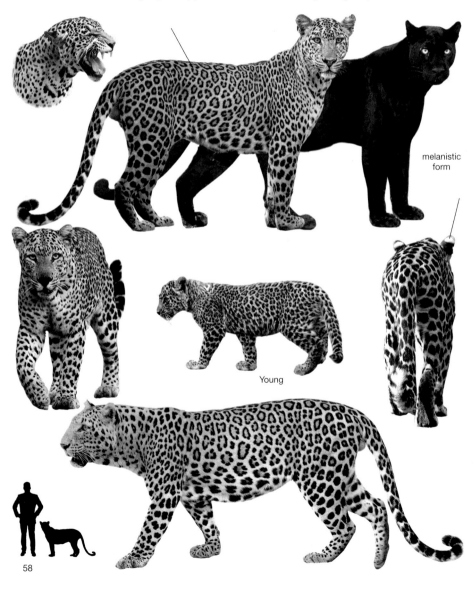

melanistic form

Young

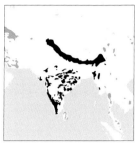

Panthera pardus fusca

OTHER NAMES Tibetan Leopard, Kashmir Leopard. *French*: Léopard indien. *German*: Indischer Leopard. *Spanish*: Leopardo indio. *Russian*: Индийский леопард. *Bengali*: Cheeta bagh. *Kannada*: Chirathe. *Tamil*: Chirutai puli. *Marathi*: Diblya wagh. *Gujarati*: Dipdo. *Mizo*: Kelral. *Kashmiri*: Khare-suh. *Naga*: Teku. *Hindi*: Tendua, chita, guldar. *Odia*: Pendra. *Malayalam*: Puli puli.

TAXONOMY Considered as a subspecies of *P. pardus* (Leopard).

REPRODUCTION *Gestation*: 90-106 days. *Young per Birth*: 1-4. *Weaning*: 100 days. *Sexual Maturity*: 22-28 months. *Life Span*: 12 years, 23 years in captivity. *Breeding Season*: Throughout the year, depending on the region. ♀ give birth in caves, crevices among boulders, hollow trees, or thickets to make a den. Cubs are born with closed eyes, which open 4-9 days after birth. Around 3 months of age, the young begin to follow the mother on hunts. Subadults start exploratory movements independent of their mother at about 13 months of age, and dispersal typically takes place at 15-19 months of age. They are known to travel long distances until they find suitable habitat patches not inhabited by larger competitors such as Tigers or by other same-sex adult Leopards.

BEHAVIOR *Social Behavior*: Solitary. *Diet*: Generalist, preferring small- to medium-sized prey within a weight range of 10–40 kg; they feed on wild ungulates (chital, sambar, nilgai, wild pig), primates (langur, macaque), hares, and birds (peafowl); they also feed on dogs and livestock around villages and other settlements, and scavenge water buffalo carcasses. *Main Predators*: Tiger. Solitary and territorial. Home range sizes vary with habitat types, prey population densities, and Tiger population densities, from 3.5 km² in Assam to 25 km² in Nagarahole (India). The juveniles share ♀ home ranges until maturity after which they disperse. Scent-marking is the primary mode of communication, including scraping, marking with feces, and spraying of urine. They hunt equally well diurnally and in the night, the former probably being an adaptation in Tiger habitat. A rasping call is a familiar nocturnal call of the Indian jungle and of the Himalayan foothills.

DISTRIBUTION *Native*: Bangladesh, Bhutan, India, Nepal, Pakistan. They occur widely in the forests of Bhutan and Nepal, and are widespread across India, except the arid parts of Kutch and Rajasthan and the high Himalayas (up to 3,000 m), occurring inside and outside protected areas.

HABITAT Deciduous and evergreen forests, scrub jungle, open country, and fringes of human habitation. Sympatric with Tigers, but more widely distributed, partly because of their ability to inhabit a variety of forested and degraded habitats and to survive by feeding on relatively small prey such as domestic dogs, goats, and pigs in the absence of large wild prey such as deer. They have colonized former human habitations, such as sugarcane fields.

CONSERVATION STATUS Vulnerable. CITES: Appendix I. Regional status: Schedule I (India), not protected in Nepal. Estimated total population of 10,000-14,000 animals. Habitat destruction, loss of wild prey, poaching for skins, bones, and claws, and poisoning carcasses of livestock killed by Leopards are a significant threat to this subspecies.

PHOTO CREDITS TL: *Sumeet Moghe*, Kabini (India); TR: *Bharath-Shreyas Photography*, Nagarahole Tiger Reserve (India); CL, CR: *Atul Dhamankar*, Tadoba Andhari (India); Young: *Aditya Singh*, Ranthambore (India); B: *Anubhab Roy* (India).

Sri Lankan Leopard

PANTHERA PARDUS KOTIYA

BL: 127-132 cm (♂), 104-114 cm (♀). TL: 77-97 cm. SH: 45-80 cm. W: 56-77 kg (♂), 29-44 kg (♀). SL: 21 cm (♂). SW: 14.7 cm (♂). DF: 30. CN: 38. A large, robust spotted cat with robust forequarters, slender hindquarters, relatively short legs, and a long tail. A large subspecies of Leopard. Pelage is golden-tawny or rusty-yellow, with dark spots and close-set rosettes, which are smaller than in Indian Leopards. Underparts white. Melanistic forms are uncommon, and have dark rosettes against a dark brown or black background. Round short ears, back with a prominent pale patch, bounded by black. Yellowish-gray eyes. Long thin tail, not bushy, white underneath, with rosettes except toward the end, where the spots form incomplete bands. Females are smaller than males, with smaller heads.

Young

60

Panthera pardus kotiya

OTHER NAMES Ceylon Leopard. *French*: Panthère de Ceylan, léopard du Sri Lanka. *German*: Sri-Lanka-Leopard. *Spanish*: Leopardo de Ceilán. *Russian*: Цейлонский леопард. *Sinhala*: Kotiya. *Tamil*: Chiruthai.

TAXONOMY Considered as a subspecies of *P. pardus* (Leopard). This subspecies has been found to be distinct in morphological analyses, but molecular analyses are conflicting (probably part of *fusca*).

REPRODUCTION *Gestation*: 90-106 days. *Young per Birth*: 1-4. *Weaning*: 100 days. *Sexual Maturity*: 22-28 months. *Life Span*: 23 years in captivity. *Breeding Season*: Throughout the year with a non-significant peak in the dry season. When a ♀ is at the peak of receptivity to mating, the ♂ will stay with her for several days and mate with her. The ♀ initiates courtship by flirting with the ♂. ♂ takes no part in bringing up the young. At about 18 months of age, ♂ cubs especially begin exploratory forays to seek a home range. After about 2 years ♂ disperse and become nocturnal in habit. Young ♀ carve out a home range near the mother.

BEHAVIOR *Social Behavior*: Solitary. *Diet*: Medium to large mammal prey (axis deer, water buffalo, wild boar, sambar, muntjac, mouse-deer), primates (purple-faced langur, toque macaque), rodents (Indian porcupine), black-naped hare, and domestic dogs; prey may also include frogs, birds, reptiles, and even insects. Sri Lanka's top terrestrial predator. More gregarious than other subspecies of Leopard, due to the lack of dominant intraguild competitors, and more often seen together, either as courting pairs or females with cubs. They hunt alone except during the mating season or when mother and cubs are encountered in the wild. Mostly crepuscular and nocturnal, but may be seen during the early mornings and late afternoons. They tree cache less often than other subspecies possibly because of the absence of intraguild competition, and the dense vegetation is more available for discreetly securing kills. In Yala, a ♂'s home range is 16–20 km², encompassing the home ranges of 3-4 ♀ whose home ranges may be 2-4 km². The core of their home range is defended rigorously. They scent-mark their home range, which enables them to avoid actual physical combat, which may be fatal. They often spray their urine upward so that it coats the undersides of leaves where it is likely to persist longer. They will also use feces and scratch marks to announce their presence. The main vocalization is a rough, rasping sound similar to that of a saw cutting wood.

DISTRIBUTION *Native*: Sri Lanka. Once found throughout the island. Owing to intense human activity they have now been extirpated from the N peninsula and the densely populated SW wet zone. Yala NP has the highest population density of Leopards in the world.

HABITAT A variety of habitats including montane, submontane, tropical rainforests, monsoonal dry evergreen, and arid zone scrub forests. They avoid dense urbanization.

CONSERVATION STATUS Endangered. CITES: Appendix I. Estimated population of 700-950 animals and declining. Despite a wide distribution within the island, it is under increasing threat from habitat destruction, forest fragmentation, and trapping and hunting.

PHOTO CREDITS TL: *Kyslynskyy*; TR: *Sergey Uryadnikov*; Young: *Mic Clark Photography*; CL: *Andrey Gudkov*; B: *Volodymyr Byrdya*. All photos taken in Yala NP (Sri Lanka).

Indochinese Leopard
PANTHERA PARDUS DELACOURI

BL: 112-132 cm (♂), 106 cm (♀). TL: 75-81 cm. SH: 45-80 cm. W: 37-55 kg (♂), 25-30 kg (♀). SL: 19.5 cm (♂), 17.2 cm (♀). SW: 13.9 cm (♂), 12.5 cm (♀). DF: 30. CN: 38. A large, robust spotted cat with robust forequarters, slender hindquarters, relatively short legs, and a long tail. A medium-sized to large, richly colored subspecies of Leopard. Pelage is short and smooth, pale buff to almost rusty-red, richer in the middle of the back, paler at the sides. Underparts white to off-white. Black rosettes, closely set, irregular in shape, thick-rimmed with much darker infuscated centers, all combining to give a darker appearance to the pelage. Solid black spots on the limbs, belly, throat, face, neck, and tail. Melanistic forms appear completely black, but the typical rosettes are still discernible in bright light. Round ears, back with a prominent pale patch, bounded by black. Long thin tail, not bushy. Females smaller than males.

melanistic for[m]

Juvenile

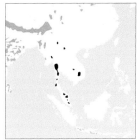

Panthera pardus delacouri

OTHER NAMES. Malayan Leopard. *French*: Panthère d'Indochine. *German*: Hinterindischer Leopard. *Spanish*: Leopardo de Indochina, leopardo de Delacour. *Russian*: Индокитайский леопард.

TAXONOMY Considered as a subspecies of *P. pardus* (Leopard). Melanistic Leopards (sometimes called Black Panthers) are seldom seen in Africa, but are not rare in S India and are quite common in SE Asia, and predominate S of the Isthmus of Kra (mainly in Malaysia). Both forms can interbreed, producing some offspring of each color. Melanisim is recessive in Leopards.

REPRODUCTION *Gestation*: 90-106 days. *Young per Birth*: 1-4. *Weaning*: 100 days. *Sexual Maturity*: 22-28 months. *Life Span*: Unknown. *Breeding Season*: Probably throughout the year. Cubs remain with mother until full grown at 1.5-2 years. One of the least known subspecies of Leopard.

BEHAVIOR *Social Behavior*: Solitary except during the breeding season. *Diet*: An opportunistic hunter, feeds mostly on hog badgers and small to medium-sized ungulates (red muntjac, wild pig, lesser mouse-deer), but also primates (langur, macaque), rodents, birds, frogs, and insects. Largely nocturnal, with activity peaks around dawn and dusk. Secretive and shy, and difficult to detect due to its excellent camouflage and secretive nature. A very fast runner and an excellent tree climber. Hunts by stalking its prey, relying on stealth and camouflage to evade detection until it is close enough to outrun the quarry, usually with a great burst of speed. Tends to dislocate using canines with nape bite or suffocate with throat bite. The ♂'s home range is large, dependent on the population density of prey species, and usually overlaps those of several ♀. Home-range estimates in Thailand and Cambodia range between 1.9 and 64 km^2.

DISTRIBUTION *Native*: Cambodia, China, Malaysia (peninsular), Myanmar, Thailand. *Possibly Extinct*: Laos, Vietnam. *Extinct*: Singapore. There are plausibly only two major strongholds remaining: Peninsular Malaysia, and the N Tenasserim Forest Complex (Myanmar and Thailand). In SE China this subspecies has recently been recorded in two nature reserves in SW Yunnan Province near the border with Myanmar but the population is low (probably fewer than 10 individuals in each reserve) and is unlikely to recover. In Cambodia it occurs only in Eastern Plains Landscape. In Vietnam, Singapore, and Laos there are no viable populations remaining.

HABITAT Dry evergreen and mixed deciduous forest near water courses, and tropical rainforests, where prey species accumulate, at lower elevations of 500–600 m. Usually avoids humans and prefers sites that are less affected by human disturbances.

CONSERVATION STATUS Endangered. CITES: Appendix I. The population of Indochinese Leopard is estimated to be 950–2,500 individuals. A recent review showed a dramatic reduction of over 80% in range. Targeted poaching for wildlife trade is the greatest threat, as Leopard parts are used as substitutes for Tiger parts for medicinal purposes in China and Southeast Asia, and Leopard skins are highly sought after as luxury items. Other important factors include depletion of prey base, and habitat loss and fragmentation.

PHOTO CREDITS TL: *Kosin Sukhum*, Kaeng Krachan NP (Thailand); TR: *Coke and Som Smith*, Huai Kha Khaeng (Thailand); CL, B: *PEET Photo* (Thailand); CR: *Super Prin*, Keang Krachan NP (Thailand).

Javan Leopard
PANTHERA PARDUS MELAS

BL: 77-122 cm (♂), 109 cm (♀). TL: 71-73 cm. SH: 45-70 cm. W: 30-60 kg. SL: 19 cm (♂), 16.1 cm (♀). SW: 13.7 cm (♂), 11.7 cm (♀). DF: 30. CN: 38. A large, robust spotted cat with relatively short legs, robust forequarters, slender hindquarters, and long tail. A small, dark and richly colored subspecies of Leopard. Pelage is short but thick and rather harsh; color is rich rusty-yellow to deep reddish in the back, paler on the flanks and dusky gray, lightly washed with buff on the limbs. Underparts are white. Rosettes are small and close set, with the centers a little darker in hue than the main background color. Solid black spots on the lower limbs, belly, throat, face, neck, and distal tail. Melanistic forms are common. Relatively small rounded head. Round ears, back with a prominent pale patch, bounded by black. Long and bushy tail. Females smaller than males.

melanistic form

Young

Panthera pardus melas

OTHER NAMES *French*: Panthère de Java, panthère noire. *German*: Java-Leopard. *Spanish*: Leopardo de Java. *Russian*: Яванский леопард. *Javanese*: Selang, meong, meong totol, sancang manik, macan kumban.

TAXONOMY Considered as a subspecies of *P. pardus* (Leopard). This subspecies has been found to be distinct from all other Asian Leopards, in both molecular and morphological analyses.

SIMILAR SPECIES The Leopard is the only pantherine cat still roaming on Java, after the Sunda Clouded Leopard (*Neofelis diardi*) went extinct during the Holocene and the Javan Tiger (*Panthera tigris sondaica*) in the 1970s.

REPRODUCTION *Gestation*: 90-106 days. *Young per Birth*: 1-4. *Weaning*: 100 days. *Sexual Maturity*: 22-28 months. *Life Span*: Over 20 years in captivity. *Breeding Season*: Probably throughout the year, but there may be a peak during October-November. There is no specific information for this subspecies, but probably similar to the Indochinese Leopard.

BEHAVIOR *Social Behavior*: Solitary. *Diet*: From small mammals (mice, bats) to medium-sized ungulates (muntjac, wild pig, Javan rusa deer), primates (long-tailed macaque, leaf monkey, gibbon), and domestic livestock (dogs, goats, and chickens). It is the apex predator in Java, after the extinction of the Javan Tiger, and shares its habitat with two other felids, the Leopard Cat and the Fishing Cat. Mainly crepuscular and diurnal, but may be nocturnal near human settlements. It marks its home range by releasing secretions from interdigital glands when leaving scratches on trees or on the ground. Population density is estimated at 1 individual per 6 km^2 in Gunung Gede Pangrango NP, and at 1 per 6.5 km^2 in Gunung Halimun-Salak NP.

DISTRIBUTION *Native*: Indonesia (Java). Endemic to the island of Java. They are commonly found in Ujung Kulon NP, Gunung Gede Pangrango NP, Gunung Halimun-Salak NP, Ceremai NP, Merbabu NP, Merapi NP, Bromo Tengger Semeru NP, Meru Betiri NP, Alas Purwo NP, and Baluran NP. Absent from Sumatra and Borneo. Historically present on the Kangean Islands, although they have not been recorded since 1983.

HABITAT A variety of habitats, from patches of dense tropical rainforest found in the SW part of the island and on the mountain tops to dry deciduous forests and scrub in the E. In central Java it inhabits several teak plantations.

CONSERVATION STATUS Critically Endangered. CITES: Appendix I. Estimated population of fewer than 350-500 individuals. Only 5% of Java Island still contains suitable habitat for this species due to anthropogenic changes. All subpopulations are small and thus vulnerable to local extinction (the largest existing population occurs in Gunung Halimun-Salak NP and has only 40-50 individuals). Human population growth and loss of habitat due to agricultural expansion are main threats. The loss of habitat also results in more frequent contacts between Leopards and people, as Leopards now more often enter agricultural areas.

PHOTO CREDITS TL: *Irawan Subingar*; TR: *Eric Iselée*; Young: *Pacific Press*, Tierpark Berlin (Germany) and *Eric Iselée*; BR: *Scott Swabey*, Bali Safari and Marine Park (Indonesia); BL: *Katerina Jisova*, Prague Zoo (Czech Republic); BR: *Puch Corinne*, Zoo de Doué (France).

Amur Leopard
PANTHERA PARDUS ORIENTALIS

BL: 107-171 cm. TL: 75-102 cm. SH: 50-78 cm. W: 32-60 kg (♂), 25-42.5 kg (♀). SL: 18.9 cm. SW: 13.8 cm. DF: 30. CN: 38. A large, robust spotted cat with robust forequarters, slender hindquarters, and long tail. A medium-sized to large subspecies of Leopard, with long limbs and long hair. Coat is soft, with long and dense hair, bright and lustrous in color, from fairly light yellow to dense yellowish-red with a golden tinge or rusty-reddish-yellow. Color on flanks and outer sides of legs lighter. Underparts white. Large, widely spaced, thick-rimmed pure black rosettes, with light-colored centers, somewhat darker than main background color. Summer pelage is shorter and brighter with more vivid coloration. Relatively small rounded head. Eyes small, with round pupils. Round ears, back with a prominent pale patch, bounded by black. Long and bushy tail. Females smaller than males. Cubs with tiny dark brown and black spots but not the distinctive rosettes.

Young

66

Panthera pardus orientalis
(Amur population)

OTHER NAMES Far Eastern Leopard. *French*: Panthère de l'Amour, léopard de l'Amour. *German*: Amur-Leopard. *Spanish*: Leopardo de Amur. *Russian*: Дальневосточный (амурский) леопард.

TAXONOMY Considered as a subspecies of *P. pardus* (Leopard). Includes *amurensis*, *chinensis*, *villosa*, and *japonensis*.

REPRODUCTION *Gestation*: 90-106 days. *Young per Birth*: 1-4. *Weaning*: 100 days. *Sexual Maturity*: 22-36 months. *Life Span*: Over 20 years in captivity. *Breeding Season*: Second half of winter. ♀ shelter for 3 months inside rock piles, caves, and under overhanging cliffs, giving birth to 2-3 cubs covered with dense, rather long fur. Cubs open their eyes at 7-9 days after birth, and at around 2 months they leave the dwelling. After their mother wanders off, they stick together until the end of the winter season. ♀ leopards can give birth once a year, but the mortality rate for cubs appears to be very high.

BEHAVIOR *Social Behavior*: Solitary. *Diet*: Medium-sized ungulates (roe deer, sika deer, wild pigs), but small mammals (rabbits, badgers, raccoon dogs), birds (pheasants, hazel grouse), and insects make up a significant portion of their diet, especially in the summer months. It is the only subspecies adapted to a cold climate and displays the greatest divergence in coat pattern from other Leopard subspecies. Mainly nocturnal, but may hunt in daytime, especially on cold and cloudy days and in winter. Home ranges overlap considerably; ♀ maintain home ranges that vary in size from 40 to 100 km², while ♂ can have territories as large as 400 km².

DISTRIBUTION *Native*: China, Russia (Primorsky Krai). *Possibly Extinct*: North Korea. *Extinct*: South Korea. Until the late 19th century, it was distributed across the S stretches of the Amur-Ussuri region in Russia, Manchuria, N China, and the Korean Peninsula, reaching as far south as Beijing. They only occur now in a large area of about 7,000 km² along the eastern slopes of the E Manchurian Mountains in the Russian Far East, on the border with China but their numbers are likely to be very low. Its status in North Korea is unknown, although it is possible that some still occur in high mountainous areas.

HABITAT Manchurian-type mixed forests of pine and deciduous broadleaf trees, preferring rugged terrain with steep slopes, protruding rocks, ridgelines, and watersheds. Snow cover is a limiting factor, and it appears that Leopards cannot survive farther N, where snow is too deep in the winter. Forest cover is important, yet much of their habitat in Russia has been converted into unsuitable savanna-like grasslands by annual fires. Leopards may avoid areas inhabited by Tigers (there have been documented kills of Amur Leopards by Amur Tigers).

CONSERVATION STATUS Critically Endangered. CITES: Appendix I. Its range was reduced dramatically during the 20th century due to habitat loss, hunting, intensive logging, elimination of prey base, poaching, and a demand for body parts used in Asian traditional medicines. It is one of the most endangered subspecies of Leopard, and faces immediate risk of extinction. Although its population may have increased recently, especially on the Chinese side of the border (Jilin Province, Heilongjiang Province), the total population is just over 80 individuals.

PHOTO CREDITS T: *Alexander Sliwa*, Marwell Zoo (UK); Young: *Sergey Chichagov*, Tallinn Zoo (Estonia); CR: *Walter Arce*; CL, B: *Warren Metcalf.*

North Chinese Leopard

PANTHERA PARDUS ORIENTALIS

BL: 106-151 cm. TL: 70-95 cm. SH: 50-75 cm. W: 25-59 kg. SL: 19.7 cm (♂), 16.5 cm (♀). SW: 13.5 cm (♂), 11.7 cm (♀). DF: 30. CN: 38. A large, robust spotted cat with robust forequarters, slender hindquarters, and a long tail. A medium-sized, less richly colored subspecies of Leopard. Coat is thick, tawny-buffy to fulvous in color, with no rusty hue on the back. Underparts white. Large, thick-rimmed black rosettes, with darker enclosed fur, and sometimes even a spot within the rosette (traits common in Jaguars, but uncommon in Leopards). Back and limbs with ovate or roundish unequal-sized black spots. Relatively small rounded head, with small, regularly disposed, black spots. Eyes small, with round pupils. Round ears, back with a prominent pale patch, bounded by black. Long legs. Long and hairy tail. Females smaller than males. Cubs with tiny dark brown and black spots but not the distinctive rosettes.

Young

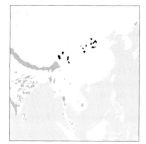

Panthera pardus orientalis
(North Chinese population)

OTHER NAMES Chinese Leopard. *French*: Panthère de Chine du Nord. *German*: Chinesischer Leopard. *Spanish*: Leopardo del norte de China. *Russian*: Северокитайский леопард. *Chinese*: Bao.

TAXONOMY Considered as a subspecies of *P. pardus* (Leopard). The subspecies *japonensis* is now included in *P. p. orientalis* by the Cat Specialist Group, as there is no clear biogeographical barrier between these two forms, which appear to form a cline in NE Asia. Includes *fontanierii* and *hanensis*.

REPRODUCTION *Gestation*: 98-105 days. *Young per Birth*: 2-3. *Weaning*: 90 days. *Sexual Maturity*: 30-36 months. *Life Span*: 20 years in captivity. *Breeding Season*: January and February in China. There is no specific information about the reproduction of this species in the wild. They are promiscuous, as both sexes have multiple mates. ♀ initiate mating by walking back and forth in front of a ♂ and brushing up against him or swatting him with her tail. ♂ mount ♀ while frequently biting her nape. Age at independence is 12-18 months. Cub mortality is quite high. Siblings may stay together for several months before separating. Home ranges are flexible and young may stay temporarily in their natal area.

BEHAVIOR *Social Behavior*: Solitary. *Diet*: Large ungulates (wild goats, argalis), but also small mammals (rodents, hares), birds (partridges), and amphibians when large prey are relatively scarce; near humans they may eat dogs, cats, sheep, and calves. There is no specific information for this population, but probably similar to the Amur Leopard. Nocturnal; although they sometimes hunt during overcast days, they are less diurnal in areas close to humans. They easily climb trees, but rarely swim. They hunt mostly on the ground and use scent-marks and vocalization to communicate. They hunt by stalking from a very low position with long periods of motionless needed; they attack from a very close range with a short burst of speed and a powerful strike of the front paw. They mark their home ranges with urine, feces, and claw marks and communicate with conspecifics by growling, roaring, and spitting when aggravated and purring when content.

DISTRIBUTION *Native*: China. This subspecies, endemic to China, now occurs only in parts of seven provinces in E and central China, presumably as far N as the Beijing area, and as far S as the Pearl River, including Sichuan and Guizhou Provinces. Historically, it was distributed throughout China, with the exception of the arid Gobi Desert and mountainous W regions at elevations > 4,000 m.

HABITAT Most commonly associated with some type of forest cover, woodlands, scrub jungles, or rocky hills. They are absent from true deserts but are found in just about any other habitat.

CONSERVATION STATUS Not assessed by IUCN, probably qualifies as Critically Endangered. CITES: Appendix I. Estimated population is probably fewer than 175-500 individuals. Subpopulations are small (fewer than 50 individuals) and fragmented, and occur mainly in isolated nature reserves. Reasons for their decline include retaliatory killings due to conflict, poaching for wildlife trade, low prey numbers (especially ungulates), and habitat loss and fragmentation.

PHOTO CREDITS TL: *Joachim S. Müller*, Zoological Gardens Karlsruhe (Germany); TR: *Jasmine Curtis*, The Big Cat Sanctuary (UK); Young: *Eric Isselée*; CR, BL: *Rufus46*, Hellabrunn Zoo (Germany); BR: *Alan Evans*, The Big Cat Sanctuary (UK).

Jaguar
PANTHERA ONCA

BL: 110-270 cm (♂), 116-219 cm (♀). TL: 44-80 cm. SH: 55-76 cm. W: 36-158 kg (♂), 36-100 kg (♀). SL: 18.6-28 cm. SW: 14-20.8 cm DF: 30. CN: 38. A large, stocky cat, with an unusually large head and short massive limbs. Body size varies across its range (the smallest Jaguars occur in the Amazon and Central and North America, while the largest individuals can be found in the Pantanal and in the Venezuelan Llanos). Coat color is pale yellow or tawny-orange, covered with large, black block-like rosettes with a darker brown interior and usually small black spots inside. White belly, throat, and inside of the limbs, marked with irregular black spots. Melanistic and albinistic individuals have been recorded. Head is short, rounded, and massively built. Ears are short and rounded with black backs and an off-white central patch. Feet are very broad and rounded. Tail is relatively short, spotted, and has several black rings from the midpoint to the tip.

melanistic
form

Young

Panthera onca

OTHER NAMES *French*: Jaguar. *German*: Jaguar. *Spanish*: Otorongo, tigre, tigre Americano, tigre Real, tigre mariposo, yaguar, yaguareté. *Russian*: Яrуар. *Portuguese*: Onça, onça pintada, onça canguçu. *Mayan*: Zac-bolay, ballum.

TAXONOMY Monotypic. Recent genetic and morphological analyses suggest four incompletely isolated phylogeographic groups: Mexico and Guatemala, S Central America, N South America N of the Amazon River, and South America S of the Amazon River.

REPRODUCTION *Gestation*: 90-103 days. *Young per Birth*: 1-4, usually 2. *Weaning*: 3-6 months. *Sexual Maturity*: 24-30 months (♀), 36-48 months (♂). *Life Span*: 15 years, 23 years in captivity. *Breeding Season*: Year-round, but may be seasonal in some areas (January to April in Venezuela). It uses rocky caves or dense thickets for den sites. Cubs open their eyes between 3 and 13 days, begin to follow their mother at 2-5 months, and travel and hunt independently within their mother's range by 15-18 months. They become independent by the age of 24 months.

BEHAVIOR *Social Behavior*: Solitary. *Diet*: Opportunistic hunters, including mammals (large ungulates, including livestock, armadillo, peccary, capybara, deer, agouti, paca, coati, tapir, sloth, monkey, anteater), reptiles (iguanas, caimans, turtles, and snakes), and birds. Largest Jaguars from open flood-plain areas (the Llanos in Venezuela and the Pantanal in Brazil) take the largest prey, while the smallest Jaguars inhabiting the dense forest areas of Central America and Amazonia take smaller prey. Primarily nocturnal, but can also be active during the day. It is an excellent swimmer, and readily catches fish, capybaras, and caimans in the water. Prey is killed by jumping from the back or side and immediately biting the nape or puncturing the braincase. Home ranges are marked with urine and feces. Home ranges vary across their geographic range, from 10 km² to more than 500 km², often according to the season and availability of resources. ♂ have larger home ranges than ♀, and often overlap with several ♀. Range overlap between individuals of the same sex has been detected but temporal avoidance is common.

DISTRIBUTION *Native*: Argentina, Belize, Bolivia, Brazil, Colombia, Costa Rica, Ecuador, French Guiana, Guatemala, Guyana, Honduras, Mexico, Nicaragua, Panama, Paraguay, Peru, Suriname, United States, Venezuela. *Extinct*: El Salvador, Uruguay.

HABITAT From rainforest to seasonally flooded swamp areas, pampas grassland, thorn scrub woodland, and dry deciduous forest. They mainly inhabit tropical lowland forest, followed by dry tropical forest, xeric habitats, and finally arable lowland pastures, up to 3,800 m. Strongly associated with water. They avoid montane forest.

CONSERVATION STATUS Near Threatened. CITES: Appendix I. Estimated total population of 68,000, with the largest subpopulation in Amazonia (89% of the total population); all other jaguar subpopulations are classified as Endangered or Critically Endangered. Threatened by habitat loss and fragmentation, killing for trophies and illegal trade in body parts, retaliatory killings associated with livestock depredation, and competition for wild prey with human hunters. Fully protected at the national level across most of its range.

PHOTO CREDITS TL: *Sergey Chichagov*; TR: *Vladimir Cech*, Pantanal (Brazil); Young: *Eric Isselée* and *Andrey Kotkin*, Leningrad Zoo (Russia); CR: *4theuk*; B, C: *Javier Amores*, Pantanal (Brazil).

Snow Leopard
PANTHERA UNCIA

BL: 99-130 cm. TL: 80-100 cm. SH: 60 cm. W: 37-55 kg (♂), 35-42 kg (♀). SL: 16.9 cm (♂), 16.2 cm (♀). SW: 12.8 cm (♂), 12.7 cm (♀). DF: 30. CN: 38. A medium-sized cat, the smallest of the large felids in the genus *Panthera*, with a remarkably long and hairy tail. Coat with dense and long fur, especially on the underside, from light gray to very light brown, with large, dark gray or black open blotches, and smaller solid black blotches on the lower legs and small black spots on the head, neck, and shoulders. Markings appear less crisp in the long winter coat. Underparts are yellowish-cream to white. No records of melanism or albinism. Head is small, broad, and rounded, with a short muzzle and high domed forehead. Eyes are distinctively pale green or gray. Ears are short and round, black on the back with a pale grayish center. Deep chest. Relatively short and robust forelegs, with very large paws. Hind limbs longer than the forelimbs. Tail is very long, tubular, thick, and well furred. Males are larger than females.

Young

Panthera uncia

OTHER NAMES Ounce. *French*: Léopard des neiges, once, panthère des neiges. *German*: Schneeleopard. *Spanish*: Pantera de la nieves. *Russian*: Снежный барс, или ирбис. *Kazakh*: Irbis. *Kirghiz*: Irbis, akilbirs, ilbirs. *Mongolian*: Irvis. *Nepali*: Hiun chituwa. *Tajik*: Babri barfi. *Tibetan*: Sah. *Urdu*: Barfani chita. *Chinese*: Xue bào. *Hindi*: Barhal he. *Ladakhi*: Shan. *Bhotia*: Burhel haye. *Kashmiri*: Sheen-e-suh.

TAXONOMY Monotypic. Three subspecies proposed by some authors based on phylogenetic studies and superficial morphological differences, but not widely recognized: *P. u. uncia* (Tian Shan, Pamir, trans-Himalaya regions); *P. u. irbis* (Altai region); and *P. u. uncioides* (core Himalaya and Tibetan Plateau). Previously placed in the genus *Uncia* based on its relatively unusual, domed skull.

REPRODUCTION *Gestation*: 90-105 days. *Young per Birth*: 1-3, rarely 1-5. *Weaning*: 5 months. *Sexual Maturity*: 24-36 months. *Life Span*: 25 years in captivity. *Breeding Season*: January to March, with most births around May. ♀ and cubs stay together for about 1-2 years.

BEHAVIOR *Social Behavior*: Solitary; groups of 2-4 may form during the breeding season, or with the birth of cubs. *Diet*: Mountain ungulates (ibex, blue sheep, argali, markhor, urial, tahr, musk deer, and occasionally gazelles, and juveniles of wild pig, wild yak, and wild ass); large kills are supplemented by small prey (marmots, hares, pikas, and game birds), especially during the summer; they may prey on domestic sheep, goats, and yak calves; also carrion. No recorded fatal attacks on humans. Generally diurnal, although they will hunt at any time of the day or night. They mostly rest near cliffs and ridges that provide vantage points and shade. Stalks in typical felid fashion before rushing prey at close range; superbly agile over extraordinarily steep and rugged terrain. Large prey is usually killed by a suffocating throat bite. Adapted completely to live in snow-covered areas: an enlarged nasal cavity warms the air that it breathes, and the long fur provides excellent insulation. Maintains stable ranges that are regularly marked. Scrape markings are the most abundant type of sign left in the wild, but they also spray urine onto sheltered patches of rock. Home ranges of both sexes may overlap and individuals share central areas of activity with conspecifics. It cannot roar, although it can growl, cough, snarl, and yowl.

DISTRIBUTION *Native*: Afghanistan, Bhutan, China (Yunnan, Qinghai, Tibet, Sichuan, Gansu, Xinjiang, Nei Mongol), India (Himachal Pradesh, Sikkim, Jammu-Kashmir, Uttaranchal, Arunachal Pradesh), Kazakhstan, Kyrgyzstan, Mongolia, Nepal, Pakistan, Russia, Tajikistan, Uzbekistan.

HABITAT Alpine as well as subalpine steppe, grassland, and scrub above the treeline. It favors lightly forested and steep terrain with rocky, broken country, from 900 to 5,800 m. Prefers areas with proximity to cliffs. They usually avoid forests, although they are occasionally observed in conifer forests and alpine shrublands.

CONSERVATION STATUS Vulnerable. CITES: Appendix I. It is naturally rare, and human populations and their livestock are increasing in its habitat. Widely killed for livestock depredation. Furs and especially body parts have commercial value, chiefly in China. Estimated population of 3,400-7,000.

PHOTO CREDITS TR: *Meunierd*; TL: *Alexander Sliwa*, Zurich Zoo (Switzerland); Young: *Glenn Nagel*, Brookfield Zoo (USA); CR: *Valeriy Maleev* (Mongolia); B: *Yelizaveta Tomashevska*, Basel Zoo (Switzerland).

Indochinese Clouded Leopard
NEOFELIS NEBULOSA

BL: 68.5-108 cm. TL: 55-91 cm. SH: 30-55 cm. W: 16-18 kg (♂),11.5-13.5 kg (♀). SL: 15.4 cm (♂), 13.1 cm (♀). SW: 10.2 cm (♂), 8.9 cm (♀). DF: 28-30. CN: 38. A medium-sized cat, with a long tail and relatively short legs. Pelage is light yellow to light gray, with large, irregular, cloud-shaped black patches on the back and sides, and black oval spots on the legs. Underside white with black spots. Two broken black stripes along the spine and six longitudinal black stripes on the neck, starting behind the ears. Head is long, crown spotted, rostrum white, dark stripes from the eye and the corner of the mouth along the sides of the head. Canines exceptionally elongated. Ears are short and rounded, black on the back with a light gray spot. Legs are short and stout, hind legs longer than forelegs, with broad feet. Very long tail, thick and plush, covered proximally with spots and becoming encircled with black rings toward the tip. Males larger than females.

Young

74

Neofelis nebulosa

OTHER NAMES Enkuli Clouded Leopard. *French*: Panthère longibande, Panthère nébuleuse. *German*: Nebelparder. *Spanish*: Pantera longibanda, pantera nebulosa de Indochina. *Russian*: Дымчатый леопард (материковый). *Chinese*: Yun bao. *Nepali*: Amchita, dhwanse chituwa. *Assamese*: Ghodaphutuki bagh. *Bengali*: Lamchita. *Bodo*: Moosa phula. *Lepcha*: Pungmar. *Mizo*: Kelral. *Bhotia*: Kung.

TAXONOMY Monotypic. The Clouded Leopard has been split into two species: *N. nebulosa* (Indochinese Clouded Leopard, restricted to mainland Southeast Asia), and *N. diardi* (Sunda Clouded Leopard, found on the islands of Sumatra and Borneo). Three subspecies previously recognized: *N. n. nebulosa* (China, SE Asia, Hainan), *N. n. macrosceloides* (Nepal, NE India, Bhutan), and *N. n. brachyura* (Taiwan, likely extinct), but they are no longer considered valid.

REPRODUCTION *Gestation*: 87-99 days. *Young per Birth*: 1-3, rarely up to 5. *Weaning*: 10 weeks. *Sexual Maturity*: 26 months. *Life Span*: 17 years in captivity. *Breeding Season*: Probably aseasonal.

BEHAVIOR *Social Behavior*: Solitary, but may hunt in pairs. *Diet*: Arboreal and terrestrial prey (hog deer, slow loris, brush-tailed porcupine, pangolin, ground squirrel, primates, muntjac, pheasants); they occasionally kill poultry; apparently not interested in carrion. Its characteristics are intermediate between small and big cats: it cannot roar and can only purr like small cat species but its feeding behavior, grooming, and body postures are similar to those of big cat species. Primarily nocturnal, with crepuscular activity peaks. Highly arboreal, but probably search for prey mainly from the ground and readily pursue arboreal species into trees as they are located. They can climb down trees head first, traverse branches upside down, and hang from branches with their hind feet. They take refuge in trees when pursued by domestic dogs. They are good swimmers. ♂ and ♀ have similar home range sizes between 16 and 40 km² in size, with smaller intensively used core areas of 3-5 km². Home ranges of ♀ and ♂ overlap substantially and also home ranges of ♂ seem to have quite high overlap. They mark their territories by clawing trees, urine spraying, scraping, and head rubbing.

DISTRIBUTION *Native*: Bangladesh, Bhutan, Cambodia, China, India (Assam, Meghalaya, Arunachal Pradesh, Tripura, Mizoram, Sikkim, and N parts of West Bengal), Laos, Malaysia (Peninsular Malaysia), Myanmar, Nepal, Thailand, Vietnam. *Extinct*: Taiwan.

HABITAT Strongly associated with forest habitat, particularly primary evergreen tropical rainforest, but there are also records from dry and deciduous forest, as well as secondary and logged forests, grassland and scrub, and mangrove swamps, up to 2,200 m in the Himalayas. It shows a preference for forest over more open habitats.

CONSERVATION STATUS Vulnerable, Endangered in China. CITES: Appendix I. Relatively widespread but its status is poorly known in most of the range, with recent declines in the majority of range countries, especially Myanmar, Vietnam, and China. Its range in China has been severely reduced, and recent confirmed records are from only a handful of sites in S and W Yunnan Province and SE Tibet, with an estimated population of only 70 individuals in S Yunnan. Its presence in Bangladesh is uncertain. Threats include exploitation for pelts and bones, and habitat loss due to deforestation.

PHOTO CREDITS Young: *Balazs Buzas*, Khao Kheow Zoo (Thailand); T, C: *Alexander Sliwa*, Khao Kheow Zoo (Thailand); CR: *Tim Sagorski*, Dortmund Zoo (Germany); B: *Frida Bredesen*, Parken Zoo (Sweden).

Sumatran Clouded Leopard
NEOFELIS DIARDI DIARDI

BL: 104 cm (♂), 87 cm (♀). TL: 77-79 cm. SH: 30-55 cm. W: 23 kg (♂), 12 kg (♀). SL: 15.7 cm (♂), 12.9 cm (♀). SW: 11.1 cm (♂), 9 cm (♀). DF: 30. CN: 38. A medium-sized cat, with a long tail and relatively short legs, overall darker, with a smaller cloud pattern than Indochinese Clouded Leopards. Pelage is gray to tawny-gray, with relatively small, irregular blotches with thick, black margins and small black spots within each blotch. Two broken black stripes along the spine. Lower legs with solid, black blotches, closely clustered. Underside white with black spots. Head is long, crown spotted, rostrum white, dark stripes from the eye and the corner of the mouth. Canines elongated. Ears short and rounded, black on the back. Legs are short and stout, hind legs longer than forelegs, with broad feet. Very long tail, thick and plush, covered proximally with spots and becoming encircled with black rings toward the tip. Males larger than females. Young with dark cloudy spots and gray background.

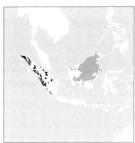

Neofelis diardi diardi

OTHER NAMES Sunda Clouded Leopard, Enkuli Clouded Leopard, Diard's Cat. *French*: Panthère nébuleuse de Sumatra. *German*: Sumatra Nebelparder. *Spanish*: Pantera nebulosa de Sumatra. *Russian*: Зондский дымчатый леопард: суматранский. *Indonesian*: Harimau dahan.

TAXONOMY Previously considered as a subspecies of the Clouded Leopard of mainland Asia (*N. nebulosa*). Two subspecies are recognized based on molecular and morphological analysis: *N. d. diardi* (Sumatran Clouded Leopard), and *N. d. borneensis* (Bornean Clouded Leopard).

SIMILAR SPECIES The Marbled Cat is much smaller, with a smaller rounded head, and smaller, more diffuse markings.

REPRODUCTION *Gestation*: Unknown. *Young per Birth*: Unknown. *Weaning*: Unknown. *Sexual Maturity*: Probably 24 months. *Life Span*: Unknown. *Breeding Season*: Aseasonal. There is little scientific information available on its reproduction in the wild.

BEHAVIOR *Social Behavior*: Solitary. *Diet*: Small to medium-sized mammals (primates, sambar, muntjac, bearded pig, mouse-deer, porcupines), and fish. Unlike the other felids of Sumatra, it can hunt entirely in the canopy, and it can jump more than 5 m between trees; it may occasionally take domestic animals. There is an overriding lack of knowledge for this subspecies in Sumatra, such as how the species exists with Tigers and other cat species, and what habitat the species uses. Largely nocturnal, with significant activity during crepuscular periods. More arboreal on the island of Sumatra than in Borneo, possibly due to sympatry with Tigers. Unlike other large cats, which kill by gripping the throat and strangling, they use their large canines to cut the spinal cord on the neck, leaving a pair of distinctive punctures on abandoned prey. They do not hold exclusive territories, and both ♂ and ♀ have overlapping ranges. There are no confirmed records of attacks on humans.

DISTRIBUTION *Native*: Indonesia (Sumatra). *Presence Uncertain*: Batu Islands. *Extinct*: Java. Before 1900, when most of Sumatra was covered in primary forest, it was probably distributed throughout the island. Now there is direct evidence of its presence in only about 3% of the island's area. Found in Barisan Selatan NP, lowland forest in the S part of Jambi province, Gunung Leuser NP, Way Kambas Game Reserve, Torgamba, Tigapulu hills, Kerinci-Seblat NP, and Gumai Pasemah Game Reserve. This subspecies probably exists at much lower population densities than on Borneo, potentially in response to predation and interspecific competition from Tigers.

HABITAT It seems to be more abundant in hilly, mountain areas than at lower elevations, but it is found in a range of forest types. Forest dependent, including disturbed forest, so long as it has high canopy closure. Oil palm plantations and areas with low canopy closure are avoided.

CONSERVATION STATUS Vulnerable. CITES: Appendix I. Estimated population around 500 in Sumatra. Main threats include habitat degradation and conversion due to commercial logging and conversion to oil palm plantations, and poaching, either directly through the use of snares, or through the reduction of prey availability by the poaching of game species. Fully protected.

PHOTO CREDITS Based on camera trap photos from *Wai-Ming Wong*, *Frankfurt Zoological Society*, and *Iding Haidir*, Kerinci Seblat National Park/Fauna & Flora International, taken in Sipurak, Kerinci Seblat NP, Sumatra (Indonesia).

Bornean Clouded Leopard
NEOFELIS DIARDI BORNEENSIS

BL: 104 cm (♂), 87 cm (♀). TL: 77-79 cm. SH: 30-55 cm. W: 23 kg (♂), 12 kg (♀). SL: 15.7 cm (♂), 12.9 cm (♀). SW: 11.1 cm (♂), 9 cm (♀). DF: 30. CN: 38. A medium-sized cat, with a long tail and relatively short legs, overall darker, with a ground color grayer than that of the Sumatran Clouded Leopard, with yellowish tinge, more frequent and bolder cloud spots, larger, more angular cloud-like blotches, with thicker black borders, neck and shoulder stripes thicker. Two broken black stripes along the spine. Lower legs with solid, black blotches, closely clustered. Underside white with black spots. Melanistic and pale individuals have been recorded. Head is long, crown spotted, rostrum white, dark stripes from the eye and the corner of the mouth. Canines elongated. Ears short and rounded, black on the back. Legs are short and stout, hind legs longer than forelegs, with broad feet. Very long tail, thick and plush, covered proximally with spots and becoming encircled with black rings toward the tip. Males larger than females. Young with dark cloudy spots and gray background.

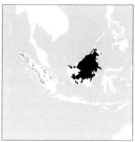

Neofelis diardi borneensis

OTHER NAMES Sunda Clouded Leopard, Diard's Cat. *French*: Panthère nébuleuse des îles de Borneo. *German*: Borneo Nebelparder. *Spanish*: Pantera nebulosa de Borneo. *Russian*: Зондский дымчатый леопард: борнейский. *Indonesian*: Harimau dahan. *Malay*: Harimau dahan, engkuli.

TAXONOMY Considered as a subspecies of Sunda Clouded Leopard (*N. diardi*). It differs in molecular, craniomandibular, and dental characteristics from the Sumatran Clouded Leopard.

SIMILAR SPECIES The Indochinese Clouded Leopard shows a distinct pelage pattern, paler and brighter with buff to rich tawny background color, and very large blotches with narrower black margins and few or no spots within the blotches.

REPRODUCTION *Gestation*: Unknown. *Young per Birth*: Unknown. *Weaning*: Unknown. *Sexual Maturity*: Probably 24 months. *Life Span*: Unknown. *Breeding Season*: Aseasonal, but peaks between December and March. There is little scientific information available on its reproduction in the wild. Cubs become independent at 10 months.

BEHAVIOR *Social Behavior*: Solitary. *Diet*: Small to medium-sized mammals (sambar, muntjac, bearded pig, mouse-deer, porcupines, primates), and fish; they may occasionally take domestic animals. Largely nocturnal, with significant activity during crepuscular periods. Semi-arboreal, resting high up along tree branch during the day. ♂ hunt mainly on the ground for bearded pigs and deer, while the much smaller ♀ hunt more for primates in the canopy. More arboreal on the island of Sumatra, possibly due to sympatry with Tigers. Unlike other large cats, which kill by gripping the throat and strangling, they use their large canines to cut the spinal cord on the neck, leaving a pair of distinctive punctures on abandoned prey. In central Kalimantan, home ranges average 35 km², with core ranges, which are used intensively, of 7.7 km². A ♀ in Sabah occupied a home range of 16.1 km² and a core range of 5.4 km². They do not hold exclusive territories, and both ♂ and ♀ have overlapping ranges. There are no confirmed records of attacks on humans. There is no evidence to indicate marking behavior in the form of scrapes or fecal deposits along roads or trails.

DISTRIBUTION *Native*: Brunei, Indonesia (Kalimantan), Malaysia (Sarawak, Sabah).

HABITAT A range of forest types: primary lowland, upland, and submontane forest, selectively logged forest, peat-swamp forest, coastal mangroves, up to 1,500 m. Forest dependent, including disturbed forest, so long as it has high canopy closure. Oil palm plantations and areas with low canopy closure are avoided.

CONSERVATION STATUS Vulnerable. CITES: Appendix I. Estimated population around 3,000 in Borneo. Main threats include habitat loss due to commercial logging and conversion to oil palm plantations, and poaching. Fully protected in Indonesia, Malaysia, and Brunei.

PHOTO CREDITS TL: *Lennart Verheuvel*, Deramakot Forest Reserve (Malaysia); CL: *Roland Wirth*, Taman Safari Bogor (Indonesia); TR, CR, B: *Mike Gordon*, Deramakot Forest Reserve (Malaysia).

Puma lineage

PUMA, JAGUARUNDI, AND CHEETAH

RECOGNITION The Puma lineage is a monophyletic clade that includes three extant species, each in its own genus, differing in size, range, and coat pattern: *Puma concolor*, *Herpailurus yagouaroundi*, and *Acinonyx jubatus* (some authors classify the Jaguarundi in the genus *Puma*, although the considerable genetic distance and morphological differences between the two species justify the genus *Herpailurus*). All species in this group have a comparatively small and short head, a long tubular tail (measuring around two-thirds of head-body length), and a relatively long body, with long hind legs, which provide increased flexion while running, and all three communicate with uncatlike whistles and chirps. Jaguarundis and adult Pumas have a plain-colored coat without body markings, while Cheetahs are covered with small, round dark spots, scattered singly over most of the body. The Cheetah is anatomically adapted for high-speed pursuit in open landscapes, having very long legs with dog-like claws (semi-retractable). The Jaguarundi is a small- to medium-sized cat with a very distinctive appearance and relatively short legs. The Puma and the Cheetah are large-sized cats. This group is sexually dimorphic in body size, with males being generally larger and heavier than females. All species have the typical felid dental formula (I 3/3, C 1/1, P 3/2, M 1/1 = 30). Chromosome number is 2n=38.

PHYLOGENY The Puma lineage diverged from other felids approximately 6.7 Ma in Eurasia. This ancestral cat produced two descendant lineages, one that evolved into Cheetahs in Africa, and another Puma-like cat that emigrated to North America, when the Bering Strait land bridge linked Asia and North America, about 5 Ma. An alternative scenario proposes a New World origin of the Puma lineage with subsequent migration of Cheetah ancestors into the Old World, but this theory has been recently challenged. The earliest specimens in the fossil record of the Cheetah (*Acinonyx* sp.) date to 4 Ma, and fossils of the living species, *A. jubatus*, appeared first in southern Africa at least 1.8 Ma. The fossil *Miracinonyx* sp., commonly known as American Cheetah, which also had long limbs and small, tall, and abbreviated skull shapes, is also part of this group, but is more closely related to Pumas than Cheetahs. The Puma and its sister-species, the Jaguarundi, diverged from a common ancestor around 4.2 Ma in North America, and spread later to South America, during the second ice age across the Panama land bridge. Pumas probably became extinct in North America in the late Pleistocene, followed by recolonization from South America. *Puma concolor* does not occur in the fossil record until 0.6 Ma.

BEHAVIOR All species in this group hunt on the ground, but can climb trees. Cheetahs and Jaguarundi are mainly diurnal, while Pumas are more crepuscular and nocturnal, although they may be seen during the day. Pumas have an extensive range of prey, reflecting their wider geographic distribution, from agoutis and armadillos to deer and guanacos, and Jaguarundis feed primarily on small vertebrates weighing less than 1 kg, such as birds and medium-sized rodents. Cheetahs are highly specialized to prey on gazelles and small to medium-sized antelopes. Pumas and Jaguarundis are solitary and probably territorial, but may be seen in pairs and may interact more regularly and predictably than previously thought. Cheetahs have a more complex social system, unique among felids, in which females are asocial and non-territorial, while males are social and often form lifelong coalitions of two to four individuals.

DISTRIBUTION The Puma and Jaguarundi are currently distributed from North to South America, while the Cheetah is restricted to Africa and Iran. The Puma has the broadest north-south distribution of any terrestrial mammal, ranging from southwestern Canada to southern Chile. It occurs in a very broad range of temperate, subtropical, and tropical habitats, provided there is vegetation or rocky terrain. The Jaguarundi lives in lowlands, in a wide range of both open and closed habitats, requiring access to dense ground cover, from northern Mexico throughout Central and South America to southeastern Brazil and central Argentina. The Cheetah is widely distributed across open habitats, from savanna to scrubland to desert, in southern and East Africa; it is rare in West and Central Africa, and is extinct in North Africa and Asia, except southern Algeria and central Iran.

CONSERVATION Pumas were eliminated from the entire eastern half of North America, except for a tiny population in Florida. It is listed as Least Concern, but the status of its populations in Central and South America is largely unknown, and many are suspected to be in decline. They are threatened by habitat loss and fragmentation, and poaching of their wild prey base, and persecuted across their range by retaliatory hunting due to livestock depredation. The Jaguarundi is much less abundant than previously perceived, with small population sizes and low densities; it is considered Near Threatened in Argentina, and threatened in Mexico, and it is probably extinct in North America. Cheetahs are extinct or Critically Endangered in North and West Africa, and have disappeared from approximately 80% of their historical range in Africa and their entire Asiatic range, except for a single population of around 50 in central Iran; total numbers are estimated at only 8,000 individuals. Conversion of habitat to farmlands with replacement of prey by livestock is a key factor driving Cheetah declines.

North American Puma
Puma concolor cougar, 84

South American Puma
Puma concolor concolor, 82

red form

Jaguarundi
Herpailurus yagouaroundi, 86

dark form

King Cheetah
color variation

Sudan Cheetah
Acinonyx jubatus soemmeringii, 90

South and East African Cheetah
Acinonyx jubatus jubatus, 88

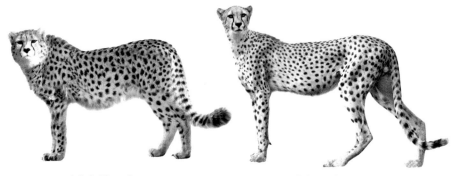

Asiatic Cheetah
Acinonyx jubatus venaticus, 94

Saharan Cheetah
Acinonyx jubatus hecki, 92

South American Puma
PUMA CONCOLOR CONCOLOR

BL: 85-150 cm. TL: 45-82 cm. SH: 66-81 cm. W: 50-65 kg (♂), 25-45 kg (♀). SL: 16.4 cm (♂), 15 cm (♀). SW: 13.9 cm (♂), 12.6 cm (♀). DF: 30. CN: 38. A large, long-tailed, unspotted cat. Coat is short and soft, silvery-gray, tawny, or reddish to dark brown in color, darkest on middle of back and tail. Individuals in temperate regions are larger and tend to have paler, light grayish coloration particularly in the long, dense winter coat. Tropical individuals tend to have rich, brick-red tones (color alone is not useful for distinguishing populations). Chin, lips, throat, and underparts whitish. No records of melanism, albinism infrequent. Relatively small head with small, rounded ears with dark brown to black back sides. Slender body with long legs and large feet. Tail is long and heavy, with a dark tip, and usually hangs down next to the hind legs. Males larger and more muscular, with a broader head. Females have 3 pairs of nipples. Young individuals have some stripes or blotches, and cubs are dark spotted and have blue eyes.

tropical form

temperate form

Young

82

Puma concolor concolor

OTHER NAMES Cougar, Mountain Lion. *French*: Puma. *German*: Puma, Silberlöwe, Berglöwe. *Spanish*: Puma de América del Sur, león americano, león bayo, león colorado, león de montaña, león sabanero, mitzli, onza bermeja. *Russian*: Южноамериканская пума. *Portuguese*: Onça vermelha, onça parda. *Guaraní*: Guasura, yaguá-pytá. *Suriname*: Reditigri.

TAXONOMY Six subspecies were formerly suggested based on genetic analysis: *P. c. cougar* (North America), *P. c. costaricensis* (Central America), *P. c. capricornensis* (E South America), *P. c. concolor* (N South America), *P. c. cabrerae* (central South America), and *P. c. puma* (S South America). Currently only two subspecies are recognized: *P. c. concolor* (South America, possibly excluding W of Andes in N), *P. c. cougar* (North and Central America, possibly N South America W of Andes).

REPRODUCTION *Gestation*: 82-98 days. *Young per Birth*: 1-4, usually 2-3. *Weaning*: 2-3 months. *Sexual Maturity*: 18-36 months. *Life Span*: 16 years, 20 years in captivity. *Breeding Season*: Throughout the year. Denning in hollows under trees, amid rocks, or in dense vegetation. Young remain with their mother for about 9-24 months. Dispersing juveniles are particularly at risk of coming into conflict with resident individuals or humans.

BEHAVIOR *Social Behavior*: Solitary. *Diet*: Large (deer, guanaco, vicuña) to medium-sized mammals (large rodents, armadillos), but in tropical rainforests also birds and reptiles (caimans, iguanas); they may also prey on livestock. In areas where the Puma co-exists with the larger Jaguar, it seems to prey more on small to medium-sized animals (hares, agoutis, marsupials, wild pigs, feral pigs, raccoons, and armadillos). They stalk very close to prey, before an explosive final rush. Active at all times of the day but typically have a more crepuscular-nocturnal activity pattern. Territorial. Home ranges are generally smaller than most reported in the USA and Canada.

DISTRIBUTION *Native*: Argentina, Bolivia, Brazil, Chile, Colombia, Costa Rica, Ecuador, French Guiana, Guyana, Paraguay, Peru, Suriname, Venezuela. *Presence Uncertain*: Uruguay. It has the largest N-S distribution of any terrestrial mammal in the W hemisphere, ranging from the Yukon-British Columbia border in SW Canada almost to the Straits of Magellan, Chile. It is extirpated from around 40% of its South American range, being absent in large areas of central-E and NE Argentina, and central and N Chile.

HABITAT All kinds of forest, woodland and scrubland, wet or dry, well-vegetated grassland savannas such as the Pantanal and pampas, and sparsely vegetated or rocky deserts, from sea level to up to 5,800 m in the Andes. Tolerant of human proximity, though they do not permanently occupy heavily modified landscapes such as croplands and monoculture plantations. They avoid open habitat, such as extensive grassland, prairie, and barren desert.

CONSERVATION STATUS Least Concern. CITES: Appendix II, Appendix I in Bolivia. Its current status in South America is relatively unknown. It is legally protected in many countries, but it is still killed because of its depredation on livestock. It can be legally hunted in some parts of Argentina and Peru. The most significant factor affecting Puma populations is the loss and fragmentation of habitat and persecution in livestock areas. Its population is decreasing.

PHOTO CREDITS TL: *Pulsar Imagens*, Pantanal (Brazil); TR, CR: *Daniel López Velasco,* Torres del Paine NP (Chile); B: *Igor Altuna,* Torres del Paine NP (Chile); Young: *Steven Metildi*, Andes (Chile).

North American Puma
PUMA CONCOLOR COUGAR

BL: 108-152 cm (♂), 80-141 cm (♀). TL: 53-92 cm. SH: 43-79 cm. W: 52-91 kg (♂), 34-57 kg (♀). SL: 16.4 cm (♂), 15 cm (♀). SW: 13.9 cm (♂), 12.6 cm (♀). DF: 30. CN: 38. A large, long-tailed, unspotted cat. The largest individuals occur in the temperate extreme of the range. Coat is short and soft, from silvery-gray, tawny, or reddish to fawn colored, darkest on middle of back and tail, and can vary greatly. Chin, lips, throat, and underparts whitish. No records of melanism, albinism is infrequent. Relatively small head, with small, rounded ears with dark brown to black back sides, without tufts. Some individuals have a prominent dark brown and white facial pattern. Slender body with long legs and large feet. Tail is long and heavy, with a dark tip, and usually hangs down next to the hind legs. Males are larger and more muscular than females, with a broader head. Females have 3 pairs of nipples. Young individuals have some stripes or blotches. Cubs are dark spotted and have blue eyes.

♀

temperate form

tropical form

Young

♂

Puma concolor cougar

OTHER NAMES Cougar, Mountain Lion, Panther, Catamount. *French*: Puma, couguar. *German*: Puma, Silberlöwe. *Spanish*: Puma, león americano, león bayo, león colorado, león de montaña, león sabanero, mitzli, onza bermeja. *Russian*: Североамериканская пума.

TAXONOMY Considered as a subspecies of Puma (*P. concolor*).

SIMILAR SPECIES The Canada Lynx and Bobcat are smaller and have mottled coats and short tails.

REPRODUCTION *Gestation*: 88-97 days. *Young per Birth*: 1-5, usually 3. *Weaning*: 2-3 months. *Sexual Maturity*: 20-24 months. *Life Span*: 16 years, 23 years in captivity. *Breeding Season*: Throughout the year, but most births occur between April and September in North America. Dens in any concealed, sheltered spot, in crevices between rocks, under overhanging banks, or beneath the roots of trees. Young open their eyes at 2 weeks, and stay with their mother for up to 2 years.

BEHAVIOR *Social Behavior*: Solitary, except for a short breeding period, but may interact more regularly and predictably than previously thought. *Diet*: Varies throughout the range, mainly native ungulates (deer, elk, bighorn, peccary), but also cattle, sheep, horses, and small mammals (rabbit, rodents); carrion is eaten rarely. They usually cover their prey and may return several times to feed. Attacks on humans are uncommon. Primarily nocturnal and crepuscular, with activity peaks at dusk and dawn. Mostly terrestrial, hunting on the ground by stalking and attacking prey at close range and from behind. It can travel extensive distances while hunting. A good climber and often escapes up trees when hunted by dogs. ♂ are territorial and ♀ express mutual avoidance; ♀ with cubs are extremely intolerant of adult ♂, who are likely to kill the cubs. Home ranges vary across their distribution (larger in arid environments), from 50 to 1,800 km². ♂ home ranges are typically twice the size of ♀'s, and overlap with several ♀. Adult ♂ make scrapes (collections of leaves, dirt, and debris formed by scratching with the hind feet), often marked with urine and feces, usually located near the margins of home ranges. Communication is primarily olfactorial. It does not roar, but is capable of a variety of vocalizations, including chirps, hisses, growls, and whistles. They are subordinate to wolves, grizzly and black bears, and Jaguars but dominant over coyotes.

DISTRIBUTION *Native*: Belize, Canada, Costa Rica, Guatemala, Honduras, Mexico, Nicaragua, Panama, USA. *Extinct*: El Salvador.

HABITAT A wide variety of habitats, from arid deserts, semi-arid brush lands, and cold coniferous forests, to seasonally flooded savannas and tropical rainforests, requiring sufficient cover for stalking prey and a lack of high human activity. They usually avoid heavily timbered areas.

CONSERVATION STATUS Least Concern. CITES: Appendix II, Appendix I in Nicaragua, Costa Rica, and Panama. In North America, it has been extirpated from most areas except the W mountains and adjacent foothills. The US population was estimated at 10,000 and the Canadian population at 3,500-5,000 in the early 1990s. The Endangered Florida subpopulation, numbering 100-180, is isolated, and has been supplemented by a reintroduction from Texas. W US population is increasing and expanding toward the E. Hunting is prohibited in Costa Rica, Guatemala, Honduras, Nicaragua, Panama, and regulated in Canada, Mexico, and the USA.

PHOTO CREDITS TR: *Lynn M. Stone* (USA); TL: *Frans Lanting*, Florida (USA); Young: *Mary McDonald*, Northern Rockies (USA) and *Volodymyr Byrdyak*; CR: *Mike Lane* (USA); B: *Mikael Males* (USA).

Jaguarundi
HERPAILURUS YAGOUAROUNDI

BL: 57-83 cm (♂), 43-73 cm (♀). TL: 27.5-59 cm. SH: 30 cm. W: 3-7.6 kg (♂), 3.5-7 kg (♀). SL: 9.4 cm. SW: 6.1 cm. DF: 30. CN: 38. A small to medium-sized, short-legged and elongated, mustelid-shaped felid, with a proportionally small head and low, rounded ears. Coat is uniformly unspotted at any age, sometimes with a grizzled appearance. Two highly variable color phases occur: dark gray (grayish or brownish-black), mostly associated with moist and dense forests, and red (rust or reddish-brown), associated with dry and open areas, which appears to be the most common; both can be found in the same litter. Head and ventral side of the neck may be slightly lighter, and some specimens show a broad black median dorsal band. Flattened head, with small rounded ears. Honey-brown eyes. Limbs are proportionally short. Slender torso. Long tail. Females have 3 pairs of nipples.

red form

Young

dark form

Herpailurus yagouaroundi

OTHER NAMES Eyra Cat, Otter Cat. *French*: Jaguarondi, chat loutre. *German*: Jaguarundi, Wieselkatze. *Spanish*: Gato colorado, gato moro, jaguarundi, leoncillo, león brenero, onza, tigrillo, yaguarundi. *Russian*: Ягуарунди. *Portuguese*: Gato-mourisco, gato-vermelho. *Guaraní*: Acutí-yaguá.

TAXONOMY Monotypic, but a recent phylogeographical study has suggested at least three possible molecular subspecies: *H. y. yagouaroundi* (wide distribution in Central and South America), *H. y. melantho* (central Andean, and their inter-valleys, Peruvian area), and *H. y. eyra* (Paraguay and N Argentina). Most closely related to the Puma and Cheetah, included in the genus *Puma* by some authors.

SIMILAR SPECIES The mustelid tayra (*Eira barbara*) has a distinct irregular ocher-yellow or orange-yellow spot on the throat, which is lacking in the Jaguarundi.

REPRODUCTION *Gestation*: 72-75 days. *Young per Birth*: 1-4, usually 2. *Weaning*: 5-6 weeks. *Sexual Maturity*: 17-26 months. *Life Span*: 15 years in captivity. *Breeding Season*: Year-round in the tropics, late-autumn period in the N part of its range. Fallen logs, dense thickets, and hollow trees are used as den sites. Young start leaving the nest at 28 days.

BEHAVIOR *Social Behavior*: Solitary, but may live in pairs. *Diet*: Small mammals (rodents, particularly rice and cotton rats, also cavies, rabbits, paca, opossums, and marmosets), birds (tinamous, quail), reptiles (lizards, iguana), and arthropods; it may prey on poultry. Mostly diurnal, hunting mainly in the morning and evening, possibly to avoid encounters with other predators or competitors. Ocelots could be important factors influencing its presence, activity, and abundance in an area. Terrestrial, but it moves about easily in trees, especially when pursued. Probably territorial. Home range size varies greatly, most ranging over 20–25 km², but up to 100 km², larger than for any other Neotropical small cat. Home ranges of ♂ are larger than those of ♀, and significant intersexual and intrasexual overlap can occur. They have a broad range of vocalizations.

DISTRIBUTION *Native*: Argentina, Belize, Bolivia, Brazil, Colombia, Costa Rica, Ecuador, El Salvador, French Guiana, Guatemala, Guyana, Honduras, Mexico, Nicaragua, Panama, Paraguay, Peru, Suriname, Uruguay, Venezuela. *Possibly Extinct*: USA (Texas, Arizona). It is the most widely distributed small felid in the W hemisphere.

HABITAT A wide range of both open and closed habitats, from Monte Desert, semi-arid thorn scrub, restinga, swamp, and savanna woodland to primary rainforest, up to 3,200 m. In open areas it sticks to vegetative cover with some protection (forest or other dense cover).

CONSERVATION STATUS Least Concern, Near Threatened in Argentina, Threatened in Mexico. CITES: Appendix II, I in Central and North America. Uncommon, with very low densities throughout its range. Main threats are habitat loss and fragmentation, especially for large-scale agriculture and pasture, and persecution for killing poultry. The skin has no commercial value. It is protected across most of its range, with hunting prohibited or regulated.

PHOTO CREDITS TR: *Sergey Chichagov*, Tallinn Zoo (Estonia); Young: *Jonas Livet*, Rare Species Conservation Centre (UK); TL, C: *Ad0bne*; B: *Daniel Heuclin*.

South and East African Cheetah

ACINONYX JUBATUS JUBATUS

BL: 108-152 cm (♂), 105-140 cm (♀). TL: 51-87 cm. SH: 73-96 cm. W: 28.5-64 kg (♂), 21-51 kg (♀). SL: 15.3 cm. SW: 14.6 (♂), 13.1 (♀). DF: 30. CN: 38. A large, slender, small-headed cat. Coat generally short and dense, longer below, with a mane along the shoulders and back. Body color is tawny-cream to pale fawn, covered with more or less uniformly sized, rounded black spots. King Cheetahs are a recessive color morph where the spots have become fused into larger brown blotches and stripes. No records of albinism, but unspotted individuals have been observed. Underparts paler with more diffuse spotting. Head is small, densely spotted, chin is white. Short muzzle, with distinct black "tear stripes" running from the inner corner of each eye to the corner of the mouth. Small ears with black and white marking behind. Long legs with partially protractile claws. Tail long and full, broader at the tip than base, black-spotted and ringed, white-tipped. Males are slightly larger than females. Cubs have an extensive mantle of longish gray hair.

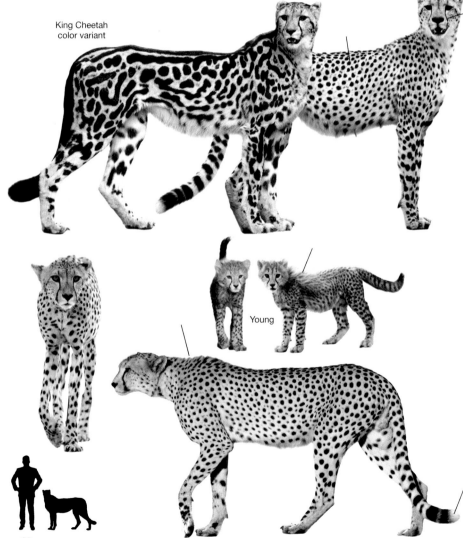

King Cheetah
color variant

Young

Acinonyx jubatus jubatus

OTHER NAMES *French*: Guépard. *German*: Gepard. *Spanish*: Guepardo de África meridional. *Russian*: Гепард (южноафриканский и восточноафриканский). *Afrikaans*: Jagluiperd. *Swahili*: Duma.

TAXONOMY Four subspecies are currently recognized: *A. j. jubatus* (S and E Africa); *A. j. soemmeringii* (NE Africa); *A. j. venaticus* (SW Asia and India); and *A. j. hecki* (W and N Africa), although the extent of morphological differences among them is minimal. This subspecies includes *fearsoni*, *raineyi*, and *velox* (East African Cheetah).

REPRODUCTION *Gestation*: 90-95 days. *Young per Birth*: 3-6. *Weaning*: 6-8 weeks. *Sexual Maturity*: 20-24 months (♀), 24-36 months (♂). *Life Span*: 14 years, 21 years in captivity. *Breeding Season*: Year-round. Cubs are born in long grass, thickets, or in a temporary "borrowed" burrow. They open their eyes at 10-14 days, and remain hidden for at least their first 6 weeks of life, being frequently carried to fresh hiding places by the mother. Cubs stay with their mother for about 2 years.

BEHAVIOR *Social Behavior*: ♀ solitary, but may be encountered with their cubs, while ♂ may form coalitions of 2-4, usually from the same litter. *Diet*: Medium to small antelope (steenbok, duiker, Thomson's gazelle, springbok, impala, reedbuck), but also prey on baboons, ground-living birds (bustards, guineafowl, spurfowl, francolin), hares, and porcupines; ♂ grouping together may hunt larger prey (wildebeest, kudu, young zebras); predation on livestock is not common; they can survive without drinking water, but will drink if available. They do not pose a threat to human life and are the most easily tamed of all the big cats. Highly vulnerable to interspecific competition with other large predators, including Lion, Hyena, and Leopard. Predominantly diurnal, with peaks of activity at sunrise and sunset. Unlike other cats, which stalk and pounce on prey, it relies on sight and speed. It sprints in for the kill at up to 100 kmph, but this speed can only be maintained for a few hundred meters. Its social and ranging behavior is unique among felids: solitary, nomadic ♀, and generally social, sedentary ♂ (some ♂ are nomadic). ♂ generally defend small discontinuous territories (37-80 km²) that overlap with ranges of several ♀. Territories and routes are marked with sprays of urine, feces, and, occasionally, by claw-raking. They use places of elevation, including rocks, termite mounds, and play trees as observation points and scent posts. ♀ are not territorial but roam over large home ranges (50-3,000 km²) that overlap with those of other ♀ whom they avoid. They have a variety of vocalizations: the two most common contact calls, chirping and churring, are unlike sounds of any other cat and are given alternately or repeatedly at varying intensity; chirping is a bird-like call. Yelps may be audible for 2 km.

DISTRIBUTION *Native*: Angola, Botswana, Kenya, Mozambique, Namibia, South Africa, Tanzania, Uganda, Zambia, Zimbabwe. *Extinct*: Malawi, Rwanda.

HABITAT Grasslands, savannas, scrub forests, semidesert steppes, woodlands, shrublands, mountainous grasslands, and montane areas.

CONSERVATION STATUS Vulnerable. CITES: Appendix I. Total Cheetah population is roughly 7,000, distributed across 33 subpopulations, with 4,190 animals in S Africa, and 1,960 in E Africa.

PHOTO CREDITS TR: *Mauro Silva*, Kruger NP (South Africa); TL: *Steve Tracy*, Tama Zoo (Japan); CL: *Ecophoto*, Kalahari (South Africa); Young: *Hedrus* (South Africa) and *Andrey Gudkov*, Serengeti (Tanzania); B: *Ecophoto*, Kalahari (South Africa).

Sudan Cheetah
ACINONYX JUBATUS SOEMMERINGII

BL: 110-140 cm. TL: 65-80 cm. SH: 51-87 cm. W: 40-60 kg. SL: 16.8 cm. SW: 13.1 cm. DF: 30. CN: 38. A large, slender, small-headed cat. A large subspecies, similar to the South and East African subspecies, slightly smaller, darker, and brightly colored, with thinner fur. Coat generally short and dense, longer below and with a mane along the shoulders and back. Overall body color is tawny-cream to pale fawn, covered with more or less uniformly sized, rounded black spots. Underparts paler with more diffuse spotting. Head is small, densely spotted, chin is white. Short muzzle, with distinct black "tear stripes" running from the inner corner of each eye to the corner of the mouth. Small ears with black and white marking behind. Long legs with partially protractile claws. Tail long and full, broader at the tip than base, black-spotted and ringed, white-tipped. Males are slightly larger than females. Cubs have an extensive mantle of longish gray hair.

Young

Acinonyx jubatus soemmeringii

OTHER NAMES Northeast African Cheetah. *French*: Guépard. *German*: Gepard. *Spanish*: Guepardo de Sudán. *Russian*: Суданский гепард.

TAXONOMY Considered as a subspecies of Cheetah (*A. jubatus*). This subspecies is more closely related to the South and East African Cheetah (*jubatus*) than to Saharan Cheetah populations (*hecki*). Includes *megabalica* and *wagneri*.

SIMILAR SPECIES The Serval is smaller, with a shorter tail and larger ears, and has spots that merge into stripes toward the back. The Leopard has blotched rosettes rather than clearly defined spots. Both species lacks the distinctive facial "tear stripes."

REPRODUCTION *Gestation*: 90-95 days. *Young per Birth*: 3-6. *Weaning*: 6 weeks. *Sexual Maturity*: 20-24 months (♀), 24-36 months (♂). *Life Span*: 10 years, 16 in captivity. *Breeding Season*: Probably year-round. There is no specific information for this subspecies, probably similar to the South and East African Cheetah. Cubs are born with a mantle on their necks, extending to mid-back, which may camouflage them in dead grass and hide from predators. Mortality rate is very high during the early weeks, and most cubs are killed by Lions, Hyenas, or eagles. Cubs leave their mother 13-20 months after birth.

BEHAVIOR *Social Behavior*: ♀ solitary unless accompanied by cubs, ♂ can be solitary or form coalitions throughout their lifetime. *Diet*: Grant's and Soemmerring's gazelles, Cape hares, guineafowls, and, occasionally, large animals like hartebeests, plains zebras, and ostriches. There is no specific information for this subspecies, but it is probably similar to East African Cheetahs. It kills its prey by tripping it during the chase, then biting it on the underside of the throat to suffocate it, as it is not strong enough to break the necks of the gazelles it mainly hunts (gazelles sometimes break their necks when they are tripped by the Cheetahs). Hunts by sight during the day using a termite mound or similar raised area as a lookout position. It devours its catch as quickly as possible before the kill is taken by stronger predators. They are subordinate to Lions, Leopards, Spotted and Striped Hyenas and wild dogs, but are dominant over jackals and golden wolves. Occupies a home range that varies with food abundance and population density. Calls include a twittering contact call, hisses and snarls when angry, and purrs.

DISTRIBUTION *Native*: Central African Republic, Chad, Ethiopia. *Possibly Extinct*: Eritrea. *Presence Uncertain*: Djibouti, Egypt, Somalia, Sudan.

HABITAT Wide open lands, grasslands, semi-arid areas, and other open habitats where prey is abundant such as in the E Sudanian Savanna.

CONSERVATION STATUS Vulnerable. CITES: Appendix I. In 2007, the population of Cheetahs living inside protected areas in Ethiopia, Sudan, and Somalia was estimated at 950 individuals. In Chad, there is a small population in Zakouma NP. The population outside protected areas is unknown. Main threats for this subspecies include poaching, illegal wildlife trade, hunting, habitat loss, and lack of prey. There is an increasing rate of cubs, mostly from Somaliland, being smuggled to Saudi Arabia, the United Arab Emirates, and Yemen.

PHOTO CREDITS T: *Nigel Swales*, Chester Zoo (UK); CL: *Paul Sebastian Ellis*, Djibouti Cheetah Refuge (Djibouti); Young: *say_cheese85*, Whipsnade Zoo (UK); CR: *Siobhan*, Chester Zoo (UK); B: *Jaime López*, Djibouti Cheetah Refuge (Djibouti).

Saharan Cheetah
ACINONYX JUBATUS HECKI

BL: 77-105 cm. TL: 55-65 cm. SH: 65 cm. W: 20-45 kg. SL: 15 cm. SW: 11.7 cm. DF: 30. CN: 38. A large, slender, small-headed cat. A small subspecies, paler than those elsewhere, with shorter coat and larger ears. Coat is very short and pale, yellowish-sand to off-white with faint rusty-colored spots on shoulders and flanks that darken to black on the back. Mane along the shoulders. Underparts and inner legs are paler with more diffuse spotting. Head is small, face is plain with indistinct spots and some clustered dark spots on top of the head. Tear stripes are present, sometimes faint. Chin and throat are white. Round ears, larger than in other subspecies. Long legs with partially protractile claws. Tail long, dark-spotted, and ringed, white-tipped, thinner than in other subspecies. Cubs have a long light gray mane spreading over the nape and part of the back.

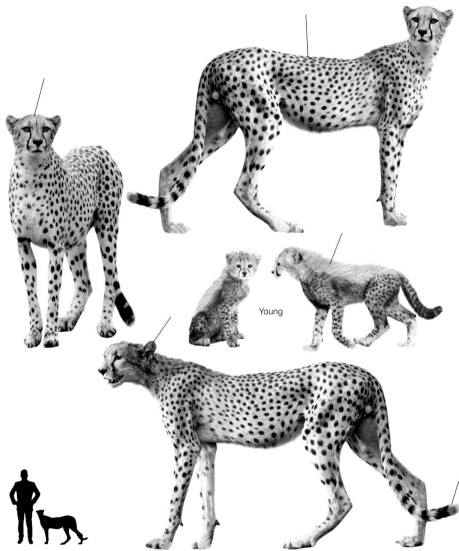

Young

Acinonyx jubatus hecki

OTHER NAMES Northern Cheetah, Central African Cheetah. *French*: Guépard d'Afrique du Nord-Ouest. *German*: Asiatischer Gepard. *Spanish*: Guepardo africano del noroeste, guepardo del Sahara. *Russian*: Сахарский гепард.

TAXONOMY Considered as a subspecies of Cheetah (*A. jubatus*). Includes *senegalensis*.

REPRODUCTION *Gestation*: 91-95 days. *Young per Birth*: 3-6. *Weaning*: 3 months. *Sexual Maturity*: 14-22 months. *Life Span*: Unknown. *Breeding Season*: During the hot season (April-June) as well as in the rainy season (July-August), with most births in the S Sahara occurring between July and November. ♂ may fight violently for the right to mate. At 6 weeks, cubs accompany their mother when she travels. Mortality is very high among the young. They leave their mother at 15-17 months.

BEHAVIOR *Social Behavior*: Solitary or small groups, ♀ generally solitary, except when with cubs or during mating, young ♂ more sociable, forming bachelor groups. *Diet*: Gazelles (dorcas, slender-horned, and young dama gazelles), addax, Barbary sheep, hares, birds, and rarely small livestock (sheep, goats, young camels); they can subsist without direct access to water, obtaining water indirectly from their prey. Most of the knowledge of Cheetahs is derived from S and E African long-term studies, but few data are available on the N African subspecies. In N Africa, densities are estimated to be 0.25-1.0 per 1,000 km², making detection difficult. This subspecies exhibits physiological and behavioral adaptations that allow it to survive in the extreme conditions of the Sahara Desert. It is more nocturnal than other subspecies, which helps it to conserve water and stay out of the daytime heat of the desert. They roam considerable distances to hunt prey. During the cold season, they hunt mainly in the plains, several km away from the massifs, while in the hot season, they do not move such a long distance from the mountains, where they can find shade, and where they can escape easily. ♂ show behaviors associated with territoriality, including urine marking trees, clawing, and defecating on branches.

DISTRIBUTION *Native*: Algeria, Benin, Burkina Faso, Chad, Central African Republic, Mali, Niger. *Presence Uncertain*: Egypt, Libya, Togo. *Extinct*: Cameroon, Côte d'Ivoire, DR Congo, Ghana, Guinea, Guinea-Bissau, Mauritania, Morocco, Nigeria, Senegal, Sierra Leone, Tunisia, Western Sahara. It was once broadly distributed across NW and central Africa, now occurs in only 9% of its former range. Individuals from Chad and Central African Republic are sometimes included under *soemmeringii*.

HABITAT Hilly and mountainous terrain in desert areas, semi-desert country, open savanna.

CONSERVATION STATUS Critically Endangered. CITES: Appendix I. This subspecies is known to be rare and threatened, with an estimated population of fewer than 250 adults in W and N Africa, but there is a lack of reliable data on its population status and distribution. Populations are very fragmented and small, with the biggest thought to be found in Algeria. Only 15 individuals are estimated to survive in the Pendjari (Benin), 10-40 in Termit (Niger), and fewer than 100 in Burkina Faso. In Chad, a small population may still exist in the Tibesti Highlands, and there may also be a small population in the Ennedi mountains; as of 1975, there was a small population in Zakouma NP.

PHOTO CREDITS T, B: *DEA/JACCOD*, Arly NP (Burkina Faso); CL: *Gunther A. Fraulob*; Young: *Stu Porter, Hedrus*.

Asiatic Cheetah
ACINONYX JUBATUS VENATICUS

BL: 100-182 cm (♂), 160-189 cm (♀). TL: 62-77 cm. SH: 51-87 cm. W: 25-38 kg (♂), 23-35 kg (♀). SL: 15.6 cm. SW: 11.4 cm. DF: 30. CN: 38. A large, slender, small-headed cat. A small subspecies, with a longer, denser, and paler coat than African subspecies. Winter mane is long and dense, less developed in summer. Overall body color is pale yellow to reddish-ocherous, slightly more intense on the back, covered with small black spots, arranged in lines on the head and nape, but irregularly scattered on body and legs. Mane is usually darker in color. Underparts paler with more diffuse spotting. Head is small, with small black spots on the top; chin and throat are white. Short muzzle, with distinct black "tear stripes" running from the inner corner of each eye to the corner of the mouth. Small ears with black and white marking behind. Long legs with partially protractile claws. Tail long and full, broader at the tip than base, black-spotted and ringed, white-tipped. Males are slightly larger than females. Cubs have an extensive mantle of longish gray hair.

winter coat

summer coat

94

Acinonyx jubatus venaticus

OTHER NAMES Iranian Cheetah, Persian Cheetah. *French*: Guépard asiatique. *German*: Gepard. *Spanish*: Guepardo asiático. *Russian*: Азиатский гепард.

TAXONOMY Considered as a subspecies of Cheetah (*A. jubatus*). Molecular studies have revealed that Asiatic Cheetahs are unambiguously separated from African subspecies some 32,000-67,000 years ago. Includes *raddei* (Trans-Caspian, now extinct).

SIMILAR SPECIES The Leopard is much more thickset, with a larger head and spots arranged in distinct rosettes.

REPRODUCTION *Gestation*: 90 days. *Young per Birth*: 1-4. *Weaning*: Unknown. *Sexual Maturity*: Unknown. *Life Span*: 15 years in captivity. *Breeding Season*: Winter (January to February), but may be year-round, with most births occurring in March-April.

BEHAVIOR *Social Behavior*: ♀ generally solitary, except when with cubs, ♂ forming small coalitions. *Diet*: Medium-sized ungulates (wild sheep, wild goat, goitered gazelle, chinkara), but also small mammals (rodents, hares); they rarely prey on livestock in this area (young camel, sheep, and goat); unlike the African subspecies, they have stopped hunting gazelles on the plains, now too scarce, and subsist on mountain ungulates living at altitude, which likely limit their hunting success. Predominantly diurnal, active mainly during early morning and late afternoon. This subspecies is extremely shy and elusive, occurs at low densities, and uses extremely large ranges (up to at least 5,000 km²), with exceptionally long movements across multiple reserves, probably due to low prey density, which could be related to poor vegetation cover in this arid climate, and to poaching. ♂, whether territorial or not, scent-mark to advertise their presence by spray-marking, scratching, and defecating on prominent features in the landscape. They hunt by sight, mainly during the day. Persian Leopards, wolves, and possibly Striped Hyenas and groups of jackals may drive Cheetahs from their kills; all five species are potential cub predators while Leopards and wolves are capable of killing adult Cheetahs as well.

DISTRIBUTION *Native*: Iran. *Extinct*: Afghanistan, India, Iraq, Israel, Jordan, Kazakhstan, Kuwait, Pakistan, Saudi Arabia, Syria, Tajikistan, Turkmenistan, Uzbekistan. This subspecies once had a distribution that extended across the Middle East, Central Asia into S Kazakhstan and across India almost to the border with Bangladesh, but currently it is distributed only throughout the arid landscapes of Iran's central plateau (provinces of Yazd, Semnan, Esfahan, North Khorasan, Razavi Khorasan, South Khorasan, and Kerman). It was declared extinct in India in 1952.

HABITAT Mosaic areas of plains and rolling mountains intersected by watercourses, even where there is a very low density of gazelles. In central Iran, the Cheetahs are known to select mountainous habitats far from open country.

CONSERVATION STATUS Critically Endangered. CITES: Appendix I. Estimated population of only 50 individuals. This subspecies is on the verge of extinction, mainly due to casualties mediated by herder persecution, poaching and road collisions, as well as prey and habitat loss. It is strictly protected in Iran.

PHOTO CREDITS TR, B: *Frans Lanting*, Miandasht Wildlife Reserve (Iran); TL: Tehran Zoological Garden (Iran); C: *Nazanim Kazemi Nava* (Iran).

Ocelot lineage

OCELOT, MARGAY, GUIÑA, COLOCOLO, AND RELATED SPECIES

RECOGNITION The Ocelot lineage consists of a monophyletic group with nine small spotted species in the *Leopardus* genus, restricted to Central and South America: Ocelot (*L. pardalis*), Margay (*L. wiedii*), Northern Tigrina (*L. tigrina*), Eastern Tigrina (*L. emiliae*), Southern Tigrina (*L. guttulus*), Geoffroy's Cat (*L. geoffroyi*), Guiña (*L. guigna*), Colocolo (*L. colocola*), and Andean Mountain Cat (*L. jacobita*). Geoffroy's Cat, Guiña, and Colocolo were formerly classified in the genus *Oncifelis,* but they are now firmly considered to represent a closely related subbranch of the *Leopardus* genus. The Colocolo was also classified in its own genus, *Lynchailurus*, while the Andean Cat was placed in *Oreailurus*; these are no longer valid genera. They are small to medium-sized, yellowish-brown to grayish spotted cats, with long tails. Melanistic forms have been described in some species, and seem to be more common in forested or wetland areas. Males are larger and heavier than females. Chromosome number is 2n=36, instead of 38 as in all the other felid species.

PHYLOGENY The ancestors of the Ocelot lineage probably diverged from a precursor to the modern Felidae 8-10 Ma in North America. Later during the second ice age of 2-3 Ma they migrated over the Panama land bridge to South America and evolved recently and rapidly, occupying all habitats available while demonstrating relatively modest morphofunctional variation. The land bridge was completely established about 3 Ma, but sea-level changes interrupted its formation several times until the mid-Pleistocene, suggesting that speciation also occurred in South America and recent diversity could be explained by a minimum of 5 or 6 immigrations. The Ocelot and its sister species, the Margay, diverged 3.3-4 Ma. The Colocolo split from a common ancestor about 1.7 Ma, and the Geoffroy's Cat and the closely related Guiña differentiated around 2.3-1 Ma, probably within southern South America. Northern and Southern Tigrinas diverged relatively recently, 0.5-0.8 Ma. An intermediate predecessor of this group (*Felis lacustris* or *F. rexroadensis*) first appears in the fossil record in North America 4-5 Ma. Fossils of present-day *Leopardus* spp. found in South America are approximately 1.5-2.5 million years old and only 0.3-0.4 million years old in southern North America.

BEHAVIOR These cats are solitary and mostly have a typical small felid socio-spatial system. They are active predominantly at night, but can also show a considerable level of diurnal activity. They are terrestrial and hunt mainly on the ground, but some are excellent climbers and escape into trees when threatened. They are opportunistic carnivores, feeding mainly on small mammals, birds, and reptiles. Most of these species are poorly studied.

DISTRIBUTION The Ocelot's distribution range extends from southern Texas, along the coast of Mexico throughout Central and South America south to northeastern Argentina and southern Brazil; it occupies a large variety of different habitats, from mangroves to high-altitude cloud forest, but tends to be more commonly associated with forests. The Margay occurs from the lowlands of northern Mexico into Central and South America to Uruguay and northern Argentina, and is strongly associated with dense forest habitats, ranging from tropical evergreen forest to tropical dry forest and high cloud forest. The Guiña occurs only in central and southern Chile, in forests with heavy understory. The Geoffroy's Cat occurs in the Andes of Bolivia, Brazil, Paraguay, Argentina, Uruguay, and southern Chile, in a wider range of habitats, with preference for areas with dense vegetation, including brush areas, open savannas, and marshes. The Northern Tigrina lives in dry and open habitats of tropical savannas and shrublands in Central America and central and northeastern Brazil, known as the Cerrado and Caatinga, while the Southern Tigrina is found in the more moist Atlantic Forest. The Colocolo has disjunct distributions in mountain areas from Ecuador into Bolivia and through portions of central Brazil south through most of Paraguay, Uruguay, Argentina, and Chile, and commonly inhabits open grassland (pampas), but is also found in evergreen forests, dense shrubland, and humid forests. The Andean Mountain Cat occurs mainly in the high Andes of Peru and Bolivia, north of Chile and northern Argentina up to 5,000 m, but it has also been found outside the Andes, in Patagonian steppe and scrub habitats at much lower altitudes.

CONSERVATION The status of most species in this group is not well known and it is difficult to judge the actual impact of threats. Research is urgently needed to plan conservation strategies more efficiently. The Andean Mountain Cat is the most threatened cat species in the Americas and is classified as Endangered; its total population is probably fewer than 1,500 animals and declining. Several species of this group are listed as Vulnerable: the Guiña (< 10,000 individuals), the Northern Tigrina (< 10,000), and the Southern Tigrina (< 6,000), all of them threatened by habitat loss and fragmentation due to deforestation, loss of prey base, and persecution by humans. The Margay and the Colocolo are listed as Near Threatened and appear to be declining in several parts of their range because of extensive loss or reduction in quality of their habitat. The Ocelot and the Geoffroy's Cat are considered to be relatively common. These species are protected in most countries of their distribution range.

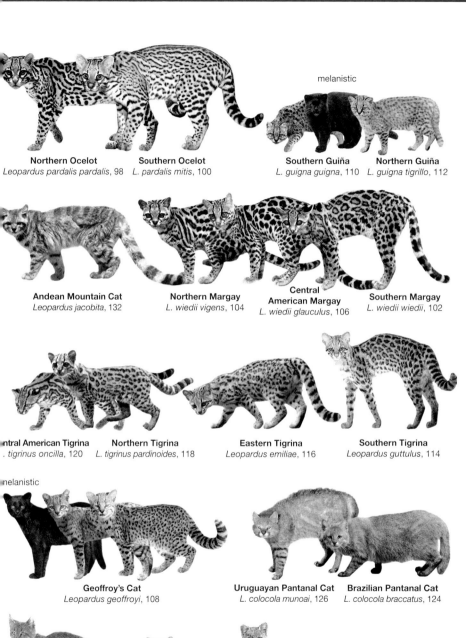

melanistic

Northern Ocelot
Leopardus pardalis pardalis, 98

Southern Ocelot
L. pardalis mitis, 100

Southern Guiña
L. guigna guigna, 110

Northern Guiña
L. guigna tigrillo, 112

Andean Mountain Cat
Leopardus jacobita, 132

Northern Margay
L. wiedii vigens, 104

Central American Margay
L. wiedii glauculus, 106

Southern Margay
L. wiedii wiedii, 102

Central American Tigrina
L. tigrinus oncilla, 120

Northern Tigrina
L. tigrinus pardinoides, 118

Eastern Tigrina
Leopardus emiliae, 116

Southern Tigrina
Leopardus guttulus, 114

melanistic

Geoffroy's Cat
Leopardus geoffroyi, 108

Uruguayan Pantanal Cat
L. colocola munoai, 126

Brazilian Pantanal Cat
L. colocola braccatus, 124

Argentinian Pampas Cat
L. colocola pajeros, 128

Northern Colocolo
L. colocola colocola, 122

Southern Colocolo
L. colocola wolfsohni, 122

Peruvian Pampas Cat
L. colocola garleppi, 130

Northern Ocelot

LEOPARDUS PARDALIS PARDALIS

BL: 55-78 cm. TL: 30-43.5 cm. SH: 35-50 cm. W: 7-15 kg (♂), 7-11 kg (♀). SL: 12.7 cm (♂), 11.3 cm (♀). SW: 8.9 cm (♂), 8.5 cm (♀). DF: 30. CN: 36. A medium-sized, solidly built, spotted cat, with a relatively short tail. Smaller and grayer than the Southern Ocelot. Coat is short and dense, variable in color, from grayish to cinnamon to buff, heavily marked with black open and solid blotches, streaks, and rosettes with russet-brown centers. Underparts white, spotted with black. Head is powerfully built, brown with black streaks and vermiculations. Blocky muzzle, especially in adult males. Two black stripes on the cheek. Eyes dark brown. Pink nose. Round ears, black with a white central spot on the back. Parallel stripes run down the nape of the neck. Fur on nape of neck runs forward. Thickset limbs. Paws heavily built, forepaws larger than hind paws. Tubular tail, typically not reaching the ground, with black partial or complete rings. Females slightly smaller than males, with 4 nipples. Young with gray fully marked coat, dark lower limbs, and blue eyes.

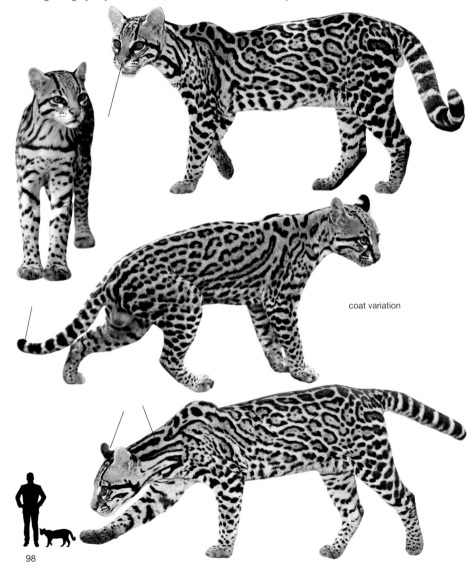

coat variation

Leopardus pardalis pardalis

OTHER NAMES *French*: Ocelot. *German*: Ozelot. *Spanish*: Gato onza, manigordo, ocelote, tigrillo, gato tigre. *Russian*: Североамериканский оцелот. *Mayan*: Zac-xicin.

TAXONOMY Two subspecies are provisionally recognized based on morphological differences, molecular data, and a biogeographical barrier, the Andes, but the fine-scale distribution of the two subspecies is not clear: *L. p. pardalis* (from Texas and Arizona S to Costa Rica); and *L. p. mitis* (South America as far S as N Argentina). Limit of range between subspecies is unclear. This species shows high genetic heterogeneity across its range, with four distinct population clusters: Central America and Mexico, N-NW South America, N-NE South America, and S South America, separated from all populations to the N by the Amazon River. This would suggest four subspecies, although up to ten are currently described, most probably invalid. This subspecies includes *albescens, pseudopardalis,* and *sonoriensis.*

SIMILAR SPECIES Margays are considerably smaller, less robust, with a longer tail, and larger eyes. Young kittens of Ocelot, Margay, and Oncilla can be very difficult to tell apart. Bobcats have a much shorter tail, and their coat is longer, with smaller spots.

REPRODUCTION *Gestation*: 72-82 days. *Young per Birth*: 1-2, exceptionally 3. *Weaning*: 8 weeks. *Sexual Maturity*: 18-24 months. *Life Span*: 10 years, 18 years in captivity. *Breeding Season*: Year-round, with most births occurring in early winter. Den in caves, hollow trees, or thorny thickets. Kittens open their eyes 14 days after birth. Kittens are slow to mature and reach independence at 17-22 months.

BEHAVIOR *Social Behavior*: Solitary. *Diet*: Small and medium-sized mammals and birds, but also reptiles, amphibians, fish, and crabs; they occasionally kill domestic animals; they frequently cache food by covering it entirely with leaf and soil debris. *Main Predators*: Puma, Jaguar, dogs. Mainly nocturnal or crepuscular, spending the day lying quietly in the branches of large trees and coming out to hunt after dark. They hunt both on the ground and in the trees. They frequent riverbanks and the shores of other bodies of water, where presumably they may catch fish. Ocelots may travel 3-6 km each night in search of food. Usually silent in the wild. Home ranges of adult ♂ typically are larger than home ranges of ♀ in the same area. Home ranges of adult ♂ usually overlap territories of several ♀, but territories of ♀ rarely overlap. Resident adults of both sexes are tolerant of their offspring, which may linger in the natal range for more than a year after independence, with some evidence of regular interaction. In Texas, average size of home range for ♂ is 2.5 km² and for ♀ 2.1 km², and in Belize, 31 km² and 15 km² respectively.

DISTRIBUTION *Native*: Belize, Costa Rica, El Salvador, Guatemala, Honduras, Mexico, Nicaragua, Panama, USA (Texas, Arizona).

HABITAT Tropical zones, from the heavy rainforest to the sparse tropical deciduous forest, up to 2,000 m in Mexico. Tolerant of modified habitat provided there is dense vegetation and prey. They do not occur regularly in arid tropical country, and mostly avoid very open areas but readily hunt in pasture and grasslands close to cover, especially at night.

CONSERVATION STATUS Least Concern. CITES: Appendix I. Endangered in Mexico and USA. Protected across most of its range, with hunting banned in Guatemala, Honduras, Mexico, Nicaragua, Panama, and USA. In Texas, population is estimated at 50-80.

PHOTO CREDITS TL: *Sergey Chichagov*, Orange County Zoo (USA); TR, B: *Martin Ruegner*, Roatan (Honduras); C: *Mike Lane45* (Belize).

Southern Ocelot
LEOPARDUS PARDALIS MITIS

BL: 65-101 cm. TL: 25.5-45 cm. SH: 40-50 cm. W: 7-15.5 kg (♂), 6.6-11 kg (♀). SL: 13.8 cm (♂), 12.4 cm (♀). SW: 9.7 cm (♂), 9 cm (♀). DF: 28-30. CN: 36. A medium-sized, solidly built, spotted cat, with a relatively short tail. Larger, with a brighter, yellower pelage than that of the Northern Ocelot. Coat is short and dense, variable in color, from tawny-yellow to reddish-gray, marked with black open and solid blotches, streaks, and rosettes with russet-brown centers. Underparts white spotted with black. No melanistic forms reported. Head is powerfully built, brown with black streaks and vermiculations. Blocky muzzle. Two black stripes on the cheek. Eyes dark brown. Pink nose. Round ears, black with a white central spot on the back. Parallel stripes run down the nape of the neck. Fur runs forward on the nape of the neck. Thickset limbs. Paws heavily built, forepaws larger than hind paws. Tubular tail, typically not reaching the ground, with black rings. Females slightly smaller than males, with 4 nipples. Young with gray fully marked coat, dark lower limbs, and blue eyes.

coat variation

Young

Leopardus pardalis mitis

OTHER NAMES *French*: Ocelot, chat tigre. *German*: Ozelot. *Spanish*: Gato onza, manigordo, ocelote, tigrillo, tirica, chivi-guazu, cuanguaro, maracaya. *Russian*: Южноамериканский оцелот. *Portuguese*: Maracajá-açu, jaguatirica, gato-maracajá, maracajá-verdadeiro. *Guarani*: Agua-tirica. *Surinam*: Hétigrikati.

TAXONOMY Considered as a subspecies of *L. pardalis* (Ocelot). Includes *aequatorialis*, *melanurus*, *pusaeus*, and *steinbachi*.

SIMILAR SPECIES Jaguars are much larger in size.

REPRODUCTION *Gestation*: 72-82 days. *Young per Birth*: 1-2. *Weaning*: 8 weeks. *Sexual Maturity*: 18-24 months. *Life Span*: 18 years in captivity. *Breeding Season*: Probably year-round, with most births May-December. Young are born in a hollow tree, rocky bluff, cave, thorny thicket, or other secluded den. ♂ have no active role in caring for the young. Subadults do not disperse until 2 years old.

BEHAVIOR *Social Behavior*: Mostly solitary, with ♂-♀ interactions during and outside breeding periods. *Diet*: Small mammals, birds, and reptiles, but also larger prey, such as agoutis, armadillos, pacas, or monkeys; they readily scavenge. *Main Predators*: Puma, Jaguar, caiman, boa, anaconda, harpy eagle, dogs. Nocturnal and crepuscular, but can also be active during daytime. Hunting is chiefly terrestrial, though they are adept climbers and some prey is taken in trees. Excellent swimmers but will not enter the water unless absolutely necessary. Home ranges of ♂ are larger than the ranges of ♀, but high variation exists in the size between regions, from 2 to 43 km². Adults patrol and scent-mark ranges that are defended against same-sex conspecifics in sometimes fatal fights. Prior to establishing their own home ranges, subadults often live in their natal ranges, tolerated by their parents.

DISTRIBUTION *Native*: Argentina, Bolivia, Brazil, Colombia, Ecuador, French Guiana, Guyana, Panama, Paraguay, Peru, Suriname, Trinidad and Tobago, Uruguay, Venezuela. Limit of range with respect to *L. p. pardalis* is unclear.

HABITAT A wide variety of habitats, strongly associated with areas of dense vegetation or forest cover: mangrove forests, coastal marshes, savanna grasslands, thorn scrubs, and tropical and subtropical forest, up to 3,000 m. Preferred habitat seems to be gallery (riverine) forests. They avoid open habitats during the day, but sometimes forage in them at night. They use similar habitat to those of Jaguars and Pumas and appear to be little affected by these species.

CONSERVATION STATUS Least Concern. CITES: Appendix I. Near Threatened in Ecuador, Vulnerable in Colombia, Argentina, and Brazil outside the Amazon. The biggest population lives in Brazil. The major threats are habitat loss and fragmentation, retaliatory killing due to depredation of poultry, and illegal trade of pets and pelts. This species is tolerant in some degree to habitat disturbance and persists in wooded patches near human settlements, but it is negatively affected by poaching and logging. Protected across most of its range, with hunting banned in Argentina, Brazil, Bolivia, Colombia, French Guiana, Panama, Paraguay, Suriname, Trinidad and Tobago, Uruguay, and Venezuela, and hunting regulations in place in Peru.

PHOTO CREDITS TL: *Erwin Blekkenhorst*, Pantanal (Brazil); TR: *Alexander Sliwa*, Quito Zoo (Ecuador); CL: *Paulo Barreiros*, Pantanal (Brazil); Young: *Sergey Chichagov*, Jerez Zoo (Spain); CR: *Sergey Chichagov*, Elmwood Zoo (USA); B: *Alexander Sliwa*, Arizona-Sonora Desert Museum (USA).

Southern Margay

LEOPARDUS WIEDII WIEDII

BL: 46-61 cm (♂), 48-62 cm (♀). TL: 30-48 cm. SH: 30-45 cm. W: 2.3-4.9 kg (♂), 2.3-3.5 kg (♀). SL: 8.4 cm. SW: 6.2 cm. DF: 30. CN: 36. A lightly built, small cat, with very large, bulging eyes, large paws, and a long tail. Coat is soft and full, from pale buff-grayish to an intensely rich ocherous-tawny and dark brownish-ocherous color, paling toward the lower part of the sides, richly marked with large, dark solid dots on the mid-back and large and complete rosettes on the sides, but there is much individual variation. Underparts whitish, with few or no spots. Throat with transverse dark lines. Hair of the nape runs forward. Rounded head with a large, bulging muzzle. Large ears, black on the back with a whitish central spot. Distinctive, very large eyes, with vertical slit pupils. Large front paws, with reversible ankle joint allowing them to descend trees head first. Long tail, with dark rings, most of them incomplete below. Males and females are about the same size. Females with 2 nipples.

Leopardus wiedii wiedii

OTHER NAMES *French*: Margay. *German*: Langschwanzkatze, Margay, Baumozelot. *Spanish*: Tigrillo, margay meridional, caucal, gato tigre, gato pintado, gato montés, gato de monté. *Russian*: Южная длиннохвостая кошка (маргай). *Portuguese*: Gato maracaja mirim peludo. *Guaraní*: Mbaracayá.

TAXONOMY Three subspecies are provisionally recognized based on phylogenetic studies: *L. w. wiedii* (South America S of the Amazon); *L. w. vigens* (South America N of the Amazon); and *L. w. glauculus* (Central America), but recent analysis of skins and skulls has failed to find any significant geographical variation, although Central American Margays appear to be smaller and grayer compared with South American. A more comprehensive molecular and morphological study is required. This subspecies includes *boliviae* (Bolivia to N Argentina), and *pardictis*.

SIMILAR SPECIES Ocelots are larger and more robust, with shorter fur, and their tail is shorter than their hind leg (Margay's tail is longer than hind leg). Geoffroy's Cats have a small solid spot or flecked pattern in the pelage and a much smaller tail. Tigrinas are smaller, less richly marked, with smaller paws, and a shorter tail.

REPRODUCTION *Gestation*: 76-84 days. *Young per Birth*: 1, rarely 2. *Weaning*: 8 weeks. *Sexual Maturity*: 24 months. *Life Span*: 24 years in captivity. *Breeding Season*: Reported as being from October to January, but is probably year-round in the South American tropics. Hollow logs and burrows are used as den sites. Young open their eyes at 11-16 days, and begin to leave the dens at 5 weeks of age.

BEHAVIOR *Social Behavior*: Solitary. *Diet*: Small mammals, but lizards and especially birds can comprise important items at some localities; larger medium-sized mammals (squirrels, rabbits, agoutis, and small monkeys) are also taken. Mainly nocturno-crepuscular, but in S Brazil it has also been recorded active during the day. More arboreal and better adapted to live in trees than other cat species. Its hind ankles can rotate through 180°, so they can descend head first down trees and hang upside down by the hind feet while handling objects with their forepaws. They demarcate home ranges with characteristic felid marking behavior, but the degree to which they defend ranges is unclear.

DISTRIBUTION *Native*: Argentina, Bolivia, Brazil, Paraguay, Peru, Uruguay.

HABITAT Strongly associated with forest habitats, from continuous forest to small forest fragments in savanna ecosystems, both evergreen and deciduous. Less tolerant of human settlement and altered habitat than the Ocelot, but may use highly disturbed forest, abandoned plantations, and other agroforestry systems that provide sufficient tree cover.

CONSERVATION STATUS Near Threatened, Vulnerable in Brazil and Argentina. CITES: Appendix I. Rare to uncommon, less abundant than previously perceived. It is declining through much of its range due to conversion of native forest habitats to agriculture, pasture, and infrastructure development. In Brazil, populations of the Atlantic Forest are more threatened than those of the Amazon. It is also negatively impacted by Ocelots, which are fairly abundant and the dominant small felid species in most areas of tropical America. Protected across most of its range, with hunting and trade prohibited.

PHOTO CREDITS T: La Senda Verde Animal Refuge (Bolivia); CR: *Roland Wirth*, Curitiba Zoo (Brazil); CL: *David Piaggio, SERFOR* (Peru); B: *Luiz Mosca*, Criadouro Bicho do Mato (Brazil).

Northern Margay
LEOPARDUS WIEDII VIGENS

BL: 53-62 cm (♂), 50-69 cm (♀). TL: 35-47 cm. SH: 30-45 cm. W: 2.6-3.4 kg. SL: 8.7 cm. SW: 6.6 cm. DF: 30. CN: 36. A lightly built, small cat, with very large, bulging eyes, large paws, and a long tail. Coat is soft and full, variable in color, from pale buff-grayish to an intensely rich ocherous-tawny and dark brownish-ocherous color, paling toward the lower part of the sides, richly marked with large, dark solid dots on the mid-back and large and complete rosettes on the sides. Color pattern in mountain areas is darker than those in lowlands, but both color patterns may occur sympatrically. Melanistic forms have been reported in Colombia and Ecuador. Longitudinal lines on the head, nape, and back. Underparts whitish. Hair of the nape runs forward. Rounded head with a large, bulging muzzle. Large ears, black on the back with a whitish central spot. Distinctive, large eyes, with vertical slit pupils. Large front paws. Long, tubular tail, with dark rings. Males and females are about the same size. Females with 2 nipples.

melanistic form

104

Leopardus wiedii vigens

OTHER NAMES *French*: Margay, chat tig, chat margay. *German*: Langschwanzkatze, Margay, Baumozelot. *Spanish*: Margay septentrional, tigrillo, burricón, gato pintado, huamburushu, cunaguaro. *Russian*: Северная длиннохвостая кошка (маргай). *Portuguese*: Gato maracaja mirim peludo. *Guyanese*: Kuichua. *Suriname*: Tigrikati, boomkat.

TAXONOMY Considered as a subspecies of Margay (*L. wiedii*). Includes *amazonicus*.

SIMILAR SPECIES The Ocelot is significantly larger, has a shorter tail, and much smaller eyes. Tigrinas are generally smaller and less richly marked. Young kittens of all these species can be very difficult to tell apart.

REPRODUCTION *Gestation*: 76-84 days. *Young per Birth*: 1, rarely 2. *Weaning*: 8 weeks. *Sexual Maturity*: 24 months. *Life Span*: 24 years in captivity. *Breeding Season*: December to February, but probably year-round.

BEHAVIOR *Social Behavior*: Solitary. *Diet*: Terrestrial and arboreal mammals, but also birds, reptiles, amphibians, and invertebrates. Mainly nocturnal, with very few records of daytime activity, resting during the day in trees. They are capable of hunting prey in the trees and possess morphological adaptations associated with this foraging strategy, such as their distinctive long tail and hind foot that can both pronate and supinate, allowing them to climb down trees head first. They are able to move rapidly along flexible vines and lianas, which they navigate by essentially running upside down at high speeds. Vision is well developed, and hearing capabilities seem to be well developed as in all other felids. Eight distinct vocalizations have been recorded: purring, meowing, barking meow, moaning, hissing, spitting, growling, and snarling. When displaying threat behavior, the back is usually kept slightly arched (rarely with straight back and hooked tail) and the hair along the middle of the back and on the tail is erected.

DISTRIBUTION *Native*: Brazil, Colombia, Ecuador, French Guiana, Guyana, Peru, Suriname, Venezuela.

HABITAT Forest-dependent, more closely associated with forest habitats than any other Neotropical cat, from lowland tropical forest to montane cloud forests, from sea level typically to 1,500 m, and exceptionally to 3,000 m in the Andes. They tolerate converted landscapes provided these are densely vegetated, such as plantations of coffee, cocoa, eucalyptus, and pine, but they cannot inhabit open agriculture including sugarcane, soy, and pasture. More sensitive to habitat disturbance than their sympatric congeners, the Ocelot and Tigrinas, potentially due to their greater utilization of available canopy for foraging and traversing the forest.

CONSERVATION STATUS Near Threatened. CITES: Appendix I. It was one of the most heavily exploited cat species in South America and from the mid-1970s to the mid-1980s a minimum of over 125,000 Margay skins were traded. In some areas illegal hunting still takes place. Less abundant than previously thought. Despite their large geographic distribution, they occur at low population densities. Continued deforestation, habitat alteration, and poaching pose a serious threat. Protected across most of their range, with hunting and trade prohibited.

PHOTO CREDITS T: *Nathalie Regnier*, Cali Zoo (Colombia); CL: *Santiago F. Burneo*, Napo (Ecuador); BL: *Alejandro Mesías* (Ecuador); CR, BR: *J. P. Bueno*, Santacruz Zoo (Colombia).

Central American Margay
LEOPARDUS WIEDII GLAUCULUS

BL: 49-72 cm (♂), 51-61 cm (♀). TL: 33-49 cm. SH: 30-45 cm. W: 3.4-4.1 kg. SL: 8.9 cm. SW: 6.7 cm (♂), 6.3 cm (♀). DF: 30. CN: 36. A lightly built, small cat, with very large, bulging eyes, large paws, and a long tail. Coat is soft and full, variable in color, pale drab gray to ocherous-tawny, usually less tawny and smaller than South American subspecies, paling toward the lower part of the sides, richly marked with large, dark solid dots on the mid-back and large and complete rosettes with narrowish dark rims on the sides. Color pattern in mountain areas is darker than those in lowlands, but both color patterns may occur sympatrically. Melanistic forms have been reported in Costa Rica. Longitudinal lines on the head, nape, and back. Underparts whitish. Throat with three transverse dark lines. Hair of the nape runs forward. Rounded head with a large, bulging muzzle. Large ears, black on the back with a whitish central spot. Distinctive, very large eyes, with vertical slit pupils. Large front paws. Long, tubular tail, with dark rings. Females with 2 nipples.

coat variation

Young

Leopardus wiedii glauculus

OTHER NAMES *French*: Margay. *German*: Langschwanzkatze, Margay. *Spanish*: Tigrillo, margay de centro América, pichigüeta, caucel, tigrillito, mabaracaya. *Russian*: Центральноамериканская длиннохвостая кошка (маргай). *Guatemala*: Mbaracaya. *Mayan*: Chulul.

TAXONOMY Considered as a subspecies of Margay (*L. wiedii*). Includes *pirrensis* (Panama), *nicaraguae* (Nicaragua), *oaxacensis* (Sierra Madre, Oaxaca, Mexico), *salvinia* (Guatemala, Belize), *yucatanicus* (Yucatan Peninsula and N Chiapas, Mexico), and *cooperi* (Texas, USA, NE Mexico).

REPRODUCTION *Gestation*: 76-84 days. *Young per Birth*: 1, rarely 2. *Weaning*: 8 weeks. *Sexual Maturity*: 24 months. *Life Span*: 24 years in captivity. *Breeding Season*: Probably year-round in tropical zones. Kittens are much darker than adults, with uniform dark spots and dark gray paws.

BEHAVIOR *Social Behavior*: Solitary. *Diet*: Arboreal mammals and birds, but also amphibians, reptiles, and other animals and plants, such as arthropods and fruits. Mainly nocturnal. In Belize, Margays show temporal segregation from Jaguarundis, being active nocturnally, whereas the latter are active diurnally. Margays also use predominantly late second-growth forests, whereas jaguarundis are commonly found in old-field habitats, and show more arboreal habits, preying mostly on arboreal species. Margay numbers tend to be lower in areas of high Ocelot concentration, even though the two species occupy different habitat zones. Mean home range sizes are 4.1 km² in Mexico and 10.9 km² in Belize. There is a high degree of home range overlap between ♂, which is unusual in many small cat species. Margays can easily hang from a tree limb by a single hind foot; in that position the cat can use its flexible ankles to turn 180° outward as needed while simultaneously manipulating an object with its front paws. They climb down tree trunks head first. They are excellent jumpers, and use their long tail to balance as they move from perch to perch. Margays use only short-range vocalizations; ♀ emit long, moaning calls to attract ♂ for mating, and ♂ respond by rapidly shaking their heads from side to side and trilling or yelping. Otherwise, the species is relatively silent. They may, however, have greater vocal abilities than previously realized.

DISTRIBUTION *Native*: Belize, Costa Rica, El Salvador, Guatemala, Honduras, Mexico, Nicaragua, Panama. *Presence uncertain*: United States. A single individual was recorded in Texas in 1852, but researchers do not believe an actual population is present in the USA.

HABITAT Strongly associated with forest habitats, including tropical evergreen forests, premontane humid and very humid forests, montane cloud forests, gallery forests, and wet-swampy savannas. In Mexico, it is also found in the arid lower tropical subzone of the Yucatan, which is characterized by alternations of open savannas with deciduous forests, and narrow strips of evergreen gallery forests. In Belize, they use late second-growth forests significantly more than abandoned cornfields and mature subclimax forest.

CONSERVATION STATUS Near Threatened, Threatened in Mexico and in Costa Rica. CITES: Appendix I. Rare throughout its range. Protected across most of its range, with hunting and trade prohibited.

PHOTO CREDITS TL: *Evangelina Laura* (Costa Rica); TR: *Mark Payne-Gill*, Gamboa (Panama); CL: *Minor Torres*, Tapantí (Costa Rica); Young: *Mandenno Photography*, Jihlava Zoo (Czech Republic); CR: *Klaus Rudloff*, Tierpark Berlin (Germany); B: *Jon G. Fuller*, Arenal (Costa Rica).

Geoffroy's Cat
LEOPARDUS GEOFFROYI

BL: 42-66.5 cm. TL: 24-40 cm. SH: 15-22.5 cm. W: 3.8-5.8 kg (♂), 3-4.2 kg (♀). SL: 9.8 cm (♂), 8.8 cm (♀). SW: 7.0 cm (♂), 6.4 cm (♀). DF: 30. CN: 36. A small, lithely built, spotted cat. Body size varies considerably across the range. Coat from silver-gray to ocher-yellow or reddish-brown, with small, solid black spots, not rosettes, which converge into longitudinal lines on the nape, chest, and lower limbs. Size, shape, arrangement of spots, and ground color vary greatly. Belly is white. Melanistic forms are common in forested or wetland areas. Flattened head. Nose is red or black. Two dark teardrop streaks on the cheeks. Eyes clear gold to amber. Crown with several dark longitudinal lines. Back of the ears black with a central white spot. Tail is relatively short, the same color as the dorsum, narrowly banded with black stripes, interspersed with small spots. Males are larger than females. Kittens are fully spotted.

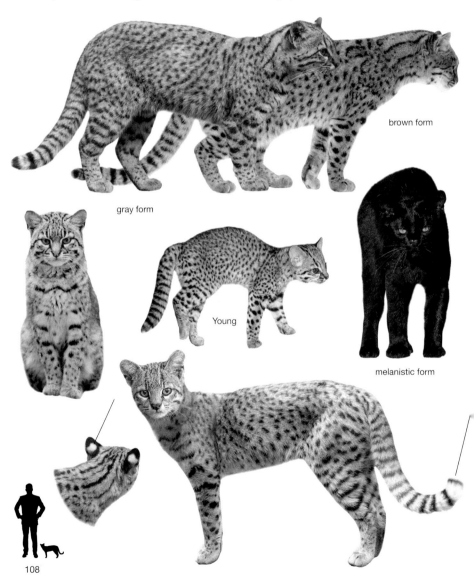

brown form

gray form

Young

melanistic form

Leopardus geoffroyi

OTHER NAMES Geoffroy's Ocelot. *French*: Chat de Geoffroy. *German*: Kleinfleckkatze, Salzkatze, Geoffroy-Katze. *Spanish*: Gato montés común, gato de mato. *Russian*: Кошка Жоффруа. *Portuguese*: Gato-do-mato-pelo-curto, gato-do-mato-grande.

TAXONOMY Monotypic. It displays a morphological cline in relation to differences in habitat throughout its range, but phylogenetic studies have found no evidence for distinct groups. Previously four subspecies were recognized, based on external morphological characters, such as color pattern of the pelage: *L. g. geoffroyi* (central to S Argentina and Chile); *L. g. salinarum* (NW Argentina), *L. g. paraguae* (Paraguay); and *L. g. euxanthus* (Bolivia and far N of Argentina). Formerly classified in the genus *Oncifelis*. It hybridizes with *L. guttulus* in S Brazil, where the two species' ranges overlap.

SIMILAR SPECIES The Guiña is very similar in appearance, but is considerably smaller, generally has richer coloration and a distinctive bushy tail, and has a quite large and conspicuous lateral rostral stripe.

REPRODUCTION *Gestation*: 72-78 days. *Young per Birth*: 1-3. *Weaning*: 8-10 weeks. *Sexual Maturity*: 24 months (♂), 18 months (♀). *Life Span*: 25 years in captivity. *Breeding Season*: No evidence for seasonality in the N part of the range, but in the S part of the range, births occur from December to May. Den in burrows, probably created usually by armadillos, in thick vegetation and possibly in tree cavities. Kittens open their eyes at about 12 days.

BEHAVIOR *Social Behavior*: Solitary. *Diet*: Small rodents and introduced hares, but also reptiles and birds; it caches large kills. *Main Predators*: Pumas, dogs. Mostly nocturnal and crepuscular, resting in thickets or in hollow trees during the day. Spends most of its time on the ground, although it can climb well, and is a good swimmer. It disperses over distances up to more than 100 km and has a home range size of 2.5-12 km². ♂ have large home ranges and move farther than ♀. Home ranges of ♀ overlap. The degree of territorial defense is unknown but they mark their ranges assiduously; they often deposit feces in certain trees, which they repeatedly mark over time, creating conspicuous arboreal middens.

DISTRIBUTION *Native*: Argentina, Bolivia, Brazil, Chile, Paraguay, Uruguay.

HABITAT A high variety of habitats, including pampas grassland, marsh grasslands, broadleafed forest, savanna, dry shrublands, arid woodland, Monte Desert, semi-desert, and arid steppe uplands, up to 3,300 m. They prefer areas with dense vegetation and may occur in highly degraded human-developed areas. Not found in tropical or temperate rainforest.

CONSERVATION STATUS Least Concern. CITES: Appendix I. Widespread and abundant over most of its range. In parts of its range, the Geoffroy's Cat seems to have benefited from the conversion of subtropical forests into croplands. They were killed in huge numbers for their furs throughout the 1970s and 1980s, but they are now fully protected across their range, with hunting and trade prohibited. Habitat loss and fragmentation, and retaliatory killing remain as the main threats. Their pelts may be seen in local illegal trade.

PHOTO CREDITS TL: *Esteban Argerich*, Colonia Carlos Pellegrini (Argentina); TR: *Tetsu Yamazaki*; CL, Y: *Alexander Sliwa*, Amersfoort Zoo (Netherlands), Wuppertal Zoo (Germany); CR: *Ricardo Fernández Chaves*, Saavedra (Argentina); B: *Jaime San Roman*, Le Parc des Felins (France).

Southern Guiña

LEOPARDUS GUIGNA GUIGNA

BL: 42-49 cm (♂), 39-45 cm (♀). TL: 19.5-25 cm. SH: 22 cm. W: 1.5-3 kg. SL: 7.9 cm (♂). SW: 5.4 cm (♂). DF: 26. CN: 36. A tiny, compactly built cat, with relatively short limbs and a thick, tubular, bushy tail. Slightly smaller and more brightly colored than the northern subspecies. Coat is gray-brown to buff, to reddish-brown, heavily patterned with small black spots on the back and flanks that coalesce into broken lines on the back and nape. Undersides are lighter and also spotted. Melanism is common, sometimes with mahogany-brown extremities on which the markings are obvious. Head small and rounded. Face distinctively marked with dark cheek stripes, eyebrow markings, and prominent dark stripes under the eyes that border the muzzle. Some individuals have prominent dark bands across the throat. Ears are relatively small, rounded, black on the back with a white central spot. Tail is bushy, black ringed, about half of the head-body length. Males are larger than females.

melanistic form

Leopardus guigna guigna

OTHER NAMES Kod-kod, Chilean Cat. *French*: Guigna, chat du Chili, kodkod. *German*: Kodkod, Chilenische Waldkzatze, Nachtkatze. *Spanish*: Guiña meridional, huiña, gato choco, gato de Santa Cruz. *Russian*: Южная чилийская кошка (гуинья).

TAXONOMY Two subspecies are currently recognized based on phylogenetic studies, with moderate morphological differences: *L. g. guigna* (Southern Guiña); and *L. g. tigrillo* (Northern Guiña). Closely related to Geoffroy's Cat; both species were formerly grouped in their own genus, *Oncifelis*, with the Colocolo.

SIMILAR SPECIES The Geoffroy's Cat, sympatric at the extreme E edge of the Guiña's range (Los Alerces NP in S Argentina, Puyehue NP in Chile), is larger with a relatively heavier head and less bushy tail.

REPRODUCTION *Gestation*: 72-78 days. *Young per Birth*: 1-3. *Weaning*: Unknown. *Sexual Maturity*: Unknown. *Life Span*: 14 years in captivity. *Breeding Season*: Possibly seasonal breeding, in early spring (August to September), with births in late October to early November, but largely unknown from the wild.

BEHAVIOR *Social Behavior*: Solitary. *Diet*: Small mammals (rodents, marsupials, and lagomorphs) but also birds, invertebrates, lizards; they occasionally take carrion and prey on poultry. *Main Predators*: Pumas, culpeo foxes, domestic dogs. It can be active day and night. They hunt mainly on the ground. In fragmented landscapes, home ranges are larger than in pristine areas: 1.3-22.4 km^2 in the fragmented landscapes of N Chiloé Island, 0.3-2.2 km^2 in Laguna San Rafael and Queulat NP. It may cover daily distances of 14 km in fragmented landscapes. Territoriality may be more prevalent among populations on Chiloé, where the availability of prey may be more limited.

DISTRIBUTION *Native*: Chile (38° to 48° S), Argentina (39° to 46° S). Restricted to S Chile, including Isla Grande de Chiloé and marginally in adjacent border areas of extreme SW Argentina.

HABITAT Strongly associated with dense, temperate rainforest and southern beech forest, particularly the distinctive Valdivian forests in S Chile characterized by dense colihue bamboo thickets and fern understory; from sea level to the treeline up to 2,500 m. They consistently avoid open land such as cultivation and areas with short vegetation except for very small patches, which they traverse to reach cover. They inhabit secondary forest, forested ravines, and coastal forest strips in heavily altered habitat, and they use small forest fragments and plantations (eucalyptus and pine), when close to native forested habitat, and provided they contain dense understory.

CONSERVATION STATUS Vulnerable. In Chile Vulnerable from Los Ríos Region to the N, Near Threatened from Los Lagos Region to the S. In Argentina it is included among the high-priority species to conserve. CITES: Appendix II. Most of its area of occupancy is suffering from increasing landscape fragmentation due to logging, habitat conversion to pine plantations, and agricultural and livestock activities. This landscape fragmentation is associated with reduced genetic diversity and population size decline. Other threats include retaliatory killings for poultry predation, road kills, diseases facilitated by increased contact with Domestic Cats, and climate change. Estimated total population for this subspecies is 3,400-50,000. Protected in Argentina and Chile.

PHOTO CREDITS TR, B: *Alexander Sliwa*, Fauna Andina (Chile); TL: *Enrique Couve,* Chiloé Island (Chile); CL: *SAG*, Huilo Huilo Biological Reserve (Chile); CR: *Eduardo Minte Hess*, Pucatrihue (Chile).

Northern Guiña
LEOPARDUS GUIGNA TIGRILLO

BL: 42-56 cm (♂), 37.4-51 cm (♀). TL: 19.5-25 cm. SH: 22 cm. W: 1.7-3.0 kg (♂), 1.3-2.1 kg (♀). DF: 26. CN: 36. A tiny, compactly built cat, with relatively short limbs and a thick, tubular, bushy tail. The smallest cat in the Americas. Larger and paler than the southern subspecies. Coat is light gray-brown to buff, to reddish-brown, heavily patterned with small black spots on the back and flanks that coalesce into broken lines on the back and nape. Undersides are lighter and also spotted. Melanism is not known to occur in this subspecies. Head small and rounded. Face distinctively marked with dark cheek stripes, eyebrow markings, and prominent dark stripes under the eyes that border the muzzle. Some individuals have prominent dark bands across the throat. Ears are relatively small, rounded, black on the back with a white central spot. Tail is bushy, black ringed, about half of the head-body length. Males are larger than females.

Leopardus guigna tigrillo

OTHER NAMES Kod-kod, Chilean Cat. *French*: Guigna, chat du Chili, kodkod. *German*: Kodkod, Chilenische Waldkzatze, Nachtkatze. *Spanish*: Guiña septentrional, huiña, gato choco. *Russian*: Северная чилийская кошка (гуинья).

TAXONOMY Considered as a subspecies of Guiña (*L. guigna*). Includes *molinae*.

SIMILAR SPECIES The Colocolo is larger, with longer hair, covered with oblique, rusty-cinnamon cheek stripes and lines on flanks, and a erectile spinal crest along the dorsal midline. The Andean Mountain Cat is also larger, with a long luxurious coat, marked with large vertical orange-brown spots on the flanks, and a longer tail.

REPRODUCTION *Gestation*: 72-78 days. *Young per Birth*: 1-3. *Weaning*: Unknown. *Sexual Maturity*: Unknown. *Life Span*: 11 years in captivity. *Breeding Season*: Possibly seasonal breeding, in early spring (August to September), with births in late October to early November, but largely unknown from the wild.

BEHAVIOR *Social Behavior*: Solitary. *Diet*: Small mammals, especially rodents, but also small marsupials, birds, and reptiles; they scavenge opportunistically on carrion. *Main Predators*: Pumas, culpeo foxes, domestic dogs. Agile hunters, mainly hunting on the ground. It can be active day and night, with a tendency to be most active at dusk into the evening. A good climber, escaping to trees when threatened. It likes to shelter in trees, in dense cover near waterways, and in thick piles of ground-level vegetation or quila thickets during inactive periods. In protected populations, range size is similar for ♂ and ♀, while in fragmented populations the ranges of ♂ are often larger than those of ♀. ♂ and ♀ home ranges largely overlap whereas home ranges of individuals of the same sex usually are exclusive; aggressive interactions appear to be rare and mild.

DISTRIBUTION *Native*: Chile (30° to 38° S). Restricted to N and C Chile.

HABITAT They occur mostly in Chilean Mediterranean matorral habitat made up of temperate forest, sclerophyll woodland, and dense scrub. Also found also in secondary forest, exotic pine and eucalyptus plantations, fragmented landscapes, and on the fringes of rural settlements and agricultural areas, but plantations are only used when close to native primary forests or regeneration understory.

CONSERVATION STATUS Vulnerable. CITES: Appendix II. Current main threats include habitat loss and fragmentation, and direct persecution by humans. Human population and deforestation are increasing in the Chilean temperate rainforest. Other threats include diseases and climate change. Protected by national legislation. Estimated population for this subspecies is 2,600-40,000 individuals.

PHOTO CREDITS T: *Alfredo Boettiger*, Buin Zoo (Chile); C: *Alexander Sliwa*, Fauna Andina (Chile); B: *Christopher Momberg*, Termas de Chillán (Chile).

Southern Tigrina

LEOPARDUS GUTTULUS

BL: 36.5-54 cm. TL: 23-35 cm. SH: 22-30 cm. W: 1-4.6 kg. SL: 8.1 cm. SW: 5.4 cm. DF: 30. CN: 36. A small cat, with a slender body, about the size of a young Domestic Cat. Coat color is dark yellowish-brown to ocherous-buff, lighter on the sides of the body, with small dark open rosettes on the body sides with thick and discontinuous black rims, rarely coalescing into small oblique bands. Belly is white or very light gray, covered with dark spots. Melanism is common. Nape hair runs backward. Large ears, black on the back with a central white spot. Tail is about 60% of the head and body length, has 7 to 13 irregular thin rings, and a black tip. Males are slightly larger than females.

Young

Leopardus guttulus

OTHER NAMES Southern Tiger Cat, Southern Little Spotted Cat, Atlantic Forest Oncilla. *French*: Oncille du sud, chat-tigre du sud. *German*: Südliche Tigerkatze, Kleinfleckenkatze, Ozelotkatze, Zwergtigerkatze. *Spanish*: Tigrillo, tirica, gato tigre. *Russian*: Южная тигровая кошка. *Guaraní*: Mbaracayá, mbaracayá-miú. *Portuguese*: Gato-do-mato, maracajá-í, pintadinho, gato-macambira, gato-maracajá.

TAXONOMY Monotypic. Formerly treated as a subspecies of *L. tigrinus*, but molecular studies showed that it is clearly a distinct species. There is an extensive hybridization zone with the Geoffroy's Cat (*L. geoffroyi*) in the state of Rio Grande do Sul, S Brazil, and with the Pantanal Cat (*L. colocola*) in central Brazil; however, there is no evidence of gene flow with the Eastern Tigrina (*L. emiliae*).

SIMILAR SPECIES The Northern Tigrina has a lighter built, with a slender body and legs, slightly smaller and less rounded rosettes, and a less conspicuous, thinly ringed tail. Geoffroy's Cat is larger, with a bulky head, and with the typical paired dots that usually do not form rosettes. The Margay has thicker fur, more richly marked, larger paws, and a distinctively longer tail.

REPRODUCTION *Gestation*: 75-78 days. *Young per Birth*: 1-4, usually 1. *Weaning*: 2-3 months. *Sexual Maturity*: 2 years. *Life Span*: 20 years in captivity. *Breeding Season*: Year-round, but could show different peaks in different areas. Kittens open their eyes at 8–17 days, and are almost adult body size at 11 months of age.

BEHAVIOR *Social Behavior*: Solitary. *Diet*: Small mammals, birds, and lizards; larger prey (small primates, agoutis, whistling-ducks) occasionally taken. Predominantly nocturnal and crepuscular, but may be active during the day, to avoid predation by the sympatric Ocelot. They are negatively impacted by the larger Ocelot, but they are not affected by the Margay and Jaguarundi. Excellent climbers, but spend most of their time on the ground. Small prey is killed with a nape bite, while larger prey is attacked first on the back; feeding starts on the head or neck. Home ranges 2-25 km², larger than would be expected, probably also to avoid other larger potential felid predators. ♀ ranges are smaller than those of ♂.

DISTRIBUTION *Native*: Argentina, Brazil, Paraguay. Absent from the Paraguayan Chaco. The N limits of its geographic range are still unclear.

HABITAT A broad variety of habitats, from dense tropical and subtropical rainforests, deciduous and mixed pine forests, to open savannas and beach vegetation, both pristine and disturbed. Mostly found in lowland areas, up to 2,000 m. It is rare in swampy savannas and marshy areas. Its occurrence near agricultural fields is limited by the presence of natural cover.

CONSERVATION STATUS Vulnerable. CITES: Appendix II. Estimated population of 6,047 individuals. Very rare, especially in protected areas, due to the negative impact of the Ocelot. Threats include habitat loss and fragmentation, prey reduction, hunting due to conflicts with rural owners, competition and diseases spread by domestic dogs, indiscriminate use of rodenticides, and road kills. It was heavily exploited for the fur trade decades ago, following the decline in Ocelot trade. Hunting is prohibited in Argentina, Brazil, and Paraguay.

PHOTO CREDITS TR: *Demis Bucci*, Núcleo Santa Virginia (Brazil); TL: Refúgio Biológico Bela Vista (Brazil); CL: *Alex Meyer*, Parc des Felins (France); CR: *Alexander Sliwa*, Dortmund Zoo (Germany); B: *Roland Wirth*, Campina Grande do Sul Parana (Brazil).

Eastern Tigrina
LEOPARDUS EMILIAE

BL: 41.5-51 cm. TL: 26-32 cm. SH: 22-30 cm. W: 1.3-3.5 kg. SL: 7.7 cm. SW: 5.5 cm. DF: 30. CN: 36. A small cat, with a slender, lightly built body, about the size of a young Domestic Cat. Coat is relatively harsh, from light yellowish-brown to pale yellow and grayish-yellow in color, with small dark rosettes surrounded by thin discontinuous black lines, not coalescing into small oblique bands. Some specimens show distinctive continuous black lines that run throughout the posterior half of the dorsum to the base of the tail, while in others these lines are not continuous or are barely perceptible. Belly is white, very light gray or slightly yellowish, with dark spots. Nose pink. Nape hair runs backward. Large ears, black on the back with a central white spot. Tail narrow, slightly longer than hind legs, with irregular thin rings, and a black tip. Males are slightly larger than females.

Young

Leopardus emiliae

OTHER NAMES Snethlage's Tigrina, Oncilla, Little Spotted Cat. *French*: Chat tigre du est. *German*: Tigerkatze. *Spanish*: Gato tigre, tigrillo, tirica, tigrillo gallinero, tigrillo lanudo, tigrillo peludo, tigrillo chico. *Russian*: Восточная тигровая кошка (онцилла). *Portuguese*: Gato-do-mato, gato-maracajá, maracajá-í, pintadinho.

TAXONOMY Monotypic. Formerly treated as a subspecies of *L. tigrinus*, but molecular studies showed that it is probably a distinct species. There is no evidence of gene flow with the Southern Tigrina (*L. guttulus*).

REPRODUCTION *Gestation*: 62-76 days. *Young per Birth*: 1-4, usually 1. *Weaning*: 3 months. *Sexual Maturity*: 2 years. *Life Span*: 21 years in captivity. *Breeding Season*: Probably year-round, but could show different peaks in different areas. There is very little information available about the reproduction of this species.

BEHAVIOR *Social Behavior*: Solitary. *Diet*: Small mammals (small rodents, shrews, small opossums), birds, and lizards. Mostly nocturnal and crepuscular, but with considerable amount of daytime activity. It may be highly diurnal in some areas of Brazil. It is generally terrestrial, but climbs with ease. Home ranges are much larger than would be expected for its small body size, 1-25 km² (♀) and 4.8-17 km² (♂).

DISTRIBUTION *Native*: Brazil. It is the only Felidae species endemic to Brazil, distributed in the N (right bank of the Amazon River), NE, and central portion of this country (states of Pará, Tocantins, Maranhão, Ceará, Rio Grande do Norte, Paraíba, Pernambuco, Alagoas, Bahia, and Goiás). Its S limits are not yet well known, as well as the extent of a possible overlap with the populations of the Southern Tigrina (*L. guttulus*).

HABITAT Caatinga, Cerrado, Amazonia, and Atlantic Forest biomes. It avoids the more open habitats and close proximity to rural settlements. In disturbed habitats, it can occur close to human settlements, as long as there is natural cover and a prey base. Its numbers are strongly negatively impacted by the larger Ocelot, its potential intraguild predator and competitor.

CONSERVATION STATUS Vulnerable, Endangered in Brazil. CITES: Appendix I. Estimated total population of 9,000. It is naturally rare to uncommon everywhere, less abundant than the Southern Tigrina, and one of the rarest of the tropical cats. It is absent from the Llanos and from the Darien Gap connecting Central and South America, and is one of the rarest species in Amazonia. It is negatively impacted by Ocelot numbers. Threats include habitat loss and fragmentation, but also disease, road-kill, illegal trade (pets and pelts), and retaliatory killing due to depredation of poultry. Hybridization with Pampas Cat in all of NE and central Brazil has been detected in 100% of all specimens evaluated, but whether this is a threat is unknown. Hunting is prohibited in Brazil, Colombia, Costa Rica, French Guiana, Suriname, and Venezuela.

PHOTO CREDITS T, B: *Gerard Lacz*; CL: *Michal Sloviak*, Praha Zoo (Czech Republic); Young: *Eric Isselée*, Mulhouse Zoo (France); CR: *Roland Wirth*, Mulhouse Zoo (France, from Guyana).

Northern Tigrina

LEOPARDUS TIGRINUS PARDINOIDES

BL: 45-56 cm. TL: 24-34 cm. SH: 22-30 cm. W: 2.4 kg. SL: 7.7 cm. SW: 5.5 cm. DF: 30. CN: 36. A small cat, with a slender, lightly built body, about the size of a young Domestic Cat. Coat is relatively harsh, from dark brown and orangish-brown to yellowish-brown and grayish-brown in color, becoming lighter on the sides of the body, with medium-sized rosettes with black or very dark brown rims on the sides of the body forming small or medium-sized oblique bands arranged in scapular-inguinal direction. Belly is white or light gray, with dark spots. Melanistic individuals have been recorded. Nose pink. Nape hair runs backward. Large ears, black on the back with a central white spot. Tail narrow, slightly longer than hind legs, with irregular thin rings, and a black tip. No sexual dimorphism.

melanistic form

118

Leopardus tigrinus pardinoides

OTHER NAMES Oncilla, Little Spotted Cat. *French*: Chat tigre du nord. *German*: Tigerkatze. *Spanish*: Gato tigre, tigrillo, tigrina, tigrillo gallinero, tigrillo lanudo, tigrillo peludo, tigrillo chico. *Russian*: Северная тигровая кошка (онцилла). *Portuguese*: Gato-do-mato, gato-maracajá, maracajá-í, pintadinho.

TAXONOMY Two subspecies are tentatively recognized: *L. t. pardinoides* (N South America, possibly as far S as Bolivia and NW Argentina, including the N Andes; and *L. t. oncilla* (Costa Rica and possibly Panama). Tigrinas from Central America may represent a distinct species, *L. oncilla*. Tigrinas from E Brazil (*L. emiliae*) and S Brazil (*L. guttulus*) are no longer considered a subspecies of *L. tigrina*.

SIMILAR SPECIES The Margay (*L. wiedii*) has similar ground color and markings and can be easily misidentified in the field, especially in a quick observation, but it is usually larger and the hairs on the nape face forward (backward in *L. tigrinus*).

REPRODUCTION *Gestation*: 62-76 days. *Young per Birth*: 1-4, usually 1. *Weaning*: 3 months. *Sexual Maturity*: 2 years. *Life Span*: 21 years in captivity. *Breeding Season*: Probably year-round, but could show different peaks in different areas. Very little information about the Tigrina's reproduction is available.

BEHAVIOR *Social Behavior*: Solitary. *Diet*: Small mammals, birds, and lizards. Mostly nocturnal and crepuscular, but with considerable amount of daytime activity. It may be highly diurnal in some areas of Brazil. It is generally terrestrial, but climbs with ease.

DISTRIBUTION *Native*: NW Argentina, Bolivia, N Brazil (left bank of the Amazon River), Colombia, Ecuador, French Guiana, Guyana, Peru, Suriname, Venezuela. There is a gap in the geographic distribution between Central American and N South American population.

HABITAT Lowland, premontane, and montane forests, but it can be found in a broad range of habitats, from Andean montane to Rupununi Savannas, from sea level up to 4,800 m. Apparently it has a marginal distribution on the open areas of Los Llanos. In Colombia it seems to be restricted to elevations above 1,500 m, and in Brazil most of the records were below 500 m. It avoids the more open habitats and close proximity to rural settlements. In disturbed habitats, it can occur close to human settlements, as long as there is natural cover and a prey base. Its numbers are strongly negatively impacted by the larger Ocelot, its potential intraguild predator and competitor.

CONSERVATION STATUS Vulnerable, Endangered in Brazil. CITES: Appendix I. Less abundant than the Southern Tigrina, and one of the rarest of the tropical cats. It is absent from the Darien Gap connecting Central and South America, and is one of the rarest species in Amazonia. It is negatively impacted by Ocelot numbers. Threats include habitat loss and fragmentation, but also disease, road-kill, illegal trade (pets and pelts), and retaliatory killing due to depredation of poultry. Hybridization with Pampas Cat in all of NE and central Brazil has been detected in 100% of all specimens evaluated, but whether this is a threat is unknown. Hunting is prohibited in Brazil, Colombia, Costa Rica, French Guiana, Suriname, and Venezuela.

PHOTO CREDITS T: *Alexander Meyer*, Zoo de Santa Cruz (Colombia); CR: Zoo de Santa Cruz (Colombia); CL: *Juan Castillo*, Zoo de Santa Fé (Colombia); B: *Alex Kantorovich*, Parque Jaime Duque (Colombia).

Central America Tigrina

LEOPARDUS TIGRINUS ONCILLA

BL: 45.2-55.6 cm. TL: 24-34.5 cm. SH: 22-30 cm. W: 2.4 kg. SL: 8.3 cm (♂), 7.9 cm (♀). SW: 5.6 cm (♂), 5.2 cm (♀). DF: 30. CN: 36. A small cat, with a slender, lightly built body, much richer and deeper in color than the Northern Tigrina, with the lateral rosettes little elongated. Coat is harsh, from dark gray-brown to light yellowish-brown orange in color, with the sides of the body usually lighter, with medium-sized rosettes on the sides of the body surrounded by thin discontinuous black or very dark brown lines, forming small or medium-sized oblique bands arranged in scapular-inguinal direction. Belly is white or light gray, with dark spots. Nose pink. Yellowish eyes. Nape hair runs backward. Large ears, black on the back with a central white spot. Feet small, forefoot broader than hind foot. Tail narrow, slightly longer than hind legs, with irregular thin rings, and a black tip.

melanistic form

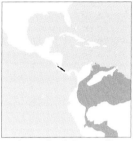

Leopardus tigrinus oncilla

OTHER NAMES Oncilla, Little Spotted Cat, Tigrillo. *French*: Chat tigre d'Amérique centrale. *German*: Tigerkatze. *Spanish*: Caucel, tigrillo. *Russian*: Центральноамериканская онцилла (малая пятнистая кошка).

TAXONOMY Considered provisionally as a subspecies of *L. tigrinus*, but there is some evidence that this Central American population may represent a different species (*L. oncilla*).

SIMILAR SPECIES Difficult to distinguish from a Central American Margay or a small Ocelot. The Margay is larger, more richly marked (larger and more boldly defined spots or streaks), and densely furred, with a distinctively longer tail, very large darker eyes, and oversized front paws. The Ocelot is much larger, with a relatively shorter tail (tail is shorter than the hind legs). In all Tigrinas the nape hair runs backward, different from both the Ocelot and Margay, but similar to Geoffroy's Cat.

REPRODUCTION *Gestation*: 62-76 days. *Young per Birth*: 1-4, usually 1. *Weaning*: 3 months. *Sexual Maturity*: 2-2.5 years. *Life Span*: Unknown. *Breeding Season*: Probably year-round, but could show different peaks in different areas. Very little information about the Tigrina's reproduction is available. The eyes are open at 8-17 days. Young are almost adult body size at 11 months of age.

BEHAVIOR *Social Behavior*: Solitary. *Diet*: Small mammals and ground-dwelling birds, including tinamous, wood-quail, sparrows, and finches; it is a generalist predator, taking advantage of the most readily available resources in the area. There are few direct observations of hunting but its prey profile indicates that it forages mainly terrestrially and nocturno-crepuscularly but with some flexibility depending on prey activity, and the presence of Ocelots, which it might avoid. Its ecology is poorly known. They are naturally rare compared to other small Neotropical felids. They are excellent climbers, but spend most of their time on the ground as most prey are terrestrial. When threatened, Tigrinas show an aggressive behavior with arched back and raised hair, besides showing the teeth and producing a "whistling-spitting" vocalization.

DISTRIBUTION *Native*: Costa Rica, Panama. *Presence Uncertain*: Nicaragua. In Costa Rica, it inhabits high-elevation forests of the Tilarán and Talamanca Mountains, Corcovado NP, Sirena Biological Station, Manuel Antonio NP, La Amistad International Park, and Chirripó NP.

HABITAT Montane forests along the flanks of volcanoes and other high mountains from 1,000 m up to the treeline (páramo), cloud forests, and high-elevation elfin forests. Their distribution pattern in Costa Rica and Panama closely resembles that of the oak-dominated forests. Up to 3,625 m in Chirripó NP in Costa Rica.

CONSERVATION STATUS Vulnerable. CITES: Appendix I. Naturally rare. Current patterns of deforestation in Mesoamerica, together with presumed low population densities and fragmented populations, make this subspecies a conservation and research priority. Hunting is prohibited in Costa Rica.

PHOTO CREDITS T, CL, B: *Kevin Schafer*, La Paz Waterfall Gardens (Costa Rica); C: *Ignacio Yúfera*, Volcán Barú NP (Panama); CR: *Jean-Francois Noblet* (Costa Rica).

Colocolo
LEOPARDUS COLOCOLA COLOCOLA AND WOLFSOHNI

BL: 56.7-67 cm. TL: 29-32.5 cm. SH: 36 cm. W: 2-4 kg. SL: 9.7 cm (♂). SW: 7.7 cm (♂). DF: 30. CN: 36. A small and stocky cat, about the size of a Domestic Cat with relatively short legs, long hair, and a shortish, thickly furred tail. Coat is reddish or dark gray in color, covered with oblique, rusty-cinnamon cheek stripes and lines (*colocola*) or rosettes (*wolfsohni*) on flanks. Conspicuous erectile spinal crest behind the shoulders, extending along the dorsal midline, black and rusty in color. Ventral markings are rusty-ocherous, on a more or less white background. Broad face, with 2 transverse dark lines crossing each cheek. Triangular ears, cinnamon dorsally, with blackish edges and black tips. Yellowish-brown eyes. Large pink rhinarium. Throat with 2 or 3 transverse dark stripes. Legs with dark brown rings and stripes, somewhat rustier colored on hind legs. Feet are cinnamon dorsally, with small dark spots. Tail with 4 or 5 reddish rings, the last 2 appearing darker (*colocola*) or not ringed (*wolfsohni*).

ssp. *colocola*

ssp. *wolfsohni*

Leopardus colocola colocola

Leopardus colocola wolfsohni

OTHER NAMES *French*: Chat des pampas. *German*: Colocolo, Pampaskatze. *Spanish*: Colocolo, gato de los Pajonales, gato montés, gato pajero. *Russian*: Пампасская кошка (колоколо): центральночилийская (*colocola*), северочилийская (*wolfsohni*) .

TAXONOMY Based on morphology, this species clusters into three major groups, sometimes classified as full species (*L. colocolo, L. pajeros*, and *L. braccatus*), but genetic data indicate only moderate differences between populations. Seven subspecies are currently recognized, but this is likely to change as more information becomes available, including the possible recognition of some as full species: *L. c. colocola* (Southern Colocolo, central Chile W of Andes); *L. c. wolfsohni* (Northern Colocolo, N Chile W of Andes); *L. c. pajeros* (central, N central, and S Argentina); *L. c. budini* (NW Argentina, Bolivia E of Andes); *L. c. garleppi* (S Colombia, Ecuador, Peru E of Andes), *L. c. braccatus* (SW and central Brazil, Paraguay); and *L. c. munoai* (Uruguay). Previously classified in its own genus, *Lynchailurus*, or as a member of the genus *Oncifelis* with the Guiña and Geoffroy's Cat, but recent molecular analyses place it firmly within the *Leopardus* genus. A zone of hybridization between *L. colocola* and *L. tigrinus* has been found through genetic analyses of specimens from central Brazil.

SIMILAR SPECIES Coat pattern of *L. c. wolfsohni*, from N Chile, is similar to that of *L. c. garleppi* (Ecuador, Peru), but examination of cranial characteristics indicates that it is closer to the central Chilean subspecies *L. c. colocola* than to any other known population of *L. colocola*. In addition, this population lives on the W drainage of the Andes, as does the central Chilean population, in isolation from *garleppi* and *budini* from the E slope. This population is separated by nearly 2,000 km from the central Chilean population.

REPRODUCTION *Gestation*: 80-85 days. *Young per Birth*: 1-3. *Weaning*: Unknown. *Sexual Maturity*: 24 months. *Life Span*: 9 years in the wild, 16 years in captivity. *Breeding Season*: Unknown. There is little information available on the reproductive behavior of these subspecies, and most of it comes from captive animals.

BEHAVIOR *Social Behavior*: Solitary. *Diet*: Small mammals (guinea pigs, small rodents, mountain vizcachas) and birds (flamingos, ground-dwelling birds). There is little information available on the ecology of this species. Nocturnal with some crepuscular and diurnal activity. It is terrestrial and hunts mainly on the ground.

DISTRIBUTION *Native*: Chile. This population lives in central Chile on the W slope of the Andes.

HABITAT Subtropical, xerophytic forests, occasionally penetrating the spiny shrublands to the N, from sea level to 1,800 m. *L. c. wolfsohni* occurs in highland shrub and grass steppes (páramos and marginal areas of puna), and occasionally penetrates dry forests in the upper part of inner Andean valleys, from 1,800 to 5,000 m.

CONSERVATION STATUS Near Threatened. CITES: Appendix II. This species group is one of the least known of the South American cats, and it is difficult to determine the extent to which populations are impacted by different threats. Estimated total population for this group is fewer than 50,000 individuals. These subspecies could be the most endangered, because their ranges are significantly smaller. Protected in Chile.

PHOTO CREDITS T, C: *Andrea Riveros*, Zoológico Nacional (Chile); B: *Verónica Araya García*, Guallatire (Chile).

Brazilian Pantanal Cat
LEOPARDUS COLOCOLA BRACCATUS

BL: 47-56 cm. TL: 23-33 cm. SH: 36 cm. W: 2.9-3.7 kg. SL: 9.1 cm. SW: 6.5 cm. DF: 30. CN: 36. A small and stocky cat, about the size of a Domestic Cat with relatively short legs, long hair, and a shortish, thickly furred tail. Coat is almost uniform brown agouti color dorsally, with some traces of dark brown rosettes on the flanks, with longer hair than in other subspecies. Spinal crest darker than ground color, sometimes rather inconspicuous. Melanism has been reported in Brazil. Underside of the chin is white. Yellowish-brown eyes. Large pink rhinarium. Ears are large and pointed, with a black band along anterointernal border, reddish on basal portion, and creamy-white over the remaining outer surface. Throat is white, becoming orangish behind the first throat stripe, and over all other ventral surfaces. Leg stripes and ventral markings are black. Feet are dorsally and ventrally black, including wrists and ankles (giving the appearance of wearing boots). Tail not ringed, darker at the tip.

melanistic form

Leopardus colocola braccatus

OTHER NAMES *French*: Chat du Pantanal. *German*: Pampaskatze. *Spanish*: Gato de los Pajonales, gato del Pantanal, gato montés. *Russian*: Бразильская пантанальская кошка. *Portuguese*: Gato-Palheiro.

TAXONOMY Considered as a subspecies of Colocolo (*L. colocola*). Formerly considered as a full species, the Pantanal Cat (*L. braccatus*), with two subspecies: *L. b. braccatus*, and *L. b. munoai*. Genetic analysis in central Brazil showed that an area of hybridization exists between this subspecies and the Northern Tigrina (*L. t. tigrinus*).

SIMILAR SPECIES *L. c. munoai* (Uruguayan Pantanal Cat) is larger than *L. c. braccatus*, has a paler color, more yellow to orangish on the back and flanks, with brown spots on flanks more noticeable, and the feet are black only on palmar and plantar surfaces. The tail of both subspecies has a dark tip, but the black tip of *L. c. munoai* is reduced.

REPRODUCTION *Gestation*: 80-85 days. *Young per Birth*: 1-3. *Weaning*: Unknown. *Sexual Maturity*: 24 months. *Life Span*: 9 years, 16.5 years in captivity. *Breeding Season*: In captivity, from April to July in the N hemisphere. There is little information available on the reproductive behavior of these subspecies, and most of it comes from captive animals.

BEHAVIOR *Social Behavior*: Solitary. *Diet*: Ground birds, small mammals, and guinea pigs, but also small reptiles, plant material, and beetles. There is little information available on the ecology of this subspecies. Diurnal with some crepuscular and only occasional nocturnal activity. It is terrestrial and hunts mainly on the ground. Home range sizes range from 3 to 37 km^2 in Brazilian grasslands. Vocalizations are similar to other small felids' and include a meow, growl, spit, hiss, gurgle, and purr.

DISTRIBUTION *Native*: NE Bolivia, SW and C Brazil, Paraguay.

HABITAT Shrubland and grassland steppes (campos limpos and sujos), dry savannas (campos cerrados), humid savannas (pantanal), and deciduous forests, between 140 and 1,240 m above sea level. This subspecies occurs in warmer and more humid habitats than do other subspecies, but it prefers drier, short grassland habitat far from water. It can be found among clumps of tall pampas grass and in low-lying swampy areas. It may also be found in pastures and agricultural fields, demonstrating that it can use human-altered habitats and adapt to changing environments. It probably does not avoid areas where Jaguars occur.

CONSERVATION STATUS Near Threatened, Vulnerable in Brazil and Argentina. CITES: Appendix II. Considered typically rare and with low population densities throughout these regions, but may be relatively common in a few areas, usually protected, such as Emas NP in the Cerrado, and Mirador State Park. In the Brazilian pampas (S portion of Rio Grande do Sul state), this felid is considered to occur only in well-preserved habitats, and is always rarer than Geoffroy's Cat. Future population declines are likely to result from land conversion of native habitat to agricultural crops, land degradation from cattle grazing, fragmentation, hunting by local farmers in retaliation for depredation of their chickens, and decline of prey populations.

PHOTO CREDITS TR, B: *Roland Wirth*, Jardim Zoológico de Belo Horizonte (Brazil); TL: *Francisco Erize* (Brazil); CL: *Alexander Meyer*, Sorocaba Zoo (Brazil); CR: *Marc Faucher*, Emas NP (Brazil).

Uruguayan Pantanal Cat

LEOPARDUS COLOCOLA MUNOAI

BL: 53 cm. TL: 29 cm. SH: 36 cm. W: 2.9-3.7 kg. SL: 9.1 cm (♂). SW: 6.6 cm. DF: 30. CN: 36.
A small and stocky cat, about the size of a Domestic Cat with relatively short legs, long hair, and a
shortish, thickly furred tail. Larger and paler than the Brazilian Pantanal Cat. Coat is almost uniform
yellowish-brown in color, more yellow to orange on the back and flanks, with brown spots on flanks more
noticeable than in the Brazilian Pantanal Cat, with longer hair than in other subspecies. Spinal crest
darker than ground color, sometimes rather inconspicuous. Underside of the chin is white. Yellowish-
brown eyes. Large pink rhinarium. Ears are large and pointed, with a black band along anterointernal
border, reddish on basal portion, and creamy-white over the remaining outer surface. Throat is white,
becoming orangish behind the first throat stripe, and over all other ventral surfaces. Leg stripes and
ventral markings are black. Feet are black only on palmar and plantar surfaces. Tail not ringed, less
dark at the tip than in the Brazilian Pantanal Cat.

Leopardus colocola munoai

OTHER NAMES *French*: Chat du Pantanal. *German*: Pampaskatze. *Spanish*: Gato de los Pajonales Uruguayo, gato del Pantanal, gato montés. *Russian*: Уругвайская пантанальская кошка. *Portuguese*: Gato-Palheiro.

TAXONOMY Considered as a subspecies of Colocolo (*L. colocola*). Formerly considered as a full species, the Pantanal Cat (*L. braccatus*), with two subspecies: *L. b. braccatus* and *L. b. munoai*. The ranges of *munoai* and *braccatus* are separated by rainforest, but the subspecific status of individuals in the S Amazon Basin, and the Atlantic Forest and grassland regions in Paraguay and the Brazilian Pantanal is not clear.

SIMILAR SPECIES *L. c. braccatus* (Brazilian Pantanal Cat) is smaller, has a darker color, with brown spots on flanks less noticeable, and the feet are dorsally and ventrally black, including wrists and ankles, giving the appearance of wearing boots. The tail of both subspecies has a darkened tip, but the black tip of *L. c. braccatus* is more extensive.

REPRODUCTION *Gestation*: 80-85 days. *Young per Birth*: 1-3. *Weaning*: Unknown. *Sexual Maturity*: 24 months. *Life Span*: 9 years in the wild, 16.5 years in captivity. *Breeding Season*: In captivity, from April to July in the N hemisphere. There is little information available on the reproductive behavior of this subspecies, and most of it comes from captive animals.

BEHAVIOR *Social Behavior*: Solitary. *Diet*: Ground birds, small mammals, and Brazilian guinea pigs, but also birds (tinamous), small reptiles, plant material, and beetles. There is little information available on the ecology of this subspecies. Diurnal with some crepuscular and only occasional nocturnal activity. It is terrestrial and hunts mainly on the ground. Home range sizes range from 3 to 37 km^2 in Brazilian grasslands. Vocalizations are similar to other small felids' and include a meow, growl, spit, hiss, gurgle, and purr.

DISTRIBUTION *Native*: Argentina (provinces of Entre Rios and Corrientes), Brazil (state of Rio Grande do Sul), Uruguay.

HABITAT Shrubland and grassland steppes (campos limpos and sujos), dry savannas (campos cerrados), humid savannas (pantanal), and deciduous forests, between 140 and 1,240 m above sea level. It prefers open fields with shrub cover and the edges of swamps for foraging terrestrial prey. It may also be found in pastures and agricultural fields, demonstrating that it can use human-altered habitats and adapt to changing environments.

CONSERVATION STATUS Near Threatened, Vulnerable in Brazil and Argentina. CITES: Appendix II. Considered typically rare and with low population densities. In the Brazilian pampas (S portion of Rio Grande do Sul state), this felid is considered to occur only in well-preserved habitats, and is always rarer than Geoffroy's Cat. Future population declines are likely to result from land conversion of native habitat to agricultural crops, land degradation from cattle grazing, fragmentation, hunting by local farmers in retaliation for depredation of their chickens, and decline of prey populations.

PHOTO CREDITS T, CR: *Juan Villalba-Macías*, Bioparque M'Bopicuá (Uruguay); CL, B: *Francisco Erize*, Bioparque M'Bopicuá (Uruguay).

Argentinian Pampas Cat
LEOPARDUS COLOCOLA PAJEROS

BL: 65 cm (♂), 54 cm (♀). TL: 23-28 cm. SH: 36 cm. W: 2-3 kg. SL: 9.9 cm (♂), 8.9 cm (♀). SW: 7.5 cm (♂), 7.2 cm (♀). DF: 30. CN: 36. A small and stocky cat, about the size of a Domestic Cat with relatively short legs, long hair, and a shortish, thickly furred tail. Coat is almost uniformly grayish to reddish-brown, paler than other subspecies, usually with no signs of dorsal spots or rings on body and tail, although some individuals show indistinct oblique darker lines or blotches on flanks and darkish tail bands. Dark brown ventral markings on a more or less white background. Some individuals have long hair forming a dorsal mane along the back. Broad face. Face with 2 transverse brown lines that cross each cheek. Underside of the chin is white. Pink rhinarium. Ears are distinctly triangular (in contrast to the rounded ears of all other small felids in South America). Dark brown-black striping on forelegs, paler on hind legs. Feet similar to the background color of the body, with some small, dark spots on the dorsal surfaces.

Young

Leopardus colocola pajeros

OTHER NAMES *French*: Chat des Pampas. *German*: Pampaskatze. *Spanish*: Gato de los pajonales, gato de las pampas, gato pajero. *Russian*: Аргентинская пампасская кошка. *Aymara*: Titi, osqollo.

TAXONOMY Considered as a subspecies of Colocolo (*L. colocola*). Formerly considered as a full species, the Pampas Cat (*L. pajeros*), with three subspecies: *L. p. pajeros*, *L. p. garleppi*, and *L. p. budini*. Includes *crucinus* (S Argentina).

SIMILAR SPECIES Individuals from S Argentina are almost uniformly grayish, usually with no signs of dorsal spots or rings on body and tail, although some individuals show indistinct oblique darker lines on flanks; stripes on front and hind legs are conspicuous and dark brown, as are ventral markings.

REPRODUCTION *Gestation*: 80-85 days. *Young per Birth*: 1-3. *Weaning*: Unknown. *Sexual Maturity*: Unknown. *Life Span*: 16 years in captivity. *Breeding Season*: Unknown. Largely unknown from the wild.

BEHAVIOR *Social Behavior*: Solitary. *Diet*: Mainly rodents, but also lizards and birds; it is an opportunistic predator feeding off the prey it finds as it moves around. *Main Predators*: Domestic dogs, Pumas. Its low population density suggests a very large home range for each individual; ranges in the Andes are likely to be larger given that prey is patchily distributed at lower population densities than in the Cerrado. Similar to some other small Neotropical felids, they deposit feces in latrines that probably have a spacing function.

DISTRIBUTION *Native*: Central, N central, and S Argentina.

HABITAT Grasslands (pampas), dry and mesophytic forests (Chaco and Espinal), shrubland steppes (Monte), and transitional areas, from sea level to 1,240 m.

CONSERVATION STATUS Near Threatened, but Vulnerable on the National Red List of Argentina. CITES: Appendix II. In Argentina, extensive habitat loss/modification due to the expansion of the agricultural frontier, mining, and oil extraction are the major threats. It appears to be declining in central Argentina, mainly due to habitat modification, and is regionally extinct in the pampas grasslands, where it only occurs in the southern and dry portion. In the Argentine Espinal, population numbers are low and distribution is largely limited to grassland habitats that are threatened by human activities. Pampas Cats are similarly rare in the adjacent S part of the Monte ecoregion. It is a naturally rare species in most of Patagonia, where records of its presence are scarce in comparison with those of other felids, such as Geoffroy's Cat. Records are very scarce in the Yungas ecoregion of NW Argentina, where it is limited to the high-altitude grasslands. The Pampas Cat was extensively hunted in Argentina for the fur trade; since 1976-1980, 78,000 skins were exported. Aymara people use skins or stuffed cats during ceremonies for marking their domestic livestock, mainly llamas or alpacas (both the Andean Cat and Pampas Cat are part of these traditions and beliefs, and in general are used indiscriminately).

PHOTO CREDITS TL, CL: *Agustín Esmoris*, Buenos Aires Province (Argentina); Young: *Escuela número 102*, Lihué Calel NP (Argentina); TR, B: *Ricardo Fernández Chaves*, Buenos Aires Province (Argentina).

Peruvian and Bolivian Pampas Cat

LEOPARDUS COLOCOLA GARLEPPI AND BUDINI

BL: 51-75 cm (♂), 46-52 cm (♀). TL: 24-28.5 cm. SH: Unknown. W: Unknown. SL: 9.0 cm (♂), 8.5 cm (♀). SW: 6.9 cm (♂), 6.5 cm (♀). DF: 30. CN: 36. A small and stocky cat, about the size of a Domestic Cat with relatively short legs, long hair, and a shortish, thickly furred tail. A small subspecies, with a strongly defined color pattern. Coat is grayish with large, reddish-brown rosettes with darker borders, arranged in oblique chains along the flanks. Spinal crest and tail rings are same color as flank spots. Stripes on legs and the ventral markings are dark brown to black on a more or less white background. Broad face. Pink rhinarium. Ears are distinctly triangular (in contrast to the rounded ears of all other small felids in South America), base of ears same color as head, otherwise ears are black with a small gray spot. Feet similar to the background color of the body, but with some small, dark spots on the dorsal surfaces. Tail ringed from base to tip.

Leopardus colocola garleppi

Leopardus colocola budini

OTHER NAMES *French*: Chat des Pampas. *German*: Pampaskatze. *Spanish*: Gato del desierto, gato montés, gato peludo, gatillo. *Russian*: Пампасская кошка: перуанская (*garleppi*), боливийская (*budini*). *Aymara*: Titi, osqollo.

TAXONOMY Considered as a subspecies of Colocolo (*L. colocola*). Formerly considered as a subspecies of Pampas Cat (*L. pajeros*), but now is included under *L. colocola*. Includes *thomasi* and *steinbachi*.

SIMILAR SPECIES The Andean Mountain Cat is slightly larger, with a longer tail, no spinal crest, incomplete rings on forelegs, and coat less heavily marked, with blotches arranged in vertical series.

REPRODUCTION *Gestation*: 80-85 days. *Young per Birth*: 1-3. *Weaning*: Unknown. *Sexual Maturity*: Unknown. *Life Span*: 16 years in captivity. *Breeding Season*: Unknown. Largely unknown from the wild.

BEHAVIOR *Social Behavior*: Solitary. *Diet*: Small and medium-sized rodents and small birds; they are also known to eat carrion, scavenging from livestock and other large mammal carcasses, and may kill domestic poultry. There is little information available on the ecology of these subspecies. They are terrestrial and hunt mainly on the ground, though they may climb, at least within lower branches. They are mostly nocturnal in the high Andes, but may be active during all hours of the day. Unlike some of the other small felids they are reputedly aggressive and not responsive to taming. The Pampas Cat populations living in the high Andes and puna ecoregions appear to be able to reach relatively high population densities (0.74-0.78 individuals/km^2) in the most productive habitat patches.

DISTRIBUTION *Native*: NW Argentina, Bolivia, Ecuador, Peru. *Presence uncertain*: Colombia. This subspecies lives on the E slope of the Andes or farther E.

HABITAT Areas of shrub and grass steppes (páramos and marginal areas of the puna), and occasionally penetrate dry forests in the upper part of inner Andean valleys, and some coastal hills, between 400 m in Arequipa and Lima, up to 5,000 m in Ancash. Also found in arid ecosystems, tolerating some degree of disturbance and the presence of other small felid species at low population densities.

CONSERVATION STATUS Near Threatened, Data Deficient in Peru, Vulnerable in Ecuador. CITES: Appendix II. The population appears to be in slight decline in Bolivia and Peru. Across their distribution ranges they face habitat loss, and the presence of feral dogs and livestock. These subspecies are also hunted for their skins, to obtain stuffed cats or body parts for use in religious ceremonies and folk dances, to decrease potential predation on waterfowl, for superstitious reasons, or for sport.

PHOTO CREDITS T: Unknown photographer (Peru); CL: *Dkadra89* (Peru); CR: *Guillaume Matthieu Dupuy* (Peru); B: *Francisco Erize* (Peru).

Andean Mountain Cat
LEOPARDUS JACOBITA

BL: 57-85 cm. TL: 41-48 cm. SH: 36 cm. W: 4-5.5 kg. SL: 9.6 cm. SW: 7.1 cm. DF: 28. CN: 36. A small, stocky cat, with a long luxurious coat, thickset limbs, and a very long banded tail. Coat is thick, ashy-gray in color, marked with large orange-brown spots, arranged in vertical series on the flanks. No spinal crest of long hair. Belly is white or creamy with light brown spots laterally and black spots medially. Head and face are gray, with cheeks and areas around the lips white, and a dark streak from nose to mouth, and a dark streak behind each eye. Three faint mid-dorsal stripes on forehead, and 2 on the neck. Nose and lips black. Dark eyes. Round ears, gray in color, with darker borders. Legs banded with 2 or 3 bars of black. Feet are well furred except for the pads. Tail is long, bushy, and cylindrical, banded with 6 to 9 distinctive thick russet bands that become paired dark brown rings, often with a russet-brown center, toward the tip. Males are slightly larger than females. Females have 2 pairs of nipples. Juveniles have a lighter coloration and more and smaller blotches.

Young

Leopardus jacobita

OTHER NAMES *French*: Chat des Andes. *German*: Bergkatze, Andenkatze. *Spanish*: Chinchay, gato montés andino, gato lince, gato de las peñas, gato chacra. *Russian*: Андская кошка.

TAXONOMY Monotypic, but recent genetic analyses have found four isolated populations that may represent distinct subspecies. Previously classified in its own genus, *Oreailurus*.

SIMILAR SPECIES Colocolo, which is sympatric over most of the Andean Cat's range, is smaller and more heavily marked (markings oriented transversely across the body), and has a much shorter, tapering tail, with fewer and narrower rings, a pink or reddish nose, and a crest of long hairs along the spine.

REPRODUCTION *Gestation*: Unknown, probably 80 days. *Young per Birth*: 1-2. *Weaning*: Unknown. *Sexual Maturity*: Unknown. *Life Span*: Unknown. *Breeding Season*: Between July and November or December, with most births between September and April.

BEHAVIOR *Social Behavior*: Solitary, but may be seen in pairs during mating season or with a kitten. *Diet*: A specialist, preying mostly on medium-sized rodents living in rocky habitats (mountain vizcachas, chinchillas, but also mice, cavies, and European hares); birds (tinamous) are also part of its diet, and it sometimes scavenges from carcasses of dead ungulates; there is little evidence for it taking domestic poultry. *Main Predators*: Pumas, dogs. It is one of the most threatened and least known felid species in the world. Mostly nocturnal with crepuscular activity peaks, although most sightings have been made during daytime. Known resting sites consist of small caves in rocky areas. They hunt on the ground, typically in very uneven, rocky habitat in which they are adept at running and jumping (mountain vizcachas and chinchillas are saltatorial rodents that evade predators by making sudden jumps in unpredictable directions). Its long tail may be an adaptation for maintaining balance while rapidly changing directions when pursuing prey. ♂ home ranges are probably larger than those of ♀, and there could be a certain degree of home-range overlap between sexes, as in other felids. Home ranges are very large, averaging 60 km^2, due to the habitat conditions and low prey abundance. They scent-mark, deposit feces, and spray urine to mark home ranges. Unlike most other cats, they primarily defecate in latrines, using the same areas; these latrines are often in dry places, like caves and small overhangs.

DISTRIBUTION *Native*: Argentina, Bolivia, Chile, Peru.

HABITAT Restricted to rocky and open, semi-arid and arid treeless areas over 3,000 m on the altiplano or the high Andes, and up to 5,100 m. They have also been recently recorded from Patagonian steppe in SW Argentina at elevations of 650-1,800 m, below the treeline, in rocky areas with scrub and steppe vegetation.

CONSERVATION STATUS Endangered. CITES: Appendix I. Critically Endangered in Bolivia. A naturally rare species, occurring at low population densities, with a very restricted distribution and narrow habitat preference. Threatened by human persecution, local elimination of major prey species, and alteration of natural habitats by livestock grazing, mining, fracking, and salt extraction. Its bioclimatic distribution may be affected by climate change. Total population estimated at 2,500 individuals, and is probably decreasing. There are none in captivity.

PHOTO CREDITS T, B: *Juan Reppucci*, Abra Granada (Argentina); Young: *Rodrigo Villalobos* (Chile); CL: *Antonio Núñez Lemos*, Salar de Surire (Chile).

Leopard Cat lineage
LEOPARD CAT, PALLAS'S CAT, AND RELATED SPECIES

RECOGNITION The Leopard Cat lineage consists of six species of small Asian cats, five of the *Prionailurus* genus (Leopard Cat, Sunda Leopard Cat, Fishing Cat, Flat-Headed Cat, and Rusty-spotted Cat), and one of the *Otocolobus* genus (Pallas's Cat). Most species of this group are small felids, about the size of a Domestic Cat. Color is highly variable, usually brownish-gray or reddish-brown, with a white chin, throat, and belly. *Prionailurus* species have small solid dark spots that often coalesce into horizontal stripes on the nape and shoulders, dark stripes on the cheek and forehead, horizontal bars on the inner legs, and a white spot on the back of the ear, as in some big cats. Pallas's Cat may have narrow vertical stripes on the back. All species have thick, medium-sized tails (half the length of the body or less). They have round and small ears, and large eyes, as an adaptation to their nocturnal or crepuscular behavior. Toes are partially webbed in some species as an adaptation to hunt in the water. Claws do not fully retract in the Flat-Headed Cat and Fishing Cat. There is usually little size dimorphism between males and females. Dentition in most species is complete although the second upper premolar is very small. All *Prionailurus* species have the typical felid dental formula (I 3/3, C 1/1, P 3/2, M 1/1 = 30); in the Pallas's Cat the first pair of upper premolars is missing (28). *Prionailuris* species have slit-like pupils, while *Otocolobus* has rounded pupils. Chromosome number is 2n=38 in all species.

PHYLOGENY The Leopard Cat lineage is one of the most recently derived groups. Between 6.7 and 6.2 Ma the Leopard Cat and Domestic Cat lineages probably diverged from Eurasian forebears that either remained in Asia or derived from American migrants that crossed the Bering Strait. This group still occurs within the zoogeographical regions of its original establishment. The Leopard Cat lineage is very poorly known in the fossil record. A few fossils probably pertaining to this lineage have been found in middle Pleistocene sites in Southeast Asia. In addition, fossils tentatively referred to *Otocolobus manul* have been recorded from Kamyk (Poland); these may be more than 1 Ma. Recent molecular evidence indicates that the Indochinese and Sundaic populations of the Leopard Cat experienced a species-level separation of more than one million years, being now considered as two different species: Mainland Leopard Cat (*P. bengalensis*) and Sunda Leopard Cat (*P. javanensis*). The Pallas's Cat belongs to a monotypic lineage that is sister taxa to the Domestic Cat and Leopard Cat lineages, but it is normally classified within this group. Pallas's Cat is estimated to have diverged from a Leopard Cat ancestor about 5.19 Ma ago.

BEHAVIOR Like most felids, they are solitary predators, forming pairs only during the breeding season. They feed on a variety of small prey, mostly small mammals, and they hunt primarily on the ground. The Fishing Cat and the Flat-Headed Cat mainly prey on fish and are very good swimmers. Most species are nocturnal or crepuscular. They are probably territorial, at least in the breeding season, and both males and females maintain a territory by scent-marking.

DISTRIBUTION This group is endemic to Asia. Pallas's Cat has a wide distribution across cold steppes of Central Asia and west into Iran, but is not common across its range and has a fragmented distribution. The poorly known Flat-Headed Cat is endemic to the lowland tropical rainforests of the Sunda region in Southeast Asia. The Rusty-Spotted Cat has a relatively restricted distribution, occurring only in India, Sri Lanka, and Nepal. The Fishing Cat has a very discontinuous distribution in wetland habitats across mainland tropical Asia, and on the islands of Sri Lanka and Java. The Mainland Leopard Cat is the most widely distributed species of the group, found in tropical, subtropical, and temperate Asia. The Sunda Leopard Cat inhabits lowland tropical evergreen forest in the Sundaland islands.

CONSERVATION Nearly every species in this group requires careful monitoring and individual consideration. Little is known about the abundance and distribution of most species, limiting its effective conservation. The Flat-Headed Cat is Endangered with an estimated population of fewer than 3,000 animals, threatened by wetland and lowland forest destruction and degradation. The Fishing Cat is also Endangered and believed to be declining within all range countries at an alarming rate, threatened by freshwater marshlands conversion and degradation. The Rusty-Spotted Cat is Near Threatened; it is not common anywhere and believed to be declining. The Pallas's Cat is Near Threatened, but it is still hunted for its fur in Mongolia and illegally exported to Russia and China, and there is also a demand as exotic pets and for traditional medicines in Mongolia and Russia; its requirement for large areas and its diet and habitat specialization make it very vulnerable to habitat fragmentation and degradation. The Leopard Cat is listed as Least Concern and is widespread in most of its range; however, it is legally harvested for fur and heavily hunted in its temperate range, and targeted for the pet trade; many island populations are small and threatened by rapid development.

Asian Pallas's Cat
Otocolobus manul manul, 136

Tibetan Pallas's Cat
Otocolobus manul nigripectus, 138

Flat-Headed Cat
Prionailurus planiceps, 140

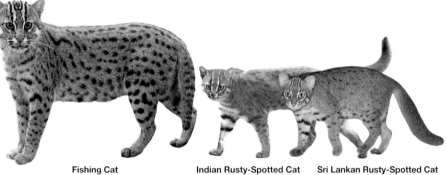

Fishing Cat
Prionailurus viverrinus, 142

Indian Rusty-Spotted Cat
P. rubiginosus rubiginosus, 144

Sri Lankan Rusty-Spotted Cat
P. rubiginosus phillipsi, 146

Sunda Leopard Cat
Prionailurus javanensis, 154

South Asian Leopard Cat
Prionailurus bengalensis bengalensis, 148

Iriomote Cat
Prionailurus bengalensis euptilurus, 152

Amur Leopard Cat
Prionailurus bengalensis euptilurus, 150

Asian Pallas's Cat
OTOCOLOBUS MANUL MANUL

BL: 45-65 cm. TL: 21-35 cm. SH: 30-35 cm. W: 2.3-4.5 kg. SL: 8.2 cm. SW: 6.8 cm. DF: 28. CN: 38. A small-sized cat, slightly larger than a Domestic Cat, with short legs, stocky compact build, thick tail, and long fur, making it appear fairly heavy and massive. Coat is long and dense, ocherous-gray to brownish-gray in color, with white hair tips producing a frosted appearance. Indistinct narrow black transverse stripes across the back, sometimes absent. Chin and belly are white. Winter coat is grayer and less patterned than the summer coat. Erythristic (reddish) forms have been described. Small head, short muzzle, and broad flattened forehead, patterned with small black spots. Cheeks with dark and white stripes. Small round ears, set low and wide apart. Large eyes, set forward, bordered with white. Legs relatively thick and short, with indistinct transverse black bands. Short claws. Tail is thick and furry, gray above and below, black-tipped, with several narrow black rings.

winter coat

summer coat

Young

136

Otocolobus manul manul

OTHER NAMES Manul, Steppe Cat. *French*: Manul, chat de Pallas. *German*: Manul. *Spanish*: Gato manul asiático, gato de Pallas asiático. *Russian*: Центральноазиатский манул. *Afghanistan*: Psk kuhey. *Bashkir*: Yalami. *Bukharian*: Malem. *Chinese*: Tu sun, wulun, manao, yang shihli. *Kazakh*: Sabanshy. *Kyrgyzstan*: Madail. *Mongolian*: Manul mii. *Soyot*: Mana. *Uygur*: Molun. *Uzbek*: Malin, dala mushugi.

TAXONOMY Two subspecies are tentatively recognized: *O. m. manul* (Asian Pallas's Cat, from Gansu, Mongolia, Central Asia and Kazakhstan, S Siberia, Iran, Afghanistan, and Pakistan, includes *ferrugineus*); and *O. m. nigripectus* (Tibetan Pallas's Cat, from Tibet, Kashmir, Nepal, and Bhutan).There have been no recent molecular or morphological studies, and it is possible that this species is monotypic and shows clinal variation in pelage coloration. Includes *ferrugineus* from Iran, an erythristic form, sometimes considered as a different subspecies.

REPRODUCTION *Gestation*: 66-75 days. *Young per Birth*: 2-6. *Weaning*: Unknown. *Sexual Maturity*: 12 months. *Life Span*: 12 years in captivity. *Breeding Season*: Highly seasonal, in December and March, with most births occurring between April and May.

BEHAVIOR *Social Behavior*: Solitary. *Diet*: Small mammals (mainly pikas, but also voles, jerboas, lambs of argali sheep, hares, marmots), insects, birds, reptiles, and carrion. *Main Predators*: Large raptors, wolf, red fox, domestic dog. Crepuscular, but can be active at any time of day. They hunt by ambush and sneaking. They have a strong dependency on marmot burrows and rock cavities as refuges, which are used for shelter and raising young. A very poor runner; when it feels threatened and no shelter is available, it remains perfectly still relying on its camouflage for protection. Both sexes mark their territories with scent of urine and feces. It has very large home ranges, 20-200 km² for ♂ in Mongolia. Home ranges of ♂ generally overlap with those of several ♀ and can also overlap with other ♂ ranges.

DISTRIBUTION *Native*: Afghanistan, Azerbaijan, China, Iran, Kazakhstan, Kyrgyzstan, Mongolia, Pakistan, Russia. *Possibly Extinct*: Armenia. *Presence uncertain*: Tajikistan, Turkmenistan, Uzbekistan. It has a wide but fragmented distribution in the grasslands and montane steppe of Central Asia. There is a strong overlap of its distribution with the distribution of pikas, their preferred prey. This subspecies occurs in Gansu (China), Mongolia, Central Asia (Kyrgyzstan, Turkmenistan, Uzbekistan, Kazakhstan, Tajikistan), S Siberia (Altai, Tuva, Transbaikalia), N Iran, Afghanistan, Baluchistan (Pakistan), and Azerbaijan.

HABITAT Montane grassland steppe and shrub steppe, with rocky cover, ravines, and hill-slopes that provide them hiding cover. Due to predation pressure they avoid open habitats. Rarely found in areas with continuous snow cover. Absent from lowland desert basins or flat plains.

CONSERVATION STATUS Near Threatened. CITES: Appendix II. Estimated total population of 15,000. Its largest population is thought to live in Mongolia. Main threats include habitat degradation and fragmentation, predation by domestic herding dogs, and depletion of their prey base (pikas and rodents) through poisoning and over-hunting. Mongolia is the only range state that permits hunting.

PHOTO CREDITS TL: *Sergey Chichagov*, Riga Zoo (Latvia); TR: *Alexander Meyer*, Cincinnati Zoo (USA); CL: *Otgonbayar Baatargal* (Mongolia); CR: *Guseynov Elchin* (Russia); B: *Eleonora Travostino*.

Tibetan Pallas's Cat
OTOCOLOBUS MANUL NIGRIPECTUS

BL: 50-61 cm. TL: 20-30 cm. SH: 28-30.5 cm. W: 2-5 kg. SL: 8.3 cm. SW: 6.9 cm. DF: 28. CN: 38. A small-sized cat, with short legs, stocky compact build, thick tail, and long fur, making it appear fairly heavy and massive, with more black in the coat than the northern subspecies. Winter coat is dense and long, silvery-gray to brownish-gray, with more black in it, with white hair tips producing a frosted appearance, although there is great variation in color. Indistinct narrow black transverse stripes across the back. Chin is white, sometimes with a distinct gray or black bib. Belly is white. Small head, short muzzle, and broad flattened forehead, spotted thickly with black. Cheeks with dark and white stripes. Small round ears, set low and wide apart. Large eyes, set forward, bordered with white. Legs relatively thick and short, with indistinct transverse black bands. Short claws. Tail is thick and furry, gray above and below, black-tipped, with distinct black stripes. Males are slightly heavier than females.

Otocolobus manul nigripectus

OTHER NAMES Himalayan Manul, Steppe Cat. *French*: Manul, chat de Pallas. *German*: Manul. *Spanish*: Gato manul tibetano, gato de Pallas del Tibet. *Russian*: Тибетский манул. *Chinese*: Tu sun, wulun, manao, yang shihli. *Ladakhi*: Ribilik, trakshan. *Nepali*: Tashi biralo. *Tibetan*: Dromba.

TAXONOMY Considered as a subspecies of Pallas's Cat (*O. manul*). There have been no recent molecular or morphological studies, and it is possible that this species is monotypic and shows clinal variation in pelage coloration.

REPRODUCTION *Gestation*: 66-75 days. *Young per Birth*: 2-6. *Weaning*: Unknown. *Sexual Maturity*: 12 months. *Life Span*: 12 years in captivity. *Breeding Season*: Probably seasonal, in December and March, with most births occurring between April and May. There is no specific information for this subspecies, but it is probably similar to the Asian Pallas's Cat. The young are born in sheltered dens lined with dried vegetation, feathers, and fur.

BEHAVIOR *Social Behavior*: Solitary. *Diet*: Small mammals (mainly pikas, marmots, and hares), but occasionally birds (chukar partridges) and insects. *Main Predators*: Snow Leopard, red fox, Tibetan wolf. Little is known about this subspecies' ecology and behavior. Active in the early morning and evening, but can be active at any time of the day. They prefer empty burrows of marmots and foxes as a den and proximity to pika habitats. They are not fast runners, and hunt primarily by ambush or stalking, using low vegetation and rocky terrain for cover. Well adapted to the extreme cold winter conditions that are typical of its habitat. The hair on its underparts is nearly twice as long as on the top and sides, to keep it warm. The coat color and markings provide excellent camouflage to blend into its surroundings. The low profile of its head is an adaptation to hunting in open country where there is little cover. It makes a hissing snarl when aroused.

DISTRIBUTION *Native*: Bhutan, China, India, Nepal, Pakistan. This subspecies occurs in E Ladakh, Tibet, Kashmir, Nepal (Manang district), and Bhutan (Wangchuck Centennial NP and W part of Jigme Dorji NP). Recent sightings and camera trap records from N Sikkim in India and Bhutan extend the species range to the E of the Himalayas and suggest a wider distribution than previously thought.

HABITAT Alpine grasslands and subalpine scrublands, open rock-strewn mountain steppe, in the vicinity of pika habitat, up to 5,500 m in Nepal. They prefer south-facing mountain slopes. Rare in snowbound areas inhabited by Lynx.

CONSERVATION STATUS Near Threatened. CITES: Appendix II. Major threats include habitat degradation and fragmentation from traditional pastoralism, unregulated tourism, infrastructural developments such as roads and petrochemical industry, and also poaching (including their prey). Climate change is also an emerging threat to the species although the potential impacts remain uncertain. The population size and trend of this subspecies remain unknown, but the global population trend is decreasing.

PHOTO CREDITS T: *Himimomi*, Qinghai-Tibet Plateau Wildlife Zoo, Xining (China); C, B: *Staffan Widstrand*, Tibetan Plateau, Qinghai (China).

Flat-Headed Cat
PRIONAILURUS PLANICEPS

BL: 41-61 cm (♂), 44-52 cm (♀). TL: 13-20 cm. SH: 23 cm. W: 1.5-2.7 kg (♂), 1.5-1.9 kg (♀). DF: 30. CN: 38. A small-sized cat, with a distinctly elongated, flattened head and small, rounded ears, superficially resembling a civet. Coat is thick, short, and soft, reddish-brown in color on top of the head, dark brown on the body, mottled white on the belly. Hairs tipped with white, giving a silvery appearance. Face lighter in color, with two prominent whitish streaks on either side of the nose. Chin and muzzle white. Narrow head and flattened forehead. Long, sloping muzzle, with relatively long, sharp, backward-facing teeth. Large, close-set eyes. Ears are small and rounded and set well down on the sides of the head. Inner portions of the legs with black spots and horizontal bands. Feet long and narrow, toes partially webbed, pads long and narrow. Claws are visible, not fully retracting into their shortened sheaths. Tail is short and heavily furred, light in color on the underside. Females with 4 sets of nipples.

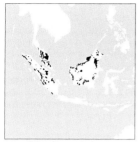

Prionailurus planiceps

OTHER NAMES *French*: Chat à tête plate. *German*: Flachkopfkatze. *Spanish*: Gato cabeciancho. *Russian*: Суматранская кошка. *Indonesian*: Kucing hutan, kucing dampak. *Malay*: Kucing hutan. *Burmese*: Gauung bya kyaung. *Thai*: Maew pa hua baen.

TAXONOMY Monotypic, but no in-depth phylogenetic analysis has been conducted. It was previously placed in the genus *Felis*.

SIMILAR SPECIES Domestic Cats are usually larger, and may also have a short, stubby tail, but their coat is spotted, while the coat of the Flat-Headed Cat is plain gray-brown and has prominent white-and-brown facial markings. The Leopard Cat (*P. bengalensis*) is similarly sized, but has longer legs, ears, and tail, a smaller head and shorter muzzle, and a spotted tawny coat.

REPRODUCTION *Gestation*: Probably 56 days. *Young per Birth*: 1-2. *Weaning*: Unknown. *Sexual Maturity*: Unknown. *Life Span*: 14 years in captivity. *Breeding Season*: Unknown. Very little information is available on the reproduction of this species. One young was born in January.

BEHAVIOR *Social Behavior*: Probably solitary. *Diet*: Preys primarily on fish, frogs, and crustaceans, but also birds, small rodents, and fruits; it has been reported to prey on domestic poultry. Very little information is available on its behavior, and most observations come from the few individuals kept in captivity, as it is extremely difficult to observe in the wild. Crepuscular. Terrestrial and semi-aquatic. Its particular dental structure (anterior upper premolars are larger and sharper) helps to grab and hold the fish that it hunts; it takes live fish with its head fully submerged and usually carries its prey at least 2 m away before consuming it, suggesting a feeding strategy to avoid letting aquatic prey escape back into water. It has been observed to wash objects as raccoons do. Most sightings have been of them walking on riverbanks. It a good swimmer that happily enters water, and it has been observed swimming across rivers.

DISTRIBUTION *Native*: Brunei, Indonesia (Sumatra, Borneo), Malaysia (Sarawak, Sabah, Peninsular Malaysia). *Possibly Extinct*: Thailand. Its distribution is thought to be very patchy and to be highly localized around water bodies.

HABITAT Strongly associated with wetlands, swampy areas, lakes, streams, and riverine forest. It also occurs in peat-swamp forest and secondary forest, at elevations mainly below 100 m and close to larger water sources.

CONSERVATION STATUS Endangered. CITES: Appendix I. It is generally seldom seen and is believed to be rare, with an estimated population of only 2,500 animals, but the status of its population is currently unknown. Hunting and trade is prohibited in Indonesia, Malaysia, and Thailand. It is currently not protected in Brunei. Main threats include habitat loss and degradation, especially through the expansion of oil palm plantations, contamination of its prey through water pollution associated with agricultural run-off and logging activities, and snaring and poisoning. Conservation of land near rivers and peat-swamp forests is of particular importance for long-term survival of this species.

PHOTO CREDITS T: *Ricky Reino*, Khao Kheow (Thailand); *CL, CR*: *Alexander Sliwa*, Khao Kheow (Thailand); B: *Bjorn Olesen*, Kinabatangan River, Borneo (Indonesia)

Fishing Cat
PRIONAILURUS VIVERRINUS

BL: 65-115 cm (♂), 57-74 cm (♀). TL: 24-40 cm. SH: 36 cm. W: 8.5-16 kg (♂), 5.1-7 kg (♀). SL: 13.3 cm (♂), 11.6 cm (♀). SW: 9.3 cm (♂), 7.7 cm (♀). DF: 30. CN: 38. A medium-sized cat, with a stocky body, short legs, and muscular tail. Coat is short and coarse, brownish-gray to olive-gray in color. Head and body conspicuously marked with nearly parallel lines of black, broken, elongated spots on the back and sides; spots vary in shape from rounded to elongate. Albinism has been reported from Bangladesh. Belly, mouth, and muzzle are white. Head is relatively big and broad, with short and small ears, black-backed with a white central spot. Pale cheeks with two darker stripes. Short legs, with 2 stripes on the inside of the forearm. Hind feet are partially webbed. Claws with incomplete sheaths so that they are not completely enveloped when retracted. Short, thick, muscular tail, banded with black. Males are larger than females.

Young

Prionailurus viverrinus viverrinus

Prionailurus viverrinus rhizophoreus

OTHER NAMES *French*: Chat pêcheur, chat viverrin. *German*: Fischkatze. *Spanish*: Gato pescador. *Russian*: Кошка-рыболов: материковая, яванская. *Assamese*: Mesheka. *Bengali*: Meccho biral. *Burmese*: Kyaung ta nga. *Hindi*: Khupya bagh. *Indonesian*: Kucing bakau. *Kannada*: Minugara bekku. *Lao*: Sua hay. *Punjabi*: Mach billi. *Tamil*: Koddi pulli. *Thai*: Sua pla. *Sinhalese*: Kola diviya, handun diviya.

TAXONOMY Two subspecies are recognized: *P. v. viverrinus* (India, Sri Lanka, Pakistan, Bangladesh, Indochina, Nepal, and possibly Bhutan); and *P. v. rhizophoreus* (Java, with a shorter skull, but no pelage coloration or marking differences; no confirmed recent records). Further research on its geographic variation is needed to clarify its taxonomy.

SIMILAR SPECIES The Leopard Cat is smaller and more gracile, has a longer tail, and completely sheathed claws; cubs from both species may be indistinguishable.

REPRODUCTION *Gestation*: 63-70 days. *Young per Birth*: 1-3. *Weaning*: 6 months. *Sexual Maturity*: 15 months (♀). *Life Span*: Up to 17 years in captivity. *Breeding Season*: January to February in NE India, with births taking place from March to May, but there is little evidence for seasonal breeding; mating is also observed in June. It dens in tree trunks and ground near water. Cubs play in the water and take solid food at 2 months. By 10 months, they become independent.

BEHAVIOR *Social Behavior*: Solitary. *Diet*: Mainly fish, but also waterfowl, frogs, rodents, snakes, snails, crustaceans, and mollusks; it may sometimes prey on small civet, wild pig, young deer, and poultry, and occasionally takes carrion. Very little is known about the ecology of this species. It is nocturnal, spending most of the time in dense cover. It dives into water to catch its prey, but despite its fishing activity, it does not show marked morphological adaptations for capturing or eating fish (its dentition is robust and typical of a more generalized felid diet, but has enlarged premolars to hold on to slippery fish and a narrow skull with a relatively long muzzle for diving into water and grabbing prey). It is also a skillful hunter of small prey on land. It travels along rivers and changes its hunting site about every 15 minutes. Home ranges of ♂ are 4 to 22 km², enclosing several ♀ home ranges. Both sexes scent-mark the territory using urine marking and rubbing.

DISTRIBUTION *Native*: Bangladesh, Cambodia, India, Myanmar, Nepal, Pakistan, Sri Lanka, Thailand. *Presence uncertain*: Bhutan, Indonesia (Java), Vietnam. A relatively wide but extremely fragmented distribution across S and SE Asia, unclear throughout its global range. It is thought to be recently extinct in many areas of former occurrence.

HABITAT Wetlands, marshes, tidal creeks, mangroves, oxbow lakes, reed beds, tidal creeks, dense jungle, and scrub but dependent on water, usually below 150 m (up to 1,800 m in Sri Lanka and the Himalayas). It may also be seen around villages in wetland areas where habitat destruction has not been significant. They do not use rice paddies and other irrigated forms of cultivation.

CONSERVATION STATUS Vulnerable; the isolated Javan population is probably Critically Endangered. CITES: Appendix II. Populations are declining at an alarming rate, particularly in SE Asia. India and Sri Lanka are the strongholds of this species. Main threats include habitat destruction, poaching, and persecution due to perceived conflict.

PHOTO CREDITS T: *Sergey Chichagov*, Tallinn Zoo (Estonia); Young: *Balasz Buzas*, Rare Species Conservation Centre (UK); CR: *Gemma Simpson* (UK); B: *Alexander Sliwa*, Port Lympne (UK).

Indian Rusty-Spotted Cat
PRIONAILURUS RUBIGINOSUS RUBIGINOSUS

BL: 35-48 cm. TL: 15-30 cm. SH: 24 cm. W: 1.5-1.6 kg (♂), 1.1-1.5 kg (♀). SL: 7 cm. SW: 5.1 (♂), 4.8 cm (♀). DF: 30. CN: 38. The smallest species of cat. Coat is short and soft, fawn-gray to rufous-brown in color, darker and drabber on back, with black spots and stripes on back and head, and brownish-black to brown spots on flanks, sometimes faint. Two color morphs: typical pale brown or rusty spots, and dark brown to blackish spots. Lips, chin, and undersides are white, but may be marked with spots. Legs and chest with horizontal bars. Round head, with relatively large eyes ringed with white. Cheeks with two dark streaks. Forehead with 4 dark stripes extending from above the eyes backward over the head to the neck. Small, round ears. Limbs paler than flanks. Tail is same color as the body, faintly ringed with rusty bands.

brown form

gray form

144

Prionailurus rubiginosus rubiginosus

OTHER NAMES Mainland Rusty-Spotted Cat. *French*: Chat rougeâtre, chat rubigineux, chat-léopard de l'Inde. *German*: Rostkatze. *Spanish*: Gato rubiginoso de India, gato rojizo de India. *Russian*: Индийская ржавая кошка (пятнисто-рыжая кошка). *Gujarati*: Bitari billi. *Kannada*: Kaadu bekku. *Malayalam*: Thurumban poocha. *Tamil*: Namali pelli. *Telugu*: Chiruta pilli.

TAXONOMY Three subspecies are recognized: *P. r. rubiginosus* (India and Nepal); *P. r. phillipsi* (wet forest zone of Sri Lanka); and *P. r. koladivius* (lowland dry zone of Sri Lanka). There has been no phylogeographical study of this species.

SIMILAR SPECIES Sympatric with the Leopard Cat, but is smaller and not as boldly marked. It may be easily mistaken for a very small Domestic Cat.

REPRODUCTION *Gestation*: 65-71 days. *Young per Birth*: 1-3. *Weaning*: 40 days. *Sexual Maturity*: 12 months. *Life Span*: Up to 18 years in captivity. *Breeding Season*: Aseasonal.

BEHAVIOR *Social Behavior*: Probably solitary. *Diet*: Probably small mammals, such as rodents, and birds; it also takes insects, lizards, and frogs opportunistically, and occasionally poultry. *Main Predators*: Jackal, foxes, other cat species, dogs. There is little information available on the behavior and ecology of this species. Probably nocturnal, lying during the day in a hollow log, tree, or thicket in small woods of heavy timber, or in thick scrub-jungles. It is an excellent climber, often seen in trees, but probably hunts mainly on the ground. When threatened, it flees into the trees or takes shelter in gaps of big boulders or stones. It also seems to be cave dwelling in some parts of its range. Vocalizations are similar to those of a Domestic Cat.

DISTRIBUTION *Native*: India, Nepal. *Presence uncertain*: Pakistan. It has been recorded from many Indian states, except NE, confirming its widespread distribution across India (Uttar Pradesh, Tamil Nadu, Rajasthan, Uttaranchal, Andhra Pradesh, Gujarat, Jammu-Kashmir, Karnataka, Kerala, Madhya Pradesh, Maharashtra, Orissa).

HABITAT It seems to have a broad habitat tolerance: moist and dry forests, tropical thorn forests, scrub forests, grasslands, rocky areas, and arid coastal belts. It prefers rocky areas and dense vegetation. It may also occur in agricultural and settled areas, and near villages. Very tolerant of human habitation, there are multiple records of it giving birth to kittens on rooftops. Absent from evergreen forests and tropical montane rainforest.

CONSERVATION STATUS Near Threatened. CITES: Appendix I, Appendix II in Nepal. Its population densities and dynamics are poorly known, but it is regarded as rare. Most of the distributional range lies outside the protected area network and in the deciduous forests of central India, which are severely disturbed. Main threats include habitat loss and deforestation. A declining prey base due to overhunting may also negatively affect this species. Hunting is prohibited in India and Nepal.

PHOTO CREDITS T: *Vickey Chauhan*, Balaram-Ambaji Wildlife Sanctuary, Gujarat (India); C: *Nayan Khanolkar*, Sanjay Gandhi NP (India); B: *Atul Dhamankar*, Tadoba Andhari Tiger Reserve (India).

Sri Lankan Rusty-Spotted Cat

PRIONAILURUS RUBIGINOSUS PHILLIPSI AND KOLADIVIUS

BL: 39-48 cm (♂), 38-41.6 cm (♀). TL: 19-25 cm. SH: 24 cm. W: 1.6 kg (♂), 1.25 kg (♀). SL: 7.1 cm (♂), 6.6 cm (♀). SW: 5.2 (♂), 4.8 cm (♀). DF: 30. CN: 38. Darker, richer, and less gray than the Indian subspecies. Coat is short and soft, fawn-gray to rufous-brown in color with rusty red-brown spots arranged in neat lines on its back, head, and flanks. There appear to be two color morphs: typical pale brown or rusty spots, and dark brown to blackish spots. Lips, chin, and undersides are white, but may be marked with spots. Legs and chest with horizontal bars. Round head, with relatively large eyes ringed with white. Cheeks with 2 dark streaks. Forehead with 4 dark stripes extending from above the eyes backward over the head to the neck. Small, round ears. Tail is same color as the body.

ssp. *phillipsi*

Young

ssp. *koladivius*

Prionailurus rubiginosus phillipsi

Prionailurus rubiginosus koladivius

OTHER NAMES Forest Rusty-Spotted Cat (ssp. *phillipsi*), Lowland Rusty-Spotted Cat (ssp. *koladivius*). *French*: Chat rougeâtre, chat rubigineux, chat-léopard de l'Inde. *German*: Rostkatze. *Spanish*: Gato rubiginoso de Sri Lanka, gato rojizo. *Russian*: Цейлонская ржавая (пятнисто-рыжая) кошка: западная (*phillipsi*), восточная (*koladivius*). *Sinhalese*: Handun diviya, kola diviya.

TAXONOMY Considered as a subspecies of Rusty-Spotted Cat (*P. rubiginosus*). Two distinct populations may exist in Sri Lanka: one in the lowland dry zone (*koladivius*) and the other in the wet zone (*phillipsi*), but variation within subspecies is unclear. *P. r. phillipsi* is usually richer, darker, and less gray, with flank spots brownish to rusty brown, while *P. r. koladivius* has a darker head, blue-gray, dorsal spots and stripes blackish, and flank spots dark brown. There appear to be two color morphs: typical pale brown or rusty spots, and dark brown to blackish spots, which is said to inhabit the lowland dry zone.

REPRODUCTION *Gestation*: 65-71 days. *Young per Birth*: 1 3. *Weaning*: 40 days. *Sexual Maturity*: 12 months. *Life Span*: Up to 18 years in captivity. *Breeding Season*: Aseasonal. They give birth in hollow trees, under rock cliffs, or in small jungle caves.

BEHAVIOR *Social Behavior*: Solitary. *Diet*: Probably small mammals, such as rodents, and birds; it also takes insects, lizards, and frogs opportunistically, and occasionally poultry. *Main Predators*: Jackal, foxes, other cat species, dogs. There is little information available on the behavior and ecology of this species. Mostly nocturnal, lying during the day in a hollow log, tree, or thicket in small woods of heavy timber, or in thick scrub-jungles. More commonly sighted in the wet season, close to or on roads. Very active, with a high basal metabolic rate. It climbs trees to hunt or rest, but most sightings are of cats patrolling on the ground. When threatened, it flees into the trees or takes shelter in gaps of big boulders or stones. It also seems to be cave dwelling in some parts of its range. Vocalizations are similar to those of a Domestic Cat. Nothing is known about home ranges or densities.

DISTRIBUTION *Native*: Sri Lanka. It has been described as widespread but its exact distribution is not yet clear. There are recent records from the Central Highlands of Sri Lanka in small, mostly isolated forest patches interspersed with tea estates but it is not known if the species occurs in or uses the tea plantation areas.

HABITAT It has been recorded from habitats throughout the island, including thorn scrub forests in the dry zone as well as from montane and lowland rainforests. In both types of forest it is often encountered along forest trails. It needs forest cover, and may live quite close to people in villages adjoining forest, but is never found where good forests are not present.

CONSERVATION STATUS Endangered. CITES: Appendix I, Appendix II in Sri Lanka. Its population densities and dynamics are poorly known, but it is regarded as rare. Main threats include habitat loss and deforestation. A declining prey base due to overhunting may also negatively affect this species. Hunting is prohibited in Sri Lanka.

PHOTO CREDITS T: *Milan Korínek*, Zoo Ostrava (Czech Republic); CR (*koladivius*): *Debankur Biswas*, Wilpattu NP (Sri Lanka); Young: *Balazs Buzas,* Rare Species Conservation Centre (UK); CL: *Michal Sloviak*, Bojnice Zoo (Slovakia); B: *Roland Wirth*, Ostrava Zoo (Czech Republic).

South Asian Leopard Cat
PRIONAILURUS BENGALENSIS BENGALENSIS

BL: 45-66 cm (♂), 36-65 cm (♀). TL: 17-26 cm. SH: 30-35 cm. W: 0.5-3.8 kg. SL: 8.4 cm (♂), 8.2 cm (♀). SW: 6.3 cm (♂), 6.0 cm (♀). DF: 30. CN: 38. A small-sized cat, with a slender body and long legs, superficially resembling a Leopard. Coat is short and thin, rich yellow to tawny-brown, ginger-brown, or gray in color, with solid black to dark brown spots or patches throughout the body, which merge into two broad streaks at the shoulders. Belly, mouth, and muzzle are white, well-spotted. Small round head, with 2 black streaks between the eyes and ears, and 2 white ones between the nose and eyes. Winter coat is thicker, with darker spots than the summer coat. There is much variation in color and spotting. Northern forms are paler, yellowish-gray in color, with a more luxuriant coat and bushy tail in winter. Complete melanism has not been reported. Round ears, black-backed with a white central spot. Toes incompletely webbed. Tail is long and ringed, black-tipped. Females slightly smaller than males.

brown form

gray form

Young

Prionailurus bengalensis bengalensis

OTHER NAMES *French*: Chat-léopard du Bengale. *German*: Bengalkatze. *Spanish*: Gato leopardo de Bengala. *Russian*: Бенгальская кошка. *Bengali*: Bon biral. *Chinese*: Bao mao, Qian mao. *Hindi*: Cheeta billi. *Kannada*: Huli bekku. *Kashmiri*: Chitin bror. *Marathi*: Waghati. *Mizo*: Keipiri. *Thai*: Maeo Dao.

TAXONOMY Two subspecies of Leopard Cat (*P. bengalensis*) are tentatively recognized: *P. b. bengalensis* (South Asian Leopard Cat, S Asia from Pakistan to China and including probably the Malay Peninsula); and *P. b. euptilurus* (Amur Leopard Cat, from Manchuria, Russian Far East, Taiwan, Iriomote and Tsushima Islands). Island Leopard Cats (Sunda Leopard Cat, *P. javanensis*) are now considered a distinct species. This species includes *horsfieldii*, *alleni*, *chinensis*, and *trevelyani*.

SIMILAR SPECIES The Fishing Cat is considerably larger and more heavily built, but may be confused with dark forms of Leopard Cat, and young cubs of both species can be indistinguishable. The Asiatic Golden Cat is much larger with a long, more tapering tail. The Domestic Cat is similar in size, but has shorter legs and a stockier body.

REPRODUCTION *Gestation*: 60-70 days. *Young per Birth*: 2-3. *Weaning*: Unknown. *Sexual Maturity*: 8-12 months. *Life Span*: Up to 17 years in captivity. *Breeding Season*: No specific breeding time is reported. In captivity, the ♂ may help in the rearing of young.

BEHAVIOR *Social Behavior*: Solitary, but they may be found in pairs. *Diet*: Small mammals, lizards, amphibians, birds, and insects. Active both day and night, probably depending on prey availability and the presence of larger carnivores or humans. Very active hunter that forages mainly on the ground and in low vegetation. It is an excellent climber and a good swimmer. Home ranges for ♂ average 3.5 km² in Thailand. ♂ ranges generally overlap one or more, smaller ♀ ranges. They urine-mark in typical felid fashion, and both sexes exhibit low to medium levels of intrasexual territoriality with little intersexual territoriality.

DISTRIBUTION *Native*: Afghanistan, Bangladesh, Bhutan, Cambodia, China, Hong Kong, India, Laos, Malaysia, Myanmar, Nepal, Pakistan, Singapore, Thailand, Vietnam. It is the most widespread of all small Asian felids.

HABITAT A wide variety of habitats with cover, from lowland tropical rainforest to dry broadleaf and coniferous forest in the Himalayan foothills as high as 3,254 m. They inhabit all kinds of woodland, scrub habitat, shrublands, marshes, wetlands, and mangroves. They usually avoid open grasslands, steppes, and rocky areas lacking vegetation. They tolerate human-modified habitats with cover including logged forest, farmlands such as sugarcane fields, and plantations of oil palm, coffee, rubber trees, and tea.

CONSERVATION STATUS Least Concern, Vulnerable in China. CITES: Appendix II, Appendix I in Bangladesh, India, and Thailand. China suspended its international trade in 1993, though they are still legally hunted outside protected areas and skins are common in Chinese fur warehouses. Hunting is illegal in subtropical and tropical Asia, but it is widely killed for fur and meat, and in retaliation for poultry predation.

PHOTO CREDITS TR: *Zaharil Dzulkafly*, Peninsular Malaysia (Malaysia); TL: *Hendrix* (China); Young: *Michal Sloviak*, Tierpark Berlin (Germany); B, CL: *Alexander Sliwa*, Saigon (Vietnam).

Amur Leopard Cat
PRIONAILURUS BENGALENSIS EUPTILURUS

BL: 60-85 cm (♂), 49-77 cm (♀). TL: 23-44 cm. SH: 31-36 cm. W: 3.1-7.1 kg (♂), 3.2-4.5 kg (♀). SL: 10 cm (♂), 9.1 cm (♀). SW: 7.2 cm (♂), 6.2 cm (♀). DF: 30. CN: 38. A small to medium-sized cat, with a slender body and long legs. The largest subspecies of Leopard Cat, more faintly spotted that the South Asian Leopard Cat. Coat is long and dense in winter, light grayish pale yellow to dull grayish-brown with a slight rusty or reddish hue, with reddish-brown elongated spots on flanks, darker and browner on hindquarters and back. There is much variation in terms of color and spotting. Summer pelage is darker, russet-brown to gray-brown in color. Chin, throat, underside of neck, belly, and inner sides of legs dirty white. Small, round head, with 2 light brown streaks between the eyes and ears, and 2 white ones between the nose and eyes. Round ears, dark brown on the back, with a white central spot. Tail is thick and bushy, with incomplete rings.

Young

Prionailurus bengalensis euptilurus

OTHER NAMES Siberian Leopard Cat, Tsushima Leopard Cat. *French*: Chat-léopard du Amur. *German*: Amurkatze. *Spanish*: Gato leopardo de Amur. *Russian*: Амурский или дальневосточный лесной кот. *Chinese*: Bao mao, Qian mao. *Japanese*: Yameneko.

TAXONOMY Considered as a subspecies of Leopard Cat (*P. bengalensis*). Includes *iriomotensis* (Iriomote Cat, from Iriomote Island in Japan), previously considered as a distinct species, and the Tsushima Cat (from Tsushima Island).

SIMILAR SPECIES Domestic Cats are slightly smaller, with shorter legs and a relatively longer tail.

REPRODUCTION *Gestation*: 60-70 days. *Young per Birth*: 1-3. *Weaning*: Unknown. *Sexual Maturity*: 8-12 months. *Life Span*: 15 years in captivity. *Breeding Season*: Apparently seasonal, with births restricted to late February-May. In Tsushima Island they breed from winter to early spring. Dens are set up in crevices among rocks and in tree hollows.

BEHAVIOR *Social Behavior*: Solitary, in pairs during the breeding season. *Diet*: Mainly murids and other small mammals (mice, voles, chipmunks, hares, squirrels), but also birds (pheasant, hazel grouse), insects, reptiles, amphibians, and plants; it may occasionally prey on domestic fowl; in Russia, it is reported to attack neonate ungulates including roe deer, sika, and long-tailed goral when unguarded by the mother; they readily scavenge. *Main Predators*: Leopards, domestic dogs, wild boar (young). Predominantly nocturnal, but it may occasionally be active during the daytime. It is a skillful climber of trees, but it hunts on the ground. It uses high ridges in mountainous areas during both day and night for catching prey. It buries unconsumed prey. Home ranges of ♂ are 0.8-4.8 km² in Iriomote Island, and 2.2-10 km² in Tsushima Island. ♂ have larger home range than ♀. ♂ tend to expand their home ranges during the mating season, while ♀ home range sizes shrink during the period when they nurse their kittens. Home ranges of same-sex adults do not overlap; ♂ and ♀ ranges may overlap.

DISTRIBUTION *Native*: China (Manchuria, the NE part of China), Japan (Tsushima and Iriomote Islands), North Korea, E Russia, South Korea, Taiwan.

HABITAT Temperate deciduous and coniferous forests, open forest with a dense cover of shrubby plants, and grasslands. They avoid large dense forests, They inhabit vegetated valleys in cold, temperate forest with winter snowfall in the N range but they are limited to areas with shallow snow. They are sensitive to human presence or disturbance, but may occasionally come into villages.

CONSERVATION STATUS Least Concern, Endangered in Korea and Taiwan (fewer than 1,000 individuals), Critically Endangered in Japan (83-115 in Tsushima, 100 in Iriomote). CITES: Appendix II. It is legally harvested for fur in its temperate range. Populations on Tsushima and Iriomote Islands are declining. Main threats include habitat loss and fragmentation, traffic accidents, diseases from Domestic Cats, and attacks by domestic dogs.

PHOTO CREDITS TL: *Sergey Chichagov*, Tallinn Zoo (Estonia); TR (Iriomote): *Nature Production*, Okinawa Zoo (Japan); CL: *G. Lacz*, Tsushima (Japan); CR: *Roland Wirth*, Chemnitz Zoo (Germany); B: *Tomasz Doron*, Olomouc Zoo (Czech Republic).

Iriomote Cat
PRIONAILURUS BENGALENSIS EUPTILURUS

BL: 50-60 cm (♂), 50-55 cm (♀). TL: 23-24 cm. SH: 20 cm. W: 3.5-5 kg (♂), 3-3.5 kg (♀). SL: 10 cm (♂), 9.1 cm (♀). SW: 7.2 cm (♂), 6.2 cm (♀). DF: 28. CN: 38. A small to medium-sized cat, with a shorter tail, longer body, shorter legs, and darker than the Mainland Leopard Cat. Coat is mostly dark gray and light brown, with dark brown spots on the sides of the body, and lighter hair on the belly and insides of the limbs. Some individuals are blackish-gray with indistinct markings except on the face and underparts. Small, round head, with 2 dark brown spots on the cheek, and 5-7 stripes spanning from the forehead to the back of the head not reaching the shoulder. Hair along the jaw is white. Eyes are light amber. Nose is large and flat, reddish-brown in color. Round ears, with black hair along the edge, dark brown on the back, with an indistinct white central spot (not present in young cats). Thick neck. There are 3-4 bands of irregular stripes on the chest. Short, thick limbs. Tail is dark brown, thick and bushy, with dark spots on the back side and a dark tip.

Prionailurus bengalensis euptilurus
(Iriomote form)

OTHER NAMES *French*: Chat d'Iriomote. *German*: Iriomote-Katze. *Spanish*: Gato de Iriomote. *Russian*: Ириомотейская кошка. *Japanese*: Iriomote-yamaneko. *Yaeyama*: Yamamayaa, meepisukaryaa.

TAXONOMY Previously recognized as a distinct species or subspecies (*P. bengalensis iriomotensis*). Based on molecular and morphological studies it is now considered as a Leopard Cat included in populations of Far East (*P. b. euptilurus*). Pelage coloration similar to that of Leopard Cats from N China. This form may have been introduced by humans, although estimated divergence times vary from 100,000 to 200,000 years ago, and more research is required to determine its distinctiveness. It was discovered in 1965.

SIMILAR SPECIES Domestic Cats are slightly smaller, with shorter legs and a relatively longer tail.

REPRODUCTION *Gestation*: 60-70 days. *Young per Birth*: 1-2. *Weaning*: 2-3 months. *Sexual Maturity*: 10-12 months. *Life Span*: 13 years. *Breeding Season*: February to May, but may be year-round; kittens are born from April to July and become independent from the mother between August and December.

BEHAVIOR *Social Behavior*: Solitary, in pairs during the breeding season. *Diet*: Opportunistic predators, with a non-selective varied diet representing prey availability with seasonal variations; birds, reptiles, amphibians, crustaceans, and insects, besides mammals; skinks constitute one of the dominant prey items during spring and summer. *Main Predators*: None. On the island, there are no autochthonous terrestrial small mammals such as rodents, which are generally the principal prey of wild felids. Thus, it is likely that there are unique characteristics of the ecology of the cat as the top predator in the ecosystem. Nocturnal and crepuscular, sleeping in tree hollows or in caves during the daytime. They hunt mainly on the ground, but occasionally prey on arboreal species, and swim well. Territorial. Home range size is 1.3-9.6 km^2 for ♂ and 1.2-5 km^2 for ♀. ♀ have stable home ranges. ♂ maintain relatively exclusive home ranges among their own sex, but overlap with those of one or two ♀. Some ♂ may roam without fixed ranges as transients. They mark their territory by urinating and defecating on rocks, tree stumps, and bushes.

DISTRIBUTION *Native*: Japan. It occurs only on the small Iriomote Island (284 km^2) of the Ryukyu Archipelago in S Japan.

HABITAT Low mountains with subtropical evergreen forest, including extensive belts of mangrove along the waterways. It also occurs in lower elevations, a mosaic of wetland, streams, and small hills, which is also where the human settlements are.

CONSERVATION STATUS Critically Endangered, Endangered in Japan. CITES: Appendix II. Population estimated at around 100 individuals in 2008. It is declining in the lower coastal area due to the accelerated rates of lowland habitat loss and increase of traffic accidents. Other threats include predation by dogs, competition with and infection from Domestic Cats, and human disturbance. It is protected.

PHOTO CREDITS T, CL, CR: *Iriomote Wildlife Conservation Center*, Iriomote Island (Japan); B: *Nature Production*, Okinawa Zoo (Japan).

Sunda Leopard Cat

PRIONAILURUS JAVANENSIS JAVANENSIS AND SUMATRANUS

BL: 39-50 cm. TL: 22 cm. SH: 30-35 cm. W: 0.5-3.8 kg. SL: 8.0 cm (♂), 7.7 cm (♀). SW: 5.8 cm (♂), 5.6 cm (♀). DF: 30. CN: 38. A small-sized cat, with a slender body and long legs, superficially resembling a Leopard, smaller than the Mainland Leopard Cat. Coat is short and thin, drab ginger-brown to dark brownish-gray in color, darker on midline of back than on flanks, with small round dark brown to black spots on flanks, and 4 dark longitudinal stripes on nape and neck. Underparts creamy-white, well-spotted. Small round head, marked with 2 prominent dark stripes and a short and narrow white muzzle. Round ears, black on the back, with central white spots. Long legs, with well-defined webs between toes. Tail short, faintly marked with spots. Females similar to or slightly smaller than males.

Young

Palawan form

154

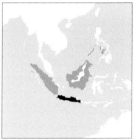

Prionailurus javanensis javanensis

Prionailurus javanensis sumatranus

OTHER NAMES Visayan Leopard Cat, Palawan Leopard Cat. *French*: Chat-léopard de la Sonde. *German*: Sundakatze. *Spanish*: Gato de las Islas de la Sonda. *Russian*: Зондская леопардовая кошка: яванская, индонезийская. *Indonesian*: Kucing batu, kucing congkok.

TAXONOMY Formerly considered as subspecies of Leopard Cat (*P. bengalensis*), now elevated to species. Two subspecies are provisionally recognized: *P. j. javanensis* (Java, ground color of pelage is brownish-gray); and *P. j. sumatranus* (Sumatra, Borneo, and Palawan, Negros, Cebu and Panay, the Philippines; pelage ground coloration variable, ranging from ferruginous to tawny, buffy-fawn, and gray-fawn; includes *borneoensis*, *heaneyi*, and *rabori*). Since Leopard Cats in Palawan and Negros show low genetic differentiation, it is possible that humans introduced this species from Palawan to Negros and adjacent islands.

SIMILAR SPECIES Domestic Cats are similar in size, but with shorter legs and a stockier body. Mainland Leopard Cats are larger in size, with longer tails, and have larger blotches filled with a lighter coloration, while Sunda Leopard Cats have small solid spots. There are some morphological variations amongst the different island populations.

REPRODUCTION *Gestation*: 56-70 days. *Young per Birth*: 1-3. *Sexual Maturity*: 10-18 months. *Breeding Season*: Probably aseasonal. Cubs open their eyes at 10 days, and start to eat solid food at 23 days.

BEHAVIOR *Social Behavior*: Solitary. *Diet*: Murids (rats) constitute the majority of the prey base, but also prey on other small mammals (squirrels, treeshrew), birds, lizards, snakes, frogs, large invertebrates, and occasionally poultry. *Main Predators*: Reticulated python, large raptors, owls, Clouded Leopard, other large cats. They prefer to hunt in oil palm plantations despite smaller number of rats because the habitat is more open with fewer places for the rats to hide. Nocturnal and crepuscular. Usually terrestrial, but highly agile in trees, where it may sleep during the day, but does not usually hunt in trees like the Marbled Cat and Clouded Leopard. A sit-and-wait predator. In captivity, they are fierce and untamable. Home ranges in Borneo average 3.5 km² for ♂ and 2.1 for ♀.

DISTRIBUTION *Native*: Brunei, Indonesia (Java, Bali, Borneo, Sumatra), Malaysia (Borneo), Philippines (Palawan, Negros, Cebu, Panay; probably introduced to Philippines with possible exception of Palawan).

HABITAT Tropical lowland rainforests, open forest habitats, altered and degraded habitats such as logged forest, forests with frequent canopy gaps, sugarcane fields, and rubber and oil palm plantations. They use plantations for hunting during the night, but probably require the forests for shelter and rest during the daytime or denning. On the island of Java the species can occur in pine plantations and shrubs, and is known to explore rice paddies for prey.

CONSERVATION STATUS Least Concern, Vulnerable in Philippines. CITES: Appendix II. Populations on the Philippine islands of Panay, Negros, and Cebu are declining. This species is stable and will readily use degraded forest and even heavily modified habitats such as oil palm and sugarcane plantations. They can be very effective rodent controllers in oil palm plantations. Protected in Indonesia. It is also targeted for the pet trade and is frequently sold in wildlife markets in Java.

PHOTO CREDITS T: *Markus Lilje*, Tabin Wildlife Reserve (Malaysia); CR: *Mark Louis Benedict*, Kinabatangan River (Malaysia); CR (young): *Lukas Blazek*; CL, BL: *Klaus Rudloff*, Tierpark Berlin (Germany); BR: *Anda Ciurezu*, Deramakot Forest Reserve (Malaysia). 155

Caracal lineage
CARACAL, SERVAL, AND AFRICAN GOLDEN CAT

RECOGNITION The Caracal lineage includes two genera, *Caracal* and *Leptailurus*, incorporating three African species: Caracal (*C. caracal*), African Golden Cat (*C. aurata*), and Serval (*L. serval*). The Caracal was formerly classified in the genus *Lynx* due to morphological similarities with Lynx, but the resemblance is superficial and they are not closely related. The African Golden Cat was grouped with the Asiatic Golden Cat in *Felis* or *Profelis*, but molecular analyses have shown they are not closely related. They are medium-sized cats, with a slender body, a relatively small, round head, and a medium-length tail measuring around a third of the body length. Servals are yellow-brown or tawny marked with black spots merging into stripes in the neck and shoulders, while Caracals are a uniform tawny-brown to brick-red, and African Golden Cats are reddish-brown or grayish and can have spotted or plain coats. Melanistic individuals have been recorded in all three species. Servals have relatively the largest ears and the longest legs in the cat family. This group is sexually dimorphic in body size, with males being larger and heavier than females. All species have the typical felid dental formula (I 3/3, C 1/1, P 3/2, M 1/1 = 30). Chromosome number is 2n=38.

PHYLOGENY The Caracal lineage is the third oldest lineage of the Felidae family and diverged at 8.5 Ma. The precursor of this lineage spread trans-continentally from Asia into Africa 10-8 Ma, when the sea level lowered to 60 m below modern levels, creating a land bridge between Africa and the Arabian Peninsula in the southern Red Sea. In Africa, the Serval diverged 5.6 Ma from the ancestor of Caracal and African Golden Cat. Around 1.9 Ma, Caracal and African Golden Cat separated and expanded in Africa. The African Golden Cat stayed in Africa but the Caracal migrated back to Asia. It is possible that this Caracal migration was contemporary with the second migration wave of felines that occurred 4-1 Ma in the late Pliocene when sea level again dropped and East Africa and Arabia were again connected.

BEHAVIOR All species in this group are solitary, and social interactions are limited to periods of mating, except for mothers with cubs. They are largely crepuscular and nocturnal, but may be active during the daytime. They hunt most of their prey on the ground. Servals prey on small mammals, especially rodents, but also birds; they generally do not take larger prey such as duikers or smaller antelope species, but may prey on domestic livestock, such as sheep and goats. Caracals prey on small to medium-sized mammals, birds, and domestic animals. They will not hesitate to kill prey larger than themselves and will occasionally feed on carrion. African Golden Cats also prey on small to medium-sized mammals, such as rodents and small duikers, but may also prey on birds, hyraxes, bats, and primates.

DISTRIBUTION The Serval is endemic to Africa, where it occurs widely throughout southern and East Africa, patchily in West Africa, and as a relict population in North Africa. They inhabit all types of savanna woodlands, grasslands, and dry-humid forests, typically close to water. Caracal and African Golden Cat have adjacent but nonoverlapping ranges, with Caracal occupying drier woodlands, rocky habitats, and steppe of Africa and parts of the Middle East, west to northwest India, and African Golden Cat inhabiting mostly the moist forests of West and Central Africa.

CONSERVATION The Serval is relatively common south of the Sahara, but it is already extinct or relict in most of the north, west, and extreme south of its original range. The Caracal is widely distributed and relatively common in southern and East Africa, and it is known to survive in many areas of North and southern Africa in spite of being rare and seldom seen. They are considered threatened in Asia. Caracals are hunted intensively in Namibia and South Africa. The African Golden Cat is considered rare in most of its geographic range, being one of the world's least-studied felids. These three species are increasingly threatened by habitat degradation, loss, and fragmentation, persecution by people, and unsustainable hunting.

South African Serval
Leptailurus serval serval, 158

East African Serval
Leptailurus serval lipostictus, 160

servaline
morph

West and Central African Serval
Leptailurus serval constantina, 162

South African Caracal
Caracal caracal caracal, 164

Asiatic Caracal
Caracal caracal schmitzi, 168

North African Caracal
Caracal caracal nubicus, 166

Central African Golden Cat
Caracal aurata aurata, 170

West African Golden Cat
Caracal aurata celidogaster, 172

South African Serval
LEPTAILURUS SERVAL SERVAL

BL: 75-92 cm (♂), 70.5-82 cm (♀). TL: 24-38 cm. SH: 54-62 cm. W: 9-13.5 kg (♂), 7-11.8 kg (♀).
DF: 30. CN: 36. A medium-sized, slender, spotted cat, with long legs and neck, small head, short
tail, and large, rounded ears. It has the longest legs of all cats. Body color and pattern variable,
yellowish-fawn, richer in color than in other subspecies, with distinct scattered black spots and
bars, extending down legs. Coat darker in moister regions but bolder markings in arid and Karoo
regions. Underparts paler, usually also spotted. Small whitish muzzle, golden-yellow face, with
small black spots on cheeks, nose black, occasionally with a pink mark. Brown or greenish eyes,
rimmed with black. White vibrissae. Very large, rounded ears, each with 2 black bands separated
by white patch at back. Short, black-banded, and black-tipped tail, only just reaching to the hocks
of the hind legs. Females less heavily built than males, with 2 pairs of abdominal and 1 pair of
inguinal nipples.

Young

Leptailurus serval serval

OTHER NAMES *French*: Serval, chat-tigre, lynx tacheté. *German*: Serval. *Spanish*: Serval sudafricano. *Russian*: Южноафриканский сервал. *Afrikaans*: Tierboskat. *Chichewa*: Njuzi. *Sepedi*: Letlotse, tetekgwe. *Sesotho*: Phaha, tlohi, qwako. *Swati*: Lindloti. *Tsonga*: Ndloti. *Tswana*: Tadi, Letlôtse. *Venda*: Didingwe, dagaladzhie. *Xhosa*: Inhlosi, ingwenkala. *Zulu*: Indlozi.

TAXONOMY Mores than 17 subspecies have been listed based on ground color and size of spots, but their validity has been brought into question. Three subspecies are now recognized, based on phylogeographical patterns, although further research is required: *L. s. serval* (S Africa), *L. s. lipostictus* (E Africa), and *L. s. constantina* (W and Central Africa). This subspecies includes *beira, capensis, hamiltoni, ingridi, kempi, larseni, lonnbergi, mababiensis*, and *robertsi*.

SIMILAR SPECIES Servals in parts of Zambia are reported to have much smaller spot patterning. Cheetahs and Leopards are larger, with proportionally shorter legs, and a much longer tail.

REPRODUCTION *Gestation*: 68-79 days. *Young per Birth*: 1-5, typically 1-3. *Weaning*: 3-5 months. *Sexual Maturity*: 17-26 months (♂), 15-16 months (♀). *Life Span*: 13 years, 20 years in captivity. *Breeding Season*: Births occur in September-April in Zimbabwe, November-March in KwaZulu-Natal. Young are born in burrows dug by other species, among long, dense grass or under bushes. They disperse at about 1 year.

BEHAVIOR *Social Behavior*: Usually solitary but also in pairs. *Diet*: Small mammals (vlei rats, striped mice, multimammate mice, but also hares and cane rats), birds, reptiles, and amphibians; perhaps young of smaller antelope species; they may kill small farm stock, and medium-sized domestic animals, such as sheep and goats. Usually nocturnal, but also active in early morning and late afternoon. Prey is located by sight or hearing (large ears to locate burrowing rodents underground and dig them up) and caught with a slap of one forepaw, or a high, arching pounce. Playing with prey seems to be common. Servals readily wade in shallow water in pursuit of prey. Mainly terrestrial but may climb. ♂ and possibly ♀ territorial. Both ♂ and ♀ scent-mark with urine, and rub their faces on grass or soil, probably depositing saliva. Feces are left exposed and the ground nearby is raked with the hind feet. Home range size varies from 1.5 km² to 30 km². When foraging, tend to follow regularly used pathways and roads.

DISTRIBUTION *Native*: Angola, Botswana, Congo, DR Congo, Gabon, Malawi, Mozambique, Namibia, South Africa, Swaziland, Zambia, Zimbabwe. Recent reintroductions have been made to conservation areas within their former coastal South African range.

HABITAT Environments with water, adjacent tall grassland, reed beds or rank vegetation fringing forest. Also areas where sugarcane is grown, because of abundance of rodents. Mainly in higher-rainfall areas from sea level to higher grassed slopes of mountain ranges.

CONSERVATION STATUS Least Concern. CITES: Appendix II. South Africa: Near Threatened. Possibly declining due to loss of wetland habitat, deaths from persecution (snaring and roadkills) in some areas of their range. Secure inside protected areas.

PHOTO CREDITS TR: *Arco*, Tenikwa (South Africa); CL: *Bernard Dupont*, Kruger (South Africa); BL: *Matthieu Gallett*, Kruger (South Africa); Young: *Ragnhild Lillehaug* (South Africa); BR: *Mike and Glen Heramb* (Botswana).

East African Serval
LEPTAILURUS SERVAL LIPOSTICTUS

BL: 60-92 cm. TL: 24-35 cm. SH: 54-62 cm. W: 8-13 kg (♂), 6-10 kg (♀). SL: 10.9-11.7 cm. SW: 8.25 cm. DF: 30. CN: 36. A medium-sized, slender, spotted cat, with long legs and neck, small head, short tail, and large, rounded ears. Body color variable, yellowish-tan, paler than in other subspecies, with bold, elongated black spots that tend to merge into longitudinal stripes on the upper neck, shoulders, and insides of the legs. Underparts white or off-white, usually also spotted. Very large, rounded ears, each with 2 black bands separated by white patch at back. Short, black-banded, and black-tipped tail, only just reaching to the hocks of the hind legs. In montane areas, fur is much denser. Melanistic individuals widely recorded in highland areas of eastern Africa (Aberdare Range north of Nairobi or in the Ethiopian highlands). Females less heavily built than males, with 2 pairs of abdominal and 1 pair of inguinal nipples.

melanistic form

Young

Leptailurus serval lipostictus

OTHER NAMES *French*: Serval, chat-tigre, lynx tacheté. *German*: Serval. *Spanish*: Serval de África oriental. *Russian*: Восточноафриканский сервал. *Kiswahili*: Mondo. *Somali*: Muq shabeel, dumad xabashi, shabeel adari, shabeel yer.

TAXONOMY Considered as a subspecies of Serval (*L. serval*). Includes *ferrarii*, *hindei*, *kempi*, *kivuensis*, *pantastica*, *phillipsi*, and *tanae*.

SIMILAR SPECIES Cheetahs and Leopards also have spotted coats, but are larger, with proportionally shorter legs, and a significantly longer tail.

REPRODUCTION *Gestation*: 67-77 days. *Young per Birth*: 2-3. *Weaning*: 3-5 months, but may begin to eat prey at 4-5 weeks old. *Sexual Maturity*: 15-24 months. *Life Span*: 11 years, 19 in captivity. *Breeding Season*: In Uganda and E DR Congo there appear to be two birth seasons, which coincide with the wet seasons, in March-April and again in September-November; however in Ngorongoro Crater the birth season appears to be in the mid to late dry season, probably so that the rains coincide with the period when the cubs are older but still dependent, and require more provisioning. Young are born with closed eyelids, in a well-hidden lair in dense vegetation, a hollow tree, or down a hole. Young are independent at around 6-8 months, and may stay within their natal range for up to and over their first year.

BEHAVIOR *Social Behavior*: Solitary. *Diet*: Small mammals (rodents, hares), but also birds, reptiles, and amphibians; they may take domestic livestock such as chickens, goats, and sheep in some regions. They sometimes cache food. Known predators include Leopard, Lion, Nile crocodile, and domestic dogs. Active at all hours of the day, with the majority of activity occurring at night. Hunts by sound and sight in long grass, pouncing with high leaps onto prey. Its long legs are not for fast running but to gain elevation for hunting in tall grass. Although the Serval can walk up to 6 km a night when prey is scarce, it normally remains in a small area and travels an average of 2 km. Territorial. Home ranges are long lasting and may persist for 4 to 9 years. ♂ have larger home ranges than ♀. The minimum home range in Ngorongoro (Tanzania) was 11.6 km² for one adult ♂ and 9.5 km² for one adult ♀. The home ranges of ♂ overlap with those of ♀ whereas the ♀ home ranges show minimal overlap. ♂ scent-mark more often than ♀. Aggressive behavior between Servals is unusual and rare.

DISTRIBUTION *Native*: Burundi, Djibouti, Eritrea, Ethiopia, Kenya, Rwanda, Somalia, Sudan, Tanzania, Uganda.

HABITAT Savanna associated with well-watered habitat, reed beds, marshes, subalpine habitat, agricultural land, and along the margin of forest, but seldom in dense forests. Also common in montane habitats including bamboo and forest, as long as they include grassy glades or moorland, up to an elevation of 3,200 m in Ethiopia and up to 3,800 m in Kenya. They can also be found in cropped fields, and hence are potentially able to adapt to changing land use patterns from pastoral to agricultural land.

CONSERVATION STATUS Least Concern. CITES: Appendix II.

PHOTO CREDITS TL: *Daniel López Velasco*, Masai Mara (Kenya); TR: *Nigel Pavitt*, Aberdare Mountains (Kenya); Young: *James Hager*, Masai Mara (Kenya); CL: *Radhakrishnan Rajagopalan*, Masai Mara (Kenya); CR: *Robin Bmann*, Ngorongoro (Tanzania); BR: *Danielle Mussman*, Masai Mara (Kenya).

West and Central African Serval

LEPTAILURUS SERVAL CONSTANTINA

BL: 84.7 cm (♂). TL: 24-35 cm. SH: 50-55 cm. W: 12 kg. SL: 10.7-11.7 cm. SW: 8.1-8.6 cm. DF: 30. CN: 36. A medium-sized, slender, spotted cat, with long legs and neck, small head, short tail, and large, rounded ears. Body color and pattern variable, rich rufous-fulvous to pale ocherous-buff, with distinct scattered black spots and bars, extending down legs. A small spotted coat pattern, the servaline morph, is known mainly from West and Central Africa, but is rare. Underparts paler, usually also spotted. Inside of limbs with blackish blotches. Very large, rounded ears, each with 2 black bands separated by white patch at back. Short, black-banded, and black-tipped tail, only just reaching to the hocks of the hind legs. Females less heavily built than males, with 2 pairs of abdominal and 1 pair of inguinal nipples.

Young

servaline form

Leptailurus serval constantina

OTHER NAMES Barbary Serval. *French*: Serval, chat-tigre, lynx tacheté. *German*: Serval. *Spanish*: Serval de África central y occidental. *Russian*: Западноафриканский сервал. *Algerian*: Ouchiak zilagla, amich boudrar. *Creole*: Onca de baga baga.

TAXONOMY Considered as a subspecies of Serval (*L. serval*). Includes *algiricus*, *brachyurus*, *faradjius*, *ogilbyi*, *poliotricha*, *pococki*, *senegalensis*, *servalina*, and *togoensis*.

SIMILAR SPECIES The servaline morph (mistakenly assigned to distinct species *L. brachyura*) seems to be associated with dense vegetation and secondary forest, while the large spotted Serval inhabits more open habitats. Servaline individuals may resemble the Caracal.

REPRODUCTION *Gestation*: 68-74 days. *Young per Birth*: 2-5. *Weaning*: 3-5 months. *Sexual Maturity*: 15-26 months. *Breeding Season*: Aseasonal but birth peaks appear to be correlated with wet seasons when prey densities are at their highest due to new vegetative growth (April-November). At 6-8 months young are independent, but are tolerated by their mothers and may circulate within their natal range for periods up to and over a year.

BEHAVIOR *Social Behavior*: Solitary, in pairs, or in small family parties. *Diet*: Rodents and birds make up the bulk of its diet; reported to be rarely involved in livestock depredation; it does not take larger prey and is only rarely observed to kill duikers and fawns of smaller antelope species. Its large ears and excellent hearing sense help it to localize its prey species and make it a very efficient hunter of small mammals and birds. Predominantly nocturnal, but increasing evidence points to crepuscular behavior. During bright, daylight hours, Servals will rest under cover, rarely visiting the same resting site twice. Almost nothing is known about this cat within the region. Territorial.

DISTRIBUTION *Native*: Benin, Burkina Faso, Cameroon, Central African Republic, Chad, Côte d'Ivoire, Gambia, Ghana, Guinea, Guinea-Bissau, Liberia, Mali, Niger, Nigeria, Senegal, Sierra Leone, Togo. *Possibly Extinct*: Algeria, Morocco. *Reintroduced*: Tunisia (with animals of East African stock).

HABITAT Marshland, well-watered savanna, and long-grass environments. Particularly associated with reed beds and other riparian vegetation types. They can penetrate dense forest along waterways and through grassy patches and are able to tolerate agricultural areas to some extent provided cover is available. Key vegetation types are wetlands, grasslands (with a preference for long, rank grass), and indigenous vegetation that can provide cover and allow dispersal. It does not occur in desert habitats or in the rainforests of Central Africa. In N Africa, it is recorded from semi-desert to cork oak forest on the Mediterranean coast.

CONSERVATION STATUS Critically Endangered. CITES: Appendix II. There are fewer than 250 mature animals in N Africa, if it still exists at all. They occur in a number of protected areas across their range. Relict populations in the N Atlas ranges of Morocco, Algeria, and Tunisia are endangered and may be extinct. In Nigeria, Servals are used in traditional medicine, while in Senegal, Gambia, and Benin, their skins are traded heavily.

PHOTO CREDITS TL: *Daniel Nelson*, Pendjari (Benin); TR: *Michael Loretz*, Zakouma (Chad); Young: *Thomas;* based on photos from RNC Boundou (Senegal) and Zakouma (Chad); BR: *Emmanuel Keller*; BL: *David Mills/Panthera/WCS*.

South African Caracal

CARACAL CARACAL CARACAL

BL: 75-108 cm (♂), 71-102 cm (♀). TL: 21-34 cm. SH: 40-45 cm. W: 7.2-28 kg (♂), 7-15.9 kg (♀). SL: 12.5 cm. SW: 9.8 cm. DF: 30. CN: 38. A medium-sized, stocky, uniformly colored cat, with dark-backed ears with distinct terminal tufts. Pelage is thick and short, from pale tawny-brown to rich red in color, unspotted. Underparts and inner legs are paler, sometimes with faint spotting or blotching. Very dark chocolate-brown individuals occur rarely and true melanism is exceptional. Head is heavily built. Face with white on the chin and throat and a black line from the eye to the nose. Ears are black on the back and distinctly tufted with long black hairs approximately 4-5 cm in length. Long legs, hind limbs being longer than the front limbs. Relatively short tail, similar in color to the dorsal aspect. Males are larger and heavier than females. Females have 3 pairs of nipples.

Young

Caracal caracal caracal

OTHER NAMES African Caracal, Desert Lynx. *French*: Caracal. *German*: Wüstenluchs, Karakal. *Spanish*: Caracal meridional, lince africano. *Russian*: Южноафриканский каракал. *Afrikaans*: Rooikat, lynx. *Ndebele*: Indabutshe. *Setswana*: Thwane. *Sotho*: Thooane. *Tsonga*: Nandani. *Venda*: Thwani. *Xhosa*: Ingqawa, ngada. *Zulu*: Indabushe.

TAXONOMY Eight subspecies were recognized in the past, based on minor differences in pelage coloration, but their validity is questionable. Three subspecies are recognized now based on phylogeographical patterns, but further research is required: *C. c. caracal* (S and E Africa); *C. c. nubicus* (N and W Africa); and *C. c. schmitzi* (Middle East to India). Closely related to the African Golden Cat and Serval; it was previously classified with *Lynx* and *Felis*, but is not closely related to them. This subspecies includes *coloniae, damarensis, limpopoensis, melanotis*, and *roothi*.

SIMILAR SPECIES The smaller African Wildcat has stripes on the legs and tail and has a proportionally longer tail. The African Golden Cat is similar in size and color, but has a longer tail and lacks the terminal black ear tufts. The Serval has distinctive spotting and barring, a ringed tail, and a large white spot on back of each ear, with terminal tuft absent.

REPRODUCTION *Gestation*: 78-81 days. *Young per Birth*: 1-4. *Weaning*: 15-24 weeks. *Sexual Maturity*: 12-15 months (♂), 14-16 months (♀). *Life Span*: 18 years. *Breeding Season*: Probably year-round, with births peaking in October-February in South Africa. Young open their eyes at 10 days, and ears stand erect by the third week.

BEHAVIOR *Social Behavior*: Solitary. *Diet*: Small to medium-sized mammals (rodents, small ungulates, small carnivores), birds, reptiles, and invertebrates; they prey on small domestic livestock and sometimes scavenge. Like Leopards, they are known to hoist their kills into trees and return to carcasses. Predominantly nocturnal, but can be observed during the day in protected areas. Territorial. Home range sizes vary by habitat type and prey abundance, with ♂ ranges typically being three times larger than those of ♀. Both sexes scent-mark by spraying urine on rocks, bushes, and tree trunks.

DISTRIBUTION *Native*: Angola, Botswana, DR Congo, Djibouti, Egypt, Eritrea, Ethiopia, Kenya, Lesotho, Malawi, Mozambique, Namibia, Somalia, South Africa, Swaziland, Tanzania, Uganda, Zambia, Zimbabwe.

HABITAT A wide variety of habitats, from semi-desert to relatively open savanna and scrubland to moist woodland and thicket, evergreen forest, montane grassland, and arid mountains, up to 3,000 m in the Lesotho and Ethiopian Highlands. They prefer wooded vegetation types, especially mountain bushveld. Absent from tropical forests and true deserts, and cover is needed wherever it occurs. They avoid areas where Leopards are prevalent. They tolerate high levels of human activity.

CONSERVATION STATUS Least Concern. CITES: Appendix II. Namibia, Botswana, and South Africa offer an important stronghold for this subspecies. They can be hunted in Namibia and South Africa. They are subject to persecution by farmers through hunting, trapping, and, in some areas, even poisoning. There are no population estimates for this subspecies, but it is considered stable.

PHOTO CREDITS TL: *Ondrej Prosický* (Botswana); TR: *Sergey Chichagov*, Tallinn Zoo (Estonia); Young: *Ivanka Blazkova* and *Stu Porter* (South Africa); B: *Andrew M. Allport* (South Africa).

North African Caracal

CARACAL CARACAL NUBICUS

BL: 60-91 cm. TL: 25 cm. SH: 40 cm. W: 5.9-18 kg. SL: 10.5 cm. SW: 8.1 cm. DF: 30. CN: 38. A medium-sized, stocky, uniformly colored cat, with dark-backed ears with distinct terminal tufts. Caracals from the Sahara Desert are smaller and paler. Pelage is thick and short, from sandy to reddish-cinnamon in color, unspotted. Mid-dorsal region scarcely darker than the flanks and limbs. Underparts and inner legs white sometimes with pale spotting. Throat pale buff. Head is heavily built. Face with white on the chin and throat and a black line from the eye to the nose. Ears are silvery-black on the back, sometimes mixed with white hairs, distinctly tufted with long black hairs. Long legs, hind limbs being longer than the front limbs. Relatively short tail, similar in color to the dorsal aspect, not black-tipped. Males are larger and heavier than females. Females have 3 pairs of nipples.

Caracal caracal nubicus

OTHER NAMES Barbary Lynx, Nubian Caracal, North African Caracal, West African Caracal. *French*: Caracal. *German*: Wüstenluchs, Karakal. *Spanish*: Caracal septentrional, lince africano. *Russian*: Североафриканский каракал. *Berber*: Warsal, bousboela, mousch, nouadhrar, aousak.

TAXONOMY Considered as a subspecies of Caracal (*C. caracal*). Includes *algira, berberorum, corylinus, lucani, medjerdae, poecilotis, spatzi.*

REPRODUCTION *Gestation*: 78-81 days. *Young per Birth*: 2-3. *Weaning*: 15-24 weeks. *Sexual Maturity*: 12-14 months. *Breeding Season*: Probably year-round, but most births are associated with seasons with an increased abundance of prey. The den is usually in a hollow under thick brush but can also be an abandoned aardvark hole, a cave, or between large rocks, usually lined with fur and feathers.

BEHAVIOR *Social Behavior*: Solitary; the only contact between adults is a very short period of mating. *Diet*: Small to medium-sized mammals (gazelles, small antelopes), reptiles, small carnivores; unlike most other carnivores, Caracal do not eat the stomach, intestines, feathers, or hairy skin; they rarely scavenge. They can survive without surface drinking water. There is no specific information for this subspecies, but probably similar to other Caracals. Extremely shy and most activity takes place at night, but may be active at dusk or during the day. During the day, lies up in rock crevices, caves, burrows, or dense bush. They are unable to run distances at a high speed but rather stalk their prey and leap onto it at the last moment with speed. Birds flying up from the ground are often taken by a powerful leap. Adults give low-pitched coughs when communicating and high-pitched chirps when handling their cubs. Ear movement also plays an important role in visual communication. Probably territorial. The home ranges of ♂ are much larger than those of ♀ and overlap those of several different ♀.

DISTRIBUTION *Native*: Algeria, Benin, Burkina Faso, Cameroon, Central African Republic, Chad, Côte d'Ivoire, Gambia, Ghana, Guinea, Guinea-Bissau, Libya, Mali, Mauritania, Morocco, Niger, Nigeria, Senegal, Sudan, Togo, Tunisia, Western Sahara. Now it is probably extinct in Libya. This subspecies' distribution is still scattered but in low densities.

HABITAT A wide variety of habitats, in arid open landscapes, coniferous forests, savanna, steppes, and subdesert mountains. Its habitat needs shelter such as hollow trees, areas under boulders, or dense vegetation to spend the day resting, and to provide sufficient cover to bring prey within range of a few jumps. It is not present in true deserts or tropical forests around the equator. In the Mediterranean area it may be found in pine and cedar forests in the Atlas Mountains.

CONSERVATION STATUS Least Concern. CITES: Appendix II. In N Africa, it is considered Critically Endangered. Its occurrence in Morocco, Algeria, and other North African countries is unusual, and it is probably on the verge of extinction. It is very rare in West Africa. Habitat destruction (agriculture and desertification) is a significant threat in Central, W, N, and NE Africa where Caracals are naturally sparsely distributed. There are no population estimates for this subspecies, but it is possibly declining.

PHOTO CREDITS T, B: Based on photos from Pendjari (Benin), *Antonella865* and *Stephen Smith*; C: *Alexander Sliwa*, Sharjah Desert Park (UAE), individual from Central Africa.

Asiatic Caracal
CARACAL CARACAL SCHMITZI

BL: 69-108 cm (♂), 56-77 cm (♀). TL: 16-32.5 cm. SH: 27-47 cm. W: 4-13.6 (♂), 5.9-9.2 kg (♀). SL: 12.3 cm. SW: 8.9 cm. DF: 30. CN: 38. A medium-sized, stocky, uniformly colored cat, with dark-backed ears with distinct terminal tufts. Paler than African subspecies, with poor development of dark marks on the underparts. Arabian Caracals are smaller. Pelage is thick and short, from light sandy to pale reddish-brown, unspotted, though seasonal variation may exist. Summer coat is coarser and shorter than the winter coat. Underparts and inner legs whitish, sometimes with indistinct spots. Face reddish-brown, with white on the chin and throat and a black line from the eye to the nose. Ears are long, silvery-black on the back, and distinctly tufted with long black hairs, inner side and margins whitish. Long legs, hind limbs being longer than the front limbs. Furry paws. Relatively short tail, similar in color to the dorsal aspect. Males are larger and heavier than females.

Young

168

Caracal caracal schmitzi

OTHER NAMES Turkmenistan Caracal, Arabian Caracal, Persian Lynx. *French*: Lynx du désert, caracal. *German*: Wüstenluchs, Karakal. *Spanish*: Caracal asiático. *Russian*: Азиатский каракал. *Dari*: Psk qarh qol. *Arabic*: Ajal, anaq al ardh, washeq, al khanaq, hirr khuwainga, tiffa. *Farsi*: Caracal. *Hindi*: Siyah ghosh. *Kutchi*: Hinotro. *Shehri*: Khanshant. *Turkish*: Karakulak. *Uzbek*: Karakulak.

TAXONOMY Considered as a subspecies of Caracal (*C. caracal*). Includes *michaelis*.

SIMILAR SPECIES Lynx have a shorter tail, longer whiskers, and fur is almost always marked with dark spots. The Jungle Cat is smaller, has a ringed and black-tipped tail, much smaller ear tufts, and a less strikingly marked face. The Leopard and Cheetah both are clearly spotted.

REPRODUCTION *Gestation*: 82 days. *Young per Birth*: 2-3, rarely up to 5. *Weaning*: 15-24 weeks. *Sexual Maturity*: 12-14 months. *Breeding Season*: Births occur in April-May in Iran and Turkmenistan. Young are hidden in the burrows of other animals or in crevices, hollow trees, thickets, and caves. Young become independent at 9-10 months.

BEHAVIOR *Social Behavior*: Solitary. *Diet*: Mostly small mammals (lagomorphs, rodents), but also medium-sized mammals (gazelles, wild sheep), ground birds, and insects; they may prey on domestic animals (especially poultry) and occasionally feed on carrion. Nocturnal and crepuscular, although in less disturbed habitats they may be active during the daytime. Its daily activity seems correlated with ambient temperature rather than the photoperiod; the warmer the temperature in summer, the more active the Caracals will be during the night. Territorial. ♂ occupy notably larger home ranges that often overlap with one to several ♀. The home range of this subspecies is considerably larger than those of Caracals from South Africa, probably because prey abundance is low.

DISTRIBUTION *Native*: Afghanistan, NE Egypt, India, Iran, Iraq, Israel, Jordan, Kazakhstan, Kuwait, Lebanon, Oman, Pakistan, Saudi Arabia, Syria, Tajikistan, Turkey, Turkmenistan, United Arab Emirates, Uzbekistan, Yemen.

HABITAT Highly adaptable, preferring drier open terrain with sufficient shelter and vegetation cover, dry riverbeds, wadis, drainage lines, and well-vegetated foothill trails. They do not seem to require extensive shelter, as do other cats in the desert. They avoid true deserts and dense tropical rainforests.

CONSERVATION STATUS Near Threatened. CITES: Appendix I (Asia). The status and population trends of this subspecies are largely unknown and there are no population estimates, but it is believed that its population is decreasing. Considered Near Threatened in the Arabian Peninsula (in Yemen they are thought to be stable), Critically Endangered in Oman, Endangered in India (probably on the verge of extinction), and Threatened in Turkey and Iran. It is legally protected in most of its range countries. Habitat loss and fragmentation are the main threats for this subspecies. In the Middle East, prey base depletion (gazelles) and hunting have a major impact too. In the Arabian Peninsula and Turkey it is perceived as a pest due to livestock predation and is shot, trapped, and poisoned. Domestic dogs are thought to be big competitors of the Caracal.

PHOTO CREDITS T: *Iman Memarian*, Tehran Zoo (Iran); CL, CR: *Alexander Sliwa*, Sharjah Desert Park (UAE); B, Young: *Balasz Buzas*, Sharjah Desert Park (UAE).

Central African Golden Cat
CARACAL AURATA AURATA

BL: 62-94 cm (♂), 63-75 cm (♀). TL: 25-37 cm. SH: 40-45 cm. W: 8-14 kg (♂), 6.2-8.2 kg (♀). SL: 11.3 cm. SW: 9.0 cm. DF: 30. CN: 38. A medium-sized, strongly built cat. Coat very variable in color and markings, with 2 color forms: reddish-brown and gray, with some intergradation between them (both colors can occur in the same litter). Melanistic individuals uncommon. Spots nearly always visible on the belly and inside limbs, but may be absent from back, nape, and shoulders. Spots vary from large and distinct circles or rosettes, to small and obscure freckles. Spotted individuals more common in West Africa, unspotted individuals are more common in East Africa. Dark mid-dorsal line absent or faint. Small, round head, short face with distinctive pale patches on the cheeks and around the eyes and mouth, and a heavy muzzle. Eyes green to golden-brown. Small and rounded ears, lack tufts, black-backed. A medium length, black-tipped tail, either not banded or indistinctly banded. Males heavier than females.

red/brown form

gray form

Caracal aurata aurata

OTHER NAMES *French*: Chat doré Africain. *German*: Afrikanische Goldkatze. *Spanish*: Gato dorado centroafricano. *Russian*: Центральноафриканская золотая кошка. *Lingala*: Gnaou ya zamba. *Gabon*: Lobwa, ebyo, ebie.

TAXONOMY Previously included in the genus *Felis* or *Profelis*, but molecular data reveal that it is more closely related to the Caracal and Serval. Not closely related to the Asiatic Golden Cat. There are probably two subspecies based on biogeographical patterns, but genetic studies are required to confirm their validity: *C. a. aurata* (E and Central Africa as far W as the River Congo); and *C. a. celidogaster* (W Africa W of Cross River). There is a large area of W Central Africa where this species is not present, between the Cross and Congo Rivers. These two subspecies may represent clinal variations, in which case no subspecies should be recognized. This subspecies includes *cottoni*.

REPRODUCTION *Gestation*: 75 days. *Young per Birth*: 2. *Weaning*: 6 weeks. *Sexual Maturity*: 18 months (♂), 11 months (♀). *Life Span*: 12 years in captivity. *Breeding Season*: Unknown. Nothing has been published on breeding in the wild. The young are well concealed, fully open their eyes at 6 days, and eat meat from day 40.

BEHAVIOR *Social Behavior*: Solitary. *Diet*: Rodents, duikers, primates, hyraxes, and gallinaceous birds (francolins, guineafowls); sometimes kill livestock. *Main Predators*: Leopard. It is one of the least known carnivores in Africa. They are seldom observed in the wild, and very little is known about their ecology and behavior. Crepuscular and nocturnal, but may also be active at any time of the day. Activity may vary according to the level of human activity and to avoid competition with Leopards. Frequent sightings in restricted localities imply regular routines and smallish home ranges, and they prefer to move along roads and well-used tracks. Adult ♂ probably hold territories that encompass all or part of the home ranges of several adult ♀. Predominantly terrestrial, it hunts on the ground by using a typical felid stalk-and-rush technique; it does not readily catch arboreal monkeys. Its vocal repertoire is extensive, and the principal vocalization is a strong, abrupt, and husky "meow."

DISTRIBUTION *Native*: Angola, Cameroon, Central African Republic, DR Congo, Equatorial Guinea, Gabon, Nigeria, Uganda. *Presence Uncertain*: Burundi, Kenya, Rwanda, Sudan, Tanzania.

HABITAT A wide range of habitats: woodland, thicket, savanna/forest mosaic, coastal forest, riverine forest, gallery forest, swamp forest, lowland forest, mid-altitude forest, montane forest, subalpine forest, and moorland, from near sea level up to 3,600 m. It is mostly associated with lowland moist forest and with the edge of forest and along rivers in outlying areas. They are tolerant of logged forest, where thick understory vegetation and higher rodent densities follow exploitation.

CONSERVATION STATUS Vulnerable. CITES: Appendix II. Little known but habitat and prey populations are known to be contracting. The low frequency of field sightings of this species is probably due largely to secretive and cryptic behavior and to dense vegetation, rather than to low densities. They are particularly susceptible to being caught in snares. This species is a forest specialist and is, therefore, vulnerable to forest degradation, loss, and fragmentation.

PHOTO CREDITS TL, CL, B: *Laila Bahaa-el-din* (Gabon); TR: *Sebastian Kennerknecht*, Kibale NP (Uganda); CR: *Nayer Youakim* (Uganda).

West African Golden Cat

CARACAL AURATA CELIDOGASTER

BL: 62-94 cm (♂), 63-75 cm (♀). TL: 25.4-37 cm. SH: 40-45 cm. W: 8-14 (♂), 6.2-8.2 kg (♀). SL: 11.5 cm. SW: 8.3 cm. DF: 30. CN: 38. A medium-sized, strongly built cat. More extensively spotted subspecies. Coat very variable in color and markings, with 2 color forms: reddish-brown and gray, with some intergradation and variation between them (both colors can occur in the same litter). Melanistic individuals uncommon. Spotting is usually all over the body. Spots range from fine freckles to large rosettes, from faint to bold, and from partial to overall. Small, round head, short face with distinctive pale patches on the cheeks and around the eyes and mouth, and a heavy muzzle. Eyes green to golden-brown. Small and rounded ears, lack tufts, black-backed. Dark mid-line along the back. Tail is banded (either distinctly or indistinctly), black-tipped. Males heavier than females.

gray form

red/brown form

Caracal aurata celidogaster

OTHER NAMES *French*: Chat doré Africain. *German*: Afrikanische Goldkatze. *Spanish*: Gato dorado de África Occidental. *Russian*: Западноафриканская золотая кошка. *Peul*: Donnou, dondou. *Mandinka*: Soukalan.

TAXONOMY Considered as a subspecies of African Golden Cat (*C. aurata*). Includes *chalybeata* (Guinea), *neglecta* (Gambia), and *rutila* (Sierra Leone).

SIMILAR SPECIES Leopard (*P. pardus*) is larger, with distinct spotting including on face and neck, back of ears with prominent pale patch, and a proportionally longer tail. Serval (*L. serval*) has larger ears, back side with broad white horizontal band, larger and thinner limbs, and distinctly banded black and beige/dirty-yellow tail, not reaching the hocks. Caracal (*C. caracal*) has larger triangular ears, blackish, with long blackish tuft on the tip. African Wildcat (*F. lybica*) has a relatively longer tail, distinctly banded gray and black, and held out well behind the body when the cat is standing, and has ears rusty-brown on the back side with blackish tip. African Golden Cat typically carries its tail so that the tip is curved away from the body.

REPRODUCTION *Gestation*: 75 days. *Young per Birth*: 2. *Weaning*: Unknown. *Sexual Maturity*: 18 months (♂), 11 months (♀). *Life Span*: 12 years in captivity. *Breeding Season*: Unknown. Very little is known about the reproductive biology of this subspecies.

BEHAVIOR *Social Behavior*: Solitary. *Diet*: Rodents, small ungulates (duikers), primates, pangolins, and birds; predation on domestic livestock such as chickens, goats, and sheep has been recorded but appears to be rather rare. This species is challenging to study due to its preference for dense forest habitat and elusive behavior. There is no specific information available for this subspecies. They probably catch most prey while on the ground, presumably by stalking and rushing, and by ambushing prey from low tree branches.

DISTRIBUTION *Native*: Côte d'Ivoire, Ghana, Guinea, Liberia, Sierra Leone. *Presence Uncertain*: Benin, Gambia, Guinea-Bissau, Togo. *Probably Extinct*: Senegal. This subspecies occurs in a number of protected areas, including Gola Forest Reserve (Sierra Leone), Mount Nimba Strict Nature Reserve (Liberia, Côte d'Ivoire, Guinea), Upper Niger NP (Guinea), Sapo NP (Liberia), and Taï and Comoé NP (Côte d'Ivoire).

HABITAT Lowland and montane rainforest, swamp forest, bamboo forest, as well as alpine moorland. Penetrates drier regions by using gallery forest along major rivers, wooded savannas, and savanna/forest mosaics. Adapts well to selectively logged areas, presumably in response to increased prey abundance in dense secondary growth; also seen on roads, in banana plantations, and near small villages.

CONSERVATION STATUS Vulnerable. CITES: Appendix II. It is generally considered as rare and no reliable density estimates exist. Hunting species is prohibited or regulated by national laws in about half the range countries. Dependence on forest cover means that habitat loss is a threat particularly in West and East Africa. The impact of hunting and trading is not clear but it could be a significant threat.

PHOTO CREDITS TL: *Alan Hill*, Artis Zoo (Netherlands); TR, CR, BL: *Terry Whittaker* (Togo); BR: *Roland Seitre*.

Wildcat lineage
DOMESTIC CAT, WILDCATS, AND RELATED SPECIES

RECOGNITION The Wildcat or Domestic Cat lineage consists of seven closely related species in one genus, *Felis*, including the European Wildcat (*F. silvestris*), Domestic Cat (*F. catus*), African Wildcat (*F. lybica*), Chinese Mountain Cat (*F. bieti*), Jungle Cat (*F. chaus*), Sand Cat (*F. margarita*), and Black-Footed Cat (*F. nigripes*). Some authors recommend that *F. silvestris* be regarded as a single polytypic species with four allopatric subspecies: the European (*F. s. silvestris*), Asian (*F. s. ornata*), African (*F. s. lybica*), and Chinese Mountain (*F. s. bieti*) Wildcats, and a domesticated form (*F. s. catus*). They are small to medium-sized cats, similar to a Domestic Cat, pale sandy-buff to dark gray-brown colored, mostly lightly marked with spotting or striations on the body, whitish underparts, and short to medium-sized black-ringed, black-tipped tails. Males are heavier and always larger than females. Chromosome number is 2n=38.

PHYLOGENY The Wildcat lineage is the most recent to diverge at 3.4 Ma, comprising mostly smaller cats under 10 kg that seem to have originated around the Mediterranean basin and W Asia. The Black-Footed Cat was the first species of the lineage to diverge, followed by the Jungle Cat and Sand Cat. European, African, and Asian Wildcats diverged from each other as recently as 20,000 years ago, being phylogenetically very close. Domestic Cats are descended from the African Wildcats (*F. lybica*), and domestication probably occurred somewhere in the Fertile Crescent (the Levant, southern Turkey, and Iraq) of W Asia, around the same time as the first agricultural village settlements (10,000 years ago). Subsequent gradual movements of cats with their human companions would spread Domestic Cats across the globe. By the time of the industrial revolution, pet cat owners were selectively mating their pet tabbies to produce breeds (Siamese, Persian, Korat, Egyptian Mau, Manx, Turkish Angora, and others). The oldest fossil record that belongs to this lineage is from Kenya, dated to > 4 Ma. The modern Wildcat is related to *F. lunensis*, whose presence in Europe is known as early as the late Pliocene, about 2 Ma. Specimens referable to *F. nigripes* have been found in early Pleistocene deposits in South Africa, and to *F. chaus* in Holocene strata of Java. No specimens referable to *F. margarita* have been found in the fossil record.

BEHAVIOR These cats are solitary except during the breeding season, territorial, and mostly crepuscular and nocturnal, resting in burrows, under cover (bushes, grass), and in depressions during the day. They are predominantly ground-dwellers and hunt on the ground, although the Wildcat and the Jungle Cat are very good climbers. Hunting involves the classical feline stalk, rush, and pounce. They feed mainly on small mammals, especially rodents, but may also take birds, reptiles, amphibians, and invertebrates, and sometimes scavenge food, or prey upon poultry and small livestock.

DISTRIBUTION The European Wildcat inhabits broadleaf and mixed forests of Europe and parts of adjoining Russia. The African Wildcat occurs in wide parts of Africa, around the periphery of the Arabian Peninsula, and in SW and Central Asia into India, China, and Mongolia, and has a very broad habitat tolerance, from deserts, savannas, and scrub grassland to open forests and mixed forests, being absent only from tropical rainforest. The Jungle Cat occurs in reed beds, grassland, and scrubland associated with swamps, wetlands, marshes, and coasts, in tropical and subtropical Asia, in the more mesic parts of Arabia, and marginally into Africa. The Chinese Mountain Cat is endemic to central China and lives in alpine habitats in the northeastern edge of the Tibetan Plateau. The Sand Cat is a desert specialist, with a discontinuous distribution in Central Asia, in the Middle East and the Arabian Peninsula, and in North Africa. The Black-Footed Cat lives in dry, open grasslands, and semidesert habitats of the southern African subregion.

CONSERVATION Two species in this group are listed as Vulnerable: the Chinese Mountain Cat and the Black-Footed Cat. The former has a very restricted range, and it is killed for its fur and by the use of poison to control rodents. The population size of Black-Footed Cat is estimated at fewer than 10,000 individuals and is threatened by habitat degradation and indiscriminate pest control methods. The European Wildcat population is fragmented and declining in some countries, being threatened by interbreeding with feral cats and loss of habitat; they have become rare in most European countries. Hybridization with Domestic Cats is also considered the main threat to the African Wildcat. The ecology and status of the other two species, the Jungle Cat and the Sand Cat, are poorly known. The Jungle Cat adapts more readily than other felids to artificial landscapes, but persecution by people and habitat degradation have caused population declines in many areas throughout its range. Degradation of arid ecosystems, being rapidly converted by human settlement and activity, seems to be the major threat to the Sand Cat. Populations of all these species are decreasing.

Caucasian Wildcat
Felis silvestris caucasica, 178

European Wildcat
Felis silvestris silvestris, 176

Domestic and Feral Cat
Felis catus, 180

Asian Wildcat
Felis lybica ornata, 186

North African Wildcat
Felis lybica lybica, 182

South African Wildcat
Felis lybica cafra, 184

Indochinese Jungle Cat
Felis chaus fulvidina, 194

Indian Jungle Cat
Felis chaus affinis, 192

Western Jungle Cat
Felis chaus chaus, 190

Chinese Mountain Cat
Felis bieti, 188

African Sand Cat
F. margarita margarita, 196

Asian Sand Cat
F. margarita thinobia, 198

Black-footed Cat
Felis nigripes, 200

European Wildcat
FELIS SILVESTRIS SILVESTRIS

BL: 43-91 cm (♂), 40-77 cm (♀). TL: 23-40 cm. SH: 26-40 cm. W: 3.5-7.3 kg (♂), 2.3-4.7 kg (♀). SL: 9.4 cm (♂), 9 cm (♀). SW: 7.1 cm (♂), 6.5 cm (♀). DF: 30. CN: 38. A medium-sized cat, similar to a domestic tabby cat, generally slightly larger, longer-legged, and more robust. Coat is long and thick in winter, grayish-brown to yellowish-brown in color, with a well-defined pattern of black stripes on the head, neck, limbs, and a distinct dorsal band. Melanistic individuals have not been recorded, and piebald, ginger, and black variants are the result of hybridization with Domestic Cats. Underparts are light gray with a light ocherous tinge. Broad head. Wide set ears, with a very short dark tuft, yellowish-white inside, reddish-brown behind. Pink nose. Forehead and crown with 4 well-developed black or brownish bands. Distinctive white chin. Some individuals have a white spot on the throat. Tail is bushy, blunt-ending, with several black rings and a black tip. Females are smaller than males.

Young

Felis silvestris silvestris

OTHER NAMES *French*: Chat forestier, chat sauvage d'Europe, chat sylvestre. *German*: Europäische Wildkatze, Waldkatze. *Spanish*: Gato montés, gato silvestre europeo. *Russian*: Европейский лесной кот.

TAXONOMY *F. silvestris* includes only the forest cats of Europe. Many subspecies have been described, but there are no recent phylogeographical studies. The following subspecies are currently recognized based on current geographical isolation: *F. s. silvestris* (Europe, including Scotland, Sicily, and Crete), and *F. s. caucasica* (Caucasus, Turkey). There is a cline in pelage flank stripes in Europe from distinctly striped animals in the W to faintly striped animals in the E. Includes *grampia* (Scottish Wildcat). It is not clear if the Domestic Cat, genetically very similar to the Wildcat, should be considered as a separate species (*F. catus*) or as a subspecies of the African or Eurasian Wildcat.

REPRODUCTION *Gestation*: 64-71 days. *Young per Birth*: 2-4. *Weaning*: 4 months. *Sexual Maturity*: 7-11 months (♂), 9-10 months (♀). *Life Span*: 18 years in captivity. *Breeding Season*: January-March, with most births taking place in April-May. Age at independence can vary from 5 to10 months.

BEHAVIOR *Social Behavior*: Solitary. *Diet*: Rodents (rats, mice, voles) and rabbits, and occasionally insects, birds, frogs, lizards, hares, and poultry or even smaller carnivores such as martens, weasels, and polecats; they also scavenge food. Mostly nocturnal, but may be active during the day in areas with little human activity, with activity peaks at dawn and dusk. It hunts almost exclusively on the ground, although it is an excellent climber, and usually stalks its prey followed by a quick attack. Territorial, with home ranges from 1 to 8.7 km². Home ranges of ♂ are larger than the ones of ♀ and overlap with the ranges of 3-5 ♀. They use scent-marks for communication, including urine spraying in both sexes and uncovered feces. Vocal communication occurs throughout the year, but most frequently in the breeding season.

DISTRIBUTION *Native*: Albania, Andorra, Austria, Belarus, Belgium, Bosnia and Herzegovina, Bulgaria, Croatia, France, Germany, Greece, Hungary, Italy, Latvia, Lithuania, Luxembourg, Macedonia, Moldova, Montenegro, Poland, Portugal, Romania, Russia, Serbia, Slovakia, Slovenia, Spain, Switzerland, Ukraine, United Kingdom. *Possibly Extinct*: Czech Republic. *Extinct*: Netherlands.

HABITAT Primarily associated with forest habitat and most abundant in broadleaf or mixed forests, up to 2,250 m in the Pyrenees. It also inhabits grassland, steppe habitats, Mediterranean maquis scrubland, riparian forest, marsh boundaries, sea coasts, or wet swampy areas. It generally avoids areas of intensive cultivation.

CONSERVATION STATUS Least Concern. CITES: Appendix II. One of the main threats is hybridization with Domestic Cats, and in some parts of the European Wildcat distribution range, probably only a few genetically pure individuals remain: in Scotland, 88% may be hybrids or feral cats, 30% in Hungary, and 8% in Italy; hybrids have also been detected in Belgium, Portugal, Germany, and Switzerland; populations of European Wildcats in Eastern Europe are generally considered to be genetically relatively pure. European Wildcat populations are often fragmented and decreasing. Strictly protected in Europe.

PHOTO CREDITS T, B: *Jesús Rodriguez-Osorio*, Palencia (Spain); CL: *Alexander Sliwa*, Edinburgh Zoo (UK); Young: *Alexander Sliwa*.

Caucasian Wildcat

FELIS SILVESTRIS CAUCASICA

BL: 63-75 cm (♂), 54-63 cm (♀). TL: 27-38 cm. SH: 26-28 cm. W: 5.2-8 kg. SL: 9.4 cm (♂), 8.7 cm (♀). SW: 7.2 cm (♂), 6.6 cm (♀). DF: 30. CN: 38. A medium-sized cat, similar to a domestic tabby cat, generally slightly larger, longer-legged, and more robust. Lighter gray in color, with a fainter pattern on the sides and the tail than in the European Wildcat. Coat is rich, dense, and soft in winter, grayish-brown to yellowish-brown in color. Transverse bands and spots on trunk usually faint or absent, but may be well defined in some individuals. Pattern on head well developed. Dorsal band present in some individuals. Underparts are light gray with a light ocherous tinge. Broad head. Wide set ears, with a very short dark tuft, yellowish-white inside, reddish-brown behind. Pink nose. Forehead and crown with 4 black or brownish bands. Distinctive white chin. Some individuals have a white spot on the throat. Tail is bushy, blunt-ending, with only 3 black transverse rings and a black tip. Females are smaller than males.

Young

Felis silvestris caucasica

OTHER NAMES *French*: Chat forestier, chat sauvage, chat sylvestre. *German*: Kaukasus Wildkatze. *Spanish*: Gato montés, gato silvestre del Caucaso. *Russian*: Кавказский лесной кот. *Armenian*: Vairi katu, antarayin katu. *Turkish*: Yaban kedisi.

TAXONOMY Considered as a subspecies of European Wildcat (*F. silvestris*). Includes *trapezia*.

SIMILAR SPECIES The Wildcat is slightly more robust than the Domestic Cat. The main difference is the color of the fur on its back: in the Wildcat, it is mostly gray-brown to yellowish-brown with distinct stripes across the back, legs, and tail; a narrow dark dorsal band runs along the back to the base of its tail; the tail is thicker, bushier, and seemingly shorter with 3-4 black transverse rings and a black tip.

REPRODUCTION *Gestation*: 64-71 days. *Young per Birth*: 2-4. *Weaning*: 3-4 months (they begin to eat meat at 1.5 months). *Sexual Maturity*: 7-11 months. *Life Span*: 18 years in captivity. *Breeding Season*: From mid-February to late March, with the young born in April or May. Den in the trunk of fallen trees, in hollows of beech trees, in rocky fissures, or in abandoned burrows of foxes and badgers. Kittens open eyes at 9-12 days. They begin to hunt with their mother at the age of 2 months and travel with her up to 1 year, after which they move independently.

BEHAVIOR *Social Behavior*: Solitary; ♂ and ♀ associate only for mating. *Diet*: Rodents (mice, voles, squirrels, rats), and birds, but also catch larger species such as hares and young deer, and insects, fish, or mollusks. Normally crepuscular and nocturnal, but are also diurnal without human disturbance, in the Yenice Forest (Turkey). The Jungle Cat is a serious competitor, but it occupies a different biotope in the lowland sections, while the Wildcat resides higher up along the mountain slopes in beech forests.

DISTRIBUTION *Native*: Armenia, Azerbaijan, Georgia, Russia, Turkey. In Turkey, it is common in mesic and mixed oak-beech forests of the Pontic Mountains, but rare in the Marmara and Aegean Sea regions. In the Taurus Mountains, it probably only occurs in deciduous forest of Kahramanmara Province. It is possibly extinct in the Eastern Anatolia Region.

HABITAT Deciduous forests, in particular beech and oak, mountain and Mediterranean mixed forests, moorland, marshland, reeds along the sea coast, and near farmland. It is not adapted to living in regions with deep, loose snow cover.

CONSERVATION STATUS Least Concern. CITES: Appendix II. The major threats are persecution by humans and hybridization with Domestic Cats, but there is no information from the Caucasus about extensive hybridization. Protected in Turkey and any form of hunting or killing is prohibited.

PHOTO CREDITS T: *Edwin Giesbers*; CL: *Georg Pauluhn*; Young: *R. Linke*; B: *Fabrice Cahez*; based on photos from Georgia and Turkey.

Domestic and Feral Cat

FELIS CATUS

BL: 40-60 cm. TL: 24-30 cm. SH: 23-25 cm. W: 3-8 kg (♂), 2-5 kg (♀). SL: 7.8-9.2 cm. SW: 5.6-7.1 cm. DF: 30. CN: 38. A small-sized cat, with a long tail, relatively short legs, and a small head. Hair color, pattern, and size are extremely variable in domesticated varieties, with some breeds even being hairless. Most feral cats have a short coat, ginger, tabby, tortoiseshell, gray, or black in color, sometimes with several broken stripes and spots. Crown with thin, fused, sometimes non-existent, stripes. White markings may be present on the feet, belly, chest, and throat; completely white feral cats are extremely rare. Pointed ears, broad at the base, usually dark gray or black-backed, without terminal tufts. Slender and tapered tail, often narrows to a point, sometimes with fused or disrupted dark bands. Males are usually larger than females. Females have 4 pairs of nipples.

Young

Felis catus

OTHER NAMES House Cat. *French*: Chat domestique. *German*: Hauskatze. *Spanish*: Gato doméstico. *Russian*: Домашняя кошка.

TAXONOMY Domesticated mostly from a lineage of *F. lybica lybica* from Mesopotamia. Treated as a distinct taxon, *F. catus*, following the International Commission on Zoological Nomenclature.

REPRODUCTION *Gestation*: 63-65 days. *Young per Birth*: 1-6, averaging 4. *Weaning*: 5-7 weeks. *Sexual Maturity*: 7-12 months. *Life Span*: 5 years, 20 years in captivity. *Breeding Season*: From spring to late autumn; they generally do not breed during winter. An adult ♀ may produce 2-3 litters per year. Multiple ♂ will be attracted to a ♀ in heat. The ♂ will fight over her for the right to mate.

BEHAVIOR *Social Behavior*: Solitary, but may be found in large colonies. *Diet*: Small mammals, birds, household food, and domestic animals, but also amphibians, reptiles, fish, and invertebrates; they prefer live prey, but will scavenge for carrion when live food is scarce; they can survive with limited access to water, as they use moisture from their prey. Although the Domestic Cat has a long history of association with humans, it retains a strong hunting instinct and can easily revert to a wild (feral) state when abandoned or having strayed from a domestic situation. Feral cats are generally nocturnal, with peak hunting activity soon after sunset and just before sunrise, and will rest during the day in den sites such as hollow logs, piles of debris, rabbit warrens, or dense scrub. Cats use two hunting strategies, either stalking prey actively, or waiting in ambush until an animal comes close enough to be captured. Prey availability is a primary factor in determining home range size for feral cats. Despite some cats cohabiting in colonies, they always hunt alone. ♂ and ♀ feral cat home ranges overlap. Territories are marked by urine spraying, by rubbing objects at head height with secretions from facial glands, and by defecation. When cats become aggressive, they try to make themselves appear larger and more threatening by raising their fur, arching their backs, turning sideways, and hissing or spitting. Domestic Cats use many vocalizations for communication, including purring, trilling, hissing, growling/snarling, and several different forms of meowing. By contrast, feral cats are generally silent.

DISTRIBUTION Worldwide, except Antarctica and some isolated islands in the Arctic Ocean and Pacific SW where they have not been introduced.

HABITAT A variety of habitat types: urban areas, forests, grasslands, tundra, coastal areas, agricultural land, scrublands, and wetlands.

CONSERVATION STATUS Domesticated. Worldwide population exceeds 500 million as of 2007. Feral cats are exceptional hunters and pose a significant threat to the survival of many native species including small mammals, birds, and reptiles. Its ability to thrive in almost any terrestrial habitat has led to its designation as one of the most invasive species. Wildlife on oceanic islands is particularly susceptible to the impact of predation by cats, and cats have played a leading role in the endangerment and extinction of many species. Hybridization with Wildcats poses a danger to the genetic distinctiveness of some Wildcat populations. Feral cats pose a serious health risk to humans, livestock, and native animals as carriers of diseases such as toxoplasmosis and sarcosporidiosis.

PHOTO CREDITS TR: *Iryna Irena*; TL: *Masajla*; CL: *Koenigpunk*; Young: *Tony Campbell*; B: *Nicolae Cirmu*.

North African Wildcat

FELIS LYBICA LYBICA

BL: 37-54 cm. TL: 26-36 cm. SH: 30-35 cm. W: 2.4-6 kg. SL: 9.1 cm. SW: 6.4 cm. DF: 30. CN: 38. A small-sized cat, with long legs and tail, and a slender body compared with Domestic Cats. There is a wide variation in coat length and color, from pale sandy-brown to grizzled light or dark gray, with gray-black or brown spots or stripes on the back and flanks and bold stripes on the legs or no spots or stripes. Dorsal line absent. Underparts whitish to buff. Chin and throat whitish. Faint stripes on cheek, crown, nape, and dorsum. Medium-sized triangular pointed ears, reddish or rusty-brown behind, with indistinct grayish-black margins, with a short apical tuft, inner hairs whitish or cream. Feet yellowish above, palm and sole black. Tail relatively long, with several distal rings and black tip.

Young

Felis lybica lybica

OTHER NAMES Arabian Wild Cat, Gordon's Wild Cat, Tristram's Wild Cat. *French*: Chat ganté, chat sauvage d'Afrique, chat orné. *German*: Nordafrikanische Falbkatze. *Spanish*: Gato silvestre norafricano, gato montés norafricano. *Russian*: Североафриканский степной кот. *Swahili*: Paka mwitu, pori, kimburu.

TAXONOMY *F. lybica* includes the steppe and bush cats of Africa and Asia. It was previously included within *F. silvestris*. Many subspecies have been described, but three distinct clades have been identified, which are tentatively considered as subspecies (sometimes as species): *F. l. lybica* (North African Wildcat, from E, W, and N Africa, Arabian Peninsula, Middle East, Corsica, Sardinia, and Crete), *F. l. cafra* (South African Wildcat, from S Africa), and *F. l. ornata* (Asian Wildcat, from SW and C Asia, Afghanistan, Pakistan, India, Mongolia, and China). This subspecies includes *foxi, gordoni, haussa, mellandi, reyi, rubida, ocreata, tristrami, syriaca, ugandae*.

SIMILAR SPECIES It hybridizes with feral Domestic Cats, which can make identification confusing; Wildcats can be identified by the russet color on the backs of the ears. Caracals are larger, have long tufts on their ears, and are more uniform in color, with proportionately shorter tails. The Sand Cat is smaller, with a broad face with large, rounded ears, and a pale sandy-buff pelage with indistinct darker markings.

REPRODUCTION *Gestation*: 56-65 days. *Young per Birth*: 1-5, usually 3. *Weaning*: 3-4 months. *Sexual Maturity*: 11 months. *Life Span*: 19 years in captivity. *Breeding Season*: In January-March in the Sahara.

BEHAVIOR *Social Behavior*: Solitary. *Diet*: Small rodents are particularly important, but they also take young hares, hyraxes, young gazelles, birds, and more rarely reptiles, insects, and fruits (dates). Mainly nocturnal and crepuscular, they lie up during the day in grass tufts and bushes, dense vegetation, rock crevices, trees, or burrows dug by other species (foxes, porcupines, etc.); they are also known to dig their own shelters. Both sexes establish, mark, and defend territories.

DISTRIBUTION *Native*: Algeria, Benin, Burkina Faso, Burundi, Cameroon, Central African Republic, Chad, Congo, DR Congo, Djibouti, Egypt, Eritrea, Ethiopia, Gambia, Ghana, Guinea-Bissau, Iraq, Israel, Jordan, Kenya, Kuwait, Lebanon, Libya, Malawi, Mali, Mauritania, Morocco, Niger, Nigeria, Oman, Rwanda, Saudi Arabia, Senegal, Sierra Leone, Somalia, Sudan, Syria, Tanzania, Togo, Tunisia, Turkey, Uganda, United Arab Emirates, Western Sahara. *Presence Uncertain*: Côte d'Ivoire. Boundaries with *F. l. ornata* in Iraq are unclear, and they probably intergrade.

HABITAT Mediterranean scrub forest on rocky slopes, sand dunes, open grassland, bushland, woodland, agricultural land, and around human settlements. They may be found in true desert, but avoid areas of thick forest. Up to 3,000 m in the mountains of Kenya and Ethiopia.

CONSERVATION STATUS Least Concern. CITES: Appendix II. Hybridization with feral Domestic Cats is widespread, and purebred *F. l. lybica* is not found in many areas. Domestic Cats are bigger and more successful in competition for living space, food, and estrous ♀. This species has no resistance again feline distemper and captive born kittens die within their first year if not vaccinated, while feral cats seem to acquire resistance early in life and can infect purebred Wildcats.

PHOTO CREDITS TL, B: *Javier Gómez Aoiz*, Serengeti NP (Tanzania); TR: *Eric François*, Parc des Félins (France); CL: *Klaus Rudloff*, Tel Aviv Zoo (Israel); Young: *Alexander Sliwa,* Wuppertal Zoo (Germany).

South African Wildcat

FELIS LYBICA CAFRA

BL: 54.5-66.5 cm (♂), 46-62 cm (♀). TL: 25-36 cm. SH: 35-50 cm. W: 3.8-6.4 kg (♂), 2.4-5.5 kg (♀). SL: 9.3 cm (♂), 8.8 cm (♀). SW: 7.6 cm (♂), 6.7 cm (♀). DF: 30. CN: 38. A small-sized cat, with long legs and tail, and a slender body compared with Domestic Cats. There is considerable variation in color and markings, from pale sandy-brown to grizzled light or dark gray, with gray-black or brown spots or stripes on the back and flanks or no spots or stripes. Dorsal line blackish. Underparts whitish to buff. Chin and throat whitish. Faint stripes on cheek, crown, nape, and dorsum. Medium-sized triangular pointed ears, reddish or rusty-brown behind, with indistinct grayish-black margins, sometimes with a short apical tuft, inner hairs whitish or cream. Legs distinctly marked with transverse black bands, and red fur behind the hind legs. Feet hairy below, except on the pads, the hair black or very dark brown. Tail relatively long, with several distal rings and black tip. Males are larger than the females.

Felis lybica cafra

OTHER NAMES *French*: Chat ganté, chat sauvage d'Afrique, chat orné. *German*: Südliche Falbkatze. *Spanish*: Gato silvestre sudafricano, gato montés sudafricano. *Russian*: Южноафриканский степной кот. *Shona*: nhiriri/nhiriri, goya. *Ndebele*: Igola.

TAXONOMY Considered as a subspecies of African Wildcat (*F. lybica*). Includes *griselda* and *mellandi*.

SIMILAR SPECIES The Black-Footed Cat is much smaller, with a proportionally large head, and distinctly marked with dark to black spots and bars on body, and tail and legs are always distinctly ringed with dark brown or black, and backs of ears are the same color as the body. Domestic Cats and hybrids lose the rich red color of the back of the ears and have shorter legs.

REPRODUCTION *Gestation*: 56-65 days. *Young per Birth*: 1-5, usually 3. *Weaning*: 3-4 months. *Sexual Maturity*: 11 months. *Life Span*: 19 years in captivity. *Breeding Season*: Throughout the year; births are mainly recorded from September to March in South Africa. Courtship and mating follow a similar pattern to that of the Domestic Cat. Kittens are born in burrows dug by other species, in rock tumbles, crevices, or amongst dense vegetation; they emerge from the den after 7-10 days, and disperse at 4-6 months. ♂ play no role in raising the young.

BEHAVIOR *Social Behavior*: Solitary, but pairs or family parties have been seen hunting together. *Diet*: Mainly small mammals (murids, hares, rabbits, squirrels, and springhares), but it may take the young of small antelope, including gazelles and domestic goat kids and sheep lambs; it may also prey on birds, amphibians, reptiles, including snakes, and insects. *Main Predators*: Lion, Leopards, Spotted Hyena, raptors. Mainly nocturnal, but may remain active until late in the morning, especially in winter months. Terrestrial although they are adept at climbing trees when they are under stress or when hunting. Their hunting technique is typically felid: the stalk, the crouch, accompanied by a settling of the hind feet to get a good grip on the ground, and then the rush in to the kill. Both sexes mark their ranges using droppings and tree scratchings in conjunction with urine spraying.

DISTRIBUTION *Native*: Angola, Botswana, Lesotho, Malawi, Mozambique, Namibia, South Africa, Swaziland, Tanzania, Zimbabwe.

HABITAT A wide variety of habitats, from sea level to about 2,400 m. In the arid W and central areas of South Africa they are commonly associated with hill ranges and isolated rock outcroppings, penetrating the surrounding plains mainly along dry watercourses. Shows strong association with a variety of woodland types. They require adequate cover to rest up in during the day. It is commonly found in and around cultivated areas and often in association with human settlements; in agriculturally developed areas, it uses the shelter of standing crops such as maize and other high-standing grain crops. Absent in tropical and montane forest.

CONSERVATION STATUS Least Concern. CITES: Appendix II. Generally common despite human persecution, and high densities may be reached in suitable areas. Threatened by hybridization with feral Domestic Cats, especially in South Africa; it is becoming increasingly difficult to find purebred African Wildcats anywhere near settled areas.

PHOTO CREDITS T: *Ecophoto*, Kalahari (South Africa); CL: *Martin Mecnarowski*, Kalahari (South Africa); CR: *Alexander Sliwa*, Karoo Cats (South Africa); B: *Steve Toon*, Kgalagadi (South Africa).

Asian Wildcat
FELIS LYBICA ORNATA

BL: 47-60 cm (♂), 46 cm (♀). TL: 25-31 cm. SH: 25-30 cm. W: 3-4 kg (♂), 2.7 kg (♀). SL: 8.7 cm (♂), 8.2 cm (♀). SW: 6.6 cm (♂), 6 cm (♀). DF: 30. CN: 38. A small-sized cat, with long legs and tail, and a stout and long body compared with Domestic Cats, smaller and more yellow or reddish in color than the European Wildcat, with characteristic small dark spots instead of stripes. Coat is pale sandy to ashy or stone-gray, with solid black or dark brown spots all over its body, and sometimes stripes. Underparts are unspotted and whitish. Winter coat is softer, fuller, and darker. Medium-sized ears, same color as the body, with a small hair-tuft at the tip. Forehead with scattered small spots, not vertical stripes. Cheeks with 2 clear, black markings. Stripes on the base of the limbs. Soles of the feet are black, sometimes extending nearly to the hock. Tail is long and thin, tipped black, with spots near the base and rings near the tip.

summer coat

winter coat

Felis lybica ornata

OTHER NAMES Indian Desert Cat, Asian Steppe Wildcat. *French*: Chat sauvage d'Asie, chat orné. *German*: Asiatische Wildkatze, Steppenkatze. *Spanish*: Gato montés asiático. *Russian*: Азиатский степной кот. *Dari*: Psk dsty. *Chinese*: Ye mao, caoyuan ban mao. *Georgian*: Velis cata. *Gujarati*: Ran biladi. *Kutch*: Jhangmeno. *Farsi*: Gorbeh yahhshi. *Kazakh*: Myshuk dala, jawa misik. *Kirgiz*: Matsyl, zhapayi mishik. *Mongolian*: Tsookhondoi. *Uygur*: Yawa müshükl. *Uzbek*: Choi pshak, sabancha, yobai pshak.

TAXONOMY Considered as a subspecies of African Wildcat (*F. lybica*). Previously considered as a subspecies of European Wildcat (*F. silvestris ornata*). Includes *iraki*, *nesterovi*, and *caudata*.

SIMILAR SPECIES The Chinese Mountain Cat is similar, but it lacks the obvious body spots, though lightly marked individuals are difficult to differentiate. The Jungle Cat is larger, with longer legs, has a distinctive white muzzle, less conspicuous body markings, no cheek stripe, a more prominent lacrimal stripe, black ear tufts, and a shorter tail.

REPRODUCTION *Gestation*: 56-68 days. *Young per Birth*: 2-4. *Weaning*: Unknown. *Sexual Maturity*: 9-12 months (first breeding probably takes place at 18-22 months). *Life Span*: 16 years in captivity. *Breeding Season*: From March to April and from November to December in India, from January to February in Central Asia, year-round in Pakistan. Kittens do not accompany their mother until 3 months of age. The mother teaches her cubs to hunt by providing them injured prey or beetles.

BEHAVIOR *Social Behavior*: Solitary. *Diet*: Rodents (jerboas, gerbils, voles, and mice), but it occasionally takes birds, amphibians, insects, and reptiles; it sometimes scavenges food, or preys upon poultry and small livestock. Mostly nocturnal but can also be observed during daytime. It rests and dens in burrows. It hunts on the ground and yet is a very good climber. Like most solitary felids, it hunts its prey by stalking followed by a quick attack. Territorial.

DISTRIBUTION *Native*: Afghanistan, Armenia, Azerbaijan, China, Georgia, India, Iran, Iraq, Kazakhstan, Kyrgyzstan, Mongolia, Pakistan, Tajikistan, Turkey, Turkmenistan, Uzbekistan. India is the SE border of its range and its occurrence is reported from the drier areas of W and central India. The W extent of its distribution is unknown.

HABITAT A wide variety of habitats, mostly in scrub deserts, mountainous areas with sufficient vegetation, as well as temperate forests, up to 3,000 m. It avoids vast deserts, dense forests, and deep snow. It usually occurs close to water sources but can also live in low-water areas. It does not avoid cultivated areas and human settlements.

CONSERVATION STATUS Least concern. CITES: Appendix II. Its status is not very clear due to its cryptic behavior and its hybridization with Domestic Cats. Recent population estimates are missing. Threatened by hybridization and competition for food with feral Domestic Cats (there may be very few genetically pure populations remaining). Other threats include poaching related to conflict with humans and for its fur, and habitat destruction. Hunting and trade are prohibited across most of its range.

PHOTO CREDITS TL: *Alexander Sliwa*, Port Lympne Reserve (UK); TR: *Vijaybabu Kaliappan*, Desert NP, Rajasthan (India); C: *Bernard Castelein*, Rajasthan (India); B: *Terry Whittaker.*

Chinese Mountain Cat

FELIS BIETI

BL: 60-84 cm. TL: 29-35 cm. SH: Unknown. W: 5.5-9 kg. DF: 30. CN: Unknown. A medium-sized cat, with a stocky body and relatively short legs, resembling a large Domestic Cat. Coat is long and thick, nearly uniform yellow-gray in winter, darkening to tawny or gray-brown in summer, with pale rufous or yellow-white underparts. Darkish dorsal midline. Some individuals may have indistinct darker stripes and blotches on the lower limbs, sides, and nape, especially in the short summer coat. Two indistinct pale rufous stripes on the cheeks. Lower lip, chin, and belly are white. Ears are triangular and relatively long, with short dark reddish tufts on the tip, reddish-brown at the back. At the base of the ear is a pale reddish-brown area. Eyes are pale blue. Bushy tail, conspicuously banded with 3-6 dark rings and a dark tip (some individuals have a pale tip).

Felis bieti

OTHER NAMES Chinese Steppe Cat, Chinese Desert Cat, Grass Cat. *French*: Chat de Biet. *German*: Graukatze, Gobikatze. *Spanish*: Gato de Biet, gato del desierto de China. *Russian*: Китайская (горная) кошка, или гобийская кошка. *Chinese*: Cao shili, huang mo mao. *Kazakh*: Shel misigi. *Uygur*: Qel müshüki.

TAXONOMY Monotypic. The taxonomy of the species remains unclear. Formerly recognized as a subspecies of Asian Wildcat (*F. lybica ornata*), it has been recently attributed species status. Includes *bieti*, *chutuchta* (probably a form of *F. lybica*), and *vellerosa* (probably *F. chaus* or *F. catus*).

SIMILAR SPECIES The species most resembles the Wildcat (*F. lybica ornata*), or a large Domestic Cat.

REPRODUCTION *Gestation*: 60 days. *Young per Birth*: Unknown. *Weaning*: Unknown. *Sexual Maturity*: Unknown. *Life Span*: Unknown. *Breeding Season*: From January to March, with most births occurring around May. Cubs become independent at 7-8 months.

BEHAVIOR *Social Behavior*: Probably solitary, except during the breeding season. *Diet*: Zokors (*Eospalax*, *Myospalax*), voles (*Microtus*), pikas (*Ochotona*), and hares (*Lepus*); it also captures birds, especially pheasants, and apparently raids poultry especially during winter; this species most probably also scavenges. *Main Predators*: Probably wolves, golden eagles, domestic dogs. Nocturnal or crepuscular. The Chinese Mountain Cat is one of the most poorly known living felids. This species occurs at high altitudes, in areas with harsh climatic seasonal extremes. They rest and den in rocky terrain, under tree roots, in dense thickets, and in the burrows of marmots and Eurasian badgers. Most such burrows have been found on S facing slopes and some at elevations of 3,600 m. Chinese Mountain Cats are reported to listen for zokors in their subterranean tunnels, and rapidly dig them out. The same technique would also work during winter when some small rodents are active in subnivean tunnels. There is no information on home range size or density.

DISTRIBUTION *Native*: China. It has a restricted distribution in central China, occurring on the NE region of the Qinghai-Tibetan Plateau (SW Gansu, Inner Mongolia, E Qinghai, and Xinjiang).

HABITAT Mountainous areas, including alpine meadow, alpine bush, edges of coniferous forests, grassy meadows, steppe forests, grasslands, and steppe, at elevations between 2,800 and 4,100 m.

CONSERVATION STATUS Vulnerable. CITES: Appendix II. It is naturally rare. There are probably fewer than 10,000 individuals, with fragmented subpopulations unlikely to contain more than 1,000 individuals. Threats include accidental killing through the control of pikas using poisons and targeted hunting for the illegal trade in furs. Its population is probably declining. Protected in China. Research on its status and distribution is urgently needed as well as further studies about its ecology and demography to enable efficient conservation measures.

PHOTO CREDITS T, B: *Daniel López-Velasco*, Sichuan (China); C: *Lianquan Yu*, Qinghai Zoo *(China)*.

Western Jungle Cat

FELIS CHAUS CHAUS

BL: 60-76 cm. TL: 19-35 cm. SH: 39.5-45 cm. W: 5-13 kg (♂), 2.5-8.9 kg (♀). SL: 12 cm. SW: 7.9 cm. DF: 28-30. CN: 38. A medium-sized, large-bodied, long-legged cat, with shortish, banded tail and large, pointed ears, larger than a Domestic Cat. The largest subspecies. Coat is plain and uniformly colored, grizzled pale gray to yellow-brown, paling toward flanks. Dorsal stripe absent. Underside and inside of legs pale cream. Fur rough in the summer coat. Head with rather elongated muzzle, buffish along nose with white patch below eye and very faint markings along forehead. Cheeks unpatterned. Eyes yellow. Throat white or light cream. Long ears with backs reddish-buff, with a short black apical tuft. Prominent black rings inside of forelegs, and pale stripes on front and hind legs. Feet ocher to brown, black below. Tail distinctly short with rounded tip, buffish with 2-3 blackish rings and black tip. Males larger than females. Females with 4 pairs of nipples. Kittens have very distinctive black markings on their coats and a very short tail.

Felis chaus chaus

OTHER NAMES Reed Cat, Swamp Cat. *French*: Chat de jungle, Chat des Marais. *German*: Rohrkatze, Sumpfluchs. *Spanish*: Gato de la jungla occidental, gato de los pantanos occidental. *Russian*: Среднеазиатский камышовый кот. *Iranian*: Gorbeh jangali. *Arabic*: Qitt barri nili. *Turkish*: Saz kedisi.

TAXONOMY Originally placed in a separate genus (*Catolynx*) due to its resemblance to the Eurasian Lynx, but was later reassigned to the genus *Felis*. Three subspecies are currently recognized, but further phylogeographical studies are required to better understand geographical variation in this species: *F. c. chaus* (Egypt and the Middle East to Turkmenistan, Uzbekistan, Kazakhstan, and Afghanistan); *F. c. affinis* (E Afghanistan, Indian subcontinent, and Sri Lanka); and *F. c. fulvidina* (SE Asia, possibly including China). Pelage characters used by classical designators vary widely. This subspecies includes *oxiana*, *nilotica*, and *furax*.

SIMILAR SPECIES The Sand Cat is much smaller, with shorter legs, paler coat, with proportionately longer tail and broader ears. The African Wildcat is smaller, with a longer tail, body markings more conspicuous, including a cheek stripe.

REPRODUCTION *Gestation*: 63-68 days. *Young per Birth*: 1-4, generally 2-3. *Weaning*: Unknown. *Sexual Maturity*: 11-18 months. *Life Span*: 20 years in captivity. *Breeding Season*: In January to February in Central Asia; in Armenia, births occur in early May, while in Egypt, births occur in January to April.

BEHAVIOR *Social Behavior*: Largely solitary, except ♀ with kittens. *Diet*: Fish, birds (waterfowl, poultry, galliform birds), and rodents, but also reptiles, amphibians, eggs, and fruit. *Main Predators*: Golden jackals, Leopards. Information on the ecology, distribution, and status of this species is still sparse. Largely nocturnal but also active at dusk and occasionally during the day, where not disturbed or in cool weather. A very good swimmer, and can hunt in water. It is also a very good tree climber. When threatened, reacts like the Wildcat, arching the back, raising the fur, and hissing. Other calls include a loud mewing at mating and the familiar purr.

DISTRIBUTION *Native*: Afghanistan, Armenia, Azerbaijan, Egypt, Georgia, Iran, Iraq, Israel, Jordan, Kazakhstan, Lebanon, Pakistan, Russia, Syria, Tajikistan, Turkey, Turkmenistan, Uzbekistan. *Presence Uncertain*: Kyrgyzstan.

HABITAT A variety of habitat types from plains and agricultural lands to the mountains. Most common in shrublands, woodlands, marshes, and reed beds. They may occur in cultivated landscapes (cane, maize fields), especially those that lead to increased numbers of rodents, and artificial wetlands. In Israel, recorded around fish ponds and tamarisk thickets.

CONSERVATION STATUS Least Concern. CITES: Appendix II. Population declines and range contraction are of concern in Egypt, the Caucasus, SW and Central Asia, and parts of Turkey. In Russia there are about 500 animals left in the wild, and very small populations persist in Georgia, Armenia, Azerbaijan, and Georgia. Main threats include habitat destruction for agricultural purposes and infrastructure development, and illegal hunting, especially in Turkey and Iran. Some illegal trade and killing still occur in Egypt and Afghanistan.

Indian Jungle Cat

FELIS CHAUS AFFINIS

BL: 55-69 cm. TL: 21-25 cm. SH: 35.5-38 cm. W: 5-12 kg (♂), 2.5-9 kg (♀). SL: 10.8 cm (♂), 9.4 cm (♀). SW: 7.8 cm (♂), 7.0 cm (♀). DF: 28-30. CN: 38. A medium-sized, large-bodied, long-legged cat, with shortish, banded tail and large, pointed ears. Much smaller and lighter than *chaus* subspecies. Coat is plain and uniformly colored, grizzled buff or yellowish-gray. Melanistic individuals occur in Pakistan and India. Individuals from Sri Lanka and southern India have a shorter, darker, and richly colored coat. Underside and inside of legs pale cream. Head with rather elongated muzzle, buffish along nose with white patch below eye. Cheeks unpatterned. Eyes yellow. Throat white or light cream. Long ears with backs reddish-buff, with a black apical short tuft. Black rings inside of forelegs, and indistinct dark stripes on the outer surface of the legs. Tail distinctly short with rounded tip, buffish with 2-3 blackish rings and black tip. Males larger than females. Females with 4 pairs of nipples.

North India coat

Sri Lanka coat

Young

Felis chaus affinis

OTHER NAMES Reed Cat, Swamp Cat. *French*: Chat de jungle, chat des Marais. *German*: Rohrkatze, Sumpfluchs. *Spanish*: Gato de la jungla indio, gato de los pantanos de India. *Russian*: Индийский камышовый кот. *Odia*: Bana bhua. *Bengali*: Bano biral. *Hindi*: Jangli billi. *Assamese*: Jongli mekuri. *Telugu*: Jungam pilli. *Gujarati*: Jungli biladi. *Kannada*: Kaadu bekku. *Tamil*: Kaattu poonai. *Manipuri*: Lam houdong. *Kashmiri*: Lesh. *Malayalam*: Pokkan. *Marathi*: Ran manjar.

TAXONOMY Considered as a subspecies of Jungle Cat (*F. chaus*). Includes *kelaarti*, *prateri*, and *kutas*.

SIMILAR SPECIES The Caracal has a uniform coat, not grizzled, with black backs to the ears, and very long, prominent ear tufts.

REPRODUCTION *Gestation*: 63-68 days. *Young per Birth*: 1-4, generally 2-3. *Weaning*: Unknown. *Sexual Maturity*: 11-18 months. *Life Span*: 20 years in captivity. *Breeding Season*: Probably year-round, in October in SW India, in the early spring, and again after the monsoon in Pakistan. Both ♂ and ♀ produce bark-like calls when females are in estrus. Den in disused burrows of other species, rock cavities, deep thickets, or dry areas in reed beds, and also in abandoned buildings. The kittens are kept in a hidden reed-bed den, lined with fur and grass, concealed and located in inaccessible areas.

BEHAVIOR *Social Behavior*: Solitary, but family groups of a ♂ with a ♀ and cubs have been seen. *Diet*: Small mammals (hares, mouse-deer, rodents), birds and eggs, reptiles, and frogs. In a semi-arid environment of W India they feed largely on rodents and less frequently on birds and invertebrates; they are also capable of hunting larger prey such as young swine, subadult gazelles, and chital fawns; they are dependent on water for drinking. It can be seen hunting early in the morning and early in the evening, although it is probably nocturnal where there is a human presence. They can climb trees if needed. As in other felids, ♂ control a home range that encompasses the home range of several ♀. When hunting, they will sit motionless, attentively listening for the sounds of their prey, and then leap vertically high in the air, landing and catching the prey. Similar leaps are also used to catch birds.

DISTRIBUTION *Native*: Bangladesh, Bhutan, China, India, Nepal, Pakistan, Sri Lanka.

HABITAT Mainly associated with dense riparian vegetation, especially reed beds and marshes, but may also occur in shrubby woodland, grassland, evergreen forests, deciduous forest, lowland dipterocarp forests, desert, agricultural lands and forest plantations, around human villages, and suburban areas up to 2,400 m in the Himalaya. Its occurrence in arid environments, such as sand deserts, is rare. Despite its name, the Jungle Cat is more of a grassland cat and is not strongly associated with closed forest. Not as dependent on burrows as *F. silvestris*.

CONSERVATION STATUS Least Concern. CITES: Appendix II. The most common cat species in India, Nepal, and Bangladesh, where the majority of the global population occurs. In India, there is evidence of continued habitat loss due to industrialization and urbanization of low intensity agricultural areas and scrubland, and ongoing poaching as a result of conflict with farmers. As a species associated with riparian habitats it can be significantly affected by extensive droughts.

PHOTO CREDITS TL, CL, B: *Vivek Sharma*, Jabalpur, Madhya Pradesh (India); TR: *Alexander Sliwa*, Dehiwala (Sri Lanka); Young: *Felineus*, Ranthambore NP (India).

Indochinese Jungle Cat
FELIS CHAUS FULVIDINA

BL: 58-76 cm. TL: 20-27 cm. SH: 35-40 cm. W: 5-13 kg. SL: 10.8 cm (♂), 10.3 cm (♀). DF: 28-30. CN: 38. A medium-sized, large-bodied, long-legged cat, with shortish, banded tail and large, pointed ears. Coat is short, plain, and uniformly colored, grizzled reddish to brownish-gray, on average tawnier than the Indian Jungle Cat. Darker stripe down the center of the back. Underside and inside of legs light clear fulvous. Winter coat is darker. Face, sides of neck, and whole outer side of limbs uniform fulvescent without spotting. Chin, throat, and inguinal region are white to light gray, grading into fulvous laterally. Chest band stronger fulvous. Head with rather elongated muzzle, with white patch below eye and very faint markings along forehead. Cheeks unpatterned. Long ears with backs reddish-buff, with small dark brown to black tufts. Prominent black rings inside of forelegs, and pale stripes on front and hind legs. Tail distinctly short with rounded tip, buffish with distinctive dark rings on the distal half, and black tip.

Felis chaus fulvidina

OTHER NAMES Reed Cat, Swamp Cat. *French*: Chat de jungle indochinois, chat des marais indochinois. *German*: Rohrkatze, Sumpfluchs. *Spanish*: Gato de la jungla indochino, gato de los pantanos de Indochina. *Russian*: Индокитайский камышовый кот. *Chinese*: Conglin mao, limao. *Burmese*: Kyaung-ba. *Arakanese*: Kyung tset-kun. *Lao*: Meo pa. *Thai*: Maew pa, sewa kratay.

TAXONOMY Considered as a subspecies of Jungle Cat (*F. chaus*). The taxonomic status of Indochinese Jungle Cats needs to be reviewed; if valid, this taxonomic distinctiveness would enhance the need to conserve the species in Indochina.

REPRODUCTION *Gestation*: 63-68 days. *Young per Birth*: 1-4, generally 2-3. *Weaning*: Unknown. *Sexual Maturity*: 11-18 months. *Life Span*: Probably 20 years in captivity. *Breeding Season*: From January to February in China; however, kittens have been observed year-round.

BEHAVIOR *Social Behavior*: Solitary. *Diet*: Rodents, lagomorphs, birds and their eggs, amphibians, fish, and reptiles; they occasionally take the young of small ungulates such as a wild pigs, gazelles, and deer fawns; where they live next to humans, they will take chickens, ducks, and geese. Very little is known about their behavior in the wild. While they can be found at all times of the day or night, they are more diurnal than most cat species. They can climb and swim, although they chiefly hunt on the ground.

DISTRIBUTION *Native*: Cambodia, China, Laos, Myanmar, Thailand, Vietnam.

HABITAT A wide variety of habitat types: tall grass, swamps, cattail thickets, and reeds, as well as wet lowland forests around lakes. Also found in dry environments along riparian ecosystems and tropical deciduous forests and shrublands. Rarely in tropical rainforests, in spite of its name. They are usually found near water and prefer dense cover, although they have been reported from desert areas with only sparse cover. Often found in agricultural areas, sugarcane plantations, and associated with gardens, hedgerows, and barns, and are seen around dwellings.

CONSERVATION STATUS Critically Endangered. CITES: Appendix II. Extremely scarce in mainland SE Asia and largely restricted to remote lowland deciduous dipterocarp forest. In Indochina, all other small and medium-sized cats are recorded much more frequently than Jungle Cat. Its preference for open scrub and grassland in S Asia makes the species more susceptible to habitat loss than cat species that also utilize denser evergreen forests.

PHOTO CREDITS T: *Parinya Padungtin*, Omkoi Wildlife Sanctuary (Thailand) and *Alex Kantorovich*, Chiang Mai Zoo (Thailand); CL: *Israel Didham*, Yadanabon Zoo (Myanmar); B: *Kobchai Matasurawit*, Chiang Mai Zoo (Thailand).

African Sand Cat

FELIS MARGARITA MARGARITA

BL: 42-45 cm (♂), 39-42 cm (♀). TL: 23.5-29 cm. SH: 25-30.5 cm. W: 2.2-2.85 kg (♂), 1.6 kg (♀). SL: 7.9-8.3 cm. SW: 6.4-7 cm. DF: 30. CN: 38. A small cat, with a broad face, large ears, short legs, and overall pale coloration. The smallest subspecies, brighter and more yellowish in color. Pelage is soft and dense, with woolly underfur, making it appear much larger, pale sandy-buff in color, finely speckled with gray over the shoulders and upper flanks, with 7-8 faint reddish-black vertical stripes, broken up into spots. Markings fade with age. Belly and throat are white. Dark horizontal bars on the legs. Head flat and broad with well-developed sideburns. Crown marked with indistinct striations, and reddish streaks from its eyes across the cheeks. Yellow eyes. Large black-tipped ears, set widely apart and low, with the tip tinted black, thick white hair inside, without tufts. Dense dark fur growing between the toes and on the foot soles, completely covering the pads. Longish tail, with 2 to 8 black rings and a black tip. Males larger and heavier than females. Four pairs of nipples.

Young

Felis margarita margarita

OTHER NAMES Sand Dune Cat. *French*: Chat des sables. *German*: Sandkatze, Wüstenkatze. *Spanish*: Gato del desierto africano, gato del Sahara. *Russian*: Североафриканский барханный кот.

TAXONOMY Two subspecies are currently recognized: *F. m. margarita* (North Africa), and *F. m. thinobia* (SW Asia and the Arabian Peninsula), as genetic data support the distinctiveness of North African Sand Cats, albeit weakly. There appear to be differences in pelage coloration and markings and skull size between North African Sand Cats and those from Pakistan, but phylogeographical studies are needed to confirm this classification.

SIMILAR SPECIES *F. lybica* is larger and darker, with longer legs, a relatively smaller and narrower head, and more vertically oriented ears; plantar and digital pads not concealed by thick mat of long hair.

REPRODUCTION *Gestation*: 59-67 days. *Young per Birth*: 2-8, usually 3. *Weaning*: 5 weeks. *Sexual Maturity*: 9-14 months. *Life Span*: 14 years in captivity. *Breeding Season*: In the Sahara, mating takes place from November to February. In Niger, the young are born from January to April. Young become independent as early as 4 months.

BEHAVIOR *Social Behavior*: Solitary, except during the mating season. *Diet*: Small desert rodents (spiny mice, jirds, jerboas, Cape hare), but also small birds (larks), reptiles (desert monitor lizards, sandfish, geckos, and snakes), and insects; it is independent of drinking water. *Main Predators*: Domestic dog, jackals, red fox, Eurasian eagle-owl (young). Nocturnal and in winter also crepuscular. In the Moroccan Sahara, they do not use dens in winter, but hide amongst rocks, under vegetation, or in birds' nests in acacia trees during the day. With its thickly furred feet, it is well adapted to the extremes of a desert environment, living in areas far from water, and tolerant of extremes of hot and cold temperatures. When they are surprised they crouch immediately behind the nearest tuft of vegetation, chin on the sand, completely motionless; some individuals are surprisingly placid when encountered, and they tame easily. Home range sizes vary according to ecological conditions and vegetation availability for prey animals. In S Morocco, home ranges were estimated at 80 to 1,300 km². Home ranges of ♂ may overlap with each other and there is a considerable overlap between seasonal ranges of ♂ and ♀. Sand Cats have been recorded to move long distances in a single night (5-15 km). ♂ utter a distinctive series of fast yap-like calls, like a small dog.

DISTRIBUTION *Native*: Algeria, Chad, Egypt, Mali, Mauritania, Morocco, Niger, Sudan, Western Sahara. No confirmed records exist from Tunisia, Libya, and W of the Nile River in Egypt.

HABITAT Sandy and stony desert, around sparse vegetation that can support small rodent prey. It is known to use burrows as resting sites and is absent from areas where the soil is compacted.

CONSERVATION STATUS Least Concern. CITES: Appendix II. This species occurs naturally at low densities, and confirmed records are sparse. Its status and the impact of threats on the species are difficult to assess. Hunting of this species is prohibited in Algeria, Mauritania, Niger, and Tunisia. Main threats include the expansion of human settlement, and the introduction of feral and domestic dogs and cats, which serve both as direct competitors and predators, as well as vectors for disease transmission.

PHOTO CREDITS T: *Alain Dragesco-Joffe,* Sahara (Niger); C, B: *Alexander Sliwa* (Morocco).

Asian Sand Cat
FELIS MARGARITA THINOBIA

BL: 44-57 cm (♂), 43-48 cm (♀). TL: 22-35.5 cm. SH: 25-30.5 cm. W: 2-2.5 kg (♂), 1.8 kg (♀). SL: 8.4-9.7 cm. SW: 6.5-7.8 cm. DF: 30. CN: 38. A small cat, with a broad face, large ears, short legs, and overall pale coloration. The largest subspecies, grayer pelage with fewer markings. Soft and dense coat, longer in winter, with a much darker dorsal overlay and a less defined stripe pattern than in summer. Overall color is pale sandy-buff, with 7-8 faint reddish-black vertical stripes, broken up into spots. Belly and throat are white. Dark horizontal bars on the legs. Head flat and broad with well-developed sideburns. Crown marked with indistinct striations. Reddish streaks from eyes across the cheeks. Large black-tipped ears, set widely apart and low, with the tip tinted black, thick white hair inside, without tufts. Dense dark fur growing between the toes and on the foot soles, completely covering the pads. Longish tail, with 2-9 black rings and a black tip. Males larger and heavier than females. Four pairs of nipples. Kittens are grayer, with the pattern better expressed.

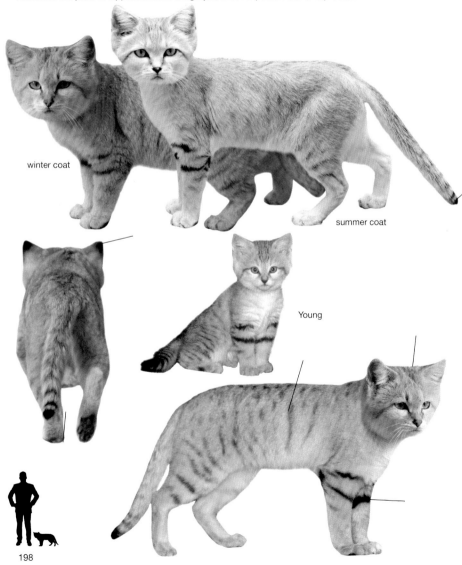

winter coat

summer coat

Young

Felis margarita thinobia

OTHER NAMES Sand Dune Cat, Barchan Cat, Arabian Sand Cat. *French*: Chat des sables. *German*: Sandkatze, Wüstenkatze. *Spanish*: Gato del desierto asiático. *Russian*: Азиатский барханный кот. *Arabic*: Qit al rimal. *Tamahaq*: Qareschtar, aghsheter. *Farsi*: Gorbeh sheni. *Hebrew*: Hattul holot. *Kazakh*: Sevin. *Uzbek*: Mushuk.

TAXONOMY Considered as a subspecies of *F. margarita* (Sand Cat). This subspecies includes *harrisoni* (Arabian Peninsula, Sinai, Israel), *thinobia* (Central Asia and Iran), and *scheffeli* (Pakistan).

SIMILAR SPECIES Jungle Cat has a sandy-brown pelage, without distinctive markings, reddish-brown hair on ear backs with short, black tufts of hair at tips.

REPRODUCTION *Gestation*: 59-67 days. *Young per Birth*: 2-8, usually 3. *Weaning*: 5 weeks. *Sexual Maturity*: 9-14 months. *Life Span*: 14 years in captivity. *Breeding Season*: April in Turkmenistan, September to October in Pakistan. Kittens begin to walk by the 21st day, and by 5 weeks they emerge from the burrow and begin to dig for food.

BEHAVIOR *Social Behavior*: Solitary, except during the mating season. *Diet*: Sand-dwelling rodents (jerboas, jirds, gerbils), but also reptiles and insects; it may cover kills with sand and return later to feed. *Main Predators*: Jackals, snakes, birds of prey. Primarily nocturnal, but has some diurnal activity in winter. Not a good climber or jumper, but an excellent digger. It may dig burrows to escape the heat of the day or adopt dens from other species. In Central Asia it withstands 40°C in summer and -25°C in winter. Burrows are shared with other individuals, but more than one cat never occupies the same burrow simultaneously. It is known to lie on its back outside the burrow to release internal heat. It has an estimated home range of about 20-51 km² in Saudi Arabia, and territories of neighboring ♂ often overlap. It has a loud mating call, which resembles the barking of a small dog.

DISTRIBUTION *Native*: Iran, Iraq, Jordan, Kazakhstan, Kuwait, Oman, Saudi Arabia, Syria, Turkmenistan, United Arab Emirates, Uzbekistan. *Presence Uncertain*: Palestine, Qatar. *Possibly Extinct*: Israel, Pakistan, Yemen.

HABITAT Sand dunes with shrubs and small trees and arid flat plains with little vegetation. In the Arabian Peninsula it also occurs in areas of hard, rocky substrate.

CONSERVATION STATUS Least Concern. CITES: Appendix II. Hunting is prohibited in Iran, Israel, Kazakhstan, Pakistan, and United Arab Emirates. Major threats include habitat loss and degradation, which may lead to population fragmentation. The micro-distribution of the small mammals that make up an important part of its diet is often found close around vegetation and does not extend into bare sand ranges, limiting the distribution and density of Sand Cats in areas devoid of vegetation or during drought years leading to a loss of vegetation. An additional threat is the introduction of feral and Domestic Cats, and human disturbance, to which Sand Cats seem to be very sensitive. Locally, the species is also threatened by the pet trade. The current captive population consists only of this subspecies.

PHOTO CREDITS TL, C, B: *Alexander Sliwa*, Parc des Félins (France); TR: *Juan José Part Oliver*, Pont Scorff Zoo (France); Young: *Alexander Sliwa*, Wuppertal Zoo (Germany).

Black-Footed Cat
FELIS NIGRIPES

BL: 37-52 cm (♂), 35-41 cm (♀). TL: 12-20 cm. SH: 25 cm. W: 1.5-2.5 kg (♂), 1-1.6 kg (♀). SL: 7.5 cm (♂), 7 cm (♀). SW: 5.8 cm. DF: 30. CN: 38. A very small-sized stocky cat (the smallest cat species in Africa). Coat is soft, longer and denser in winter, from cinnamon-buff to pale tawny in color, with numerous prominent dark brown to black spots and bars on body, legs, head, and tail. Underparts pale buff or white. Throat white with 2 or 3 distinct dark bands. Broad head. Small nose, red in color, black in kittens. Margins of eyes, ears, and mouth white. Two black cheek stripes. Eyes dark yellow to light greenish. Large, widely spaced, rounded ears, back same color as body, without markings. Short legs. Soles are black. Short tail, narrowly black-tipped. Males are larger than females. Females with 3 pairs of nipples.

Young

Felis nigripes

OTHER NAMES Small-Spotted Cat. *French*: Chat à pieds noirs. *German*: Schwarzfußkatze. *Spanish*: Gato de pies negros, gato patinegro. *Russian*: Черноногая кошка. *Afrikaans*: Klein gekolde kat, swart-poot kat, miershooptier. *Sesotho*: Tsetse. *Tswana*: Sebalabolokwane, sebalabala, kêkêtlane. *Xhosa*: Ingwe yeziduli.

TAXONOMY Monotypic. Two subspecies have been traditionally described: *F. n. nigripes* (smaller and paler, with less distinct striping, found in SE Namibia, Botswana, Northern Cape, North West Cape, Gauteng, Limpopo, and Mpumalanga) and *F. n. thomasi* (more tawny appearance with bolder patterning, found in Eastern Cape, W to the S regions of the Northern Cape and the Free State), but are now considered invalid and represent a geographical cline. There are no obvious ecological or geographical barriers between the ranges.

SIMILAR SPECIES The conspecific and more common African Wildcat (*F. silvestris*) is considerably larger, with longer legs and tail, and no clear spotting, but also has black under feet.

REPRODUCTION *Gestation*: 63-68 days. *Young per Birth*: 1-4, typically 2. *Weaning*: 2 months. *Sexual Maturity*: 24 months (♂), 12 months (♀). *Life Span*: 5-6 years. *Breeding Season*: Year-round, with a distinct season from late July to March, with most births in September and October, coinciding with rains and food availability. Kittens are independent after 3-4 months, but remain within the range of their mother for extended periods.

BEHAVIOR *Social Behavior*: Solitary, except when with kittens or during brief mating periods. *Diet*: Small rodents (large-eared mouse, ground squirrels) constitute the most important prey class, followed by larger mammals and small ground-roosting birds, but may also consume amphibians and reptiles. Extremely secretive and strictly crepuscular and nocturnal, resting mostly within dens during daylight. They are predominantly ground-dwellers and will not readily take to trees. Home ranges of ♂ average 20 km² while those of ♀ 9 km², and ♂ home ranges overlap with those of ♀. In arid regions home ranges can be considerably larger, since range size is dependent on available prey resources. Both sexes spray-mark, particularly during mating season. The species prefers hollowed out abandoned termite mounds when available, but will use dens dug by other animals such as springhares, ground squirrels, and aardvark.

DISTRIBUTION *Native*: Botswana, Namibia, South Africa. *Presence uncertain*: Angola.

HABITAT Dry, open savanna, grasslands, and Karoo semi-desert with sparse shrub and tree cover and a mean annual rainfall of 100-500 mm at altitudes up to 2,000 m above sea level. It is not found in the driest and sandiest parts of the Namib and Kalahari Deserts.

CONSERVATION STATUS Vulnerable. CITES: Appendix I. Rare compared to the other small cats of S Africa, with a total population estimated at 10,000 mature individuals. There is a higher density in the central part of South Africa. Main threats include intraguild predation, diseases, declining prey populations due to habitat degradation, and unsuitable farming practices. The majority of the distribution occurs outside of formally protected areas.

PHOTO CREDITS T: *Alexander Sliwa*, Wuppertal Zoo (Germany); C, Young, B: *Alexander Sliwa* (South Africa).

Lynx lineage

LYNX AND BOBCAT

RECOGNITION The Lynx lineage is a monophyletic group that includes four extant species in one genus, *Lynx*, including the Iberian Lynx (*L. pardinus*), Canada Lynx (*L. canadensis*), Eurasian Lynx (*L. lynx*), and Bobcat (*L. rufus*). They are medium-sized cats, sharing a short tail (less than one-third body length), muscular body, long legs in relation to body length, a relatively small head with a short face, characteristic tufted ears, and beard-like ruffs. All species of Lynx have white fur on the chest, belly, and on the insides of the legs, and spotted coats, especially on the limbs. One distinguishing characteristic of this group is the absence of a set of upper premolars, which gives them 28 teeth (I 3/3, C 1/1, P 2/2, M 1/1 = 28) instead of the usual 30 found in other felines. Chromosome number is 2n=38.

PHYLOGENY Paleontological evidence points toward a North American origin of this group. The Lynx lineage descends from a common ancestor that diverged from other cat species and dispersed to the Americas via the reopening of the Bering land bridge. *Lynx issiodorensis*, the oldest known Lynx, first appeared in North America about 4 Ma before spreading to the continents of Asia and Europe where it persisted throughout time. The first species of Lynx to evolve was the Bobcat about 2.5 Ma when it scattered across North America. In Asia, the Eurasian Lynx emerged, the species that would later spread across Europe. The European population of *L. issiodorensis* led to the appearance of the Iberian Lynx 1.5 Ma, when the Iberian Peninsula became a refuge from the Quaternary glaciation. Most recently, in the last 0.2 Ma, the Eurasian Lynx dispersed through the Bering Strait across North America, thus giving rise to the Canada Lynx, which displaced the Bobcat toward more southern latitudes.

BEHAVIOR Lynx are solitary hunters, mostly crepuscular and nocturnal, although in winter they may be active during the daylight hours in response to the activity of their prey. Lynx stalk their prey before pouncing on it, utilizing dense cover, but ambush hunting is occasionally used as well. All species may climb trees. The Eurasian Lynx eats a wide range of prey, including roe deer, various other small mammals, birds, and, quite rarely, domestic livestock. The Bobcat is also a generalist carnivore, eating a wide variety of small mammals, birds, and reptiles. In contrast, the Iberian Lynx preys almost exclusively on rabbits, and the Canada Lynx depends almost exclusively on snowshoe hares.

DISTRIBUTION The Iberian Lynx was formerly distributed throughout Spain and southern France, but today is restricted to two disjunct regions of southwestern Spain. The Eurasian Lynx is a very widespread species, ranging from China in the southeast to Norway in the northwest; in the recent past, it was spread throughout Europe, but as a result of harassment by man its range became restricted to heavily forested regions in the eastern and northern parts of the continent. The Canada Lynx extends from the northern United States northward through Canada and Alaska. The Bobcat extends from Mexico through the United States and northward into Canada; this large area of distribution shows that it has adapted to a wide range of environments, from subtropical swamps to arid areas and temperate forest.

CONSERVATION The Iberian Lynx, one of the most threatened species of carnivore, experienced a severe population decline during the 19th and the early 20th centuries, bringing it to the edge of extinction. Between 2002 and 2017, its population size increased from 52 to 500 individuals, and it no longer qualifies as Critically Endangered. Today, the Iberian Lynx is listed as Endangered and it may become extinct within 35 years in the absence of reintroductions. Canada Lynx populations are considered stable in the northern portion of their range, being managed for the fur trade throughout Alaska and most of Canada. However, in the southern part of their range, they are less abundant and as a result are protected from harvest. Threats to this species include competition from the coyote, aggressive logging, road-building, and habitat destruction. The Eurasian Lynx, once widespread in the forest and forest-steppe regions of the Old World, has been eradicated from many parts of its former range in Europe, and it was intensively hunted for its fur and considered a threat to other wildlife populations. By 1950, the Eurasian Lynx was considered extinct from central, southern (except Balkans), and western Europe. Thanks to conservation programs and reintroductions, it has slowly recolonized these parts of Europe. These populations still appear small and endangered. Its status in China and in Asia is not well known due to a lack of data. Threats to this species include habitat fragmentation, loss of prey species, activities related to human population growth, and poaching. The Bobcat is the most abundant of North American wild felids, and it is widely distributed.

summer coat **Canada Lynx** winter coat
Lynx canadensis, 204

large-spotted form **Iberian Lynx** small-spotted form
Lynx pardinus, 208

southern form **Eurasian Lynx** northern form
Lynx lynx, 208

summer coat **Bobcat** winter coat
Lynx rufus, 220

Canada Lynx

LYNX CANADENSIS

BL: 80-105 cm (♂), 76-96.5 cm (♀). TL: 5-13 cm. SH: 48-56 cm. W: 6-15 kg (♂), 5-12 kg (♀). SL: 13.4 cm. SW: 9.4 cm (♂), 8.9 cm (♀). DF: 30. CN: 38. A medium-sized, long-legged cat, with thick fur, and large paws. Winter pelage is dense and has a grizzled appearance with grayish-brown mixed with buff or pale brown fur on the back, and grayish-white or buff-white fur on the belly, legs, and feet. Summer pelage is more reddish to gray-brown. No melanistic forms have been reported. Relatively small head with a flared facial ruff. Back of the ears black at the base, ear tips prominently marked with an elongated tuft of black hair. Short, completely black-tipped tail. Long legs, with the hind limbs longer than the forelimbs. Snowshoe-like paws, that can be spread widely. Fur covering the paws long and dense. Males are slightly larger and heavier than females.

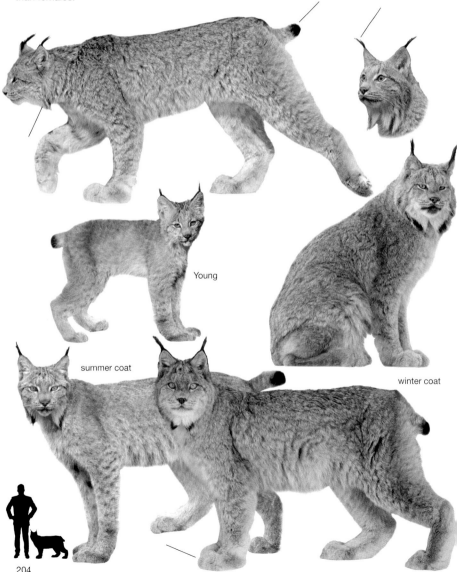

Young

summer coat

winter coat

Lynx canadensis

OTHER NAMES *French*: Lynx du Canada, loup-cervier. *German*: Kanadaluchs. *Spanish*: Lince de Canadá. *Russian*: Канадская рысь.

TAXONOMY Monotypic. Three subspecies were previously recognized: *L. c. canadensis* (mainland Canada and N US); *L. c. mollipilosus* (Alaska, browner and less gray, very dense, soft, woolly pelage, narrower skull); and *L. c. subsolanus* (island of Newfoundland, smaller, darker and richer color). These are no longer considered valid. Formerly considered as conspecific with Eurasian Lynx. It may hybridize with Bobcats in the wild.

SIMILAR SPECIES Bobcat is similar in size and appearance, but has small, less furred paws, smaller or no ear tufts, and a longer tail.

REPRODUCTION *Gestation*: 60-70 days. *Young per Birth*: 1-8. *Weaning*: 5 months. *Sexual Maturity*: 33 months (♂), 21 months (♀). *Life Span*: 15 years, 21 years in captivity. *Breeding Season*: March to early April; most births occur in the last third of May and early June. Dens are found in hollow logs, stumps, timber clumps, or root tangles. When hares are abundant, adult fecundity is high, litter size averages 4–5, cub survival is high, and yearling Lynx reproduce. ♂ do not participate in parental care. Young are altricial at birth, and remain with the mother until next mating season; siblings may remain together for a while after separation from the mother.

BEHAVIOR *Social Behavior*: Solitary, except for ♀ with offspring. *Diet*: Snowshoe hares form most of the diet; may also prey on small rodents and ground birds; ungulates are mostly eaten as carrion; larger food items may be cached under snow or brush and visited later. Almost entirely nocturnal, hiding during the day. Territorial, they maintain exclusive intrasexual territories, based on social intolerance and mutual avoidance. ♂ home ranges may include the range of 1 or more ♀ and their young. Ranges vary in size from 11 to 300 km². They may use feces and sprayed urine with anal secretions to mark home ranges and to provide information that may reduce confrontations. They hunt by either stalking and rushing at their prey, or ambushing it from "ambush beds" established near the trails of prey.

DISTRIBUTION *Native*: Canada, United States. Primarily found in Canada, Alaska, and into portions of the N contiguous USA. In Canada, it has been extirpated from Prince Edward Island, New Brunswick, and mainland Nova Scotia. In the contiguous USA, populations are smaller, with resident breeding populations in Idaho, Colorado, Maine, Minnesota, Montana, and Washington.

HABITAT Boreal, subboreal, and western montane forests, preferring older regenerating forests and generally avoiding younger stands. They also need persistent deep snow, which limits competition from other hare predators. They can tolerate human disturbance.

CONSERVATION STATUS Least Concern. CITES: Appendix II. Widespread and abundant over most of its range. Trapped for its fur across much of Canada. In the S part of its range it is less abundant, and is listed as Endangered in New Brunswick and Nova Scotia, and as Threatened in USA. Populations undergo dramatic fluctuations roughly every ten years, following the regular cycles of population increase and decline of their primary prey, the snowshoe hare.

PHOTO CREDITS TL: *Ron Gallagher*, Sault Ste. Marie (Canada); TR: *Nicolas Grevet*, Laurentian Maple Forest (Canada); Young: *Warren Metcalf*; CR: *Mikael Males* (Canada); BL: *Angela Meyers*, Binder Park Zoo (USA); BR: *Michael Quinton*, Alaska (USA).

Iberian Lynx

LYNX PARDINUS

BL: 68-88 cm (♂), 68-75 cm (♀). TL: 12.5-16 cm. SH: 40-51.5 cm. W: 7-14.6 kg (♂), 8.7-10.4 kg (♀). SL: 12.1 cm (♂), 11 cm (♀). SW: 9.5 cm (♂), 8.6 cm (♀). DF: 30. CN: 38. A medium-sized, long-legged cat, with a prominent facial ruff, and a short, black-tipped tail. Coat is relatively sparse, short, and coarse, heavily spotted. Coat color is bright yellowish-red or tawny, overlaid with dark brown or black spots. Underparts are white. Two color patterns occur: small-spotted (small spots on the back and sides, about 10 mm in diameter, rows indistinct); and large-spotted (larger and more distinct spots, rows containing only about a dozen spots between the shoulder and base of tail). Head is relatively small. Prominent facial ruff. Ears tipped with long, erect tufts of black hair. Short tail, black-tipped. Long legs. Males are heavier and larger than females, with longer ear tufts.

large-spotted
coat

small-spotted
coat

Young

small-spotted
coat

Lynx pardinus

OTHER NAMES Spanish Lynx, Pardel Lynx. *French*: Lynx pardelle, lynx d'Espagne. *German*: Pardelluchs. *Spanish*: Lince ibérico. *Russian*: Пиренейская или иберийская рысь.

TAXONOMY Monotypic. Formerly considered as a subspecies of the Eurasian Lynx, but currently accepted as a distinct species.

SIMILAR SPECIES It is about half the size of the Eurasian Lynx. It is the most heavily spotted Lynx.

REPRODUCTION *Gestation*: 60-70 days. *Young per Birth*: 1-4. *Weaning*: 10 weeks. *Sexual Maturity*: 24 months (♀). *Life Span*: 15 years. *Breeding Season*: From December to February, with the peak birthing season in March and April. Dens are found at the base of hollow cork oak trees. Cubs stay in the natal den for the first 20 days, after which their mother moves them to as many as 3-4 other dens. This protects them against predators as fecal material and smells build up and may also help avoid parasite buildup. Cubs become independent around 10 months of age. Independent cubs often remain in their mother's territory until 20 months of age. ♂ and ♀ usually don't breed until they acquire their own territory, and they may have to wait until a resident animal dies, or moves on.

BEHAVIOR *Social Behavior*: Solitary, except for ♀ with offspring and mating pairs. *Diet*: European rabbit (*Oryctolagus cuniculus*) accounts for 90% of its diet; only when the rabbit population crashes due to viral outbreaks it may also prey on small rodents, birds, and the young of wild boar, red deer, fallow deer, and wild sheep; leaves, soil, and other debris is scraped over large kills to be consumed later. In summer they are nocturnal and crepuscular but in winter they are active during the daylight hours. Their overall activity patterns are closely synchronized with those of the rabbits. Home ranges average 9.5 km² for ♀, and 18.2 km² for ♂. ♂ territories overlap those of several ♀. Occupancy of ranges is indicated primarily by scent-marking with urine and feces.

DISTRIBUTION *Native*: Spain. *Reintroduced*: Portugal. Found only in two separate regions of SW Spain: E Sierra Morena (Andújar-Cardeña) and the coastal plains W of the lower Guadalquivir (Doñana-Aljarafe). More than 100 individuals have been reintroduced since 2014 in the Spanish regions of Ciudad Real, Toledo, Badajoz, and the Portuguese Guadiana Valley.

HABITAT Mediterranean shrubland containing dense rabbit populations. Other essential habitat elements include natural cavities that are used as natal dens. Forestry landscapes, farmland, or open land devoid of native shrubs is rarely used.

CONSERVATION STATUS Endangered. CITES: Appendix I. It was once well distributed throughout the Mediterranean areas of the Iberian Peninsula and SE France. By the turn of the century fewer than 100 individuals remained in two isolated subpopulations in S Spain, Doñana NP and the E Sierra Morena Mountains. Since 2002, the population size has steadily increased, with an estimated population of 580 in 2017. The current recruitment rate is low, due to the scarcity of rabbits, which reduces the species' reproductive potential. Future range expansion and population increase depend upon continued reintroductions. Road casualties typically produce several losses each year.

PHOTO CREDITS TL: *Peter Dunn*, Doñana (Spain); TR, B: *Alex Martín Ros*, Sierra Morena (Spain); CL: *Jesús Rodríguez-Osorio*, Sierra Morena (Spain); Young: *Antonio Rivas*, Programa de Conservación ex-situ (Spain).

Northern Lynx

LYNX LYNX LYNX

BL: 76-108 cm (♂), 73-99 cm (♀). TL: 10-24 cm. SH: 55-62 cm. W: 16-23 kg (♂), 8-21 kg (♀). SL: 13.9 cm (♂), 13 cm (♀). SW: 10.1 cm (♂), 9.5 cm (♀). DF: 28. CN: 38. The largest species of Lynx. A medium-sized, long-legged cat, with a stocky body, and a short, black-tipped tail. Individuals from the northern and eastern part of its range are generally bigger. Ground color ranges from grizzled gray to gray-brown, and spotting is quite variable, from a few indistinct spots to large, well-defined spots. Coat is short and reddish-brown in summer, thicker and silvery gray-brown in winter. Throat and underparts are a white to light gray color. Wide fringe of long hair from ears to throat. Distinctly long legs, with hind limbs appearing longer than forelimbs. Ears have distinctively long tufts, backs of the ears have a central light gray spot, and inside is covered with white hairs. Tail is very short, with a black tip. There are 3 pairs of nipples.

Young

coat variation

Lynx lynx lynx

OTHER NAMES Eurasian Lynx. *French*: Lynx commun, lynx boréal. *German*: Nordluchs. *Spanish*: Lince boreal. *Russian*: Европейская рысь. *Finnish*: Ilves. *Norwegian*: Gaupe. *Swedish*: Lodjur.

TAXONOMY There is no broad consensus on the number of recognized subspecies of *Lynx lynx* and their geographical distributions. On the basis of current evidence the following six subspecies have been proposed, although this number may be further reduced in the future: *L. l. lynx* (Northern Lynx); *L. l. balcanicus* (Balkan Lynx); *L. l. carpathicus* (Carpathian Lynx); *L. l. dinniki* (Caucasian Lynx); *L. l. isabellinus* (Central Asian Lynx); and *L. l. wrangeli* (Siberian Lynx). Includes *melinus* (Finland, European Russia, W Siberia).

REPRODUCTION *Gestation*: 67-74 days. *Young per Birth*: 1-4. *Weaning*: 5-6 months. *Sexual Maturity*: 33-36 months (♂), 22-24 months (♀). *Life Span*: 20 years, 25 years in captivity. *Breeding Season*: From January to April. Polygamous. The young remain with their mother for 10 months. Both sexes may disperse, though ♀ are more likely than ♂ to establish ranges within or close to those of their mothers.

BEHAVIOR *Social Behavior*: Solitary. *Diet*: Small ungulates (roe deer, chamois, reindeer); when ungulates are rare, it relies on smaller prey (hares, foxes, marmot, wild boar, and birds); in N Scandinavia, semi-domestic reindeer are in some areas the most frequent prey; depredation on livestock (sheep, goats, poultry) occurs occasionally, but more frequently in Norway; in European Russia and W Siberia, where roe deer are absent, mountain hares and tetraonids are its main prey. Mainly silent; most sightings are simply an observation of tracks, scat, or the remnants of prey. It is a stalking predator, but will occasionally ambush victims. Because they have exceptionally acute vision, the cats will sometimes climb to a high point and scan the surrounding area for targets. ♂ ranges are larger than ♀ ranges, and overlap between ♂ is greater than between ♀. Both sexes demarcate territorial boundaries with urine-marks. Little is known about territorial defense but encounters between adults are occasionally fatal. Range size increases from S to N reflecting the availability of prey, with the largest ranges occurring in areas where Lynx depend mainly on hares. These populations are also subject to dramatic, cyclical fluctuations in hare numbers (as for the Canada Lynx).

DISTRIBUTION *Native*: Belarus, Estonia, Finland, Kazakhstan, Latvia, Lithuania, Norway, Mongolia, Poland, Russia (European part, E to the Yenisei River), Ukraine, Sweden.

HABITAT Dense, thick, boreal forests, but also occurs in deciduous forest, steppe, mountains, and alpine regions. Summer range includes steep slopes with rock outcrops and talus slopes overgrown with forests.

CONSERVATION STATUS Least Concern. CITES: Appendix II. The status of the Eurasian Lynx varies greatly within its range. Populations in Fennoscandia, the Baltic States, and European Russia are largely intact and stable. Estimated population is: 2,000 in Scandinavia, 2,500 in Finland, 1,600 in Baltic States, and 22,510 in Russia. Sweden, Latvia, and Finland allow a limited cull of Lynx by hunters. In Norway and Russia it is a game species. In Russia the Lynx is still important for the pelt industry.

PHOTO CREDITS TL: *Ulli Joerres*, Zoo Gelsenkirchen (Germany); TR: *Kjetil Kolbjornsrud* (Norway); CR, Young: *Sergey Chichagov, Riga Zoo* (Latvia); BL: *Blickwinkel* (Norway); BR: *Kyslynskyy (Norway)*.

Siberian Lynx

LYNX LYNX WRANGELI

BL: 87-108 cm. TL: 17-25 cm. SH: 55-70 cm. W: 14-45 kg. SL: 14.8 cm (♂), 13.6 cm (♀). SW: 11.6 cm. DF: 28. CN: 38. A medium-sized, long-legged cat, with a stocky body, and a short, black-tipped tail. It is the largest subspecies of Eurasian Lynx. Fur luxuriant and dense. Ground color is a light, dull, grayish-reddish to silvery white, either monochromatic (without spots) or with small, vague, brownish-black spots. Winter coat is longer and thicker, usually paler and less noticeably marked than in summer, but extremely diverse in color and degree of spottiness. Northern populations tend to be paler. Throat and underparts are white to light gray. Head is heavily built. Wide fringe of long hair from ears to throat. Feet are wide, in winter the undersides of are covered with long, dense hair. Ears have distinctively long tufts, backs of the ears have a central light gray spot, and inside is covered with white hairs. Tail is very short, with a black tip.

Young

Lynx lynx wrangeli

OTHER NAMES Yakutian Lynx, Altai Lynx, Baikal Lynx. *French*: Lynx commun. *German*: Sibirischer Luchs. *Spanish*: Lince boreal de Siberia. *Russian*: Сибирская рысь.

TAXONOMY Considered as a subspecies of Eurasian Lynx (*Lynx lynx*). The taxonomic status of the Lynx in the Altai, the Baikal region, and the Amur region needs further investigation and clarification. Includes *kozlovi* (Baikal Lynx, central Siberia, from the Yenisei River to Lake Baikal), *neglectus* (Amur Lynx, Russian Far East, Ussuri and Amur territories, North Korea, Manchuria in NE China), *stroganovi*, and *wardi* (Altai Mountains, sometimes included under *isabellinus*).

REPRODUCTION *Gestation*: 63-73 days. *Young per Birth*: 1-5, with an average of 2-3 per litter. *Weaning*: 3-6 months. *Sexual Maturity*: 36 months (♂), 24 months (♀). *Life Span*: 23 years. *Breeding Season*: February to early April with a peak in the second half of March, and births usually take place around end of May and the beginning of June. At the age of 2 months the cubs follow the mother to the kill; ♀ do not bring food to the den. The mother leaves the cubs at the age of around 10 months during the next mating period.

BEHAVIOR *Social Behavior*: Solitary. *Diet*: Small to medium-sized ungulates, but hares, marmots, and birds are important prey also in other Central Asian regions where habitats are drier and less forested; they will also actively seek out and kill foxes. They are mostly active at dawn and dusk. They usually avoid water, and may travel up to about 10 km per day. They are excellent tree climbers and use forest trails, logs, and rock outcroppings when hunting. Home range size varies in response to prey abundance and density, and to the regional population status. ♂ home ranges generally include 1-2 ♀ home ranges. Scent-marks and calls are used for communication purposes. It is an efficient hunter that can kill prey up to 3-4 times its own size. It hunts by stalking and ambushing its prey, and is known to migrate up and down slopes following ungulates and hares to areas of lesser snow cover. It has an excellent sense of hearing and very good eyesight to find its prey. It has no natural enemies; sporadic cases of Lynx killed by wolves, wolverines, Amur Leopards, and Tigers have been reported.

DISTRIBUTION *Native*: China, Mongolia, North Korea, Russia (E of the Yenisei River).

HABITAT Dense, thick, boreal forests, but also occurs in deciduous forest, steppe, mountains, and alpine regions. Summer range includes steep slopes with rock outcrops and talus slopes overgrown with forests. In the Altai Mountains, Lynx are found in the taiga zone with snow cover not deeper than 40–50 cm. To a great extent, hare and small ungulate distribution determines Lynx distribution.

CONSERVATION STATUS Least Concern. CITES: Appendix II. In China the population is considered to be decreasing; it is not known if it still occurs in the Chinese region of Inner Mongolia. In 2003 the population in the Siberian region was estimated to be 6,390, 5,890 in the Russian Far East, and 10,000 in Mongolia. In Russia it is still important for the skin market and the pelt industry, and it is subject to hunting.

PHOTO CREDITS TL: *Alex Kantorovich*, Tierpark Berlin (Germany); TR: *Alexander Sliwa*, Tierpark Berlin (Germany); Young: *Nagel Photography*; BL: *Alex Kantorovich*, Karagandy Zoo (Kazakhstan); BR: *Alexander Silwa*, Wuppertal Zoo (Germany).

Central Asian Lynx

LYNX LYNX ISABELLINUS

BL: 80-130 cm. TL: 11-25 cm. SH: 55-62 cm. W: 18-38 kg. SL: 13 cm. SW: 10.7 cm. DF: 28. CN: 38. A medium-sized, long-legged cat, with a stocky body, and a short, black-tipped tail. Smaller than other Asian subspecies, similar in size to the Carpathian Lynx. Coat is dense and soft, color is variable, from monochromatic, light gray, or white-brownish without spots or only faintly visible pale brown spots, to deep brown with distinct patches (this pattern is more common in individuals from Xinjiang, Tian Shan, Qinghai, and Tibet). Coat is short and reddish-brown in summer. Throat and underparts are white to light gray in color. Wide fringe of long hair from ears to throat. Ears have distinctively long tufts, backs of the ears have a central light gray spot, and inside is covered with white hairs. Feet are wide, in winter the undersides of are covered with long, dense hair. Tail is very short, with a black tip. There are 3 pairs of nipples.

summer coat

winter coat

Lynx lynx isabellinus

OTHER NAMES Himalayan Lynx, Tibetan Lynx, Turkestan Lynx. *French*: Lynx commun. *German*: Himalayaluchs. *Spanish*: Lince tibetano, lince del Himalaya. *Russian*: Туркестанская рысь. *Ladakhi*: Eeh. *Kashmiri*: Patsalam. *Dun*: Jungle Billi. *Lahul*: Phiauku. *Mongolian*: Shleleisin.

TAXONOMY Considered as a subspecies of Eurasian Lynx (*Lynx lynx*). Further investigations are needed in order to declare whether it is a separate subspecies or not; it sometimes is considered as consubspecific with the Altai Lynx (*wardi*). Includes *kamensis* (W of Sichuan Province), and *tibetanus*.

REPRODUCTION *Gestation*: 63-74 days. *Young per Birth*: 1-5. *Weaning*: 3-6 months. *Sexual Maturity*: 36 months (♂), 24 months (♀). *Life Span*: 15 years in captivity. *Breeding Season*: Probably in January and February, with most births between May and June. It breeds once a year for 2-3 years and then skips one year.

BEHAVIOR *Social Behavior*: Solitary. *Diet*: Hares, marmots, pikas, small ungulates (roe deer, blue sheep, Tibetan antelope, Tibetan gazelle), and birds; during the winter their diet may focus more on small ungulates; they will also actively seek out and kill foxes. Solitary and nocturnal, they usually avoid water, and may travel more than 10 km per day. They are ambush predators, and are known to migrate up and down slopes following ungulates and hares to areas of lesser snow cover. Lynx are rare where wolves are numerous. They can leap over 2.3 m in dense shrub habitat. They are excellent tree climbers and use forest trails, logs, and rock outcroppings when hunting.

DISTRIBUTION *Native*: Afghanistan, Bhutan, China (Gansu, Qinghai, Sichuan, and Shaanxi), India (limited to Ladakh, parts of the upper Indus in Jammu and Kashmir, and Sikkim), Kazakhstan, Kyrgyzstan, Nepal, N Pakistan (Chitral, Gilgit-Baltistan, Azad Jamu, and Kashmir), Tajikistan, Turkmenistan, Uzbekistan. It is believed to occur throughout the N slopes of the Himalaya and most parts of the Hindu Kush. The border between *L. l. isabellinus* and *L. l. lynx* (*wardi*) is not clear; it seems to be around the Irtysh Valley.

HABITAT Dry temperate mixed forests, but it also occurs in more open, thinly wooded, and alpine habitats (it is the only subspecies living in a treeless environment), cold desert, scrub woodland, and barren outcrops of rock above the treeline (2,745-5,500 m). On the Tibetan Plateau it occurs sporadically. Rarely found on S slopes. Shelters in willow and reed patches.

CONSERVATION STATUS Least Concern. CITES: Appendix II. The status of this subspecies in China and in Asia is not well known and trends in many countries are poorly understood due to a lack of data. Chinese population was estimated at around 27,000 in 2009 and is listed as Vulnerable. In Kyrgyzstan populations are thought to be stable. In Nepal, Pakistan, and Uzbekistan it is thought to be decreasing, and in Tajikistan it is considered rare. Main threats include habitat loss and fragmentation, mainly due to livestock farming and infrastructure development, and poaching, mainly as retaliatory killing due to livestock depredation, or for the fur trade. In some Asian countries, such as Azerbaijan, Mongolia, and Pakistan, prey base depletion due to poaching is considered a major threat too. Protected in China.

PHOTO CREDITS T: *Axel Gomille*, Celestial Mountains (Kyrgyzstan); C: *Stephen Lioy*, NABU Rehabilitation Centre, Ananyevo (Kyrgyzstan); B: Based on photos from Qi Jingde, Hoh Xil, Qinghai (China).

Carpathian Lynx

LYNX LYNX CARPATHICUS

BL: 87-105 cm (♂), 80-99 cm (♀). TL: 12-22 cm. SH: 55-62 cm. W: 11.7-29 kg (♂), 13-23 kg (♀). SL: 13.9 cm (♂), 13.1 cm (♀). SW: 10.7 cm (♂), 10.2 cm (♀). DF: 28. CN: 38. A medium-sized, long-legged cat, with a stocky body, and a short, black-tipped tail. Fur moderately rich and soft. Winter coat is longer, denser, and more luxuriant. Ground color reddish to chestnut-red or rusty-brown. Very intense spottedness predominates, with little variability, but different types of spotting can occur in the same population. Throat and underparts are white. Head is heavily built. Wide fringe of long hair from ears to throat. Ears have distinctly long tufts, backs of the ears have a central light gray spot, and inside is covered with white hairs. Distinctly long legs, with hind limbs appearing longer than forelimbs. Feet are wide, in winter the undersides are covered with long, dense hair. Tail is short, with a black tip.

coat variation

Young

summer
coat

214

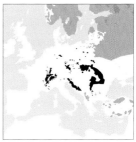

Lynx lynx carpathicus

OTHER NAMES European Lynx. *French*: Lynx commun. *German*: Karpatenluchs. *Spanish*: Lince boreal, lince de los Cárpatos. *Russian*: Карпатская рысь.

TAXONOMY Considered as a subspecies of Eurasian Lynx (*L. lynx*). Recent genetic analyses have shown that this subspecies is isolated from the other populations.

REPRODUCTION *Gestation*: 67-74 days. *Young per Birth*: 1-5, most often 2-3. *Weaning*: 3-6 months. *Sexual Maturity*: 36 months (♂), 24 months (♀). *Life Span*: 17 years, 25 years in captivity. *Breeding Season*: From February to mid-April, with most births in late May. ♂ follow the ♀ to check their reproductive status. Estrus lasts about 3 days, and a ♂ accompanies the ♀ all that time, and they copulate often. Cubs follow their mother until the next mating season and leave the mother at an age of 10 months.

BEHAVIOR *Social Behavior*: Solitary, except for ♀ and the young of the year. *Diet*: Small ungulates (roe deer, chamois) and hares; in areas with low ungulate availability, lagomorphs, birds, and rodents; when it has a fresh kill, it stays in its proximity for several days. They are mainly active at dusk and at night, and rest during the daytime, except for the rutting period when they are active also during the daytime. Both ♂ and ♀ occupy individual home ranges, which they mark with gland secretions, urine, and feces. Home range sizes vary considerably depending on habitat type, composition of prey community, and availability of prey, averaging 230 km². ♀ usually travel over short distances while nursing kittens (late spring to summer). Home ranges of ♂ are larger than those of ♀; they monopolize 1 or 2, rarely more ♀. Home ranges of ♂ overlap, whereas ranges of ♀ overlap only slightly.

DISTRIBUTION *Native*: Austria, Bosnia and Herzegovina, Bulgaria, Croatia, Czech Republic, France, Germany, Hungary, Italy, Liechtenstein, Poland, Romania, Serbia, Slovakia, Slovenia, Switzerland, Ukraine. It occurs in E and C Europe. Lynx for the reintroductions in the Alps, the Vosges, the Dinaric, and the Bohemian-Bavarian Mountains were taken from the Carpathian population. Other occurrences are of unknown origin (as in the German Harz Mountains and Kampinoski NP in Poland).

HABITAT Extended temperate and boreal forests, which support good ungulate populations and provide enough cover for hunting, from sea level up to the N treeline.

CONSERVATION STATUS Least Concern (some subpopulations are Critically Endangered or Endangered). CITES: Appendix II. Populations in Europe are generally small and fragmented. In central Europe a relatively large but isolated population is found in the Carpathian Mountains. Extirpated from most of W Europe, and reintroduced in several countries, while in others it has recovered partly due to an increase in small ungulate populations and reduction of threats. Estimated population is fewer than 2,500 (Vosges Palatinian: 19, Jura: 100, Alpine: 130, Carpathian: 2,300-2,400, Bohemian-Bavarian: 50, Slovenia: 100). Strictly protected in Europe. Threats includes conflicts with hunters and livestock farmers, persecution, habitat loss and fragmentation, poor management structures, and accidental mortality.

PHOTO CREDITS TL: *Juniors Bildarchiv* (Germany); TR: *Tambako the Jaguar*, Wildpark Pforzheim (Germany); Young: *Bildagentur Zoonar* (Germany); BL: *Jonas Livet*, Zoologischer Garten Magdeburg (Germany); BR: *Image Broker*, Bavarian Forest NP (Germany).

Balkan Lynx

LYNX LYNX BALCANICUS

BL: Unknown. TL: 12-22 cm. SH: 50 cm. W: 9-22 kg (♂). SL: 13.6 cm (♂), 12.7 cm (♀). SW: 10.6 cm (♂), 9.9 cm (♀). DF: 28. CN: 38. A medium-sized, long-legged cat, with a stocky body, and a short, black-tipped tail. It is the smallest subspecies of Eurasian Lynx. Coat is dense and soft, color is variable, from yellowish-red with small elongated black spots to monochromatic white-brownish without spots or only faintly visible spots. Throat and underparts are white to light gray in color. Head is heavily built. Wide fringe of long hair from ears to throat. Ears have distinctively long tufts, backs of the ears have a central light gray spot, and inside is covered with white hairs. Distinctly long legs, with hind limbs appearing longer than forelimbs. Feet are wide. Tail is very short, with a black tip. Females have 3 pairs of nipples.

Lynx lynx balcanicus

OTHER NAMES *French*: Lynx. *German*: Balkanluchs. *Spanish*: Lince de los Balcanes. *Russian*: Балканская рысь. *Macedonian*: Балкански рис.

TAXONOMY Considered as a subspecies of Eurasian Lynx (*Lynx lynx*). The subspecies status of the Balkan Lynx is questionable, but new genetic research has confirmed that it is different from the Carpathian Lynx (*L. l. carpathicus*) and should be considered a distinct subspecies. Includes *martinoi*.

REPRODUCTION *Gestation*: 67-74 days. *Young per Birth*: 1-5, but most often 2-3. *Weaning*: 3-6 months. *Sexual Maturity*: Probably 24 months. *Life Span*: Unknown. *Breeding Season*: From January to February, with most births in late May-early June. Kittens are born in a well-sheltered den that is dry and has only 1 to few entrances. Cubs are moved several times to different dens before they start following the mother on their own. Dens can be found in a rock heap, a rock lair, a rootstock, or an earth lair. ♀ does not bring food to the den; the cubs only start eating meat when they can follow the ♀ to the kill, at about the age of 3 months.

BEHAVIOR *Social Behavior*: Solitary, except for ♀ and the young of the year. *Diet*: Rock partridge, hare, chamois (mostly juvenile specimens), roe deer, capercaillie, thrush, and micromammals (the prey of Carpathian subspecies is much less diverse); attacks on livestock are almost unknown (the Carpathian population is more inclined to feed on domestic animals, mostly sheep). Mainly active at dusk and at night, and rest during the daytime, except for the mating season when they are active also during the daytime. Home range size averages 30 km² for this subspecies.

DISTRIBUTION *Native*: Albania, Kosovo, Macedonia, Montenegro. It is restricted to the SW Balkans (the basic part of the contemporary population is concentrated in Kosovo, W Macedonia, and E Albania). Some sporadic observations have been reported from Greece along the border with Macedonia. No Balkan Lynx are believed to remain in Bulgaria. The border between *L. l. balcanicus* and the larger *L. l. carpathicus* seems to be around the Danube River.

HABITAT Hill and mountain regions at an altitude range of 550-2,500 m in scarcely populated forest and rocky-forest areas, while the Carpathian Lynx is mostly found in forest and rocky forests in hills or mountains at an altitude range from 100-1,000 m. Both populations often live in beech, oak, and other deciduous forests, and also in thickets, gorges, and rocky terrain.

CONSERVATION STATUS Critically Endangered. CITES: Appendix II. It is the smallest and the most threatened Eurasian Lynx population in Europe, with an estimated population size of 27-52 animals. Its presence is only confirmed for Macedonia (Mavrovo NP) and Albania in two separate subpopulations. Its presence in Kosovo, Montenegro, and Greece is presently regarded as unlikely. It is completely protected. Major threats to the Balkan Lynx population are small population size, limited prey base, habitat degradation (especially in Albania), and poaching. In Bosnia and Herzegovina, Lynx immigrated from the reintroduced population of Slovenia, and in E Serbia Lynx are immigrating from the Carpathian Mountains of Romania (*L. l. carpathicus*); these populations are increasing and expanding, but are not part of the autochthonous population.

PHOTO CREDITS Based on photos from the Balkan Lynx Recovery Programme.

Caucasian Lynx
LYNX LYNX DINNIKI

BL: 80.5-95 cm (♂), 84-92 cm (♀). TL: 14-21 cm. SH: 50 cm. W: 12.2-22 kg (♂), 14.8-24 kg (♀). SL: 12.5-13.2 cm. SW: 9.9 cm. DF: 28. CN: 38. A medium-sized cat, with a stocky body, elongated legs, and a very short, black-tipped tail. A small subspecies, intermediate in size between Carpathian and Balkan Lynx, similar in color to the Iberian Lynx. Coat is sparse, short, and coarse. Coat color is bright yellowish-red overlaid with bright black spots and stripes. Reddish color predominates in winter coat. Throat and underparts are white. Head is heavily built. Wide fringe of long hair from ears to throat. Ears have distinctively long tufts, backs of the ears have a central light gray spot, and inside is covered with white hairs. Distinctly long legs, with hind limbs appearing longer than forelimbs. Feet are wide. Tail is very short, with a black tip. Females have 3 pairs of nipples.

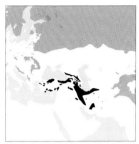

Lynx lynx dinniki

OTHER NAMES Oriental Lynx, Anatolian Lynx. *French*: Lynx commun. *German*: Kaukasusluchs. *Spanish*: Lince del Cáucaso. *Russian*: Кавказская рысь. *Turkish*: Vasak, üsek. *Armenian*: Lusan. *Georgian*: Potskhveri. *Farsi*: Siahh goosh. *Azerbaijani*: Meshag.

TAXONOMY Considered as a subspecies of Eurasian Lynx (*Lynx lynx*) and a very morphologically distinct form, which has been geographically isolated for a long time. The geographical distribution of *L. l. dinniki* may have reached SE Europe and preliminary genetic analyses have shown that *L. l. balcanicus* and *L. l. dinniki* are perhaps consubspecific. It was formerly considered to be a member of the species *L. pardina* (Iberian Lynx) based on the spotted coat pattern. Includes *orientalis*.

SIMILAR SPECIES Distinguished from Caracal by its much shorter tail, the presence of a bushy facial ruff, the retention of the white patch on the back of the ear, and the spotting on the pelage.

REPRODUCTION *Gestation*: 67-74 days. *Young per Birth*: 1-5, typically 2-3. *Weaning*: 4 months. *Sexual Maturity*: 24 months (♀). *Life Span*: 24 years in captivity. *Breeding Season*: From February to April, with most births in May.

BEHAVIOR *Social Behavior*: Solitary. *Diet*: Small ungulate species (roe deer, red deer, chamois, wild goat, wild boar); in contrast to most Eurasian Lynx populations in Europe, Lynx populations in Turkey strictly rely on brown hares; they may prey on livestock (domestic goat); intraspecific killing and cannibalism have been described in Turkey. Most active during early morning and the evening. When they are not active, they spend their time resting under the cover of thick brush, tall grasses, or in trees. Very secretive, and rarely seen. They stalk their prey from the cover of thick vegetation and pounce with a bite to the neck. Mainly terrestrial but are adept at climbing and may swim. They scent-mark locations concentrating on the borders of neighboring territorial animals; fecal marking increases in the mating season.

DISTRIBUTION *Native*: Armenia, Azerbaijan, Georgia, Iraq, Iran, Russia, Turkey. It occurs in the Caucasus Mountains S to Turkey, N Iraq, and Iran (Alborz and Zagros Mountains), formerly also in the Kopet-Dag, Turkmenistan.

HABITAT Large deciduous mixed and coniferous forest, open wooded regions, mixed forest-steppe.

CONSERVATION STATUS Least Concern. CITES: Appendix II. Its population is probably declining. The estimated population in the N Caucasus in 2013 was 680 mature individuals. Vulnerable in Iran. There have been no observations from Iraq since 2011. Status in Turkey is data-deficient, but it is probably present as several subpopulations, some of which are isolated from each other. In Armenia it is thought to be a common species and it is not protected, but it is rarely seen. In Azerbaijan populations are thought to be stable. It is protected and hunting is prohibited in Azerbaijan, Georgia, Iran, Turkey, and in Russia in the N Caucasus and in the S region. In Iraq it may be hunted. Fragmentation of forest, depletion of prey base, poaching, and vehicle collisions represent significant threats to this subspecies. In Turkey, local people and local authorities use poison to exterminate it, as it is seen as a threat to unattended domestic goat herds.

PHOTO CREDITS T, CR: *Alex Kantorovich*, Yerevan Zoo (Armenia); CL: Yerevan Zoo (Armenia); B: Based on photos from *WWF Azerbaijan,* Zangezur NP (Azerbaijan).

Eastern Bobcat

LYNX RUFUS RUFUS

BL: 85-120 cm (♂), 51-95 cm (♀). TL: 9-19.8 cm. SH: 43-58 cm. W: 8.9-13 kg (♂), 5.8-9.2 kg (♀). SL: 11.7 cm (♂), 11 cm (♀). SW: 9 cm (♂), 8.4 cm (♀). DF: 28. CN: 38. A medium-sized, stocky cat. The largest individuals occur in the northern latitudes of the range. Coat is short, soft, and dense, with a variable background color from buff, brown, reddish, or yellowish-brown to light gray, with distinct dark brown or black spots covering the back and legs. Underparts are white, with distinct black spots. They molt twice a year, with some populations exhibiting a reddish coat during the summer and a grayer coat in winter. Melanistic and albinistic forms have been reported. Relatively small head. Facial ruff, frequently streaked with black. Ears tipped with a very short tuft of black hairs, with a large white spot on the back of each ear. Short tail, white underneath with dark bands on top. Legs relatively long. Males are longer and heavier than females.

winter coat

summer coat

Young

Lynx rufus rufus

OTHER NAMES Bay Lynx, Barred Bobcat, Pallid Bobcat, Red Lynx. *French*: Chat sauvage, lynx roux. *German*: Rotluchs. *Spanish*: Gato montés, lince rojo oriental. *Russian*: Восточная рыжая рысь.

TAXONOMY Twelve subspecies are currently described based largely on superficial differences that are unlikely to be valid. Genetic analyses of populations in the contiguous USA suggest two subspecies: *L. rufus rufus* (Western Bobcat), and *L. rufus fasciatus* (Eastern Bobcat), with a transition zone in the Great Plains grasslands of the central USA. The status of Mexican Bobcats needs to be clarified. Includes *superiorensis*, *floridanus*, and *gigas*.

SIMILAR SPECIES Canada Lynx can be distinguished by their larger feet, slightly shorter tail, longer black ear tufts, and less well defined spots on the coat. The fur of the Canada Lynx is grayer than the reddish-brown of the Bobcat. The Bobcat's tail is banded only on the upper surface, whereas the tail of the Lynx is brownish or pale buff-white and ends in black that entirely encircles the tip.

REPRODUCTION *Gestation*: 63 days. *Young per Birth*: 1-6. *Weaning*: 2-3 months. *Sexual Maturity*: 24 months (♂), 12-24 months (♀). *Life Span*: 12 years, 25 years in captivity. *Breeding Season*: Usually from February through July. Polygamous mating system. Dens are found in rock piles, caves, or hollow logs.

BEHAVIOR *Social Behavior*: Solitary. *Diet*: They hunt small animals (rabbits, hares, opossums, rats, and mice), but also fawns and deer, especially in the NE USA; they are not known to be serious predators of livestock. One of the most widespread and adaptable carnivores in North America. Crepuscular, but they may be active at any time of the day. They are not well adapted to living and hunting in deep soft snow, and they also have a hard time regulating their body temperature in cold weather. They are good climbers. Home range sizes are highly variable even within the same geographical region (13-201 km² in Minnesota). ♀ appear to have smaller home ranges than ♂. ♀ ranges do not overlap while ♂ home ranges will overlap with ♀ and other ♂.

DISTRIBUTION *Native*: Canada, United States. In USA they have been documented in every state except Alaska, Hawaii, and Delaware. They range into Canada as far north as central British Columbia in the W and the Gaspé Peninsula in the E.

HABITAT A wide variety of habitats, including swamps, boreal coniferous forest, and mixed hardwood forest in the N; chaparral, sagebrush-grasslands, and desert scrub in the W; and bottomland hardwoods, brushlands, and mixed agricultural-forest areas in the S. They prefer areas with dense cover or uneven, broken terrain.

CONSERVATION STATUS Least Concern. CITES: Appendix II. Legally harvested for the fur trade in 38 US states, and in 7 Canadian provinces. Endangered in Ohio. Downgraded to threatened in Iowa, it is now harvested in many counties. In Illinois, it was removed from the state's list of threatened species in 1999 and it is now found in nearly all counties. Indiana has sightings in much of the state and it was downgraded to special concern in 2005. There is some concern in the NE USA about interspecific competition with expanding coyote populations.

PHOTO CREDITS TL: *FLPA*, MN (USA); TR: *Bjfirestorm*, FL (USA); Young: *McKenzie Greenly*, MN (USA); CL: *Andy Morffew*, Bird Rookery Swamp, FL (USA); C: *Diego Centeno*, FL (USA); B: *Richard and Pam Winegar*, Sebastian Inlet, FL (USA).

Western Bobcat
LYNX RUFUS FASCIATUS

BL: 63-101 cm (♂), 77 cm (♀). TL: 14.6 cm. SH: 43-53 cm. W: 7-13 kg (♂), 4.5-8 kg (♀). SL: 11 cm. SW: 8.7 cm. DF: 28. CN: 38. A medium-sized, stocky cat. Coat is rather short, soft, and dense, with a variable background color from reddish-brown to light gray, streaked with black. There is considerable coat variation between individuals. Underparts are white, spotted with black. Inside of front legs with several black bars. Relatively small head. Facial ruff, frequently streaked with black. Ears tipped with a short tuft of black hairs, with a distinctive large white spot on the back of each ear. Short tail, tip black above and white below, with 3-4 blackish bars above just in front of the tip. Legs relatively long. Males are longer and heavier than females.

summer coat

winter coat

Young

Lynx rufus fasciatus

OTHER NAMES Bay Lynx. *French*: Chat sauvage, lynx roux. *German*: Rotluchs. *Spanish*: Gato montés, lince rojo occidental. *Russian*: Западная рыжая рысь.

TAXONOMY Considered as a subspecies of Bobcat (*L. rufus*). Includes *pallescens*, *baileyi*, *californicus*, *peninsularis*, and *texensis*.

SIMILAR SPECIES Canada Lynx has large furry pads, slightly shorter tail, with tip black all around, longer ear tufts, and less well-developed spots on the coat. Mountain Lion cubs, although spotted, have no elongated hair on the side of the face, and have long tails.

REPRODUCTION *Gestation*: 62-70 days. *Young per Birth*: 2-5. *Weaning*: 7-8 weeks. *Sexual Maturity*: 12-18 months (♂), 12-24 months (♀). *Life Span*: 23 years, 32 years in captivity. *Breeding Season*: January through June (December through February in California), with breeding peaking from February through May, but may vary. Most births occur between April and July. Polygamous mating system. Dens are found in caves, rock crevices, or hollow logs or trees; the den is carefully lined with dry leaves, moss, or grass formed into a shallow depression. Cubs are raised solely by the ♀ and disperse when they are about 9-24 months old.

BEHAVIOR *Social Behavior*: Solitary; excluding ♀ and their young, they generally avoid one another except during the breeding season. *Diet*: Small mammals (mice, voles, rabbits, gophers, mountain beaver, yellow-bellied marmots), fawns (mule deer, white-tailed deer, wild sheep); also insects, reptiles, birds, and carrion; they will cover the remains of a large kill with debris such as snow, grass, or leaves. Crepuscular, but may be active before sundown. Active year-round. They hunt primarily by sight and sound, and spend much of their time sitting or crouching, watching, and listening. Once they locate prey, they stalk within range of a quick dash and then pounce. Great horned owls may kill young Bobcats, and adults occasionally are taken by Mountain Lions and domestic dogs. Bobcats and coyotes may compete, and when coyote numbers are reduced by predator control, Bobcat numbers may increase. They are territorial. Home ranges average 2 km² for California, 9 km² for Arizona, and 45.3 km² in Idaho. ♀ generally have smaller home ranges than ♂. The home ranges of ♂ and ♀ may overlap, but home ranges of ♀ rarely overlap with each other. Seasonal range differences may also occur. In California, winter ranges of ♂ are smaller than summer ranges. Scent-marking appears to reduce actual contact, and fighting is very unusual.

DISTRIBUTION *Native*: Canada, Mexico, United States.

HABITAT A wide variety of habitats including swamps, deserts, and mountain ranges. They prefer rocky canyons at elevations from 1,400 to 2,100 m with ledges and areas of dense vegetation. They are adapted to even the driest deserts if shade is available. Prey abundance, protection from severe weather, availability of rest areas and cover, and freedom from human intrusion are key factors in Bobcat habitat selection.

CONSERVATION STATUS Least Concern. CITES: Appendix II. Population estimates indicate that the US population is 725,000-3,500,000.

PHOTO CREDITS TR: *Philip Schermeister*, Yellowstone NP, WY (USA); TL: *Tin Man Lee*, Salton Sea, CA (USA); C: *Matthew Rhodes*, Sierra, CA (USA); Young, BR: *Josh Whaley*, Del Valle Regional Park, CA (USA).

Mexican Bobcat

LYNX RUFUS ESCUINAPAE AND OAXACENSIS

BL: 58-70 cm. TL: 10.5-17 cm. SH: 46 cm. W: 5-12 kg. SL: 9.9-11.3 cm. SW: 7.6-8 cm. DF: 28. CN: 38. A medium-sized, stocky cat. The smallest subspecies of Bobcat. Coat is short and soft, with a variable background color from pale buffy to rusty-red, with some indistinct reddish-brown spots and lines covering the back and legs. Underparts are white, with numerous elongated black spots and lines. Relatively small head. Facial ruff, frequently streaked with black. Orbital ring, lips, and chin white. Ears tipped with a short tuft of black hairs, with a distinctive large white spot on the back of each ear. Short tail, white underneath with dark bands on top. Legs relatively long. Males are longer and heavier than females.

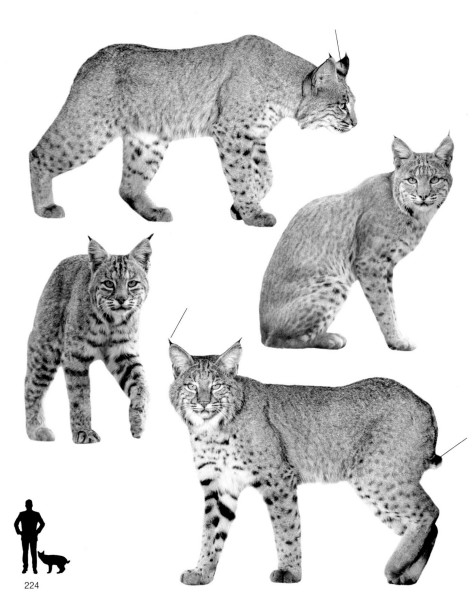

Lynx rufus escuinapae and
oaxacensis

OTHER NAMES Bay Lynx. *French*: Chat sauvage, lynx roux. *German*: Rotluchs. *Spanish*: Gato montés, lince rojo mexicano. *Russian*: Мексиканская рыжая рысь.

TAXONOMY The status of Bobcats in Mexico (*L. r. escuinapae* and *L. r. oaxacensis*) needs to be clarified. They may not constitute separate subspecies and may not constitute a distinct population segment.

REPRODUCTION *Gestation*: 60-70 days. *Young per Birth*: 1-6, with an average of 3 per litter. *Weaning*: 2 months. *Sexual Maturity*: 12 months (♂), 12-24 months (♀). *Life Span*: 14 years. *Breeding Season*: Breeding can take place any time of the year, but usually in winter. They generally have 1 litter per year, but ♀ may be capable of producing a second litter if the first one is lost after birth.

BEHAVIOR *Social Behavior*: Solitary. *Diet*: Mainly lagomorphs (hares and rabbits), followed by rodents (woodrats, porcupines), reptiles (snakes, lizards), and birds. Primarily crepuscular, being most active before and after sunset and sunrise with their lowest activity at midday hours. Behaviors of Bobcats in hot desert environments do not differ in general from those in more N populations. They are relentless hunters, stalking their prey and pouncing with a swift bite to the neck. ♀ home ranges typically do not overlap each other; ♂ home ranges often overlap those of other ♂. For mating purposes, neighboring ♂ and ♀ typically overlap home ranges. Average home range size was 25.9 km² in the Chihuahuan Desert. They appear to only breed successfully when they have a well-established home range. Subadults may disperse up to 100 km or more from their natal ranges when establishing home ranges in unoccupied territory that offers adequate cover and prey.

DISTRIBUTION *Native*: Mexico. Found throughout Mexico, but primarily in Baja, W Mexico, and S from the Sonoran Desert. It is also found in the Mexican states of Sinaloa and Nayarit, as well as parts of Sonora, Jalisco, Durango, San Luis Potosí, Nuevo León, Hidalgo, Morelos, Puebla, Tlaxcala, Tamaulipas, Michoacán, Guerrero, Veracruz, and Oaxaca.

HABITAT Coastal swamps, deserts, scrublands, old lava flows, and hardwood forests. They usually avoid open understories. Their habitat must provide suitable cover, forest shelter, escape cover, and protection from weather. Only large, intensively cultivated areas appear to be unsuitable habitat, presumably because of reductions in the availability of prey.

CONSERVATION STATUS Least Concern. CITES: Appendix II. *L. r. escuinapae* was previously included in Appendix I, but was transferred to Appendix II (1992); the US Fish and Wildlife Service published a proposed rule to remove this subspecies from the list of species protected under the Endangered Species Act. Bobcat conservation status in Mexico remains unclear, but there is no evidence of population declines in central and S Mexico (one of the most disturbed parts of the country) during the past 25 years. It is threatened by habitat destruction, rural development, illegal trapping and shooting, and militarization of the US-Mexico border. Legally hunted in small numbers as a trophy animal. No population estimates are available, as censusing of Bobcats is difficult because of their secretive nature, low densities, and wide dispersal.

PHOTO CREDITS *Sam Carrera*, Altiplano Potosino (Mexico).

Bay Cat lineage

ASIATIC GOLDEN CAT, MARBLED CAT, AND BORNEO BAY CAT

RECOGNITION The Bay Cat lineage consists of three species in the *Catopuma* and *Pardofelis* genera: the Asiatic Golden Cat (*Catopuma temminckii*), the poorly known Bay Cat (*C. badia*), and the Marbled Cat (*Pardofelis marmorata*). The Bay Cat was once considered a small, island subspecies of the Asiatic Golden Cat, but now the two species are recognized as distinct. The Asiatic Golden Cat has traditionally been suggested to be closely related to the African Golden Cat based on morphological traits, but phylogenetic analyses have revealed that these two species are distantly related. Similarly, the Marbled Cat was once considered a close relative of the Clouded Leopard, but genetic analyses have also shown the species belongs in this lineage. They are small to medium-sized long-bodied cats, with a long tail, a broad face, and rounded ears. Asiatic Golden Cat and Bay Cat have largely unmarked, golden-brown to gray coats, except for rich facial stripes and spotting on the chest, belly, and inner limbs. The Marbled Cat is morphologically very distinct, with a irregular blotched pattern on its coat and a extremely long, bushy tail. Completely melanistic individuals occur in the three species. Chromosome number is 2n=38.

PHYLOGENY The Bay Cat lineage is the second oldest Felidae lineage to diverge from the ancestral cat species in Asia at 9.4 Ma, and three species evolved in Southeast Asia. The Marbled Cat split from the Asiatic Golden Cat and the Bay Cat about 5.5 Ma. Asiatic Golden Cat and Bay Cat split during the late Pliocene, approximately 3.2 Ma. At this time, Borneo was still connected to other parts of the Sunda Shelf and Southeast Asia. During the late Pliocene, however, the Isthmus of Kra was submerged by high sea levels for an extended period of time, geographically dividing mainland Southeast Asia and Sundaland. Subsequently, these two emerging species responded differently to the changing environmental conditions: Bay Cat specialized and became more adapted to tropical evergreen rainforests, whereas the Asiatic Golden Cat remained a more generalist species due to the higher habitat diversity in Indochina. The Asiatic Golden Cat expanded southward to the Sunda Shelf using land bridges that were temporarily available during glacial periods of the late Pleistocene. The Bay Cat lineage has a very poor fossil record: the Asiatic Golden Cat has a single record in the late Pleistocene of Lang Trang (Vietnam).

BEHAVIOR This group is one of the least studied and the ecology of these species is very poorly known. Most camera-trap records are of lone adult individuals suggesting a typical, solitary felid socio-spatial pattern. They are somewhat more active by day, but camera-trap records occur around the clock. Asiatic Golden Cats and Bay Cats are thought to be mostly terrestrial, though they may take some prey arboreally. Marbled Cats are highly agile climbers, able to rapidly descend trees head first, and presumably hunt both in the trees and on the forest floor. Their diet is composed of small to medium-sized mammals, mainly rodents, but also birds and reptiles.

DISTRIBUTION These species inhabit the forests of Southeast Asia. The Asiatic Golden Cat is distributed from Sumatra and Malaysia, north to Nepal, Burma, and China, but it does not occur on Borneo. It is found primarily in forested habitats, including lowland and upland rainforest, dry deciduous forest, evergreen forest, and montane forest. The Bay Cat is found only on the island of Borneo, and it is closely associated with dense lowland forest and riverine forest habitats, but also occurs in upland forest. The Marbled Cat occurs south of the Himalayas from eastern Nepal through northern India, Bhutan, and southwest China, and patchily throughout Indochina from northern Burma to the Malay Peninsula, Borneo, and Sumatra. They are restricted to forested habitats in undisturbed evergreen, deciduous, and tropical forest. All these species seem to be able to occur at low densities in secondary and logged forest, but they do not permanently occupy heavily modified habitats, such as oil palm plantations.

CONSERVATION There is a general lack of information on the status of these species, as well as a low level of public awareness. More investigations are urgently needed to understand their ecology and distribution. They are forest-dependent, being particularly vulnerable to habitat loss which is very prevalent throughout their range; Southeast Asia has the world's fastest deforestation rate due to logging and conversion for human settlement and agriculture, including plantations, especially of oil palm. An additional important threat is wildlife trade for their skin and bones and for the pet markets. They are also threatened by indiscriminate snaring. Their populations are thought to be decreasing and are at critical risk of local extinction. The Asiatic Golden Cat and the Marbled Cat are listed as Near Threatened and protected over parts of their range. The Borneo Bay Cat, one of the rarest and least known felids, is classified as Endangered and is fully protected over most of its range; its limited distribution renders it very vulnerable.

Sunda Golden Cat
Catopuma temminckii temminckii, 228

Mainland Golden Cat
Catopuma temminckii moormensis, 230

red form

gray form

Bay Cat
Catopuma badia, 232

Borneo form

Sunda Marbled Cat
Pardofelis marmorata marmorata, 234

Mainland Marbled Cat
Pardofelis marmorata longicaudata, 236

Sunda Golden Cat
CATOPUMA TEMMINCKII TEMMINCKII

BL: 67-76 cm. TL: 42.5 cm. SH: 50 cm. W: 9 kg (♂), 8.1 kg (♀). SL: 12.2 cm. SW: 8.9 cm. DF: 28-30. CN: 38. A medium-sized cat, with a relatively long, slender tail and a stocky body. Coat is dense, soft, and short, variable in color, usually golden-brown to rich russet-brown, largely unmarked except for light speckling on the chest, abdomen, and inner side of the upper legs, and distinct white lines bordered with dark brown to black running across the cheeks, from the nostrils toward the cheeks, at the inner corner of the eyes, and up the crown. Completely melanistic individuals occur. No blotched morphs have been reported for this subspecies. Rounded ears, black-backed with a gray spot. Legs usually gray to black at the distal end. Underside of tail is conspicuously bright white with a dark upper tip, often carried with the end curled dorsally. Males are larger than females.

Young

228

Catopuma temminckii temminckii

OTHER NAMES Temminck's Golden Cat. *French*: Chat de Temminck, chat doré d'Asie. *German*: Asiatische Goldkatze. *Spanish*: Gato dorado asiático. *Russian*: Зондская кошка Темминка. *Malaysian*: Kucing tulap, harimau anjing. *Indonesian*: Kucing emas.

TAXONOMY Two subspecies are currently recognized: *C. t. temminckii* (Sumatra and the Malay Peninsula, S of the Isthmus of Kra, smaller, typical reddish coloration); and *C. t. moormensis* (from Nepal to N Burma, China, Tibet, and SE Asia, larger, pelage very variable ranging from blotches and spots to dark gray, blackish, brown, and reddish morphs). Asiatic Golden Cats cannot be assigned to any subspecies based on their coloration, but blotched forms only occur in mainland, particularly in northern, populations. This species resembles superficially the African Golden Cat, but it is not closely related. It has been suggested that it should be grouped in the genus *Pardofelis*, because of the evident close genetic relationship with the Marbled Cat, but is retained in *Catopuma*, as this species lacks the flexible ankle joint and elongated tail found in *Pardofelis*.

SIMILAR SPECIES The Bay Cat closely resembles a small Asiatic Golden Cat but the two species are not sympatric.

REPRODUCTION *Gestation*: 78-81 days. *Young per Birth*: 1-2. *Weaning*: 9 months. *Sexual Maturity*: 24 months (♂), 18 months (♀). *Life Span*: 20 years in captivity. *Breeding Season*: No reports on breeding season exist. Not much is known about the reproductive behavior of this elusive species in the wild and most of what is known has been learned from individuals in captivity. It breeds in tree hollows or in burrows among rocks.

BEHAVIOR *Social Behavior*: Solitary except during mating. *Diet*: Large rodents, but also amphibians, insects, birds, leaf monkeys, reptiles, and small ungulates (muntjac, mouse-deer); they sometimes raid poultry. Little is known about the ecology and behavior of this species. It was once thought to be primarily nocturnal; however, recent data indicate that it may be more crepuscular or diurnal. Foraging is mostly terrestrial, though they are very capable climbers and presumably take some prey arboreally.

DISTRIBUTION *Native*: Indonesia (Sumatra), Malaysia, Thailand.

HABITAT Tropical and subtropical moist evergreen forests, mixed evergreen forests, and dry deciduous forests. It may occur also in open areas such as shrub or grasslands, or open rocky areas, and in degraded or fragmented forest landscapes. Found both at low elevations and in montane forests. In Sumatra, they are found at higher elevations than other sympatric felids (Sumatran Tigers, Sunda Clouded Leopards, Marbled Cats, and Leopard Cats), up to 2,500 m on Mount Kerinci.

CONSERVATION STATUS Near Threatened. CITES: Appendix I. Its population is believed to be declining across its range, although some surveys in Sumatra indicate that it is more common than sympatric small cats, suggesting that it is more numerous than previously believed. The most significant threats are habitat loss and poaching, as it is often targeted for the sale of its pelt and bones, and killed in retribution for preying on poultry. It is also threatened by indiscriminate snaring.

PHOTO CREDITS TL: *Bram Demeulemeester*, Gunung Kerinci Sumatra (Indonesia); Young: *Alexander Sliwa*; TR, CR, B: *Alex Kantorovich*, Pata Zoo (Thailand).

Mainland Golden Cat
CATOPUMA TEMMINCKII MOORMENSIS

BL: 75-109 cm (♂), 66-94 cm (♀). TL: 42.5-58 cm. SH: 56 cm. W: 12-15.7 kg (♂), 8.5 kg (♀). SL: 13.2 cm (♂), 11.4 cm (♀). SW: 8.4 cm (♂), 7.9 cm (♀). DF: 28-30. CN: 38. A medium-sized cat, with a relatively long, slender tail and a stocky body. Largest subspecies, with a more luxuriant and longer coat. Coat is variable in color, usually fox-red to golden-brown, but it can also be dark brown, pale cinnamon, bright red, or gray, largely unmarked. Distinct white lines bordered with dark brown to black running across the cheeks, from the nostrils toward the cheeks, at the inner corner of the eyes, and up the crown. Melanistic individuals occur. A richly spotted form (ocelot morph) with light grayish fur and large russet blotches with dark borders has been recorded from Bhutan, China, and Burma. Northern populations seem to be particularly polymorphic. Rounded ears, black-backed with a gray spot. Legs usually gray at the distal end. Tail is bushy, underside is conspicuously bright white with a dark upper tip, often carried with the end curled dorsally. Males are larger than females.

melanistic form

gray form

Young

Catopuma temminckii moormensis

OTHER NAMES Temminck's Golden Cat. *French*: Chat de Temminck, chat doré d'Asie. *German*: Asiatische Goldkatze. *Spanish*: Gato dorado asiático. *Russian*: Кошка Темминка (материковый подвид). *Chinese*: Jin mao. *Manipuri*: Tokpa. *Bengali*: Shonali biral. *Assamese*: Xonali mekoori. *Lao*: Sua meo, sua pa. *Shan*: Hso hpai, miao thon.

TAXONOMY Considered as a subspecies of Asiatic Golden Cat (*C. temminckii*). Includes *bainesi* (Yunnan), *dominicanorum* (S China), and *tristis* (Tibet, Sichuan, and Upper Burma).

SIMILAR SPECIES The "ocelot" morph form is similar to the Marbled Cat, which is smaller with a distinctive very long, tubular tail. This form is also known as *tristis*, reflecting its early classification as a separate but invalid subspecies.

REPRODUCTION *Gestation*: 78-81 days. *Young per Birth*: 1-2. *Weaning*: 9 months. *Sexual Maturity*: 24 months (♂), 18 months (♀). *Life Span*: 23 years in captivity. *Breeding Season*: No reports on breeding season exist. It breeds in tree hollows or in burrows among rocks.

BEHAVIOR *Social Behavior*: Solitary except during mating; in captivity sometimes live in pairs. *Diet*: Small prey items, such as rodents, birds, reptiles, and sometimes common barking deer; it may take down large prey including domestic sheep, goats, and buffalo calves. *Main Predators*: Tigers, Leopards, possibly Clouded Leopards, and dholes are potential predators. Little is known of its behavior due to its secretive habits. Mostly diurnal and crepuscular. Terrestrial species but can climb well. ♂'s territory is larger and overlaps those of several ♀. The home ranges in Thailand were 33 km² (♀) and 48 km² (♂), with significant overlapping.

DISTRIBUTION *Native*: Bangladesh, Bhutan, Cambodia, China, NE India (Sikkim, Assam, Arunachal Pradesh), Laos, Myanmar, Nepal, Thailand, Vietnam.

HABITAT Tropical and subtropical deciduous and evergreen forests, at elevations up to 3,960 m in the Himalayas. They prefer dense vegetation cover and are seldom observed in open habitat.

CONSERVATION STATUS Near Threatened. CITES: Appendix I. Its presence in India, Bangladesh, and Nepal is limited and patchy. It is reported infrequently from E Cambodia, Laos, Vietnam, and S China. It is distributed more widely throughout Bhutan, Myanmar, Thailand, Malaysia, and Indonesia, but it is thought to be experiencing population declines. Legal hunting is prohibited over most of its range, in Bangladesh, Cambodia, China, India, Indonesia, Myanmar, Nepal, Thailand, and Vietnam, and is regulated in Laos. However, it is illegally hunted for its meat, pelt, and body parts used in Asian traditional medicine; populations are considered to be declining. There are an estimated 3,000-5,000 left in China.

PHOTO CREDITS TL, B: *Gerard Lacz*; Melanistic form: *Jonas Livet*, Lao Zoo (Laos); Young: *Eric Isselée* and *Alexander Sliwa*, Wuppertal Zoo (Germany); CL: *Balazs Buzas* (UAE).

Bay Cat
CATOPUMA BADIA

BL: 53-66 cm. TL: 32-40 cm. SH: 37 cm. W: 3-5 kg. SW: 6.4 cm. A small-sized cat, with a relatively long, slender tail and a slender body, similar in appearance to the Asiatic Golden Cat, but much smaller. Coat is variable in color, usually chestnut-red but gray individuals with red undertones are also known. Both color morphs may occur in the same area, and there is some intergradation between forms. Some individuals may change coloration during their lives. Largely unmarked, except for faint spotting along the transition between the upper body color and pale underparts. Forehead with faint dark stripes, light markings at the inner corners of the eyes, and 2 faint brown stripes on the cheeks. Chin is white. Undersides are lightly colored. Dark melanistic individuals have been recorded. Round head with small rounded ears, dark grayish behind, without white spot, set rather low on the side of the head. Long tail, with a bright whitish stripe running down the ventral surface of the terminal half and a dark dorsal tip, often carried straight and low.

gray form

red form

Catopuma badia

OTHER NAMES Borneo Bay Cat. *French*: Chat bai. *German*: Borneo-Katze. *Spanish*: Gato rojo de Borneo. *Russian*: Калимантанская кошка. *Indonesian*: Kucing merah.

TAXONOMY Monotypic. Previously considered as a small island form of the Asiatic Golden Cat (*Catopuma temminckii*), but genetic analysis leaves no doubt that the two species are distinct.

SIMILAR SPECIES The Asiatic Golden Cat is much larger, and it does not occur in Borneo.

REPRODUCTION There is no information on reproduction for this species. It has never bred in captivity.

BEHAVIOR *Social Behavior*: Probably solitary. *Diet*: Unknown, but it has never been seen in a tree, which indicates that it hunts for medium to small terrestrial birds and mammals; its relatively small size allows it to creep into underground tunnels used by mouse-deer, which would be inaccessible to Clouded Leopards; it may prey on domestic poultry (pheasants). *Main Predators*: Potential predators include Sunda Clouded Leopard, perhaps large reptiles including reticulated python and estuarine crocodile, and domestic dogs; however there are no known records and predation is likely to be uncommon. It is one of the least studied of the wild cats, and there is almost no information available about its behavior, ecology, or social or spatial structure. It is rarely observed. It appears to be primarily diurnal in nature, with occasional nocturnal activity. Terrestrial. It has been suggested that it may be specialized in hunting mouse-deer, chasing them into rivers, although this has yet to be recorded; its plain counter-shaded coloring matches that of the mouse-deer exactly.

DISTRIBUTION *Native*: Indonesia, Malaysia. *Presence uncertain*: Brunei. It is endemic to the island of Borneo. It has been recorded in Sabah in Deramakot Forest Reserve, Danum Valley Conservation Area, Ulu Segama Forest Reserve, Malua Forest Reserve, Tabin Wildlife Reserve, Tawau Hills NP, Kuching, Gunung Mulu NP, Lanjak Entimau Wildlife Sanctuary, Upper Baram River, Upper Rejang River, and in Kalimantan, in Mount Palung NP, Kutai, and Kayan Mentarang.

HABITAT Forest dependent, restricted to densely natural and semi-natural forests, with records in primary, riverine, swamp, and mangrove forests, from lowland to hill forest, up to 1,400 m in the Kelabit Highlands. It avoids oil palm plantations, but tolerates regenerating logged forest.

CONSERVATION STATUS Endangered. CITES: Appendix II. This species is naturally rare and very infrequently seen or detected during wildlife surveys. No population estimates exist, but there are possibly fewer than 2,500 individuals. Main threats include habitat loss due to commercial logging and conversion to oil palm plantations, as this species is dependent on dense forests. Poaching, particularly the use of snares, also poses a significant threat. It is fully protected across most of its range, and hunting and trade are prohibited in Indonesia and Malaysia, but enforcement is minimal. In Brunei there is no legal protection outside of protected areas. No known Bornean Bay Cat lives in captivity.

PHOTO CREDITS T: *Sebastian Kennerknecht*, Tawau Hills Park, Sabah, Borneo (Malaysia); CL: *Pierre de Chabannes*, Taman Safari, Cisarua (Indonesia); CR: *Johannes Pfleiderer*, Taman Safari, Cisarua (Indonesia); B: *Jim Sanderson*, Sarawak (Malaysia).

Sunda Marbled Cat
PARDOFELIS MARMORATA MARMORATA

BL: 45.7-65.8 cm. TL: 49.2-73.6 cm. SH: 30-38 cm. W: 2.5-5 kg. SL: 8.9 cm (♂), 7.9 cm (♀). SW: 7.1 cm (♂), 6.3 cm (♀). DF: 30. CN: 38. A small-sized cat, with a very long, thick, and furry tail, resembling a small-sized Clouded Leopard. Coat is full and soft, tawny brownish-gray in color, usually grayer than in mainland subspecies, with large irregular dark distinct blotches on the back and flanks ("marbling"), longitudinal stripes on the neck, and black dots scattered on the legs, forehead, and tail. Melanistic forms have been reported in Sumatra. Blotches and patches on the flanks are more defined in individuals from Borneo than in Sumatra and Malaysia. Relatively small, rounded head with a broad, short face. White eye patches around the eyes. Short rounded ears, black behind, with a central white spot. Paws are large and broad. Very long, thick, and bushy tail, almost the same length as the head and body and held almost horizontal while walking.

Borneo form

Pardofelis marmorata marmorata

OTHER NAMES *French*: Chat marbré. *German*: Marmorkatze. *Spanish*: Gato jaspeado de Sonda. *Russian*: Зондская мраморная кошка.

TAXONOMY Two subspecies are tentatively recognized, but a more in-depth molecular and morphological study awaits, which may show that there are two distinct species and a possible new subspecies on Borneo: *P. m. marmorata* (restricted to Borneo, Sumatra, and the Malay Peninsula S of Isthmus of Kra and S Thailand, grayer with large distinct blotches), and *P. m. longicaudata* (Nepal to Assam, Bangladesh, SE Asia N of the Isthmus of Kra, rich to pale ocherous brown). The pelage of these two forms is consistently distinct and geographically separated, and there could be differentiation between Sumatra (grayer) and Borneo (browner) populations, which may be recognized as distinct undescribed subspecies. It was once considered a close relative of the Clouded Leopard based on superficial morphological similarities, but genetic analyses show conclusively the species belongs in the Bay Cat lineage.

SIMILAR SPECIES The Clouded Leopard is larger and heavy-headed, with the fur more distinctly marked in clear clouds, and a larger tail; patches in the Marbled Cat have pale borders unlike the black-edged pattern of the Clouded Leopard, and even young animals have thin stripes from eye to crown, instead of a row of spots like the Clouded Leopard.

REPRODUCTION *Gestation*: 66-82 days. *Young per Birth*: 1-4. *Weaning*: Unknown. *Sexual Maturity*: 21-22 months. *Life Span*: 12 years in captivity. *Breeding Season*: Unknown.

BEHAVIOR *Social Behavior*: Probably solitary, but largely unknown. *Diet*: They probably prey primarily on rodents, including flying squirrels, and birds; they have been reported as poultry pests; it is unknown if they scavenge, but a captive individual refused carrion. This species is poorly known, with few observations in the wild. It appears to be primarily diurnal. Arboreal, but not clearly restricted to the trees and may be seen on the ground. Its relatively large tail indicates that it is a specialist hunter of canopy mammals, and large flying squirrels probably make up a large part of its diet. They can climb down bare tree trunks head first, due to their reversible ankle joints and highly elastic tendons in their hips and ankles, allowing them to flatten their bodies against tree trunks and use their claws to grip the curve of a trunk.

DISTRIBUTION *Native*: Brunei, Indonesia, Malaysia, Thailand.

HABITAT Forest dependent, primarily associated with moist and mixed deciduous-evergreen tropical forest, and may prefer hill forest, over a wide elevation range and in rugged areas. It may tolerate disturbed areas, including recently logged forest, but avoids oil palm plantations.

CONSERVATION STATUS Near Threatened. CITES: Appendix I. There are no published estimates of population, although it is probably declining. Main threats include forest loss and degradation across its range from logging and expansion of human settlements and agriculture, including oil palm plantations. Targeted and indiscriminate snaring, and illegal wildlife trade are prevalent throughout much of the range. Protected by national legislation across most of its range. Hunting is prohibited in Indonesia, Malaysia, and Thailand.

PHOTO CREDITS T, CL: *Joel Sartore* (Malaysia); CR: Johan Bordonné, Al Bustan Zoo (UAE); B: *Sebastian Kennerknecht*, Tawau Hills Park (Malaysia).

Mainland Marbled Cat
PARDOFELIS MARMORATA LONGICAUDATA

BL: 45-60 cm. TL: 35-55 cm. SH: 30-38 cm. W: 2-5 kg. SL: 8.1 cm. SW: 6.1 cm. DF: 30. CN: 38. A small-sized cat, with a very long, thick, and furry tail, resembling a small-sized Clouded Leopard. Coat is full and soft, rich ocherous-brown in color, usually browner, thicker and longer than that of Sunda subspecies. Large, well-defined dark blotches on the back and flanks ("marbling"), edged with black behind and sometimes in front, and separated by grayish-buff wavy lines. Longitudinal stripes on the neck, and black dots scattered on the legs, forehead, and tail. Relatively small, rounded head with a broad, short face. White eye patches around the eyes. Short rounded ears, black behind, with a central white spot. Paws are large and broad. Very long, thick tail, almost the same length as the head and body and held almost horizontal while walking.

Young

Pardofelis marmorata longicaudata

OTHER NAMES Himalayan Marbled Cat. *French*: Chat marbré. *German*: Marmorkatze. *Spanish*: Gato jaspeado. *Russian*: Мраморная кошка (материковый подвид). *Chinese*: Yunmao shu. *Tibetan*: Sikmar.

TAXONOMY Considered as a subspecies of Marbled Cat (*P. marmorata*). Includes *charltoni*. Marbled Cat from Borneo and from the mainland and Sumatra are probably two separate, closely related species.

SIMILAR SPECIES The Clouded Leopard is larger and heavy-headed, with the fur more distinctly marked in clear clouds, and a larger tail; patches in the Marbled Cat have pale borders unlike the black-edged pattern of the Clouded Leopard, and even young animals have thin stripes from eye to crown, instead of a row of spots like the Clouded Leopard.

REPRODUCTION *Gestation*: 66-82 days. *Young per Birth*: 1-4. *Weaning*: Unknown. *Sexual Maturity*: 21-22 months. *Life Span*: 12 years in captivity. *Breeding Season*: Unknown.

BEHAVIOR *Social Behavior*: Probably solitary, but largely unknown. *Diet*: Birds may play an important role in its diet due to their arboreal nature, although rodents, smaller mammals, lizards, and frogs are also part of it; they have been observed hunting arboreal squirrels. *Main Predators*: Potential predators include large cats and domestic dogs but there are no known records. Probably diurnal, but may be active at night, probably depending on the presence of larger felids and people. It has a typical arched back stance when it freezes or is resting. Its morphology suggests a high degree of arborealism. They are highly agile climbers able to rapidly descend trees head first, and there are brief sightings of them hunting in trees. They also move about on the ground and they presumably hunt both on the forest floor and in trees.

DISTRIBUTION *Native*: Bangladesh, Bhutan, Cambodia, China, India, Laos, Myanmar, Nepal, Thailand, Vietnam. It is found from the Himalayan foothills in Nepal E into SW China, S throughout mainland Southeast Asia. There are only a handful reports of Marbled Cats in China, including the tropical and subtropical forests in S and W Yunnan Province and SE Tibet. In India, this species is restricted to E Himalayan foothills, especially Arunachal Pradesh and Assam. It may occur in extreme N Bangladesh but there are no certain records.

HABITAT Forest dependent, found in moist and mixed deciduous and evergreen tropical forest. In the E Himalayan foothills it is associated with moist deciduous and semievergreen forest habitats at 1,500-3,000 m.

CONSERVATION STATUS Near Threatened. CITES: Appendix I. It is naturally rare and forest dependent, suggesting it is particularly vulnerable to habitat loss and deforestation due to logging and conversion for human settlement and agriculture, including plantations especially of oil palm. Indiscriminate hunting and poaching appears to be increasing region-wide, particularly in Laos and Vietnam, where trade-driven intensive snaring is likely impacting wild felids, including the Marbled Cat. Protected by national legislation across most of its range. Hunting is prohibited in Bangladesh, Cambodia, China (Yunnan only), India, Indonesia, Malaysia, Myanmar, Nepal, and Thailand, and regulated in Laos.

PHOTO CREDITS T, B: *Narong Suwannarong*, Dong Phayayen-Khao Yai (Thailand); Young: *Kedar Nath Timsina*, Assam (India); C: *Alexander Sliwa*, Saigon Zoo (Vietnam).

Hyenas

HYENAS AND AARDWOLF

RECOGNITION The family Hyaenidae comprises four living species: three species with a craniodental morphology adapted to cracking the bones of prey and carcasses, the Spotted Hyena (*Crocuta crocuta*), the Brown Hyena (*Parahyaena brunnea*), and the Striped Hyena (*Hyaena hyaena*), all belonging to the subfamily Hyaeninae; and the Aardwolf (*Proteles cristata*), a termite-feeding specialist and the only surviving member of the subfamily Protelinae. Despite their dog-like appearance, these animals are more closely related to cats and other feliform taxa than to caniform carnivores, such as dogs or bears. Hyenas are medium to large in size, 8-80 kg, with a large head and long neck, a blunt muzzle, and large ears. Forequarters are relatively larger than hindquarters, with shoulders being higher than the hindquarters. All hyenas have four digits on the forelimbs and hind limbs, with the exception of the Aardwolf, which has five digits on the forelimbs. Their claws are blunt and non-retractile. They have a shaggy, striped or spotted coat, a dorsal mane, and a short, bushy tail. Females of Spotted Hyenas are larger than males and have male-like genitalia. The jaws of the Brown, Spotted, and Striped Hyenas are very powerful, and their dentition is adapted to both meat-eating and bone-crushing (dental formula is I 3/3, C 1/1, P 4/3, M 1/1 = 34), but the Aardwolf, which is uniquely adapted to an insectivorous diet, displays a reduced dentition (I 3/3, C 1/1, P 3/2-1, M 1/1-2 = 28-32). Chromosome number is 2n=40.

PHYLOGENY Fossil data suggest that the Hyaenidae last shared a common ancestor with their feliform sister taxa 29 Ma, in the middle Oligocene. All four extant hyaenid species apparently originated in Africa, their ancestors having arrived there earlier from Eurasia via the Gomphotherium land bridge in what is now Saudi Arabia. Bone-cracking forms appeared relatively late in the history of the hyena family, during the late Miocene, and the extant bone-cracking forms all first appear in the fossil record in the late Pliocene. The Aardwolf is also recently derived, first appearing in the Pleistocene. Modern Spotted Hyenas first appear in the fossil record less than 1 Ma.

BEHAVIOR Spotted Hyenas live in large maternally dominated clans whose members hunt cooperatively. Although they scavenge opportunistically, they are very efficient hunters, and directly kill most of the food they eat, regularly capturing prey larger than themselves. Brown and Striped Hyenas are nocturnal and may form small clans, but both species forage alone. These two species are primarily scavengers, although they will also hunt prey smaller or larger than themselves. Bone-cracking hyenas, particularly the Spotted Hyena, can generate enormous bite forces. All three species of bone-cracking hyenas are capable of eating and digesting all parts of their prey except hair, hooves, and the keratin sheaths of antelope horns; bones are digested completely and only the inorganic components are excreted. Aardwolves are socially monogamous, but primarily solitary foragers; they are uniquely adapted to a diet consisting nearly exclusively of harvester termites. Hyenas as a group communicate through vocalizations, body posture, and scent-marking, the last of which is highly developed in the Brown Hyena and consists of two components, which dry to different colors and consistency on prominent vegetation.

DISTRIBUTION Spotted Hyenas occur throughout Africa south of the Sahara Desert, except for the dense rainforest in Central Africa and a large part of South Africa, where they were exterminated. They live in many different habitats, including savannas, swamps, woodlands, and montane forests. Striped Hyenas are found over a widespread geographical range, extending through the Middle East, Caucasus region, Central Asia, and the Indian subcontinent, with their southern and western limits in Africa. They are found in forest and grassland ecosystems, mostly preferring areas that are open and with low shrubs. Brown Hyenas are confined to southern Africa, in a large variety of habitats, from savanna and bushveld to arid and semi-arid areas. The Aardwolf inhabits open grassy plains or bushy areas, being rare in desert areas and forests; it has a disjunct geographical distribution, with populations in East Africa widely separated from those in southern Africa.

CONSERVATION Negative attitudes toward hyenas prevail across Africa and elsewhere, with many ranchers and farmers shooting, poisoning, trapping, and hunting them. The Striped Hyena is listed as Near Threatened, with a population size estimated at fewer than 10,000 individuals. Major reasons for its decline include retaliatory killings, persecution, depleted prey populations, and loss of habitat with changes in livestock practices. The Brown Hyena is also listed as Near Threatened as the global population size is estimated to be only 5,000-8,000. The Spotted Hyena is listed as Least Concern, with a total population exceeding 10,000 individuals, but its population is also declining, even inside some protected areas, primarily due to persecution and habitat loss. The Aardwolf is reasonably widespread and present in numerous protected areas, and listed as Least Concern.

Spotted Hyena
Crocuta crocuta, 240

Brown Hyena
Parahyaena brunnea, 242

East African Striped Hyena
Hyaena hyaena dubbah, 252

Indian Striped Hyena
Hyaena hyaena hyaena, 244

Barbary Striped Hyena
Hyaena hyaena barbara, 248

Syrian Striped Hyena
Hyaena hyaena syriaca, 246

Arabian Striped Hyena
Hyaena hyaena sultana, 250

South African Aardwolf
Proteles cristatus cristatus, 254

East African Aardwolf
Proteles cristatus septentrionalis, 256

Spotted Hyena
CROCUTA CROCUTA

BL: 95-165 cm. TL: 13-31 cm. SH: 75-85 cm. W: 54-79 kg (♂), 55-81 kg (♀). SL: 23.6 cm. SW: 17.1 cm. DF: 34. CN: 40. A large-sized, strongly built, dog-like hyena, with a large head, a massive neck, and back slightly sloping. The largest extant hyena. Coat is coarse, pale buff, ocherous to tawny, or grayish-brown, with dark irregular brown spots all over the body and upper half of the limbs. Individual variation is considerable. Spots become fainter with age. Head, throat, chest, and feet unspotted. Short erect mane on the neck and shoulders. Large head with a black muzzle with several rows of vibrissae. Rounded ears. Forequarters are large with a massive neck, the back is sloping, and the hindquarters are rather weakly developed. Claws not retractable. Bushy tail, medium in length, basally like the back in color, with a few dark spots, black tipped. Females are larger and heavier than males, with fully masculinized genitals (it is not easy to distinguish the sexes in the field). Young animals are dark colored, with large spots and dark feet.

Young

Immature

Crocuta crocuta

OTHER NAMES Laughing Hyena. *French*: Hyène tachetée. *German*: Tüpfelhyäne, Fleckenhyäne. *Spanish*: Hiena manchada, hiena moteada. *Russian*: Пятнистая гиена. *Afrikaans*: Gevlekte hiëna. *Sepedi*: Phiri. *Swahili*: Nyangao, fisi.

TAXONOMY Nearly 30 subspecies were recognized based on differences in morphology, size, and pelage, but their validity is questionable. Usually considered monotypic, but recent phylogenetic studies have demonstrated significant variation between W, S, and E populations, suggesting at least three subspecies: *C. c. crocuta* (W African form), *C. c. capensis* (S form), and *C. c. habessynica* (E form). Individual variation is considerable, and regional characteristics, if they exist, have yet to be identified.

REPRODUCTION *Gestation*: 110 days. *Young per Birth*: 1-2, rarely 3. *Weaning*: 14-18 months. *Sexual Maturity*: 24-30 months (♂), 24-36 months (♀). *Life Span*: 19 years, 41 years in captivity. *Breeding Season*: Non-seasonal, with a peak in late summer. All the ♀ in a clan breed. They mostly dig their own communal dens and in exceptional cases use caves or crevices in rocky country. Cubs den together but each ♀ suckles only her own cubs. Cubs are precocious and fight savagely. Adults bring very little food to the den. ♀ remain with the natal clan for life; ♂ will emigrate after they become reproductively mature.

BEHAVIOR *Social Behavior*: Clans from 3 to 80 individuals, led by a dominant ♀, containing multiple adult ♀, their offspring, and one to several resident immigrant adult ♂. *Diet*: They both hunt and scavenge, with a very varied diet: medium-sized and large ungulates, but also smaller mammals, birds, reptiles, fruit, eggs, insects, and garbage; they also frequently steal kills from other carnivores. *Main Predators*: Lions, but these rarely eat them. Mostly active at night, traveling as much as 80 km. Highly social, with ♀ dominating all ♂. Flexible hunters, cooperating to bring down larger prey or steal carcasses from other predators, but may forage alone for smaller items. Territorial; territory size varies with food supply; territories are demarcated by anal gland scent-marks and middens, and defended against neighboring clans. They utter begging calls and growls or screams in a variety of social situations.

DISTRIBUTION *Native*: Angola, Benin, Botswana, Burkina Faso, Burundi, Cameroon, Central African Republic, Chad, Congo, DR Congo, Côte d'Ivoire, Djibouti, Equatorial Guinea, Eritrea, Ethiopia, Gambia, Ghana, Guinea, Guinea-Bissau, Kenya, Malawi, Mali, Mauritania, Mozambique, Namibia, Niger, Nigeria, Rwanda, Senegal, Sierra Leone, Somalia, South Africa, South Sudan, Sudan, Swaziland, Uganda, Zambia, Zimbabwe.

HABITAT Predominantly a savanna species, but it occurs in a wide range of habitats, including semi-desert, open woodland, and dense dry woodlands, excluding only dense forest. In many parts of its range, it occurs in close association with human habitation.

CONSERVATION STATUS Least Concern. CITES: Not listed. Near Threatened in South Africa. Total global population is 27,000-47,000. Many populations in E and W Africa, even in protected areas, are declining. The largest known populations occur in the Serengeti and Kruger NP. Generally regarded as vermin. Threats include incidental snaring and poisoning, persecution by humans, and habitat loss.

PHOTO CREDITS TL: *Eugen Haag* (Kenya); TR: *Bob Steiner*, Kruger (South Africa); Young: *Patrice Correia*, Kruger (South Africa); C: *Chris Eason*, Limpopo (South Africa); BL: *Dominique Salé*, Kruger (South Africa); BR: *Gualtiero Boffi*; Luangwa (Zambia).

Brown Hyena

PARAHYAENA BRUNNEA

BL: 110-135 cm (♂), 110-126 cm (♀). TL: 18.7-26-5 cm. SH: 64-88 cm. W: 35-49.5 kg (♂), 28-47.5 kg (♀). SL: 25.4 cm. SW: 16.3 cm. DF: 34. CN: 40. Medium-sized animal, with typical hyena build, higher at shoulders than at hindquarters, giving appearance of a sloping back. Coat is long and shaggy, dark brown to black in color, with indistinct stripes on the legs, and no body spots. Neck and shoulders are off-white to tawny, as are underparts and insides of limbs. Broad and short muzzle, black in color, with long and black whiskers, forehead lighter. Heavy mane. The long hair along the mid-dorsal line can be raised in a conspicuous display. Ears are long and pointed. Heavy forequarters. Longer front legs, give a sloping outline to the back. Tail dark and bushy. Females are slightly smaller than males, with 2 pairs of abdominal nipples. Juveniles are gray, with markings unobscured by mane.

Immature

Young

Parahyaena brunnea

OTHER NAMES Strandwolf. *French*: Hyène brune. *German*: Braune Hyäne, Strandwolf. *Spanish*: Hiena parda. *Russian*: Бурая гиена. *Afrikaans*: Bruinhiëna, strandjut. *Ndebele*: Impisi. *Sepedi*: Sephiribjôkwane, phiribjôkwane. *Sesotho*: Phiribjokwane, thamahane. *Tswana*: Lefiritshwana, mosonokwane, sethenekwane. *Swati*: Imphisi. *Tsonga*: Mhisi. *Venda*: Tshivhingwi. *Zulu*: Isidawana.

TAXONOMY Monotypic. Previously placed in the genus *Hyaena*, now placed in its own genus, *Parahyaena*. Five subspecies named but none recognized: *fusca, makapani, melampus, striata*, and *villosa*.

SIMILAR SPECIES The sympatric Spotted Hyena is larger, with spots on body, round ears, and a short coat. The Striped Hyena is slightly smaller, with a pale gray to beige pelage and darker vertical stripes on the body and legs, but is not sympatric.

REPRODUCTION *Gestation*: 97 days. *Young per Birth*: 1-5, usually 2. *Weaning*: 15 months. *Sexual Maturity*: 30 months. *Life Span*: 16-20 years, 32 years in captivity. *Breeding Season*: Non-seasonal, but mainly from May to August, with most births occurring from August to November. Young open their eyes after 8-15 days and emerge from the den after 3 months. Young of several litters are raised together in a communal den. Lactating ♀ suckle any cub and all ages and sexes bring home food and share it.

BEHAVIOR *Social Behavior*: Small clans of 4-14 individuals, composed of one dominant ♂, a dominant unrelated ♀, several additional ♀, natal ♂ adults, subadults, and cubs, but they are solitary foragers who spend much of their time alone. *Diet*: Primarily scavengers, consuming a wide range of vertebrate remains, but also fruits, insects, ostrich eggs; they occasionally kill small animals, including seal pups; excess food is often cached; their impact on domestic livestock is usually small; independent of drinking water. Almost entirely nocturnal, with some crepuscular activity, hiding up during the day in secluded places such as aardvark holes or thickets. Home ranges are very large, from 240 to 480 km², defended against other hyenas. Vocalizations, visual displays, and dominance behavior closely resemble those of the Striped Hyena. Lion kills provide scavenging opportunities for Brown Hyenas, although they are dominated by Lions. Brown Hyena is usually dominant over Leopards, Cheetahs, and Caracals and often appropriates the kills of these species. The Spotted Hyena is dominant over the Brown Hyena.

DISTRIBUTION *Native*: Angola, Botswana, Namibia, South Africa, Zimbabwe. Endemic to S Africa. Absent from Lesotho and Swaziland.

HABITAT Desert areas with annual rainfall less than 100 mm, particularly along the coast, semi-desert, open scrub, and open woodland savanna with a maximum rainfall up to about 700 mm. It shows an ability to survive close to urban areas. It requires some type of cover in which to lie up during the day. Typically avoids agricultural and heavily urbanized habitats.

CONSERVATION STATUS Near Threatened. CITES: Not listed. Total population size estimated at fewer than 10,000, with Botswana having the largest population. It currently occupies about half of its original range. It is regarded as a threat to livestock in some areas, and it is shot, poisoned, trapped, and hunted with dogs, or inadvertently killed in non-selective control programs.

PHOTO CREDITS TR, CL, B: *Wolf Avni*, Kgalagadi (South Africa); TL: *Gerrie van Vuuren* (South Africa); Young: *Armand Meling* (Namibia).

Indian Striped Hyena

HYAENA HYAENA HYAENA

BL: 100-115 cm. TL: 25-46 cm. SH: 66-75 cm. W: 26-41 kg (♂), 26-34 kg (♀). SL: 20.2-22.4 cm. SW: 14.3-16.4 cm. DF: 34. CN: 40. A medium-sized hyena, with a large head, long pointed ears, sloping back, and a long, bushy tail. Coat is long, coarse, and shaggy, pale gray to light brown or buff in color, with black vertical stripes on flanks, horizontal stripes on legs, and a distinctive dark patch on the throat. Black-tipped mane from neck to rump can be erected to make the animal look larger. Pelage coloration varies by region and seasonally in colder parts of its range. Large and broad head, a black pointed muzzle, and massive jaws. Long, pointed ears. Thick neck. Heavyset body. Hind legs shorter than forelegs. Feet with 4 toes, non-retractable short claws. Tail long and shaggy. Well-developed anal pouch can be everted and be visible at times. Females are somewhat larger than males.

Hyaena hyaena hyaena

OTHER NAMES Asiatic Striped Hyena. *French*: Hyène rayée. *German*: Indische Streifenhyäne. *Spanish*: Hiena rayada india. *Russian*: Индийская полосатая гиена. *Kumaoni*: Atariyal. *Telugu*: Domulagundu. *Odia*: Heta, bagha. *Gujarati*: Jharak. *Kannada*: Kadu keeruba. *Hindi*: Lakkad bagga. *Malayalam, Tamil*: Kazhutha puli. *Marathi*: Taras.

TAXONOMY Five subspecies are provisionally recognized here: *H. h. hyena* (from India), *H. h. barbara* (from NW Africa), *H. h. dubbah* (from NE Africa), *H. h. sultana* (from the Arabian Peninsula), and *H. h. syriaca* (from Syria). These subspecies are distinguished mainly by differences in size and pelage, but their validity is uncertain. This subspecies includes *bilkiewiczi, bokharensis, indica, satunini, striata,* and *zarudnyi*.

REPRODUCTION *Gestation*: 90-91 days. *Young per Birth*: 1-4. *Weaning*: 12 months. *Sexual Maturity*: 24-36 months. *Life Span*: 24 years in captivity. *Breeding Season*: Non-seasonal. Cubs are reared in dens and intense digging behavior in the ♀ announces parturition. Dens may be holes dug by the mother, holes formed and abandoned by other species, or deep, natural, and sometimes complex caves. ♀ carry food back to the den for their cubs and prepare meat for cubs by biting off pieces.

BEHAVIOR *Social Behavior*: Solitary, pairs, and groups of 5-15. *Diet*: Omnivorous, feeding on a wide variety of vertebrates, invertebrates, vegetables, fruit, and human-originated organic wastes; they have been reported chasing hares, porcupines, domestic cats, Cheetah cubs, dik-dik, reedbuck, and young gazelles, may kill small livestock; caching of food under bushes has also been observed. Nocturnal. Spends day in den in a natural cave, crevice, or overhang, which can be recognized by the accumulation of bones. The dorsal mane is erected in a defensive posture or when threatened and, when aggressive, both the mane and the tail hairs are erected.

DISTRIBUTION *Native*: Afghanistan, Armenia, Azerbaijan, Georgia, India, Iran, Iraq, Nepal, Pakistan, Tajikistan, Turkey, Turkmenistan, Uzbekistan. *Extinct*: Bangladesh, Kazakhstan, China.

HABITAT Open scrub and dry thorn forests, often found near human habitation. They prefer arid to semi-arid environments and avoid open desert and dense thickets. Habitat preference is linked to availability of denning sites, which could be caves in rocky terrain, burrows dug by them, or even those of porcupines. Within the Indian subcontinent, they occur widely in diverse habitats except the moist forests of the NE region, up to 2,500 m in hilly terrain, but in Pakistan they have been reported at more than 3,000 m.

CONSERVATION STATUS Near Threatened. CITES: Appendix III (Pakistan). Estimates of its abundance are complicated by the limited amount of information available on the species, due to its shy, nocturnal, mostly solitary nature, its apparent affinity for rugged terrain, and its generally negative reputation. Total population estimated at 5,000-14,000 individuals. Indian population estimate 1,000 to 3,000 individuals representing around 20% of the total world population. Populations are generally declining throughout its range. It occurs at low densities across most of its range. It is apparently absent from much of the NW and W provinces of Iran. Population is declining in many places due to persecution and hunting for utilization.

PHOTO CREDITS T, BR: *Andrew M. Allport*, Gujarat (India); BL: *Vickey Chauhan,* Gujarat (India); C: *Sourabh Bharti*, Jhalana Forest Reserve (India).

Syrian Striped Hyena

HYAENA HYAENA SYRIACA

BL: 85-130 cm. TL: 25-40 cm. SH: 65-80 cm. W: 20-50 kg. SL: 21.5 cm. SW: 14.9 cm. DF: 34. CN: 40. A medium-sized hyena, with a large head, long pointed ears, sloping back, and a long, bushy tail. A large subspecies of Striped Hyena, with a more elaborate crest and tail hairs, and a long and luxuriant winter coat. Coat is long, coarse, and shaggy, gray-whitish to yellowish-brown in color, with black vertical stripes on flanks, horizontal stripes on legs, and a distinctive dark patch on the throat. In summer the stripes are more visible because the hairs are shorter. Black-tipped mane from neck to rump can be erected to make the animal look larger. Large and broad head, with 2 black cheek stripes, a black pointed muzzle, and massive jaws. Long, pointed ears. Thick neck. Heavyset body. Tail long and shaggy. Well-developed anal pouch, visible at times. Females with 2 pairs of nipples. Young are pale white, maneless, but with stripes.

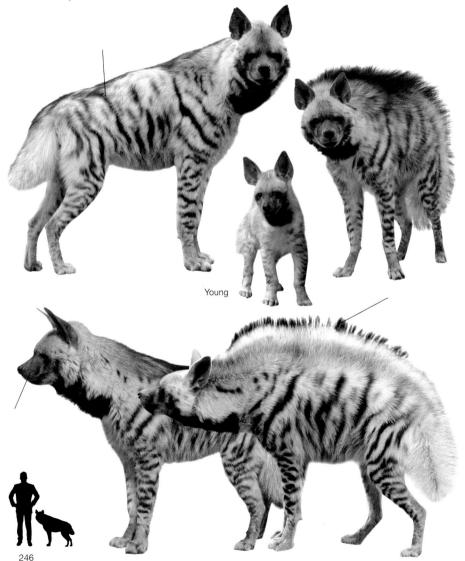

Young

246

Hyaena hyaena syriaca

OTHER NAMES *French*: Hyène rayée. *German*: Syrische Streifenhyäne. *Spanish*: Hiena rayada siria. *Russian*: Сирийская полосатая гиена. *Arabic*: Dab' moukhattat.

TAXONOMY Considered provisionally as a subspecies of Striped Hyena (*H. hyaena*). The subspecific variations are not sharply defined among these different subspecies. Includes *vulgaris* and *suilla*.

SIMILAR SPECIES Differences in pelage across the species/subspecies range appear minimal, although the Lebanese population is reported to have a reddish base coat color and hyenas on the Arabian Peninsula are described as having a yellow mark below the eyes and the dorsal crest is mixed gray and black rather than predominantly black. The golden jackal (*Canis aureus*) is much smaller and lighter, has a sharp snout, longer tail, and lacks the distinctive markings.

REPRODUCTION *Gestation*: 90-91 days. *Young per Birth*: 1-5. *Weaning*: 12 months. *Sexual Maturity*: 24-36 months. *Life Span*: 24 years in captivity. *Breeding Season*: Non-seasonal; most births occur in spring. Cubs are raised in dens, which may be either holes dug by the mother, holes formed and abandoned by other species, deep, natural, and sometimes complex caves, or simple rock depressions less than a meter deep. When large caves are not available, mothers may relocate cubs to a new den within the first few days after birth and do not reuse the same dens for subsequent litters. Both parents care for the young initially.

BEHAVIOR *Social Behavior*: Solitary or in pairs; in Israel, groups converge at feeding sites. *Diet*: Omnivorous, including small mammals, birds, reptiles, fish, eggs, large insects, fruit (dates, tomatoes, watermelons), and carrion; also human rubbish, animal bones, and even droppings; may hide excess food; drinks when water is available but can reportedly survive without for extended periods (thus, in desert areas, food, not water, may be the limiting factor). Fruit and vegetable crop raiding is considered a serious problem in Israel. They are nocturnal and hide during the day in the dense vegetation or in dens and cracks inside rocks. Hearing and smell very good. Sight good. Not territorial but occupies a home range marked by scent. They are more vocal in Israel than in East Africa. Vocalizations are similar to those of the Spotted Hyena and include whining by cubs before suckling, giggling when frightened, yelling when being chased by conspecifics, lowing in a defensive position, growling when play- or food-fighting, and a call by the mother to her cub.

DISTRIBUTION *Native*: Iraq, Israel, Jordan, Lebanon, Syria, Turkey.

HABITAT A wide variety of habitats, from coastal regions and uplands to deserts. The presence of rocky habitat that provides shelter for the animal limits its distribution. Middens frequented by hyenas are located on wadi banks of soft crumbling sediment or in stony deserts.

CONSERVATION STATUS Near Threatened. CITES: Not listed. It occurs at low densities across most of its range. Main threats include habitat alteration and destruction, and persecution (poisoning, killing, and hunting). Different parts of this species are also used to cure physical and mental diseases among the Bedouins and villagers in this area.

PHOTO CREDITS *Sergey Chichagov*, Tallinn Zoo (Estonia).

Barbary Striped Hyena

HYAENA HYAENA BARBARA

BL: 102-116 cm. TL: 30.5-33 cm. SH: 72 cm. W: 40-55 kg. SL: 22.1 cm. SW: 15.6 cm. DF: 34. CN: 40. A medium-sized hyena, with a large head, long pointed ears, sloping back, and a long, bushy tail. A large subspecies. Coat is long, coarse, and shaggy, buff to gray in color, with blackish vertical stripes on flanks, horizontal stripes on legs, and a distinctive dark patch on the throat. In summer the stripes are more visible because the hairs are shorter. Black-tipped mane from neck to rump can be erected to make the animal look larger. Large and broad head, with 2 black cheek stripes, a black pointed muzzle. Long, pointed ears. Thick neck. Heavyset body. Hind legs are shorter than forelegs. Tail long and shaggy. Well-developed anal pouch. Females with 2 pairs of nipples. Young are pale white, maneless, but with stripes.

Hyaena hyaena barbara

OTHER NAMES *French*: Hyène rayée. *German*: Nordafrikanische Streifenhyäne. *Spanish*: Hiena rayada de Berbería. *Russian*: Берберийская (североафриканская) полосатая гиена.

TAXONOMY Considered provisionally as a subspecies of Striped Hyena (*H. hyaena*). The subspecific variations are not sharply defined among these different subspecies. Includes *suilla*.

REPRODUCTION *Gestation*: 90-91 days. *Young per Birth*: 1-4. *Weaning*: 12 months. *Sexual Maturity*: 24-36 months. *Life Span*: 24 years in captivity. *Breeding Season*: Non-seasonal, although in some areas births may show seasonal peaks. Cubs are reared in dens and intense digging behavior in the ♀ announces parturition. Mothers carry food back to the den for their cubs and prepare meat for cubs by biting off pieces. There is some evidence of helpers being present to raise cubs.

BEHAVIOR *Social Behavior*: Solitary, occasionally pairs; in some areas they may hunt in groups and probably live in loosely associated groupings within a shared home range, but usually forage alone. *Diet*: Opportunistic, taking a wide range of animal and plant foods; in some areas it actively hunts larger prey such as sheep and goats; it is also a scavenger, and in some areas is a regular visitor to town rubbish dumps; it is reported to dig up human corpses from freshly dug graves. Nocturnal, during the day they lie up in natural caves or in burrows that are preferably dug by other animals but can be self-dug. They are shy, yet approach closely camps or dwellings in search of food. Territories are marked with secretions from the anal glands and delimited, but there is little evidence that territories are defended using physical force. In places where they live in groups the social structure is organized so that ♂ are dominant over ♀, as opposed to the Spotted Hyena where the ♀ is dominant. Overall, the evidence indicates Striped Hyenas in Africa are solitary nocturnal foragers for which fruit and vegetable matter, where available, may play a significant part. Striped Hyenas also regularly consume insects, invertebrates, and small vertebrates, and actively hunt small mammals and ground-nesting and/or ground-feeding birds. In addition, they scavenge off carcasses of larger mammals and this activity appears to account for a significant portion of the bones collected at den sites.

DISTRIBUTION *Native*: Algeria, Burkina Faso, Cameroon, Chad, Libya, Mali, Mauritania, Morocco, Niger, Nigeria, Senegal, Tunisia. Its presence is uncertain in Benin, Central African Republic, Guinea, and Western Sahara.

HABITAT Dry areas, often in association with rocky outcrops and within savanna. Records are few from the central areas of the major deserts, although they are present in and around the major massifs such as Ahaggar, Tassili, and Aïr. In some areas this species is also found on coastal plains, especially in Western Sahara.

CONSERVATION STATUS Near Threatened. CITES: Not listed. It is commercially hunted in Morocco for use in traditional medicine, with various parts being used (especially the brain).

PHOTO CREDITS T, C: *Ronny Graf*, Friguia Park (Tunisia); B: *Tomasinski73*, Friguia Park (Tunisia).

Arabian Striped Hyena

HYAENA HYAENA SULTANA

BL: 103.8 cm. TL: 30.8 cm. SH: 65-80 cm. W: 18-20 kg. SL: 20.6 cm. SW: 14.7 cm. DF: 34. CN: 40. A medium-sized hyena, with a large head, long pointed ears, sloping back, and a long, bushy tail. The smallest subspecies, with pelage richer and darker than in other subspecies. Coat is relatively short and coarse, buffish to yellowish-tawny in color, with black vertical stripes on flanks, horizontal stripes on legs, and a distinctive dark patch on the throat. In summer the stripes are more visible because the hairs are shorter. Dorsal mane mixed gray and black in color rather than predominantly black. Large and broad head, with 2 black cheek stripes, a black pointed muzzle. Long, pointed ears. Thick neck. Heavyset body. Hind legs are shorter than forelegs. Tail long and shaggy. Well-developed anal pouch. Females with 2 pairs of nipples. Young are pale white, maneless, but with stripes.

Hyaena hyaena sultana

OTHER NAMES *French*: Hyène rayée. *German*: Arabische Streifenhyäne. *Spanish*: Hiena rayada árabe. *Russian*: Аравийская полосатая гиена. *Arabic*: Dab' moukhattat.

TAXONOMY Considered provisionally as a subspecies of Striped Hyena (*H. hyaena*). The subspecific variations are not sharply defined among these different subspecies. On the basis of skull size, the five currently recognized subspecies of the Striped Hyena probably form two larger groups, a NE African-Arabian group composed of *H. h. sultana* and *H. h. dubbah*, and a NW African-Asian group composed of *H. h. barbara*, *H. h. syriaca*, and *H. h. hyaena*.

REPRODUCTION *Gestation*: 90-91 days. *Young per Birth*: 1-5. *Weaning*: 12 months. *Sexual Maturity*: 24-36 months. *Life Span*: 24 years in captivity. *Breeding Season*: Non-seasonal. Dens are used over extended periods while breeding and subadult animals from a previous litter are known to help feed young siblings. Solitary individuals are less attached to a single den. Cubs are born with shut eyelids, white to gray fur, and clear black stripes. Eyes open at 7-8 days, and teeth erupt at 21 days; cubs start to eat meat after the first month.

BEHAVIOR *Social Behavior*: Solitary or in pairs. *Diet*: Various well-protected vertebrates, such as tortoises, are easily killed and eaten, and invertebrates, including grasshoppers and termites, are taken. Palm dates, heglig (*Balanites*), and other fruits, including cucurbits (which may be taken primarily for the moisture they contain) are also eaten and, in some areas, scraps from garbage dumps make up the main diet. Nocturnal. Spends day in den in a natural cave, crevice, or overhang, which can be recognized by the accumulation of bones. Normally quiet but has a long, low howl when afraid or threatened. Also growls and whines.

DISTRIBUTION *Native*: Oman, Saudi Arabia, Yemen. Its presence is uncertain in Kuwait and Qatar. *Extinct*: United Arab Emirates.

HABITAT Open habitat or light thorn bush country in arid to semi-arid environments. They avoid open desert, such as the center of the Arabian desert, dense thickets, and forests. Unafraid of humans and frequently forage on garbage and carrion near human habitation.

CONSERVATION STATUS Near Threatened. CITES: Not listed. It occurs at low densities across most of its range. In the Arabian Peninsula it has been heavily persecuted but still survives in parts, associated especially with the coastal plain and adjoining mountain ranges. Estimated population between 300 and 400 animals in Saudi Arabia. Increased farming activities and the bulldozing of new routes to facilitate easier access to these farms in this area result in human-predator conflict and the decimation of this species. There is also illegal trade in skins, and body parts for use in traditional medicine, and they are often kept in cages for display purposes.

PHOTO CREDITS TL: *Tommy Pedersen*, Sir Bani Yas (United Arab Emirates); BL: *Klaus Rudloff*, Tierpark Berlin (Germany); TR, BR: *Arjan Haverkamp*, Safaripark Beekse Bergen (Netherlands).

East African Striped Hyena

HYAENA HYAENA DUBBAH

BL: 100-120 cm. TL: 23-35 cm. SH: 65-80 cm. W: 25-35 kg. SL: 21.3 cm. SW: 15 cm. DF: 34. CN: 40. A medium-sized hyena, with a large head, long pointed ears, sloping back, and a long, bushy tail. A small, longer-haired subspecies. Coat is long, coarse, and shaggy, pale buff to gray-white in color, with narrow blackish vertical stripes on flanks, horizontal stripes on legs, and a distinctive dark patch on the throat. In summer the stripes are more visible because the hairs are shorter. Black-tipped mane from neck to rump can be erected to make the animal look larger. Large and broad head, with 2 black cheek stripes, a black pointed muzzle. Long, pointed ears. Thick neck. Heavyset body. Hind legs are shorter than forelegs. Tail long and shaggy, usually white at the tip. Well-developed anal pouch. Females with 2 pairs of nipples. Young are pale white, maneless, but with stripes.

Young

Hyaena hyaena dubbah

OTHER NAMES Sudanese Striped Hyena. *French*: Hyène rayée. *German*: Ostafrikanische Streifenhyäne. *Spanish*: Hiena rayada de África oriental. *Russian*: Восточноафриканская полосатая гиена. *Arabic*: Dab' moukhattat. *Swahili*: Fisi.

TAXONOMY Considered provisionally as a subspecies of Striped Hyena (*H. hyaena*). Includes *hyaenomelas*, *bergeri*, *dubia*, *rendilis*, *vulgaris*, and *schillingsi*.

SIMILAR SPECIES The Spotted Hyena has spotted pelage and back not maned, with a relatively a short tail, short, rounded ears, and a much heavier head and jaws. The Aardwolf is smaller, with more gracile build, and relatively large pointed ears, and finer coat hairs appear glossier than the coarse coat of the Striped Hyena.

REPRODUCTION *Gestation*: 90-91 days. *Young per Birth*: 1-5. *Weaning*: 12 months. *Sexual Maturity*: 24-36 months. *Life Span*: 24 years in captivity. *Breeding Season*: Non-seasonal. Dens are in natural caves and cracks or among boulders or blocks of stone and are recognizable by accumulations of bones.

BEHAVIOR *Social Behavior*: Solitary, but in Kenya it is seen resting in pairs and occasionally in groups of up to 4 individuals; these groups never include more than 1 adult ♀, and adults within a group are typically unrelated or distantly related. *Diet*: Omnivorous and opportunistic but primarily adapted to coping with bones and carrion; there are reports of them taking sheep and goats in Tanzania, although this behavior is rare. Foraging activity in Kenya and Tanzania was restricted entirely to nighttime except during rain and/or unusually dark and cloudy weather. Where it co-exists with Spotted Hyena, the Striped Hyena is quieter, more retiring, and perhaps more solitary and cryptic with regard to dens and raising young. Mature adults of both sexes are intolerant of other members of their own sex, but they are probably non-territorial. During conflicts with other individuals, they will often erect their long mane hairs, which makes them appear larger than usual. Home range sizes are very large (44 to 72 km² in Kenya and Tanzania), with no significant difference in home range size between sexes. Individuals leave anal scent-marks on boulders or plants along habitually used paths.

DISTRIBUTION *Native*: Djibouti, Egypt, Ethiopia, Kenya, Libya, Tanzania, Uganda. Its presence is uncertain in Eritrea, Somalia, and Sudan.

HABITAT Arid steppes and subdesert, *Acacia* scrub and dry savannas, open montane habitats and rocky escarpments, up to an altitude of 3,300 m. Desert margins along Nile Valley or around oases descending to cultivated areas at night. Formerly in desert areas along camel trains but has disappeared from these areas as caravans ceased. They can tolerate high and very cold climates if they are also dry.

CONSERVATION STATUS Near Threatened. CITES: Not listed. The total African population estimate of 2,450 to 7,850 individuals represents roughly half of the total worldwide estimated population. Only Egypt and Kenya have estimated populations over 1,000 animals. Human persecution (by poisoning, shooting, and stoning), combined with reduction in prey species and habitat destruction, has greatly reduced this species.

PHOTO CREDITS T, CL: *Sergey Chichagov*, The Living Desert Zoo (USA); Young: *Aditya "Dicky" Singh*, Ndutu Lake (Tanzania); B: *Peter Satanley*, Serengeti (Tanzania).

South African Aardwolf

PROTELES CRISTATUS CRISTATUS

BL: 55-80 cm. TL: 19-28 cm. SH: 47-50 cm. W: 7.8-12 kg (♂), 7.7-13 kg (♀). SL: 13.4-14.1 cm. SW: 79-81 cm. DF: 32. CN: 40. A medium-sized, lightly built, jackal-sized hyena. Shaggy coat, with a long erectile mane from behind the head down the middle of the back to the tip of the tail. Color is pale buff to yellowish-gray, with 4-6 narrow, vertical, light brown to black stripes on the body and irregular horizontal black stripes on the upper limbs. Pelage larger and denser in winter. Dog-like head, with a broad, naked gray-black muzzle. Large eyes. Neck is long and muscular, sometimes with black spots or stripes. Large pointed ears, brown-black on the back, white in front. Sloping back with forelegs longer than the hind legs. Legs are lightly built. Small feet, black in color, with 5 toes on the forefeet and 4 on the hind feet. Bushy tail, with a broad black tip. No sexual dimorphism in size. Females have 2 pairs of inguinal teats.

erected mane

Young

Proteles cristatus cristatus

OTHER NAMES Civet Hyena. *French*: Protéle. *German*: Erdwolf. *Spanish*: Lobo de tierra, proteles. *Russian*: Южноафриканский земляной волк. *Afrikaans*: Maanhaarjakkals. *Ndebele, Swati, Zulu*: Isambane. *Sesotho, Tswana*: Thikhoi, thakadu, kgarangwê. *Shona*: Mwena. *Tsonga*: Xomboni, ndloti. *Venda*: Thagalu, didingwe. *Damara*: Gîb.

TAXONOMY Two subspecies are recognized: *P. c. cristatus* (S Africa), and *P. c. septentrionalis* (E and NE Africa), but their validity requires confirmation. Formerly placed in its own family, Protelidae. Includes *canescens*, *harrisoni*, *hyenoides*, *lalandii*, *transvaalensis*, and *typicus*.

REPRODUCTION *Gestation*: 90 days. *Young per Birth*: 2-5. *Weaning*: 4 months. *Sexual Maturity*: 24 months. *Life Span*: 12 years, 15 years in captivity. *Breeding Season*: Mating generally occurs in the second half of June and the first half of July (during the dry winter months of decreased resource availability), with most births occurring between mid-September and December. Socially monogamous, but sexually polygamous with numerous extra-pair copulations occurring in the short winter mating period. The ♀ gives birth in a den (enlarged springhare burrows or excavations) where the cubs remain for up to a month before emerging. ♂ will assist in the rearing of the young by guarding the young against predators (black-backed jackals). Between 12 and 16 weeks, the cubs will forage with an adult throughout the territory. They share their parents' territory until they are a year old.

BEHAVIOR *Social Behavior*: Monogamous pairs share a territory, but forage and sleep alone. *Diet*: Insectivorous, feeding almost exclusively on nasute harvester termites (*Trinervitermes*), occasionally supplemented with the harvester termite (*Hodotermes mossambicus*), and other insects; they do not prey on mammals and their teeth are too small to chew meat; largely independent of water, obtaining their moisture requirements from termites. *Main Predators*: Leopard, Cheetah, python, black-backed jackals kill unguarded cubs. Mainly nocturnal. They feed alone except when accompanying their young cubs. It has lost the general hyaenid characteristic of strong jaws and bone-crushing molar teeth, but instead has adaptations to termite eating: special papillae on the tongue, large salivary glands, and a muscular stomach. They do not dig, but lick the termites off the soil surface. Home ranges vary from 1 to 6 km^2, which are aggressively defended by pairs and scent-marked with anal gland secretion. During fights and chases the mane is often fully erected, nearly double its apparent size; they are also able to utter a very loud ferocious roar, an explosive bark, or a deep growl. Communication is mainly by odor via scent-marks. Feces are buried in middens.

DISTRIBUTION *Native*: Angola, Botswana, Mozambique, Namibia, South Africa, Swaziland, Zambia, Zimbabwe. No recent records from Lesotho, but may occur there.

HABITAT Open, grassy plains, where there is high termite abundance, but also most habitats having a mean annual rainfall of 100-600 mm. Absent from forests, *Baikiaea* woodland, or pure desert.

CONSERVATION STATUS Least Concern. CITES: Appendix III (Botswana). Its population is stable. Loss of habitat through urbanization or expansion of industrial agriculture may have negative impacts. Locust control with insecticides kills Aardwolves by secondary poisoning and can cause serious local losses.

PHOTO CREDITS TL: *Alexander Sliwa* (South Africa); TR: *Ole Jorgen Liodden* (Botswana); C: *Pierre Steenberg*, Kalahari (Botswana); Young: *Nigel Dennis*, Kapama (South Africa); B: *Cathy Withers-Clarke*, Eastern Cape (South Africa).

East African Aardwolf

PROTELES CRISTATUS SEPTENTRIONALIS

BL: 65-80 cm. TL: 19-28 cm. SH: 45-50 cm. W: 8-14 kg. SL: 13-14.4 cm. SW: 8-8.5 cm. DF: 32. CN: 40. A medium-sized, lightly built, jackal-sized hyena. More slender, with shorter and paler fur and more defined stripes than the South African subspecies. Shaggy coat, with a long erectile mane from behind the head down the middle of the back to the tip of the tail. Color is sandy to pale yellowish-gray, with 4-6 narrow, vertical, light brown to black stripes on the body and irregular horizontal black stripes on the upper limbs. Underparts almost white. Dog-like head, with a broad, naked gray-black muzzle. Large eyes. Neck is long and muscular, sometimes with black spots or stripes. Large pointed ears, brown-black on the back. Sloping back with forelegs longer than the hind legs. Legs are lightly built. Small feet, brown to black in color, with 5 toes on the forefeet and 4 on the hind feet. Bushy tail, with a broad black tip. No sexual dimorphism in size. Females have 2 pairs of inguinal teats.

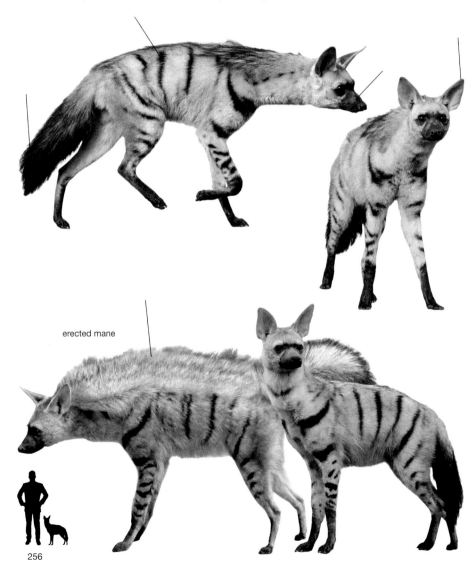

erected mane

Proteles cristatus septentrionalis

OTHER NAMES *French*: Protéle. *German*: Ostafrikanischer Erdwolf. *Spanish*: Lobo de tierra, proteles. *Russian*: Восточноафриканский земляной волк. *Arabic*: Dib, 'Usbar. *Swahili*: Fisi ya nkole.

TAXONOMY Considered as a subspecies of Aardwolf (*P. cristatus*). Includes *pallidior* and *termes*.

SIMILAR SPECIES The Striped Hyena, sympatric in E and NE Africa, also has vertical body stripes, but is nearly twice as large, has a comparatively larger and heavier head, a distinct black throat patch, and the stripes are more irregular.

REPRODUCTION *Gestation*: 90 days. *Young per Birth*: 2-5. *Weaning*: 4 months. *Sexual Maturity*: 24 months. *Life Span*: 15-20 years in captivity. *Breeding Season*: Much less restricted than South African Aardwolves, due to the warmer winters, and can mate and give birth year-round. Monogamous, but ♂ are promiscuous. Old aardvark, porcupine, or any other suitable burrows are used as dens, but they can dig their own den in soft soil. Cubs emerge from the den at about 4 weeks, and begin foraging for termites around the den at 9 weeks.

BEHAVIOR *Social Behavior*: Solitary when feeding, but probably territorial in pairs. *Diet*: Insectivorous, feeding almost exclusively on harvester termites (*Trinervitermes bettonianus*), occasionally supplemented with other termites (*Odontotermes*, *Macrotermes*) and insects during the wet season, when *Trinervitermes* are less active; they do not prey on mammals; largely independent of water, obtaining their moisture requirements from termites. They do not dig for their prey, but lick them off the soil surface. They are shy and active at dusk and at night, spending the day in a burrow. Sight, smell, and scent good, but hearing, with which it locates its prey, excellent. Monogamous, forming stable adult pairs that share a territory with their most recent offspring. Average territory size in E Africa is 1-4 km². The actual size of the range depends to some degree on the available food supply, but breeding requirements are the main determinants of its range size. Territories have at least one active den where the pair has protection from excessive cold in the winter and heat in the summer. Territories marked by strong-smelling anal gland. When threatened, erects mane and exposes anal glands. Fights are rare, except between ♂ in the mating season. Although the cheek teeth are reduced to a few small pegs, the canine teeth are very sharp and well developed and they can inflict injuries to other Aardwolves. They have many vocalizations (purr, roar, lip smack, jaw cluck).

DISTRIBUTION *Native*: Egypt, Eritrea, Ethiopia, Kenya, Somalia, South Sudan, Sudan, Tanzania, Uganda.

HABITAT Open dry grassland and bushland, with virtually no trees. May be found in rocky areas, but avoids mountainous country.

CONSERVATION STATUS Least Concern. CITES: Not listed. Not common within this range, and population trends are unknown. Main threats includes poisoning, particularly from agricultural pesticides. Sometimes killed and eaten by humans. Grassland burning and livestock overgrazing result in a gross increase in the population of *Trinervitermes*, so they may benefit in areas where management strategies favor these conditions.

PHOTO CREDITS T, C: *Robert Kok*, Masai Mara (Kenya); *Andrey Kotkin*, Berlin Tierpark (Germany); BL: Andrey Kotkin, Berlin Tierpark (Germany); BR: *Joe McDonald*, Serengeti NP (Tanzania).

SKULLS OF FELIDS

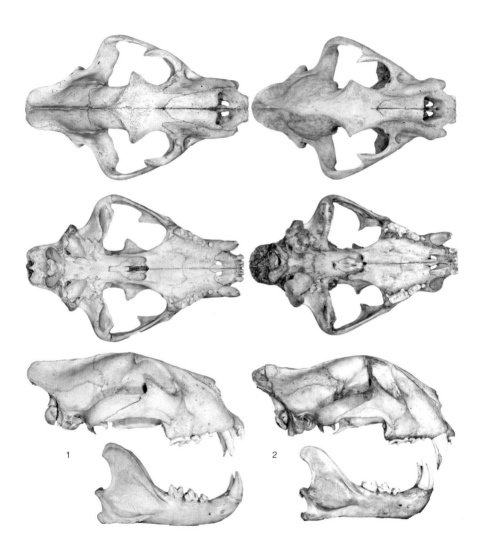

1- **South and East African Lion** Panthera leo melanochaita (SL: 32 cm, SW: 23.4 cm). 2- **Tiger** Panthera tigris (SL: 28.9 cm, SW: 22.3 cm). Photo credits: Phil Myers, Museum of Zoology, University of Michigan-Ann Arbor, USA. To the same scale.

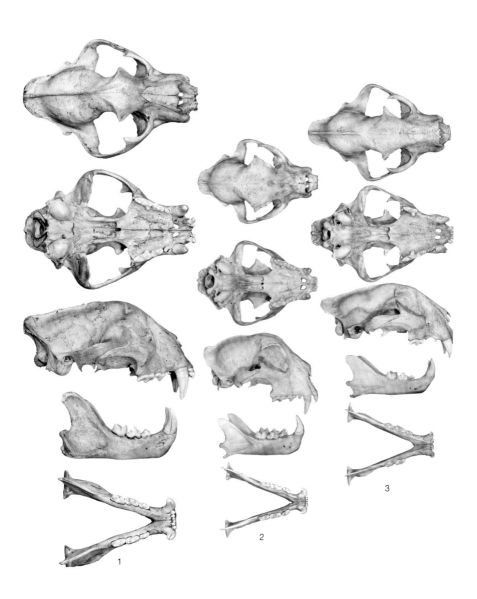

1- **Jaguar** *Panthera onca* (SL: 24 cm, SW: 17.5 cm). 2- **Snow Leopard** *Panthera uncia* (SL: 16.9 cm, SW: 12.8 cm). 3- **Leopard** *Panthera pardus* (SL: 19.1 cm, SW: 13.7 cm). Photo credits: *Phil Myers*, Museum of Zoology, University of Michigan-Ann Arbor, USA. To the same scale.

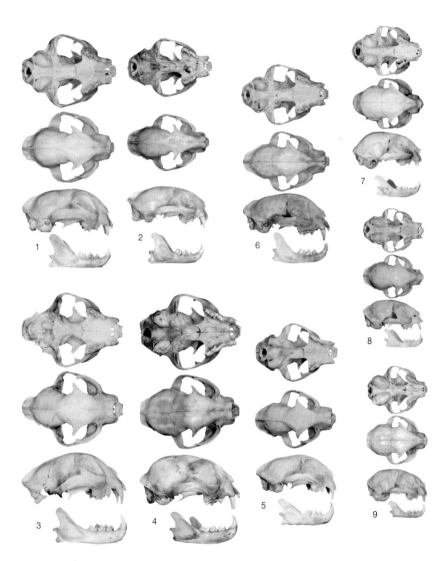

1- **Southern African Caracal** *Caracal caracal caracal* (SL: 12.5 cm, SW: 9.8 cm). 2- **Serval** *Leptailurus serval* (SL: 11.2 cm, SW: 8.4 cm). 3- **Eurasian Lynx** *Lynx lynx* (SL: 13.9 cm, SW: 10.1 cm). 4- **Canada Lynx** *Lynx canadensis* (SL: 9.4 cm, SW: 8.9 cm). 5- **Eastern Bobcat** *Lynx rufus rufus* (SL: 11.7 cm, SW: 9 cm). 6- **Western Jungle Cat** *Felis chaus chaus* (SL: 12 cm, SW: 7.9 cm). 7- **Eurasian Wildcat** *Felis sylvestris* (SL: 9.4 cm, 7.1 cm). 8- **Domestic Cat** *Felis catus* (SL: 8.6 cm, SW: 6.7 cm). 9- **Asian Sand Cat** *Felis margarita thinobia* (SL: 8.6 cm, SW: 7.1 cm). Photo credits: *Phil Myers*, Museum of Zoology, University of Michigan-Ann Arbor, USA. To the same scale.

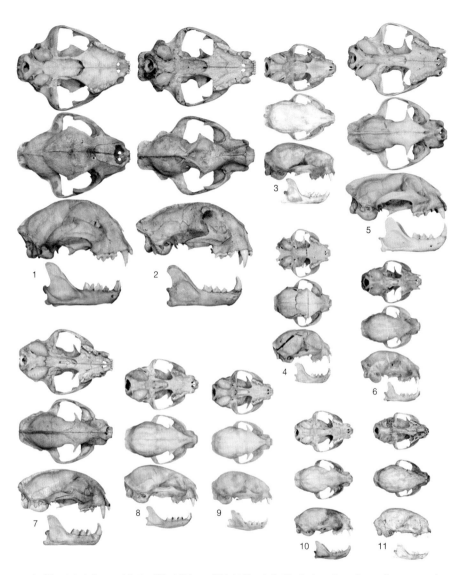

1- **Cheetah** *Acinonyx jubatus* (SL: 15.7 cm, SW: 14.7 cm). 2- **North American Puma** *Puma concolor cougar* (SL: 16.4 cm, SW: 13.9 cm). 3- **Jaguarundi** *Herpailurus yagouaroundi* (SL: 9.4 cm, SW: 6.1 cm). 4- **Pallas's Cat** *Otocolobus manul* (SL: 8.2 cm, SW: 6.8 cm). 5- **Fishing Cat** *Prionailurus viverrinus* (SL: 13.3 cm, SW: 9.3 cm). 6- **Sunda Leopard Cat** *Prionailurus javanensis sumatranus* (SL: 8 cm, SW: 5.8 cm). 7- **Northern Ocelot** *Leopardus pardalis pardalis* (SL: 12.7 cm, SW: 8.9 cm). 8- **Geoffroy's Cat** *Leopardus geoffroyi* (SL: 9.8 cm, SW: 7 cm). 9- **Southern Margay** *Leopardus wiedii wiedii* (SL: 8.4 cm, SW: 6.2 cm). 10- **Guiña** *Leopardus guigna* (SL: 7.9 cm, SW: 5.4 cm). 11- **Central American Tigrina** *Leopardus tigrinus oncilla* (SL: 8.3 cm, SW: 5.6 cm). Photo credits: *Phil Myers*, Museum of Zoology, University of Michigan-Ann Arbor, USA. To the same scale.

SKULLS OF HYENAS

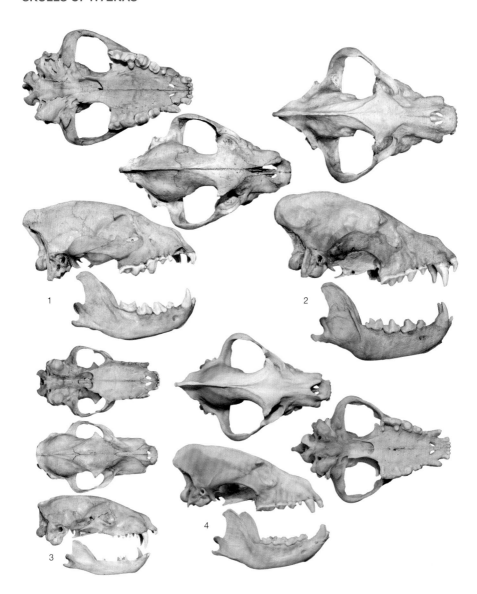

1- **Spotted Hyena** *Crocuta crocuta* (SL: 23.6 cm, SW: 17.1 cm). 2- **Brown Hyena** *Parahyaena brunnea* (SL: 25.4 cm, SW: 16.3 cm). 3- **East African Aardwolf** *Proteles cristatus septentrionalis* (SL: 13.5 cm, SW: 8.3 cm). 4- **Striped Hyena** *Hyaena hyaena* (SL: 21.1 cm, SW: 15.3 cm). Photo credits: *Phil Myers*, Museum of Zoology, University of Michigan-Ann Arbor, USA. To the same scale.

GLOSSARY

Albinistic Absence or reduction of pigmentation, resulting in a completely or partly white animal.

Alloparenting A system of parenting in which individuals other than the parents act in a parental role.

Allopatry Occurring in separate, non-overlapping geographic areas.

Alpha The reproductively dominant member of a social unit.

Altricial A mammal that is born with little, if any, hair, is unable to feed itself, and initially has poor sensory and thermoregulatory abilities.

Arboreal Living or active in trees.

Auditory bulla The rounded bony capsule surrounding the inner ear of many mammals. Also knows as tympanic bulla.

Baculum A rod-shape bone that strengthens the penis in some mammalian species.

Boreal Coniferous or needle-leaf forest zone predominant between the Arctic and the temperate deciduous forest zone.

Cache A hiding place used for storing food if there is an abundance of meat from a kill.

Camouflage The way an animal blends into its environment in order to sneak up on prey and hide from predators.

Canid A member of the family Canidae, which includes dogs, wolves, and foxes.

Canine The sharp, pointed teeth, immediately behind the incisors, which carnivores use to pierce and tear the flesh of their prey.

Carnassials Pair of shearing teeth for processing meat formed by the upper fourth premolar and the lower first molar. All carnivorans possess a pair of carnassial teeth.

Carnivoran A member of the order Carnivora; used to distinguish these member species from other meat-eaters, or carnivores.

Carnivorous Animals whose diet comprises predominantly animal matter, including insects and crustacea, as opposed to vegetable matter.

Carrion Decaying flesh of dead animals.

Cerrado A vast tropical savanna ecoregion in the center of Brazil, which includes forest savanna, wooded savanna, park savanna, gramineous-woody savanna, wetlands, and gallery forests.

Chatter A low-amplitude, smacking sound created by rhythmically clashing the jaws.

Chirp A short, high-pitched call described as similar to a bird chirping.

CITES (abbrev.) The Convention on International Trade in Endangered Species of Wild Fauna and Flora.

Clade Group of organisms with a common ancestor, often equal to a monophyletic group or lineage. The family Felidae is a clade, and each lineage within the cats is also a clade.

Cline A gradient in a measurable characteristic, such as size and color, showing geographic differentiation.

Coalition A small group of male Cheetahs or Lions, often brothers, that live, hunt, and defend a territory together.

Color phase The color of an animal's pelage (fur), which is determined by genetics and may vary within a population.

Commensal A relationship between species in which one benefits and the other is neither benefited nor harmed.

Conspecific A member of the same species.

Convergent evolution Similar features or behaviors evolved independently by distantly related animals.

Crepuscular Active in twilight, including dawn and dusk, but avoiding the darkest hours of night.

Den A shelter, often a small cave or hole dug out of the ground, to protect the breeding female and her young pups from weather and other animals.

Dewclaw A vestigial digit found on the foot of most mammals, normally growing high on the animal's leg in digitigrade species, that has become functionless through evolution.

Digitigrade Walking on its toes and not touching the ground with its heels.

Disjunct Not occurring continuously over a region, but localized into widely separated populations.

Dispersal The movements of animals, often as they reach maturity, away from their previous home range.

Distal Situated away from the center of the body or point of attachment.

Diurnal Active during the day.

Dorsal On or referring to the upper side or back of an animal.

Ecosystem A community of organisms and their physical environment.

Endemic A group or taxon that is local and of limited distribution.

Estrus The period when a female mammal is ready to copulate with a male. Estrus usually occurs around the time a female ovulates, or produces an egg or eggs that can be fertilized by male sperm.

Extant Still in existence; not destroyed, lost, or extinct.

Extinct Refers to a species that no longer survives anywhere.

Felid A member of the family Felidae, or cats.

Feral Domesticated animals that have gone wild.

Flehmen A behavior in which cats curl their lips into a grimace after sniffing another cat or its scent-mark.

Forb Broad-leaved, non-woody plant.

Fulvous Tawny; dull yellow, with a mixture of gray and brown.

Gallery forest Trees and other vegetation lining watercourses, thereby extending forested habitat into savanna and arid zones.

Gestation Period of development between conception and birth.

Growl A low-pitched, throaty, rumbling noise produced while the mouth is closed.

Grunt Short, throaty, atonal call.

Guard hairs The long outer hairs of an animal's coat that keep the downy underfur from getting dirty or wet.

Gurgle Short, pulsed sound, described as similar to a person gargling their throat.

Hibernation A deep state of reduced metabolic activity and lowered body temperature that may last for weeks or months.

Hierarchy A social structure in which the animals in a group can be arranged according to dominance.

Hiss A drawn-out, low-intensity hissing sound produced by rapid expulsion of air from a cat's mouth, usually during exhalation.

Hock The backward-pointing joint in the hind leg of a quadrupedal animal between the knee and the hoof.

Holarctic The Palearctic and Nearctic biogeographic regions combined.

Home range The area that an animal travels over during the course of a year to find food and shelter, to find mates, and to rear young.

Hybrid The offspring of parents from two closely related species.

Hypercarnivores Animals that eat only meat, like cats.

Infanticide Killing young animals of the same species.

Inguinal Of or in the groin.

Insectivorous Animals whose diet comprises predominantly invertebrates.

Lagomorph A member of the order Lagomorpha, which includes rabbits, hares, and pikas.

Latrine A place where animals regularly deposit their excrement.

Leucism Light or white coloration of skin, hair, fur, and feathers, such as the white fur of white tigers.

Lineage A group of animals whose members all derived from a common ancestor; also called a clade.

Mammae Milk-secreting organs usually arranged in pairs on the ventral surface of the body.

Maquis Dense secondary scrub dominated by heathers and strawberry trees (Mediterranean).

Melanism Color variation in which black pigment predominates to such an extent that the pelage of the animal is partly or entirely black.

Mew The distinctive meow call that is typical of cats. Mews can differ considerably between species, and vary in tone, duration, pitch, and structure.

Midden A pile of dung droppings, deposited regularly to mark an individual's territory.

Miocene The geological time period that lasted from about 23.8 to 5.6 million years ago.

Molars Permanent cheek teeth near the back of the jaws in mammals. Molars are not replaced during life.

Monoestrous Having only one estrous cycle per year.

Monogamous A breeding system in which a male and female mate only with one another.

Monophyletic A group (or clade) that shares a common ancestor.

Monotypic A taxonomic category that includes only one form (e.g., a genus that includes only one species; a species that includes no subspecies).

Montane Of or inhabiting the biogeographic zone of relatively moist, cool upland slopes below timberline dominated by large coniferous trees.

Nearctic The biogeographic region that includes temperate North America.

Neotropical The biogeographic region that includes South and Central America, the West Indies, and tropical Mexico.

New World A general descriptive term encompassing the Nearctic and Neotropical biogeographic regions.

Niche The role of an organism in its environment; multidimensional, with habitat and behavioral components.

Nocturnal Active during the night.

Old World A general term that usually describes a species or group as being from Eurasia or Africa.

Oligocene The geologic time period occurring from about 33.7 to 23.8 million years ago.

Omnivorous Feeding on both animal material (insects or meat) and vegetable matter.

Opportunistic Referring to animals that capitalize on opportunities to gain food with the least expenditure of energy.

Pair bond The social tie that keeps members of a mated pair together, usually reinforced by mutual grooming, marking, calling, aggression toward outsiders, etc.

Pelage An animal's coat of fur or hair.

Phylogeny Genealogical relationships that attempt to reconstruct historical relationships among various lineages of organisms.

Pleistocene In general, the time of the great ice ages; geological period variously considered to include the last 1 to 1.8 million years.

Pliocene The geological period preceding the Pleistocene; the last subdivision of the Tertiary period; lasted from 5.5 to 1.8 million years ago.

Poaching Hunting animals illegally.

Polyandry A breeding system in which one female mates with two or more males.

Polyestrous Having more than one estrous cycle during a specific time of the year.

Polygyny A breeding system in which one male mates with two or more females.

Premolars Cheek teeth near the front of the jaws in mammals; deciduous (milk) premolars or permanent premolars.

Pride A group of female Lions and their young. The females in a pride are usually related. Males attach themselves to prides of females.

Protractile claws Claws passively retracted within the paw, which can be actively extended out of the paw.

Purr Low, continuous rhythmical tone produced during respiration while a cat's mouth is closed. Creates a murmuring sound.

Rainforest A forest that receives at least 2.5 meters of rainfall annually. Most rainforests are in tropical regions of the world.

Regurgitation Disgorging partially digested food, as nourishment mainly for pups and young animals.

Rendezvous site An aboveground area where pups are taken when they are old enough to leave the birth den.

Rhinarium The anterior naked part of the snout, usually in fur-covered mammals the most rugose pad surrounding the nostrils.

Riparian Occurring on the banks of a river, stream, or wetland.

Roar High-intensity call that differs between species but consists of a main call and grunting sounds. In the Lion, the call may be described as moaning, full-throated, and thundering.

Rodent A member of the order Rodentia, which includes rats and mice.

Rostrum The facial part of the skull in front of the orbits.

Sagittal crest A ridge of bone developed along the midline of the top of the skull, usually enabling attachment of stronger temporal muscles.

Sarcoptic mange A skin condition caused by a parasitic mite, characterized by intense itching and hair loss, resulting in hypothermia and death.

Savanna A major biome or ecological zone where annual rainfall is insufficient to support forest cover, but where grass predominates and there may be scattered xerophytic trees but no closed canopy.

Scats Solid fecal matter or feces.

Scavenger An animal that eats animals it did not kill directly but that have died from other causes such as disease, starvation, or predation.

Scent-mark Act of marking an area with body odor, scent from a gland, or urine or scat.

Sexual dimorphism The condition in which the two sexes of the species exhibit different characteristics beyond the differences in their sexual organs.

Snarl A sound emitted when a cat bares its teeth; similar to a growl, butthe mouth is open and the sound is usually louder, shorter, and higherin pitch than a growl.

Solitary Unsocial, referring to animals that do not live in social groups.

Species Basic unit of taxonomic classification that describes a group of similar organisms that share similar genes, capable of interbreeding and producing viable offspring.

Spit A sudden, short, explosive exhalation resulting in a burst of noise, often accompanied by a violent movement.

Steppe A somewhat discontinuous grassland, harboring scattered shrubs or stunted trees.

Subordinate Lower ranking in power, control, and privilege.

Subspecies A population that has been isolated from other populations of the same species long enough to develop genetic differences sufficiently distinctive to be considered a separate race.

Sympatry Condition of overlapping geographic distribution; applies to related species that coexist without interbreeding.

Tapetum lucidum A structure in the eye that reflects light back through the eye so that the cells responding to light get a second chance to respond to and use that light. Many nocturnal mammals and most carnivorans have this structure. This is what causes the "eyeshine" of cats when they look into a light at night.

Tarsal Pertaining to the tarsus bones in the ankle, articulating between the leg and the foot.

Taxon (pl. taxa) Any unit of scientific classification (e.g., species, genus, family, order).

Taxonomy The science of defining groups of biological organisms on the basis of shared characteristics and organizing them into a classification system.

Terrestrial Living or active on solid ground.

Territory Any defended area. It may include the entire home range, only the area immediately around a den, or only a feeding area.

Thermoregulation An ability to regulate body temperature when the temperature of the surroundings changes.

Ungulates Large, plant-eating mammals with hooves, including elephants, rhinoceroses, horses, deer, antelope, wild cattle, and their relatives.

Ventral On or referring to the underside or belly of an animal.

Vestigial Small and imperfectly formed, disappearing.

Vibrissae Stiff, coarse hairs richly supplied with nerves, found especially around the snout and with a sensory (tactile) function.

Vocalization Calls or sounds produced by the vocal cords of a mammal, and uttered through the mouth. Vocalizations differ with the age and sex of mammals but are usually similar within a species.

Whiskers See Vibrissae.

Xerophytic A plant that shows a capacity to withstand drought.

Yearling A young animal between 1 and 2 years of age (referring to species that take at least 2 years to mature).

Yowl A long, drawn-out vocalization of variable pitch, intensity, duration, and tonality.

Zygomatic arch The narrow arched bones (cheekbones) on either side of the skull situated below the eyes.

REFERENCES

The references listed below have been consulted during the work on this guide. Without them, this work would have been much more difficult and the end result less good. For reasons of space and to avoid repetition, references are not listed at the end of each species account.

Abdukadir A. et al. 2010. Asiatic wild cat (*Felis silvestris ornata*) is no more a 'Least Concern' species in Xinjiang, China. Pakistan Journal of Wildlife 1(2):57-63.

Aghili A. 2008. First record of Pallas's Cat in northwest Iran. Cat News 49:8-9.

Ahmed S. et al. 2016. Rediscovering the Arabian sand cat (*Felis margarita harrisoni*) after a gap of 10 years using camera traps in the Western Region of Abu Dhabi, United Arab Emirates. European Journal of Wildlife Research 62(5):627-631.

Alam S. 2011. Status, ecology and conservation of Striped Hyena *Hyaena hyaena* in Gir National Park and Sanctuary, Gujarat. Dissertation. Aligarh Muslim University.

Alderton D. 1998. Wild Cats of the World. London, UK: Facts on File, Inc.

Alekperov K. M. 1989. Manul. In Adygezalov B. M. (ed.). Red book of the Azerbaijan SSR. Ishyg, Baku, Azerbaijan (in Azeri and Russian), 37-38.

Ali Adibi M. et al. 2014. Study of seasonal changes in habitat suitability of *Caracal caracal schmitzi* (Maschie 1812) in the central desert of Iran. Journal of Biodiversity and Environmental Sciences 5(3):95-106.

Allen G. M. 1938. The Mammals of China and Mongolia. New York: The American Museum of Natural History.

Allen J. A. 1904. Mammals of southern Mexico and Central and South America. Bulletin of the American Museum of Natural History 20:29-80.

Allen J. A. 1915. New South American mammals. Bulletin of the American Museum of Natural History 34:625-634.

Allen J. A. 1916. List of mammals collected in Colombia by the American Museum of Natural History expeditions, 1910-1915. Bulletin of the American Museum of Natural History 35:191-238.

Allen J. A. 1919. Notes on the synonymy and nomenclature of the smaller spotted cats of tropical America. Bulletin of the American Museum of Natural History 41:341-419.

Anco C. et al. 2018. Historical mitochondrial diversity in African leopards (*Panthera pardus*) revealed by archival museum specimens. Mitochondrial DNA 29(3):455-473.

Anderson C. 2015. An Introduction to the Ocelot and Margay and Other Rare Wild Cats, Including Caracal, Clouded Leopard, Black Footed Cat, Fishing Cat and Iberian Lynx. Poole, UK: EKL Publishing.

Anderson S. 1997. Mammals of Bolivia, taxonomy and distribution. Bulletin of the American Museum of Natural History 231:1-652.

Andrews C. J. et al. 2019. Reproductive biology of the 38 extant felid species: A review. Mammal Review 49:16-30.

Appel A. et al. 2018. Proceedings of the First International Small Wild Cat Conservation Summit, 11–14 September 2017, UK. Wild Cat Network, Bad Marienberg, Germany, Sálim Ali Centre for Ornithology and Natural History, Coimbatore, India, and Borneo Nature Foundation, Oxford, UK.

Apps P. 2012. Smither's Mammals of Southern Africa: A Field Guide. 4th ed. Cape Town, South Africa: Struik Nature.

Arx M. et al. 2001. Status and conservation of the Eurasian lynx (*Lynx lynx*) in Europe in 2001. KORA Bericht 19.

Ashraf N. V. K. et al. 1995. Asiatic Lion *Panthera leo persica*. Population & Habitat Viability Assessment P.H.V.A. and Global Animal Survival Plan Workshops 18-21 October 1993, Baroda, India.

Atay E. et al. 2017. Status of striped hyaena (*Hyaena hyaena*) in Hatay and Sanlıurfa-Turkey. Turkish Journal of Agriculture-Food Science and Technology 5(10):1165-1172.

Avenant N. L. et al. 2016. A conservation assessment of *Caracal caracal*. In Child M. F. et al. (eds.). The Red List of Mammals of South Africa, Swaziland and Lesotho. South African National Biodiversity Institute and Endangered Wildlife Trust, South Africa.

Azlan J. M. and Sanderson J. 2007. Geographic distribution and conservation status of the bay cat *Catopuma badia*, a Bornean endemic. Oryx 41:394-397.

Bahaa-el-din L. 2015. Ecology and conservation of the African golden cat *Caracal aurata*. Dissertation. University of KwaZulu-Natal.

Bahaa-el-din L. et al. 2015. The African golden cat *Caracal aurata*: Africa's least-known felid. Mammal Review 45:63-77.

Bailey, T. N. 2005. The African Leopard: Ecology and Behaviour of a Solitary Felid. Caldwell, NJ: The Blackburn Press.

Barnett R. et al. 2014. Revealing the maternal demographic history of *Panthera leo* using ancient DNA and a spatially explicit genealogical analysis. BMC Evolutionary Biology 14:70.

Barstow A. and Leslie Jr. D. M. 2012. *Leopardus braccatus* (Carnivora: Felidae). Mammalian Species 44(891):16-25.

Barycka E. 2007. Evolution and systematics of the feliform Carnivora. Mammalian Biology 72(5):257-282.

Begum N. et al. 2014. National Studbook: Asiatic Lion (*Panthera leo persica*). Wildlife Institute of India.

Bellani G. 2019. Felines of the World: Discoveries in Taxonomic Classification and History. Cambridge, MA: Academic Press.

Bellier L. et al. 1972. Quelques donnes nouvelles concernant le chat dore Afrique, *Profelis aurata* (Temminck, 1827) en Cote D'Ivoire. Biologia Gabonica 8(2):191-192.

Bertola L. D. et al. 2015. Autosomal and mtDNA markers affirm the distinctiveness of lions in west and central Africa. PLoS ONE 10(10):e0137975.

Bertola L. D. et al. 2016. Phylogeographic patterns in Africa and high resolution delineations of genetic clades in the lion (*Panthera leo*). Scientific Reports 6:1-11.

Bohm T. and Hofer H. 2018. Population numbers, density and activity patterns of servals in savannah patches of Odzala-Kokoua National Park, Republic of Congo. African Journal of Ecology 56(4):841-849.

Bothma J. P. and Walker C. 1999. Larger Carnivores of the African Savannas. Berlin Heidelberg, Germany: Springer-Verlag.

Breitenmoser U. et al. 2000. Action plan for the conservation of the Eurasian lynx (*Lynx lynx*) in Europe. Nature and Environment, No. 112. Council of Europe Publishing.

Breitenmoser U. et al. 2005. Balkan Lynx Field Handbook. EURONATUR.

Breitenmoser-Würsten C. and Breitenmoser U. 2001. The Balkan lynx population: History, recent knowledge on its status and conservation needs. KORA Bericht 7.

Burt W. H. and Grossenheider R. P. 1976. A Field Guide to the Mammals, North America North of Mexico. 3rd ed. Boston, MA: Houghton Mifflin Company.

Butynski T. M. et al. 2012. Identification, distribution and conservation status of the African golden cat *Caracal aurata* in Kenya. Journal of East African Natural History 101(1):3-16.

Cabrera A. 1910. Ll.—On two new Carnivora from North-east Africa. Annals and Magazine of Natural History Series 8, 6(35):461-465.

Cabrera A. 1914. Fauna Ibérica: Mamíferos. Madrid, Spain: Museo Nacional de Ciencias Naturales.

Cabrera A. 1958. Catálogo de los mamíferos de América del Sur. Revista del Museo Argentino de Ciencias Zoológicas "Bernardino Rivadavia," Ciencias Zoológicas 4(1):1-307.

Cabrera A. 1961. Los félidos vivientes de la República Argentina. Revista del Museo Argentino de Ciencias Naturales "Bernardino Rivadavia," Ciencias Zoológicas 6(5):160-247.

Cameron-Beaumont C. et al. 2002. Evidence suggesting preadaptation to domestication throughout the small Felidae. Biological Journal of the Linnean Society 75:361-366.

Caragiulo A. et al. 2014. Mitochondrial DNA sequence variation and phylogeography of Neotropic pumas (*Puma concolor*). Mitochondrial DNA 25(4):304-312.

Castillo-Martínez L. S. et al. 2016. Plan de conservación de los felinos silvestres del territorio CAR. Corporación Autónoma Regional de Cundinamarca (CAR). Bogotá, D. C.

Charruau P. et al. 2011. Phylogeography, genetic structure and population divergence time of cheetahs in Africa and Asia: Evidence for long-term geographic isolates. Molecular Ecology 20:706-724.

Chester S. 2008. A Wildlife Guide to Chile. Princeton, NJ: Princeton University Press.

Christiansen P. 2008. Evolution of skull and mandible shape in cats (Carnivora: Felidae). PLoS ONE 3(7):e2807.

Christiansen, P. 2008. Phylogeny of the great cats (Felidae: Pantherinae), and the influence of fossil taxa and missing characters. Cladistics 24:977-992.

Christiansen P. 2008. Species distinction and evolutionar differences in the clouded leopard (*Neofelis nebulosa*) and Diard's clouded leopard (*Neofelis diardi*). Journal of Mammalogy 89(6):1435-1446.

Chynoweth M. W. et al. 2015. Conservation of a new breeding population of Caucasian lynx (*Lynx lynx dinniki*) in eastern Turkey. Turkish Journal of Zoology 39:541-543.

Clark E. L. and Javzansuren M. 2006. Mongolian Red List of Mammals. World Bank's Netherlands-Mongolia Trust Fund for Environmental Reform.

Clavijo A. and Ramírez G. F. 2009. Taxonomía, distribución y estado de conservación de los felinos sudamericanos: Revisión monográfica. Boletín Científico Museo Historia Natural 13(2):43-60.

Cossios D. et al. 2012. Population structure and conservation of a high-altitude specialist, the Andean cat *Leopardus jacobita*. Endangered Species Research 16:283-294.

Croteau E. K. 2009. Population genetics and phylogeography of bobcats (*Lynx rufus*) using microsatellites and mitochrondrial dDNA. Dissertation. Southern Illinois University.

Croteau E. K. et al. 2010. Fine-scale population structure and sex-biased dispersal in bobcats (*Lynx rufus*) from southern Illinois. Canadian Journal of Zoology 88:536-545.

Croteau E. K. et al. 2012. Microsatellites and mitochondrial DNA reveal regional population structure in bobcats (*Lynx rufus*) of North America. Conservation Genetics 13:1637-1651.

Cuff A. R. et al. 2015. Big cat, small cat: Reconstructing body size evolution in living and extinct Felidae. Journal of Evolutionary Biology 28:1516-1525.

Culver M. et al. 2000. Genomic ancestry of the American puma (*Puma concolor*). Journal of Heredity 91:186-197.

Dhendup T. et al. 2019. Distribution and status of the manul in the Himalayas and China. Cat News 13:31-36.

Din J. U. and Nawaz M. A. 2010. Status of the Himalayan lynx in District Chitral, NWFP, Pakistan. The Journal of Animal & Plant Sciences 20(1):17-22.

Din J. U. et al. 2015. Population assessment of Himalayan lynx (*Lynx lynx isabellinus*) and conflict with humans in the Hindu Kush mountain range of District Chitral, Pakistan. Journal of Biodiversity and Environmental Sciences 6(2):31-39.

Dragesco-Joffé A. 1993. Le guépard saharien, un félin égaré en enfer. In La Vie Sauvage du Sahara. Lausanne: Delachaux et Niestlé, 119-126.

Driscoll C. A. et al. 2007. The Near Eastern origin of cat domestication. Science 317(5837):519-523.

Driscoll C. A. et al. 2009. Mitochondrial phylogeography illuminates the origin of the extinct Caspian tiger and its relationship to the Amur tiger. PLoS ONE 4(1):e4125.

Duckworth J. W. et al. 2005. The jungle cat *Felis chaus* in Indochina: A threatened population of a widespread and adaptable species. Biodiversity and Conservation 14:1263-1280.

Durant S. M. et al. 2006. The Tanzania Small Carnivore Conservation Action Plan. Arusha, Tanzania: Tanzania Wildlife Research Institute.

Eder T. 2002. Mammals of Washington and Oregon. Edmonton, Canada: Lone Pine Publishing.

Eizirik E. et al. 2001. Phylogeography, population history and conservation genetics of jaguars (*Panthera onca*, Mammalia, Felidae). Molecular Ecology 10:65-79.

Eizirik, E. at al. 2003. Molecular genetics and evolution of melanism in the cat family. Current Biology 13:448-453.

Elliot D. G. 1883. A Monograph of the Felidae, or Family of the Cats. London, UK.

Eroglu H. E. 2017. The comparison of the Felidae species with karyotype symmetry/asymmetry index (S/AI). Punjab University Journal of Zoology, 32(2):229-235.

Estes R. D. 1999. The Safari Companion: A Guide to Watching African mammals. White River Junction, VT: Chelsea Green Publishing Company.

Ewer R. F. 1973. The Carnivores. New York: Cornell University Press.

Farhadinia M. 2007. Identifying existence of the Asiatic cheetah, *Acinonyx jubatus venaticus* and its potential ranges in Miandasht Wildlife Refuge, Iran. Final report. Rufford Small Grants Foundation.

Farhadinia M et al. 2008. Is food availability a reliable indicator of cheetah presence in Iran? Cat News 49:14-18.

Farhadinia M. et al. 2016. A review of ecology and conservation status of Asiatic cheetah in Iran. Cat News 10:18-26.

Farhadinia M. et al. 2017. The critically endangered Asiatic cheetah *Acinonyx jubatus venaticus* in Iran: A review of recent distribution, and conservation status. Biodiversity and Conservation 26:1027-1046.

Firouz E. 2005. The Complete Fauna of Iran. London, UK: I. B. Tauris.

Fitzgerald J. P. et al. 1994. Mammals of Colorado. Denver: Denver Museum of Natural History and University Press of Colorado.

Foley C. et al. 2014. A Field Guide to the Larger Mammals of Tanzania. Princeton, NJ: Princeton University Press.

Foreman G. E. 1988. Behavioral and genetic analysis of Geoffroy's cat (*Felis geoffroyi*) in captivity. Dissertation. The Ohio State University.

Francis C. M. 2016. Mammals of South-East Asia. London, UK: Bloomsbury.

Freer R. A. 2004. The spatial ecology of the güiña (*Oncifelis guigna*) in southern Chile. Dissertation. University of Durham.

Gade D. W. 2006. Hyenas and humans in the Horn of Africa. Geographical Review 96(4):609-632.

García-Perea R. 1994. The pampas cat group (genus *Lynchailurus* Severtzov, 1858) (Carnivora, Felidae), a systematic and biogeographic review. American Museum Novitates 3096:1-36.

García-Perea R. 2002. Andean mountain cat, *Oreailurus jacobita*: Morphological description and comparison with other felines from the altiplano. Journal of Mammalogy 83(1):110-124.

Gardner A. L. 1971. Notes on the little spotted cat, *Felis tigrina oncilla* Thomas, in Costa Rica. Journal of Mammalogy 52(2):464-465.

Gay S. W. and Best T. L. 1995. Geographic variation in sexual dimorphism of the puma (*Puma concolor*) in North and South America. The Southwestern Naturalist 40(2):148-159.

Giordano A. J. 2016. Ecology and status of the jaguarundi *Puma yagouaroundi*: A synthesis of existing knowledge. Mammal Review 46(1):30-43.

Gippoliti S. and Meijaard E. 2007. Taxonomic uniqueness of the Javan leopard; an opportunity for zoos to save it. Contributions to Zoology 76(1):55-58.

Goldman E. A. 1943. The races of the ocelot and margay in Middle America. Journal of Mammology 24(3):372-385.

Goldman E. A. 1946. The puma, mysterious American cat - Part II: Classification of the races of the puma. In Young, S.P. and Goldman, E.A. (eds.). The Puma, Mysterious American Cat. Washington, DC, American Wildlife Institution, 174-358.

Gomercic T. et al. 2010. Cranial morphometry of the Eurasian lynx (*Lynx lynx* L.) from Croatia. Veterinarski Arhiv 80(3):393-410.

González-Maya J. F. et al. 2018. Margays also hide their spots: First records of melanistic *Leopardus wiedii* from Colombia and Costa Rica. Revista Mexicana Biodiversidad 89:587-589.

Goodhart C. B. 1975. Does the aardwolf mimic a hyena? Zoological Journal of the Linnean Society 57:349-356.

Goodwin G. G. 1963. A new subspecies of Bobcat (*Lynx rufus*) from Oaxaca, Mexico. American Museum Novitates 2139:1-7.

Grassman Jr. L. I. 1999. Ecology and behavior of the Indochinese leopard in Kaeng Krachan National Park, Thailand. Natural History Bulletin Siam Society 47:77-93.

Grassman Jr. L. I. et al. 2005. Ecology of three sympatric felids in a mixed evergreen forest in north-central Thailand. Journal of Mammalogy 86:29-38.

Groves C. P. 1997. Leopard-cats, *Prionailurus bengalensis* (Carnivora: Felidae) from Indonesia and the Philippines, with the description of two new subspecies. Z. Säugetierkunde 62:330-338.

Gugolz D. et al. 2008. Historical DNA reveals the phylogenetic position of the extinct Alpine lynx. Journal of Zoology 275:201-208.

Haas S. K. et al. 2005. *Panthera leo*. Mammalian Species 762:1-11.

Hall E. R. 1981. The Mammals of North America. 2nd ed. New York: John Wiley and Sons.

Hansen K. 2007: Bobcat: Master of Survival. New York: Oxford University Press.

Harper F. 1886. Extinct and Vanishing Mammals of the Old World. New York: American Committee for International Wild Life Protection.

Harrison D. L. 1968. Cheetah. In Harrison D.L. (ed.). The Mammals of Arabia: Carnivora, Artiodactyla, Hyracoidea. London: Ernest Benn Limited, 308-313.

Hassan-Beigi Y. et al. 2014. Phylogeny and genetic diversity of caracal in Iran. Wildlife Middle East 7(1).

Hassan-Beigi Y. 2015. Conservation biology of the caracal (*Caracal caracal*) in Iran: Action plan and conservation genetics. Dissertation. Universidade de Lisboa.

Hemmer H. 1978. The evolutionary systematics of living Felidae: Present status and current problems. Carnivore 1:71-79.

Heptner V. G. and Naumov N. P. 1991. Mammals of the Soviet Union. Vol. II. New Delhi: Amerind Publishing Co. Pvt. Ltd.

Hoath R. 2008. A Field Guide to the Mammals of Egypt. Cairo: The American University in Cairo Press.

Holliday J. A. 2007. Phylogeny and character change in the feloid carnivora. Dissertation. Florida State University Libraries.

Hornocker M. and Negri S. 2010. Cougar: Ecology and Conservation. Chicago: University of Chicago Press.

Horsfield T. 1855. Brief notices of several new or little-known species of Mammalia, lately discovered and collected in Nepal, by Brian Houghton Hodgson. The Annals and Magazine of Natural History 16:101-114.

Howard-McCombe J. et al. 2019. A mitochondrial phylogeny of the sand cat (*Felis margarita* Loche, 1858). Journal of Mammalian Evolution:1-10.

Hunnicutt A. et al. 2016. A conservation assessment of *Crocuta crocuta*. In Child M. F. et al. (eds.). The Red List of Mammals of South Africa, Swaziland and Lesotho. South African National Biodiversity Institute and Endangered Wildlife Trust, South Africa.

Hunter L. 2013. Cats of Africa: Behaviour, Ecology and Conservation. Cape Town, South Africa: Struik Nature.

Hunter L. 2015. Wild Cats of the World. London, UK: Bloomsbury.

Hunter L. and Barret P. 2011. A Field Guide to the Carnivores of the World. 2nd ed. London, UK: Bloomsbury.

IUCN. 2015. IUCN Red List of Threatened Species. Version 2019-2.

Janecka J. E. et al. 2017. Range-wide snow leopard phylogeography supports three subspecies. Journal of Heredity 108:597-607.

Janecka J. E. et al. 2018. The validity of three snow leopard subspecies: Response to Senn et al. Heredity 120:586-590.

Jenks J. A. 2018. Mountain Lions of the Black Hills: History and Ecology. Baltimore: Johns Hopkins University Press.

Johnson W. E. and O'Brien S. J. 1997. Phylogenetic reconstruction of the Felidae using 16S rRNA and NADH-5 mitochondrial genes. Journal of Molecular Evolution 44(1):S98-S116.

Johnson W. E. et al. 2000. Disparate phylogeographic patterns of molecular genetic variation in four closely related South American small cat species. Molecular Ecology 8:S79-S94.

Johnson W. E. et al. 2006. The late miocene radiation of modern Felidae: A genetic assessment. Science 311(5757):73-77.

Joslin P. 1973. The Asiatic lion: A study of ecology and behavior. Dissertation. University of Edinburgh.

Kasparek M. 2004. On the status and distribution of the striped hyaena, *Hyaena hyaena*, in Turkey. Zoology in the Middle East 33:93-108.

Kays R. W. and Wilson D. E. 2009. Mammals of North America. 2nd ed. Princeton, NJ: Princeton University Press.

Kenmuir D. and Williams R. 1975. Wild Mammals: A Field Guide and Introduction to the Mammals of Zimbabwe. Ardbennie, Zimbabwe: Longman.

Khalatbari L. et al. 2017. The current status of Asiatic cheetah in Iran. Cat News 66:10-13.

Khalatbari L. et al. 2018. Availability of prey and natural habitats are related with temporal dynamics in range and habitat suitability for Asiatic cheetah. Hystrix, the Italian Journal of Mammalogy 29(1):145-151.

Kingdon J. 2015. The Kingdon Field Guide to African Mammals. 2nd ed. London, UK: Bloomsbury.

Kingdon J. et al. 2013. Mammals of Africa, Volume V. London, UK: Bloomsbury.

Kitchener A. C. 1991. The Natural History of Wild Cats. New York: Comstock Publishing Associates.

Kitchener A. C. et al. 2017. A revised taxonomy of the Felidae. The final report of the Cat Classification Task Force of the IUCN/SSC Cat Specialist Group. Cat News Special Issue 11.

Kitchener A. C. and Yamaguchi N. 2010. What is a Tiger? Biogeography, morphology and taxonomy. In Tilson, R.L. and Nyhus, P. Tigers of the World: The Science, Politics and Conservation of *Panthera tigris*. 2nd ed. London, UK: Academic Press, 53-86.

Kleiman D. G. and Eisenberg J. F. 1973. Comparisons of canid and felid social systems from an evolutionary perspective. Animal Behavior 21:637-659.

Kleiman D. G. et al. 2003. Grzimek's Animal Life Encyclopedia. 2nd ed. Vol. 14. Mammals III. Farmington Hills, MI: Gale Group.

Koehler C. E. and Richardson P. R. K. 1990. *Proteles cristatus*. Mammalian Species 363:1-6.

Koepfli K-P. et al. 2006. Molecular systematics of the Hyaenidae: Relationships of a relictual lineage resolved by a molecular supermatrix. Molecular Phylogenetics and Evolution 38:603-620.

Krausman P. R. and Morales S. M. 2005. *Acinonyx jubatus*. Mammalian Species 771:1-6.

Kruuk H. and Sands W. A. 2008. The aardwolf (*Proteles cristatus* Sparrman 1783) as a predator of termites. African Journal of Ecology 10(3):211-227.

Krystufek B. 2013. Valid name for the Balkan lynx: *Lynx lynx martinoi* Miric, 1978, is a junior synonym of *Lynx lynx balcanicus* Bureš, 1941. Folia Zoologica 62(2):121-124.

Laguardia A. et al. 2015. The current distribution and status of leopards *Panthera pardus* in China. Oryx 51(1):153-159.

Lariviere S. and Walton L. R. 1997. *Lynx rufus*. Mammalian Species 563:1-8.

Laundré J. W. and Hernández L. 2010. What We Know about Pumas in Latin America. In Cougar Ecology and Conservation. Chicago: University of Chicago Press.

Leopold A. S. 1959. Wildlife of Mexico: The Game Birds and Mammals. Berkeley: University of California Press.

Leyhausen P. 1979. Cat behavior: The predatory and social behavior of domestic and wild cats. New York: Garland Publishing Inc.

Leyhausen P. and Pfleiderer M. 1999. The systematic status of the Iriomote cat (*Prionailurus iriomotensis* Imaizumi 1967) and the subspecies of the leopard cat (*Prionailurus bengalensis* Kerr 1792). Journal of Zoological Systematics and Evolutionary Research 37:121-131.

Li G. et al. 2016. Phylogenomic evidence for ancient hybridization in the genomes of living cats (Felidae). Genome Research 26:1-11.

Li J. et al. 2016. Climate refugia of snow leopards in high Asia. Biological Conservation 203:188-196.

Life Iberlince. 2016. Protocolo de selección de áreas de reintroducción de Lince Ibérico (*Lynx pardinus*) dentro del proyecto Life Iberlince. Servicio de Espacios Naturales de la Consejería de Agricultura, Medio Ambiente y Desarrollo Rural de Castilla-La Mancha.

Lim L. B. 2002. Distribution and food-habits of the golden cat (*Catopuma temminckii*) in peninsular Malaysia. Journal of Wildlife and Parks 20:43-48.

Liu Y.-C. et al. 2018. Genome-wide evolutionary analysis of natural history and adaptation in the world's tigers. Current Biology 28:3840-3849.

López González C. A. and González Romero A. 1998. A synthesis of current literature and knowledge about the ecology of the puma (*Puma concolor* Linnaeus). Acta Zoológica Mexicana 75:171-190.

Lumpkin S. 1993. Small Cats Facts on File. New York.

Luo S. et al. 2004. Phylogeography and genetic ancestry of tigers (*Panthera tigris*). PLoS Biol 2:e442.

Lydekker R. 1896. A handbook to the carnivora: Part 1: Cats, civets, and mongooses. London, UK: E. Lloyd.

Lydekker R. 1908. The Game Animals of Africa. London: Rowland Ward, Ltd.

Macdonald D. W. and Loveridge A. J. 2010. Biology and Conservation of Wild Felids. Oxford, UK: Oxford University Press.

Marker L. L. and Dickman A. J. 2003. Morphology, physical condition, and growth of the cheetah (*Acinonyx jubatus jubatus*). Journal of Mammalogy 84(3):840-850.

Mattern M. Y. and McLennan D. A. 2000. Phylogeny and speciation of felids. Cladistics 16:232-253.

Matthews L. H. 1939. The subspecies and variation of the spotted hyaena, *Crocuta crocuta*. Journal of Zoology 109(2):237-260.

Mazzolli M. 2008. Status of the Arabian leopard (*Panthera pardus nimr*) in Dhofar, Sultanate of Oman. Expedition Report. Biosphere Expeditions.

McShea W. J. et al. 2018. Guide to the Wildlife of Southwest China. Washington, DC: Smithsonian Institution Scholarly Press.

Melisch R. et al. 1996. Distribution and status of the fishing cat (*Prionailurus viverrinus rhizophoreus* Sody, 1936) in West Java, Indonesia (Mammalia: Carnivora: Felidae). Faun. Abh. Mus. Tierkd. Dresden 20(17):311-319.

Melovski D. et al. 2012. Distribution and conservation status of the Balkan lynx (*Lynx lynx balcanicus* Bureš, 1941). Proceedings of the 4th Congress of Ecologists of Macedonia with International Participation, Ohrid. Macedonian Ecological Society.

Mengüllüoglu D. et al. 2018. Foraging ecology of Eurasian lynx populations in southwest Asia: Conservation implications for a diet specialist. Ecology and Evolution 8:9451-9463.

Menon V. 2014. Indian Mammals: A Field Guide. Gurgaon, India: Hachette Book Publishing India.

Miller S. et al. 2016. A conservation assessment of *Panthera leo*. In Child M. F. et al. (eds.). The Red List of Mammals of South Africa, Swaziland and Lesotho. South African National Biodiversity Institute and Endangered Wildlife Trust, South Africa.

Mills G. and Hofer H. 1998. Hyaenas: Status Survey and Conservation Action Plan. IUCN/SSC Hyaena Specialist Group. IUCN, Gland, Switzerland and Cambridge, UK. 154 pp.

Mohamed A. J. et al. 2009. Records of five Bornean cat species from Deramakot Forest Reserve in Sabah, Malaysia. Cat News 51:14–17.

Moqanaki E. M. et al. 2010. Distribution and conservation status of the Eurasian lynx in Iran. Cat News 53:32-35.

Moqanaki E. M. et al. 2016. The caracal in Iran: Current state of knowledge and priorities for conservation. Cat News 10:27-32.

Morales M. M. and Giannini N. P. 2010. Morphofunctional patterns in Neotropical felids: Species co-existence and historical assembly. Biological Journal of the Linnean Society 100:711-724.

Morris D. 2014. Leopard. London, UK: Reaktion Books.

Mukherjee S. et al. 2010. Ecology driving genetic variation: A comparative phylogeography of jungle cat (*Felis chaus*) and leopard cat (*Prionailurus bengalensis*) in India. Plos ONE 5:1-16.

Mukherjee S. et al. 2012. Survey of the fishing cat *Prionailurus viverrinus* Bennett, 1833 (Carnivora: Felidae) and some aspects impacting its conservation in India. Journal of Threatened Taxa 4(14):3355-3361.

Murdoch J. D. 2006. Pallas' cat ecology and conservation in the semi-desert steppes of Mongolia. Cat News 45:18-19.

Murray J. L. and Gardner G. L. 1997. *Leopardus pardalis*. Mammalian Species 548:1-10.

Myers S. 2016. Wildlife of Southeast Asia. Princeton, NJ: Princeton University Press.

Napolitano C. et al. 2014. Phylogeography and population history of *Leopardus guigna*, the smallest American felid. Conservation Genetics 15:631-665.

Nascimento F. O. 2010. Revisão taxonômica do gênero *Leopardus* Gray, 1842 (Carnivora, Felidae). Dissertation. Instituto de Biociências da Universidade de São Paulo.

Nascimento F. O. 2014. On the morphological variation and taxonomy of the Geoffroy's cat *Leopardus geoffroyi* (d'Orbigny & Gervais, 1844) (Carnivora, Felidae). Papéis Avulsos de Zoologia 54(11):129-160.

Nascimento F. O. 2017. Taxonomic revision of the tigrina *Leopardus tigrinus* (Schreber, 1775) species group (Carnivora, Felidae). Papéis Avulsos de Zoologia 57(19):231-264.

Nimalrathna T. S. et al. 2019. First photographic record of the rusty-spotted cat *Prionailurus rubiginosus* (I. Geoffroy Saint-Hilaire, 1831) (Mammalia: Carnivora: Felidae) in Horton Plains National Park, Sri Lanka. Journal of Threatened Taxa 11(4):13506-13510.

Nowak R. M. 2011. Walker's Mammals of the World. 6th ed. Baltimore: Johns Hopkins University Press.

Nowell K. and Jackson P. 1996. Wild Cats: Status Survey and Conservation Action Plan. Gland, Switzerland: IUCN/SSC Cat Specialist Group.

Nyhus P. J. 2018. Cheetahs: Biology and Conservation. London, UK: Academic Press.

O'Brien S. J. et al. 2008. State of cat genomics. Trends in Genetics 24(6):268-279.

Ognev S. I. 1926. A systematic review of the mammals of Russia. Annales Musei Nationalis Hungarici 23:202-233.

Ognev S. I. 1962. Mammals of Eastern Europe and Northern Asia. Vol. 2: Carnivora (Fissipedia). Washington, DC: Smithsonian Institution.

Ojeda R. A. et al. 2012. Libro Rojo de Mamíferos Amenazados de la Argentina. Argentina, Sociedad Argentina para el Estudio de los Mamíferos (SAREM).

Oliveira T. G. 1998. *Herpailurus yagouaroundi*. Mammalian Species 578:1-6.

Oliveira T. G. 1998. *Leopardus wiedii*. Mammalian Species 579:1-6.

Orozco M. M. 2015. El Aguará Guazú (*Chrysocyon brachyurus*) en Argentina. Buenos Aires: Fundación de Historia Natural Félix de Azara.

Osborn D. J. and Helmy I. 1980. The contemporary land mammals of Egypt (including Sinai). Fieldiana Zoology New Series, No. 5, Field Museum of Natural History.

Palacios R. 2007. Manual para Identificación de Carnívoros Andinos. Guía de Campo. Wildlife Conservation Network.

Palei H. S. et al. 2018. The vulnerable fishing cat *Prionailurus viverrinus* in Odisha, eastern India: Status and conservation implications. Zoology and Ecology 28(2):1-6.

Palomo L. J. et al. 2007. Atlas y Libro Rojo de los Mamíferos Terrestres de España. Madrid: Dirección General para la Biodiversidad - SECEM-SECEMU.

Patel K. 2006. Observations of rusty-spotted cat in eastern Gujarat, India. Cat News 45:27-28.

Patel R. P. et al. 2016. Two species of Southeast Asian cats in the genus *Catopuma* with diverging histories: An island endemic forest specialist and a widespread habitat generalist. Royal Society Open Science 3:1-15.

Patel R. P. et al. 2017. Genetic structure and phylogeography of the leopard cat (*Prionailurus bengalensis*) inferred from mitochondrial genomes. Journal of Heredity 108(4):1-12.

Payán-Garrido E. 2012. Los Felinos de Colombia. Bogotá: Ministerio de Ambiente y Desarrollo Sostenible, Instituto de Investigación de Recursos Biológicos Alexander von Humboldt, Panthera Colombia.

Payán-Garrido E. et al. 2015. Plan de acción para la conservación de los felinos en el Valle del Cauca, Colombia (2016-2019). Panthera Colombia y Corporación Autónoma Regional del Valle del Cauca, Cali, Colombia.

Pendragon B. and Winkler N. 2011. The family of cats: delineation of the feline basic type. Journal of Creation 25(2):118-124.

Perez I. et al. 2006. Critically Endangered Arabian leopards *Panthera pardus nimr* in Israel: Estimating population parameters using molecular scatology. Oryx 40(3):295-301.

Pocock R. I. 1917. The groups of the small and medium-sized South American Felidae. The Annals and Magazine of Natural History Series 8(20):43-47.

Pocock R. I. 1929. Tigers. The Journal of the Bombay Natural History Society 33:3-4.

Pocock R. I. 1930. The panthers and ounces of Asia. Part II. The Journal of the Bombay Natural History Society 34:307-336.

Pocock R. I. 1934. The races of the striped and brown hyænas. Proceedings of the Zoological Society of London 104(4):199-825.

Pocock R. I. 1939. The races of jaguar (*Panthera onca*). Novitates Zoologicae 41:406-422.

Pocock R. I. 1940. The races of Geoffroy's cat (*Oncifelis geoffroyi*). The Annals and Magazine of Natural History Series 11(6):350-355.

Pocock R. I. 1941. Some new geographic races of *Leopardus*, commonly known as ocelots and margays. The Annals and Magazine of Natural History Series 11(8):234-239.

Pocock R. I. 1941. The races of the ocelot and the margay. Field Museum of Natural History, Zoological Series 27:319-369.

Pocock R. I. 1941. The examples of the colocolo and of the pampas cat in the British Museum. The Annals and Magazine of Natural History Series 11(7):257-273.

Pocock R. I. 1941. The Fauna of British India, including Ceylon and Burma. Mammalia vol. II: Carnivora. London, UK: Taylor and Francis.

Pocock R. I. 1944. Three races, one new, of the serval (*Leptailurus*) from North Africa. Journal of Natural History Series 11(82): 690-698.

Pocock R. I. 1951. Catalogue of the Genus *Felis*. London: British Museum Natural History.

Poole K. G. 2003. A review of the Canada lynx, *Lynx canadensis*, in Canada. The Canadian Field-Naturalist 117(3):360-376.

Prater S. H. 1971. The Book of Indian Animals. 3rd ed. Bombay, India: The Bombay Natural History Society and Oxford University Press.

Qarqaz M. A. et al. 2004. Status and ecology of the striped hyaena, *Hyaena hyaena*, in Jordan. Zoology in the Middle East 33 (1): 5-10.

Queirolo D. et al. 2013. Avaliação do risco de extinção do gato-palheiro *Leopardus colocolo* (Molina, 1782) no Brasil. Biodiversidade Brasileira 3(1):91-98.

Rabinowitz A. 2014. An Indomitable Beast: The Remarkable Journey of the Jaguar. Washington, DC: Island Press.

Ramesh T. et al. 2016. A conservation assessment of *Leptailurus serval*. In Child M. F. et al. (eds.). The Red List of Mammals of South Africa, Swaziland and Lesotho. South African National Biodiversity Institute and Endangered Wildlife Trust, South Africa.

Redford K. H. and Eisenberg J. F. 1992. Mammals of the Neotropics: The Southern Cone. Vol. 2. Chile, Argentina, Uruguay, Paraguay. Chicago: University of Chicago Press.

Reding D. M. 2011. Patterns and processes of spatial genetic structure in a mobile and continuously distributed species, the bobcat (*Lynx rufus*). Dissertation. Iowa State University.

Reding D. et al. 2012. Pleistocene and ecological effects on continental-scale genetic differentiation in the bobcat (*Lynx rufus*). Molecular Ecology 12:3078-3093.

Renard A. et al. 2015. *Felis nigripes* (Carnivora: Felidae). Mammalian Species 47(925):78-83.

Rieger I. 1979. A review of the biology of striped hyaenas, *Hyaena hyaena* (Linne, 1758). Saugetierkundliche Mitteilungen, 272:81-95.

Riordan P. et al. 2015. Predicting global population connectivity and targeting conservation action for snow leopard across its range. Ecography 38:1-8.

Roberts T. J. 2005. Field Guide to the Large and Medium-Sized Mammals of Pakistan. Karachi, Pakistan: Oxford University Press.

Rodriguez-Martínez L. et al. 2007. Primer registro del gato montés (*Lynx rufus*) en el Parque Nacional La Malinche, Tlaxcala, México. Revista Mexicana de Mastozoología 11:80-84.

Rohland N. et al. 2005. The population history of extant and extinct hyenas. Molecular Biology and Evolution 22(12):2435-2443.

Rosevar D. R. 1974. The Carnivores of West Africa. London, UK: Trustees of the British Museum (Natural History).

Ross J. et al. 2010. A framework for a Wild Cat Action Plan for Sabah. Global Canopy Programme, Oxford, UK.

Rueness E. K. et al. 2014. Large-scale genetic structuring of a widely distributed carnivore: The Eurasian lynx (*Lynx lynx*). PLoS ONE 9(4): e93675.

Ruiz-García M. et al. 2018. Mitogenomics of the jaguarundi (*Puma yagouaroundi*, Felidae, Carnivora): Disagreement between morphological subspecies and molecular data. Mammalian Biology 93:153-168.

Russel Cole F. and Wilson D. E. 2015. *Felis margarita* (Carnivora: Felidae). Mammalian Species 47(924):63-77.

Sakamoto M. 2010. Phylogenetically structured variance in felid bite force: The role of phylogeny in the evolution of biting performance. Journal of Evolutionary Biology 23:463-478.

Salles L. O. 1992. Felid Phylogenetics: Extant Taxa and Skull Morphology (Felidae, Aeluroidea). American Museum Novitates 3047.

Sanderson J. G. and Watson P. 2011. Small Wild Cats: The Animal Answer Guide. Baltimore: John Hopkins University Press.

Santos A. S. and Eizirik E. 2018. Phylogeographic analyses of the pampas cat (*Leopardus colocola*; Carnivora, Felidae) reveal a complex demographic history. Genetics and Molecular Biology 41(1):273-287.

Saranholi B. H. et al. 2017. Evidence of recent fine-scale population structuring in South American *Puma concolor*. Diversity 9(4):44.

Schmidly D. J. 1994. The Mammals of Texas. Rev. ed. Austin: University of Texas Press.

Schmidt K. et al. 2011. The importance of genetic variability and population differentiation in the Eurasian lynx *Lynx lynx* for conservation, in the context of habitat and climate change. Mammal Review 41(2):112-124.

Schneider A. et al. 2015. Recurrent evolution of melanism in South American felids. PLoS Genetics 10(2).

Seidensticker J. and Lumpkin S. 2004. Cats in question. Washington, DC: Smithsonian Books.

Senn H. et al. 2017. RE: Response to range-wide snow leopard phylogeography supports three subspecies. Heredity 108(6):597-607.

Seymour K. L. 1999. Taxonomy, morphology, paleontology and phylogeny of the South American small cats. Dissertation. University of Toronto.

Shawl T. et al. 2008. Field Guide Mammals of Ladakh. WWF-India.

Sheil D. 2011. An encounter with an African golden cat *Caracal aurata*: One of the world's least known felids. African Journal of Ecology 19(3):367-369.

Sheng G.-L. et al. 2014. Pleistocene Chinese cave hyenas and the recent Eurasian history of the spotted hyena, *Crocuta crocuta*. Molecular Ecology 23:522-533.

Shrestha B. 2014. Nepal's first Pallas's cat. Cat News 60:23-24.

Shrivastav A. B. and Singh K. P. 2017. Big Cats. Rijeka, Croatia: InTech.

Sicuro F. L. and Oliveira L. F. 2011. Skull morphology and functionality of extant Felidae (Mammalia: Carnivora): A phylogenetic and evolutionary perspective. Zoological Journal of the Linnean Society 161:414-462.

Sikes R. S. and Kennedy M. L. 1992. Morphologic variation of the bobcat (*Felis rufus*) in the eastern United States and its association with selected environmental variables. American Midland Naturalist 128:313-324.

Sillero-Zubiri C. et al. 2015. Saharan cheetah *Acinonyx jubatus hecki*, a ghostly dweller on Niger's Termit massif. Oryx 49(4):591–594.

Silva L. G. et al. 2016. Biogeography of polymorphic phenotypes: Mapping and ecological modelling of coat colour variants in an elusive Neotropical cat, the jaguarundi (*Puma yagouaroundi*). Journal of Zoology 299:295-303.

Skinner J. D. and Chimimba C. T. 2005. The Mammals of the Southern African Subregion. Cambridge, UK: Cambridge University Press.

Skinner J. D. and Ilani G. 1979. The striped hyaena *Hyaena hyaena* of the Judean and Negev Deserts and a comparison with the brown hyaena *H. brunnea*. Israel Journal of Zoology 28(4):229-232.

Slattery J. P. et al. 1994. Phylogenetic reconstruction of South American felids defined by protein electrophoresis. Journal of Molecular Evolution 39:296-305.

Sliwa A. 1996. A functional analysis of scent marking and mating behavior in the aardwolf, *Proteles cristatus* (Sparrman, 1783). Dissertation. University of Pretoria.

Sliwa A. 2013. *Felis nigripes* Burchell. In: Kingdon, J.S. and Hoffmann, M. (eds). The Mammals of Africa Vol 5. Carnivora, Pholidota, Perissodactyla. Amsterdam: Academic Press.

Sliwa A. et al. 2010. Black-footed cats (*Felis nigripes*) and African wild cats (*Felis silvestris*): A comparison of two small felids from South African arid lands. Case study 26. In Macdonald D. and Loveridge A. (eds.). Biology and Conservation of Wild Felids. Oxford, UK: Oxford University Press.

Smith A. T. and Xie Y. 2013. Mammals of China. Princeton, NJ: Princeton University Press.

Snow Leopard Network. 2014. Snow Leopard Survival Strategy. Revised 2014 Version. Seattle: Snow Leopard Network.

Sogbohossou E. A. 1978. Lions of West Africa: Ecology of lion (*Panthera leo* Linnaeus 1975) populations and human-lion conflicts in Pendjari Biosphere Reserve, North Benin. Dissertation. Leiden University.

Sogbohossou E. A. et al. 2018. Spatio-temporal niche partitioning between the African lion (*Panthera leo leo*) and spotted hyena (*Crocuta crocuta*) in western African savannas. European Journal of Wildlife Research 64: 1.

Sousa, K. S. and Bager A. 2008. Feeding habits of Geoffroy's cat (*Leopardus geoffroyi*) in Southern Brazil. Mammalian Biology 73:303-308.

Spassov N. et al. 2006. The discovery of an extinct species: Data for the recent presence of the lynx (*Lynx lynx* L.) in Bulgaria and discussion of its status since 1941. Historia Naturalis Bulgarica 17:167-176.

Srinivasulu C. 2019. South Asian Mammals: An Updated Checklist and Their Scientific Names.

Boca Raton, FL: CRC Press, Taylor & Francis Group.

Srinivasulu C. and Srinivasulu B. 2012. South Asian Mammals: Their Diversity, Distribution, and Status. New York: Springer.

Stein A. B. and Hayssen V. 2013. *Panthera pardus* (Carnivora: Felidae). Mammalian Species 45(900):30-48.

Sterndale R. A. 1884. Natural History of the Mammalia of India. Calcutta: Thacker, Spink, and Co.

Stroganov S. U. 1962. Carnivorous mammals of Siberia. Jerusalem: Israel Program for Scientific Translations.

Stuart C. and Stuart T. 2011. Field Guide to the Mammals of Southern Africa. 4th ed. Cape Town, South Africa: Random House Struik.

Stuart C. and Stuart T. 2016. Mammals of North Africa and the Middle East. London, UK: Bloomsbury.

Stuart C. T. 1982. Aspects of the biology of the caracal (*Felis caracal* Schreber, 1776) in the Cape Province, South Africa. Dissertation. University of Natal.

Stuart C. T. and Wilson V. J. 1988. The Cats of Southern Africa. IUCN/SCC Cat Specialist Group, African Carnivore Survey and Chipangali Wildlife Trust. Bulawayo, Zimbabwe: Chipangali Wildlife Trust.

Sunquist F. and Sunquist M. 2014. The Wild Cat Book. Chicago: University of Chicago Press.

Swanepoel L. H. et al. 2016. A conservation assessment of *Panthera pardus*. In Child M. F. et al. (eds.). The Red List of Mammals of South Africa, Swaziland and Lesotho. South African National Biodiversity Institute and Endangered Wildlife Trust, South Africa.

Sweeney J. 2014. The Pampas cat (*Leopardus pajeros*). BBIO 485 Conservation Biology.

Taylor I. R. et al. 2016. The conservation status of the fishing cat *Prionailurus viverrinus* Bennett, 1833 (Carnivora: Felidae) in Koshi Tappu Wildlife Reserve, Nepal. Journal of Threatened Taxa 8(1):8323-8332.

Tilson R. and Nyhus P. J. 2010. Tigers of the World: The Science, Politics, and Conservation of *Panthera tigris*. Cambridge, MA, USA: Academic Press.

Trajce A. et al. 2009. Conservation of the critically endangered Balkan lynx: Achievements and aspirations. Proceedings of the International Conference on Biological and Environmental Sciences, 2008.

Traylor-Holzer K. et al. 2005. Asiatic Golden Cat in Thailand Population and Habitat Viability Assessment: Final Report. IUCN/SSC Conservation Breeding Specialist Group, Apple Valley, MN.

Trigo T. C. et al. 2013. Molecular data reveal complex hybridization and a cryptic species of Neotropical wild cat. Current Biology 23(24): 2528-2533.

Tumlison R. 1987. *Felis lynx*. Mammalian Species 269:1-8.

Turner, A. and Anton, M. 1997. The Big Cats and Their Fossil Relatives. New York: Columbia University Press.

Uphyrkina O. et al. 2001. Phylogenetics, genome diversity and origin of modern leopard, *Panthera pardus*. Molecular Ecology 10:2617-2633.

Valdmann H. 2006. Lynx (*Lynx lynx*) and wolf (*Canis lupus*) in the Baltic region: Diets, helminth parasites and genetic variation. Dissertation. University of Tartu, Estonia.

Vigne J. D. 2016. Earliest "domestic" cats in China identified as leopard cat (*Prionailurus bengalensis*). PLoS ONE 11(1):e0147295.

Villalba L. et al. 2004. The Andean cat: Conservation Action Plan. La Paz, Bolivia: Andean Cat Alliance.

Vries J. L. et al. 2016. A conservation assessment of *Proteles cristata*. In Child M. F. et al. (eds). The Red List of Mammals of South Africa, Swaziland and Lesotho. South African National Biodiversity Institute and Endangered Wildlife Trust, South Africa.

Wagner A. P. 2006. Behavioral ecology of the striped hyena (*Hyaena hyaena*). Dissertation. Montana State University.

Watts H. E. and Holekamp K. E. 2007. Hyena societies. Current Biology 17(16):R657-660.

Weidong B. 2010. Eurasian lynx in China: Present status and conservation challenges. Cat News 5:22-25.

Werdelin L. 1981. The evolution of lynxes. Annales Zoologici Fennici 18:37-71.

Werdelin L. and Olsson L. 1997. How the leopard got its spots: A phylogenetic view of the evolution of felid coat patterns. Biological Journal of the Linnean Society 62:383-400.

Westbury M. V. et al. 2019. Aardwolf population diversity and phylogenetic positioning inferred using complete mitochondrial genomes. African Journal of Wildlife Research 49:27-33.

Wijeyeratne G. D. 2016. Mammals of Sri Lanka. London, UK: Bloomsbury.

Wildlife Institute of India. 1998. Smaller cats of India. ENVIS Wildlife and Protected Areas, Vol. 1, No. 2. Chandrabani, India: Wildlife Institute of India.

Wilms T. 2015. International Register and Studbook for the Rusty-Spotted Cat *Prionailurus rubiginosus phillipsi* (Pocock, 1939). Frankfurt Zoo.

Wilson B. 2015. The black-footed cat *Felis nigripes* (Burchel, 1824): A review of the geographical distribution and conservation status. Dissertation. Pretoria, South Africa: Tshwane University of Technology.

Wilson B. et al. 2016. A conservation assessment of *Felis nigripes*. In Child M. F. et al. (eds.). The Red List of Mammals of South Africa, Swaziland and Lesotho. South African National Biodiversity Institute and Endangered Wildlife Trust, South Africa.

Wilson D. E. and Mittermeier R. A. 2009. Handbook of the Mammals of the World. Vol. 1 Carnivora. Barcelona, Spain: Lynx Edicions.

Wilson D. E. and Reeder D. M. 2005. Mammal Species of the World: A Taxonomic and Geographic Reference, 3rd ed. Baltimore: Johns Hopkins University Press.

Wilting A. et al. 2007. Clouded leopard phylogeny revisited: Support for species recognition and population division between Borneo and Sumatra. Frontiers in Zoology 4:15-25.

Wilting A. et al. 2011. Geographical variation in and evolutionary history of the Sunda clouded leopard (*Neofelis diardi*) (Mammalia: Carnivora: Felidae) with the description of a new subspecies from Borneo. Molecular Phylogenetics and Evolution 58:317-328.

Wilting A. et al. 2015. Planning tiger recovery: Understanding intraspecific variation for effective conservation. Science Advances 1(5):1-13.

Wurster-Hill D. H. and Centerwall W. R. 1982. The interrelationships of chromosome banding patterns in canids, mustelids, hyena, and felids. Cytogenetics and Cell Genetics 34:178-192.

Yamaguchi N. et al. 2004. Craniological differentiation between European wildcats (*Felis silvestris silvestris*), African wildcats (*F. s. lybica*) and Asian wildcats (*F. s. ornata*): Implications for their evolution and conservation. Biological Journal of the Linnean Society 83:47-63.

Yarnell R. W. et al. 2016. A conservation assessment of *Parahyaena brunnea*. In Child M. F. et al. (eds.). The Red List of Mammals of South Africa, Swaziland and Lesotho. South African National Biodiversity Institute and Endangered Wildlife Trust, South Africa.

Yensen E. and Seymour K. L. 2000. *Oreailurus jacobita*. Mammalian Species 644:1-6.

Yerramreddy A. 2017. Determining sexual dimorphism in the cheetah (*Acinonyx jubatus* spp.) through cranial and dental morphology. Dissertation. Allegheny College.

Yu L. and Zhang Y. 2005. Phylogenetic studies of pantherine cats (Felidae) based on multiple genes, with novel application of nuclear beta-rinogen intron 7 to carnivores. Molecular Phylogenetics and Evolution 35:483-495.

Zhou Y. et al. 2017. Comprehensive species set revealing the phylogeny and biogeography of Feliformia (Mammalia, Carnivora) based on mitochondrial DNA. PLoS ONE 12(3):1-19.

INDEX

The index includes the common English and scientific names. Scientific names are in italics.

A

Aardwolf
    East African 256
    South African 254
Acinonyx jubatus
    hecki 92
    jubatus 88
    soemmeringii 90
    venaticus 94
Andean Mountain Cat 132

B

Bay Cat 230
Black-Footed Cat 200
Bobcat
    Eastern 220
    Mexican 224
    Western 222

C

Caracal
    Arabian 169
    Asiatic 168
    North African 166
    South African 164
Caracal aurata
    aurata 170
    celidogaster 172
Caracal caracal
    caracal 164
    nubicus 166
    schmitzi 168
Catopuma badia 232
Catopuma temminckii
    moormensis 230
    temminckii 228
Cheetah
    Asiatic 94
    Central African 93
    East African 88
    Iranian 95
    Northeast African 91
    Northern 93
    Persian 95
    Saharan 92
    South African 88
    Sudan 90
Chinese Mountain Cat 188
Clouded Leopard
    Bornean 78
    Indochinese 74
    Sumatran 76
Colocolo 122
Cougar 83
Crocuta crocuta 240

D

Desert Cat
    Chinese 189
    Indian 187
Domestic Cat 180

E

Eyra Cat 87

F

Felis bieti 188
Felis catus 180
Felis chaus
    affinis 192
    chaus 190
    fulvidina 194
Felis lybica
    cafra 184
    gordoni 183
    lybica 182
    ornata 186
Felis margarita
    margarita 196
    thinobia 198
Felis nigripes 200
Felis silvestris
    caucasica 178
    grampia 177
    silvestris 176
Feral Cat 180
Flat-Headed Cat 140

G

Geoffroy's Cat 108
Golden Cat
    Central African 170
    Mainland 230
    Sunda 228
    Temminck's 229
    West African 172
Guiña
    Northern 112
    Southern 110

H

Herpailurus yagouaroundi 86
House Cat 180
Hyaena hyaena
    barbara 248
    dubbah 252
    hyaena 244
    sultana 248
    syriaca 246
Hyena
    Arabian Striped 250
    Asiatic Striped 245
    Barbary Striped 248
    Brown 242
    East African Striped 252
    Indian Striped 244
    Spotted 240
    Syrian Striped 246

I

Iriomote Cat 152

J

Jaguar 70

Jaguarundi 86
Jungle Cat
    Indian 192
    Indochinese 194
    Western 190

K

Kod-kod 111

L

Leopard
    African 52
    Amur 66
    Arabian 54
    Caucasian 57
    Chinese 69
    Indian 58
    Indochinese 62
    Javan 64
    Kashmir 59
    Malayan 63
    North Chinese 68
    Persian 56
    Sri Lankan 60
Leopard Cat
    Amur 150
    Palawan 155
    Siberian 151
    South Asian 148
    Sunda 154
    Tsushima 151
    Visayan 155
Leopardus colocola
    braccatus 124
    budini 130
    colocola 122
    garleppi 130
    munoai 126
    pajeros 128
    wolfsohni 122
Leopardus geoffroyi 108
Leopardus guigna
    guigna 110
    tigrillo 112
Leopardus guttulus 114
Leopardus jacobita 132
Leopardus pardalis
    mitis 100
    pardalis 98
Leopardus tigrinus
    oncilla 120
    pardinoides 118
Leopardus wiedii
    glauculus 106
    vigens 104
    wiedii 102
Leptailurus serval
    constantina 162
    lipostictus 160
    serval 158

Lion
Asiatic 48
Central African 46
East African 50
South African 50
West African 46
Lynx
Altai 211
Anatolian 219
Baikal 211
Balkan 216
Bay 221
Canada 204
Carpathian 214
Caucasian 218
Central Asian 212
Desert 165
Eurasian 209
European 215
Himalayan 213
Iberian 206
Northern 208
Pardel 207
Persian 169
Red 221
Siberian 210
Spanish 207
Lynx canadensis 204
Lynx lynx
balcanicus 216
carpathicus 214
dinniki 218
isabellinus 212
lynx 208
wrangeli 210
Lynx pardinus 206
Lynx rufus
escuinapae 224
fasciatus 222
oaxacensis 224
rufus 265

M
Manul 136
Marbled Cat
Himalayan 237
Mainland 236
Sunda 234
Margay
Central American 106
Northern 104
Southern 102
Mountain Lion 83

N
Neofelis diardi
borneensis 78
diardi 76
Neofelis nebulosa 74

O
Ocelot
Northern 98
Southern 100
Oncilla 117
Atlantic Forest 115

Otocolobus manul
manul 136
Otter Cat 87
Ounce 73

P
Pallas's Cat
Asian 136
Tibetan 138
Pampas Cat
Argentinian 128
Bolivian 130
Peruvian 130
Pantanal Cat
Brazilian 124
Uruguayan 126
Panther 83
Panthera leo
leo 46
melanochaita 50
persica 49
Panthera onca 70
Panthera pardus
delacouri 62
fusca 58
japonensis 68
kotiya 60
melas 64
nimr 54
orientalis 66
pardus 52
tulliana 56
Panthera tigris
altaica 36
amoyensis 38
corbetti 40
jacksoni 42
sumatrae 44
tigris 34
Panthera uncia 72
Parahyaena brunnea 242
Pardofelis marmorata
longicaudata 236
marmorata 234
Prionailurus bengalensis
bengalensis 148
euptilurus 150
Prionailurus javanensis
javanensis 154
sumatranus 154
Prionailurus planiceps 140
Prionailurus rubiginosus
koladivius 146
phillipsi 146
rubiginosus 144
Prionailurus viverrinus
rhizophoreus 142
viverrinus 142
Proteles cristatus
cristatus 254
septentrionalis 256
Puma
North American 84
South American 82

Puma concolor
concolor 82
cougar 84

R
Rusty-Spotted Cat
Forest 146
Indian 144
Lowland 146
Mainland 144
Sri-Lankan 146

S
Sand Cat
African 194
Arabian 197
Asian 196
Serval
Central African 162
East African 160
South African 158
West African 162
Small-Spotted Cat 201
Snow Leopard 72
Steppe Cat 136
Chinese 189
Strandwolf 243
Swamp Cat 191

T
Tiger
Amoy 39
Amur 36
Bengal 34
Indochinese 40
Korean 37
Malayan 42
Manchurian 37
Northern Indochinese 41
Siberian 37
South China 38
Southern Indochinese 43
Sumatran 44
Tiger Cat
Southern 115
Tigrillo 119
Tigrina
Central American 118
Eastern 116
Northern 118
Southern 114

W
Wildcat
Arabian 183
Asian 185
Asian Steppe 187
Caucasian 178
European 176
Gordon's 183
North African 182
South African 184
Tristram's 183